The PhD Handbook

The PhD Handbook

**How to take care of yourself,
your research project and your future**

Dr Rosie Doyle and Dr Fraser Robertson

Open University Press

Open University Press
McGraw Hill
Unit 4,
Foundation Park
Roxborough Way
Maidenhead
SL6 3UD

email: emea_uk_ireland@mheducation.com
world wide web: www.openup.co.uk

First edition published 2024

Copyright © Open International Publishing Limited, 2024

Fistral Training and Consultancy Ltd retain copyright and IP for all templates, tables, images and activities (unless otherwise stated).

All rights reserved. Except for the quotation of short passages for the purposes of criticism and review, no part of this publication may be reproduced, stored in a retrieval system, or transmitted, in any form or by any means, electronic, mechanical, photocopying, recording or otherwise, without the prior written permission of the publisher or a licence from the Copyright Licensing Agency Limited. Details of such licences (for reprographic reproduction) may be obtained from the Copyright Licensing Agency Ltd of Saffron House, 6–10 Kirby Street, London EC1N 8TS.

A catalogue record of this book is available from the British Library

ISBN-13: 978-0-3352-5209-1
ISBN-10: 0335252095
eISBN: 978-0-3352-5210-7

Commissioning Editor: Sam Crowe
Editorial Assistant: Hannah Jones
Content Product Manager: Hannah Cartwright, Ali Davis
Marketing Manager: Bryony Waters

Library of Congress Cataloging-in-Publication Data
CIP data applied for

Typeset by Transforma Pvt. Ltd., Chennai, India

Fictitious names of companies, products, people, characters and/or data that may be used herein (in case studies or in examples) are not intended to represent any real individual, company, product or event.

Praise page

"Those who've successfully attained a PhD stress intense frustration experienced as well as the need for self-criticism and awareness. Sustaining initial enthusiasm and maintaining positivity, especially during 'dark days' when things aren't going well, is essential. The PhD Handbook by Doyle and Robertson is superbly honest about what achieving a doctorate really involves. It admirably, and elegantly, guides readers through the stages students undergo through presentation of a supportive narrative combined with easy-to-understand diagrams and vignettes. As the subtitle emphasises, students need to understand that success requires them to look after themselves in a what will be life changing and hugely rewarding process. It will undoubtedly become a must read for every PhD student."

Dr Steven McCabe, Associate Professor, Birmingham City University, UK

"Undertaking a PhD is an enormous professional and personal challenge for almost everyone: Being in charge of a cutting-edge research project, often in international collaboration, creates a large number of challenges. 'The PhD Handbook' is an essential read to make this journey easier and more structured: It helps understand the roles of various stakeholders better and introduces essential tools and techniques to be successful. The authors adapt a hands-on approach and build on their personal experiences when describing the different stages of the PhD project."

Prof Dr Carsten P Welsch, Head of Physics Department, University of Liverpool, UK

"Is it possible to write a guide for PhD candidates that does not overlap with what is already available? It's almost impossible.... but Doyle and Robertson did it! Many PhD candidates regard the planning of a project as the supervisor's weaker spot. This book pays a lot of attention to this aspect of a PhD trajectory. The career after the defense of the dissertation.... often a neglected child in the guidance. But here in the spotlight. Other highlights: the attention to stress and how to deal with it, and the power elements in the relationship with the supervisors. It's also a must-read for every supervisor and will facilitate the communication with the candidate in an inspiring way."

Dr Hans Sonneveld, Netherlands Center of Expertise for Doctoral Education, NL

"Like many books in the 'how to get a PhD genre', this one is packed with sound advice that researcher developers wish everyone would follow. The standout value of this book over the many other competing titles are the sections devoted to project management. These chapters an excellent primer on getting clarity on a big project before you start - and how to keep the various stakeholders happy throughout. There's good visual tools, diagrams and worksheets that I will be using in my own teaching practice with new candidates and even PostDocs. A great addition to any supervisor or student's bookshelf"

Professor Inger Mewburn, Director of Researcher Development,
Australian National University, Australia

"Focused on the project management of PhD study, this highly interactive and practical handbook to the PhD is full of action items and templates, designed for the student who wants a detailed map for a successful start towards a successful completion."

Dr Katherine Firth, *The University of Melbourne, Australia*;
Author of How to Fix Your Academic Writing Trouble: A Practical Guide
and Your PhD Survival Guide: Planning, Writing, and Succeeding in Your Final Year

"The PhD Handbook is a vital companion to PhD studies in any discipline. It provides a guide to those aspects of PhD study that research methods courses don't cover - how to build a support network, how to manage the complexity of the PhD project, how to maintain a good work-life balance, how to cope with the emotional and social aspects of PhD studies, and so much more. Most importantly, it recognises that every PhD student is an individual, and that you need to find your own approach to effective working. To support this, it is packed with interactive exercises. These allow you to reflect on the various stages in the PhD journey, and build your own path to success - both during the PhD and beyond, whether in academia or elsewhere."

Colin G. Johnson, Associate Professor, University of Nottingham,
and co-author of *How to Get a PhD*

Contents

List of templates xii
Acknowledgements xiii

INTRODUCTION xiv
How to ... Make the most of this book
    The purpose of the book xiv
    What this book is xv
    What this book isn't xv
    The structure of the book xvi
    How to use the book xviii
    Finally xviii

PART 1: HOW TO MAKE A GOOD START   **1**

1. WHAT TO EXPECT   3
   How to ... Stop worrying and start working
      Getting started 4
      What will it be like? 5
      The conscious competence framework 7
      Summary 14
      Further resources 14

2. CLARIFY YOUR PERSONAL GOALS   15
   How to ... Find your direction even when you don't know where you're going
      What next? Life after your PhD 16
      Set your goals and identify actions to achieve your goals 19
      Summary 23
      Further resources 23

3. ESTABLISH SUPERVISORY RELATIONSHIPS   24
   How to ... Actively shape a positive supervision partnership
      What is the supervision relationship? 25
      How to get what you need from supervision 29
      Summary 36
      Further resources 36

4. PLOT YOUR COURSE   37
   How to ... Create a useful plan when you don't know what you're doing
      The purpose of PhD planning 38
      What is a 'good' plan for you? 39
      Creating a high-level PhD plan 41
      Summary 48
      Further resources 48

5. CREATE GOOD HABITS — 49
How to ... Start as you mean to go on
- Your PhD is your job — 49
- The secrets of habit formation — 50
- Establish good habits for your PhD — 51
- Summary — 58
- Further resources — 58

6. BUILD SUPPORT NETWORKS — 59
How to ... Surround yourself with the people you need
- Why support networks are vital for your PhD — 59
- The importance of social connection for humans — 60
- Social support networks — 60
- Professional support networks — 66
- Summary — 70
- Further resources — 70

PART 2: HOW TO GET GOING — 71

7. LAY THE FOUNDATIONS — 75
How to ... Create the underpinnings of a successful PhD plan
- Initiation — 76
- The project triangle — 77
- Stakeholder identification — 79
- Summary — 85
- Further resources — 86

8. SET YOUR SCOPE — 87
How to ... Figure out what you need to do
- Identify stakeholder expectations — 88
- Your research impact — 89
- The convergence method — 90
- Prioritise scope — 94
- Determine your deliverables — 98
- Write your statement of scope — 102
- Summary — 105
- Further resources — 105

9. IDENTIFY TASKS — 106
How to ... Work out how to do what you need to do
- The work breakdown structure — 107
- Estimate task durations — 111
- Summary — 118
- Further resources — 118

10. SCHEDULE TASKS — 119
How To ... Decide what to do when
- The network diagram — 120
- The Gantt chart — 127
- Summary — 135
- Further resources — 135

11. BULLETPROOF YOUR PLAN	136
How to … Plan for things not going as planned	
Identify risks	138
Assess risks	141
Respond to risks	143
Summary	147
Further resources	147
12. TAKE CHARGE OF YOUR TIME	148
How to … Get the most out of every day	
Take charge of your week	148
Get the most out of every day	155
Summary	161
Further resources	162
13. COMMUNICATE PERSUASIVELY	163
How to … Get what you need from other people	
Leverage your personal power	163
The seven bases of power	164
Influencing tactics	169
Summary	173
Further resources	174
PART 3: HOW TO KEEP GOING	**175**
14. BOOST YOUR RESILIENCE	177
How to … Be ready for the demands of a PhD	
Stress, the brain and the body	177
Manage your thoughts to reduce stress	178
The power of happiness	182
Support your well-being	186
Summary	189
Further resources	190
15. OVERCOME PROCRASTINATION	191
How to … Get going again if you get stuck	
Fear and anxiety	192
Disorganisation	196
Overwhelm	198
Perfectionism	199
Lack of motivation	200
Habit	202
Summary	204
Further resources	205
16. TRACK YOUR PROGRESS	206
How to … Know what and when to change	
Tracking progress	207
Updating your plan	208
Dealing with unexpected issues	210
How often should you review your plan?	214
Summary	218
Further resources	218

17. LOOK AHEAD — 219
How to ... Get a head start on your future career
- Build your CV — 220
- Networking: it's not (just) what you know; it's who you know — 227
- Summary — 232
- Further resources — 232

18. DEAL WITH SETBACKS — 233
How to ... Bounce back when things go wrong
- Stress and the brain, revisited — 233
- Manage your thoughts — 235
- Take action to overcome setbacks — 238
- Summary — 246
- Further resources — 246

19. HANDLE CONFLICT AND CONFRONTATION — 247
How to ... Have those difficult conversations
- Conflict management strategies — 248
- Communication skills for conflict management — 254
- Summary — 261
- Further resources — 262

PART 4: HOW TO GET IT FINISHED — 263

20. GET IT ALL DONE — 265
How to ... Plan the final stage
- Scoping — 265
- Determine the feedback process — 270
- Network diagram — 271
- Gantt chart — 272
- Summary — 274
- Further resources — 274

21. HANG IN THERE — 275
How to ... Keep moving and stay motivated
- How to handle the stress — 275
- How to sustain your productivity — 281
- How to stay motivated — 283
- How to generate momentum in your writing — 285
- Summary — 291
- Further resources — 292

22. GET READY FOR THE VIVA — 293
How to ... Prepare yourself to perform confidently
- Your chance to shine — 293
- Preparing yourself for the Viva — 294
- Get ready: the day before your Viva — 307
- Get ready: the day of your Viva — 307
- Summary — 308
- Further resources — 309

23. TAKE THE NEXT STEP	310
How to ... Use your PhD as the launch pad for your future career	
Identify your skills	312
Articulate your skills	316
Evidence your skills	317
Summary	321
Further resources	321
Afterword	322
Glossary	323
Index	329

List of templates

Conscious competence framework	13
Goal-setting planner	22
Supervision needs analysis	31
Supervision ground rules	34
High-level PhD timeline	47
Social support network development planner	65
Community of practice development planner	69
Stakeholder identification	82
Convergence table	93
Prioritisation	97
Deliverables	101
Scope statement	104
Three-point estimation	117
Risk register	146
Power base assessment	168
Influencing tactics assessment	171
The ABC method	181
Happiness planner	185
Change assessment	213
Lessons learned review	217
CV development plan	226
Circle of control assessment	241
Effort-impact assessment	245
Conflict management mode assessment	253
Prioritisation for final six months	268
Well-being planner	280
Devil's advocate technique	302
Skill identification	315
STAR assessment	320

Acknowledgements

> Throughout this book, you will find references to the Online Learning Centre, which can be found here: https://www.mheducation.co.uk/professionals/open-university-press/olc/doyle-robertson-the-phd-handbook. We have made this companion website to reinforce your learning and to enhance your understanding. On this site, you will find templates to provide opportunities for you to practise what you have learnt.

There are so many people we would like to thank for helping to bring this book together. Sam and Hannah of Open University Press for their infinite patience in answering all of our questions; Greig from Business Glasgow for his assistance and support; Jamie of Harper McLeod for his advice and guidance; Steph, Shannan, Gabrielle and Vici from the University of Strathclyde Researcher Development Programme for all their help and encouragement. To Chloe, Gabi, Jessica, Kelly and Marcella for letting us pick their brains. We would also like to thank our own supervisors from whom we learned so much and without whom we would never have been in the position to write this book.

Rosie would personally like to thank: everyone at Fistral Training for such stimulating opportunities and great teamwork; Fraser, co-author extraordinaire – who had the 'great idea' to write a book; the Confident Futures gang – the best colleagues ever with whom I learned so much that has inspired this book. Also, my parents, sadly no longer here: my Mum, who taught me to be fascinated by what makes people tick, and my Dad, who passed on his love of ideas and writing; my sister Janet for her steadfast support and writing advice; dear friends – you know who you are – for all the long conversations that got me though the writing of this book. Finally, my wonderful husband Colin – always by my side, with love and cups of coffee.

Fraser wants to extend his personal thanks to: Paul, without whom there would be no Fistral and therefore no book. Rosie – it's been a blast! We complement (and compliment) each other so well. Pauline for her unwavering patience, love and support – as well as her fantastic proofreading abilities! To Zoe and Daniella who inspire me every day. And my parents: Dad for his sage advice, and Mum for her continual encouragement – she was so proud to see the book available for preorder but sadly didn't get to see it published.

Finally, our heartfelt thanks to all the PhD students who have come on our courses over the years. You taught us as much as we taught you.

Introduction

How to ... Make the most of this book

> It's not just the research – Sharpen your saw – Get the benefit of our experience – Make it yours – Transferable skills – A workbook, not a textbook

There is a popular saying that a PhD is 90 per cent persistence and 10 per cent intelligence. This book is aimed at making the 90 per cent easier so you can make the most of the 10 per cent! Of course, you have to be 'bright' to do a PhD, but it demands much more than the intellectual skills of academic research. You have to be able to plan and manage your work, ensure you produce the necessary outputs, keep on track and accommodate changes and unexpected problems. Your PhD is also a demanding personal undertaking: you will need motivation and resilience, not least in the face of the inevitable challenges and setbacks you will meet along the way. A PhD should also be a stepping-stone to the next phase of your career, whether in academia or elsewhere. Our aim in this book is to equip you, wherever you are on your PhD journey, to:

Take care of yourself, take care of your research project and take care of your future.

We have been delivering training courses to thousands of PhD and research students all over the world for the best part of two decades, and this book captures, in printed form, some of the key tools, tips and techniques that our course attendees benefit from the most. However, our courses, and this book, aren't just based on our professional background in management and training. Our work is informed by our own experiences as doctoral students. We know from personal experience what it takes to successfully complete a PhD.

We both completed our own PhD degrees in what might tactfully be called 'mid-life'. We came to our studies after long careers in other settings. We knew we would have to grapple with the intellectual skills of academic research. We weren't prepared, however, for how much we would need to draw on the skills we had developed during our professional lives to manage the work and to rise to the personal challenges of a PhD. There was plenty of help available for the academic demands of doctoral study, but less for these other aspects. We realised that other PhD students might be helped by our experience and knowledge.

This is the book we wish we'd had when we did our PhDs!

The purpose of the book

Whether you're just starting your PhD, part-way through or nearing completion or submission, this book will help you to manage your research effectively, take the personal demands of a PhD in your stride and set yourself up for your future career. We aim to take some of the stress out of your PhD, so you can focus your efforts on the research itself while making the most of the opportunities offered by a PhD and enjoying it as much as you can.

This book isn't discipline- or methodology-specific. Whatever your field of research, the techniques provided will help you navigate the challenges that characterise the PhD experience in general.

The tools in this book will help you complete your PhD successfully and ease the transition to your next step. These tools are also very transferable and can be applied in any work setting. By working through the book and learning to use all the techniques, you will build up a toolbox of skills prized by employers. Wherever your PhD takes you in future, the skill set provided by this book will continue to be useful and help you get the best out of yourself. See this book as a way of 'sharpening your saw':

> Imagine you're walking through a forest and you encounter a woodcutter who has a big pile of logs to saw up into firewood. They are sawing away with a blunt saw, and not getting on very quickly. You ask, 'Why don't you sharpen your saw?' The woodcutter replies, 'I don't have time to stop and sharpen my saw, I have all this firewood to cut!'

A PhD will take a lot of work, and, at times, you may feel as though you don't have time to do the very things that would make your PhD easier. There is a lot in this book and you might think, 'How can I possibly do all of this as well as work on my PhD?' All of the techniques in this book are ways of 'sharpening your saw'. They may take time and effort to set up, but, we assure you, they will allow you to complete your PhD more efficiently and with less stress. It is an *investment* that will *save* you time and effort.

What this book is

The book provides a range of tools presented in workbook form, to help you with everything *except* the research skills of a PhD. It helps you with 'the other 90 per cent' that you need to successfully complete your PhD.

This ranges from planning work effectively (estimating, creating timelines, tracking progress) to managing relationships (communicating with supervisors, managing expectations, dealing with conflict); from coping when unexpected things happen (replanning, dealing with change, maintaining personal resilience) to managing yourself (time management, motivation, dealing with stress). We've crammed the book with techniques to deal with the many different situations that you could (and most probably will) encounter during your PhD.

What this book isn't

If you're looking for guidance on research methods, completing funding applications, or defining a good question or hypothesis, then this isn't the book for you!

This is *not* a book that tells you *how* to do the research. It is *not* a textbook. There are already many excellent books on how to complete a PhD from the perspective of research skills, methods and writing, and your own institution will also have specific procedures, arrangements and training to support your through process of completing the PhD.

Of course, when we say we aren't offering help with research, we don't mean that our approaches won't contribute to your research work. The content of this book will ensure that you are in a strong position to complete your research to a high standard. You will be able to manage your work and your time efficiently, develop

> **What's in a name?**
> Although we use the term PhD for simplicity, this book is written for all doctoral degree students: whether PhD, discipline-specific (such as EngD or EdD) or professional doctorate (DBA, for example); full-time or part-time; and whether returning to academia as a mature student or embarking on the journey early in your career.

confidence and self-belief, and set motivating personal goals. This will drive the quality of your PhD just as much as a tightly focused research question and well-founded methodology.

The structure of the book

We've organised the book to follow a very rough chronology that reflects the stages of the degree process in general:

If you have found this book at the start of your PhD, it will act as a companion guide throughout your PhD journey. If you are already part-way through your research, we would still recommend reading from the beginning, rather than jumping in halfway through. The techniques provided for the earlier stages of the PhD are best used throughout the whole degree process. In addition, some of the ideas in later chapters build on techniques that are introduced earlier in the book.

You can also use the book for specific, focused advice for particular situations. The chapter subtitles, beginning 'How to …', reflect the most common issues PhD students encounter. For example, if you are having disagreements with your supervisor about how to proceed and need help to navigate a tricky discussion, you could go directly to Chapter 19, 'Handle Conflict and Confrontation – How to … have those difficult conversations'. Use these subtitles, the Contents, Index and chapter takeaway summaries to help you navigate the content of the book and find the most useful techniques when you need them.

The book is organised into four parts that reflect the common phases of a PhD. Each part provides tools and techniques to help you successfully meet the challenges of the phase.

Part 1: How to Make a Good Start

Part 1 is designed to help you use the first weeks and months to lay the groundwork for a successful PhD. There can be a lot of uncertainty at the start of a PhD. Some students feel a little stranded, with no clear direction, and frustrated that they aren't making more progress. However, this early stage should be focused on orientation and familiarisation, rather than the production of substantive research outputs. Part 1 explains what you can expect in the early phase of your PhD, and provides tools to help reduce your anxieties and take the opportunity to create firm foundations for your work. In particular, Part 1 addresses:

- Clarifying your direction and personal goals
- Establishing your supervision relationships
- Creating an overarching plan for the duration of your PhD
- Developing productive working habits from the start
- Building support networks.

By the end of Part 1, you will have found your feet and prepared yourself for getting going on your research.

Introduction   **xvii**

Part 2: How to Get Going

Part 2 helps you to understand what you need to do to produce an excellent PhD, and then to ensure that you do it. The main focus is a planning framework for use from the very outset of your PhD and throughout, creating a repeated process of planning–doing–reviewing. We provide techniques for making the most of your time and communication techniques to help you get what you need from others to successfully complete your PhD. The content of Part 2 will mean you can work efficiently and move confidently towards your goals, including:

- Laying the foundations of successful planning
- Clarifying the outputs necessary for a successful PhD
- Working out exactly what to do, and when, to achieve your PhD
- Anticipating and avoiding potential problems
- Taking productivity measures
- Getting what you need from other people.

By the end of Part 2, you will be ready to move through your PhD efficiently and productively. If you are part-way through your PhD, you may have missed the opportunity to apply these ideas early on, but you can easily use them to plan the remaining stages of your research.

Part 3: How to Keep Going

No PhD runs completely smoothly. Part 3 helps you to deal with the demands of a PhD and the problems you might face. Every PhD student needs to be ready to deal with setbacks and stay on track in the face of difficulties. Part 3 provides techniques for dealing with the practical and psychological challenges of a PhD, not least the stamina to hang in there when the going gets tough. There are tools to help you accommodate changes in your plans without compromising the schedule of your research. You will learn how to cope with the sustained demands of your work over the long term, how to bounce back from setbacks and handle conflicts promptly and effectively. We also guide you to use the middle period of your PhD to position yourself well for your future career. Part 3 specifically addresses:

- Building stamina and well-being
- Dealing with change
- Enhancing your career opportunities
- Handling the practical and psychological fallout of setbacks
- Resolving conflicts and protecting your interests.

By the end of Part 3, you will be better equipped to handle whatever challenges your PhD throws at you.

Part 4: How to Get It Finished

Part 4 provides the tools you will need to get your thesis over the line. Submitting *on time* and submitting a *high-quality thesis* are equally important and shouldn't be mutually exclusive. As a well as planning the final months of work and juggling the multiple demands of this period, we provide support with maintaining your productivity and motivation as the pressure increases. The theme of good planning continues here in helping you to plan your preparation for the Viva and ensure you are in the best position to do yourself proud. We also help you to manage your anxiety and build your confidence so that you can perform well. Finally, Part 4 demonstrates how to capitalise on the skills you have developed during your PhD, and by reading this book, to achieve your career aims. Part 4 addresses in particular:

- Creating a comprehensive plan to finish your thesis
- Maintaining momentum during the final months
- Handling the challenge of writing up
- Building confidence for the Viva
- Leveraging your professional skills in the employment market.

By the end of Part 4, you will be ready to celebrate your PhD success and take the next steps into your future.

How to use the book

This book is designed to be *used*, not just read. It is set up as a workbook, with activities for you to complete and apply to your own life and work. Write all over it, use it, make it your own. Make sure that you attempt all of the activities, because it's only in trying that you truly understand how to use the tools and techniques, how they are relevant to you and how to fully realise their value. Experiment with all the techniques at least once before deciding which you prefer and find most useful.

You will see different kinds of content in the book to help bring the techniques to life:

Boxed info – Additional ideas to help you make the most of the book.

Action – Quick pointers on how to apply the techniques in your own life.

Activities – Structured activities for you to do in order to learn and apply the techniques yourself.

Templates – Forms you can use again and again as you implement the techniques. Fill them out in the book or access electronic versions on the OLC available at: https://www.mheducation.co.uk/professionals/open-university-press/olc/doyle-robertson-the-phd-handbook.

Transferable skills – These flag up techniques or skills that can be used in all employment settings.

PhD stories – These examples, insights and anecdotes demonstrate that everything recommended in the book has proven its worth with real PhD students: both us and the people who have come on our courses.

Our primary aim for this book is for it to be accessible and practical. As a result, we have taken the decision to exclude references, unless there is a direct link to a published work – as a source or a recommendation. Our purpose is to provide tried-and-trusted techniques rather than engaging in theoretical debates on the relative merits of extant models. We hope our PhD supervisors will excuse our pragmatism – and that you, as academic readers, will see the value of this – and not use it as a guide on academic referencing! At the end of each chapter, you will find a list of additional resources to follow up for more information about the ideas and techniques.

Finally

We hope that by investing your precious time in reading this book and using the techniques, your PhD will be easier, less stressful and more successful as a result. We also know that what you learn from this book will give you an edge in your life after your PhD. We work with clients in many different fields, not just academic research. We use the tools and techniques in this book with them all, as well as PhD students, and we know how useful and valued they are. At the risk of mixing our metaphors, you aren't just 'sharpening your saw' but collecting a full toolbox that you will be able to pull from in whatever field you end up working.

Writing this book together has been as much of a learning opportunity for us as we hope it will be for you. Probably the most powerful learning has been how much our work is improved through ongoing feedback, critique and revision. During the book, we will come back to this point again and again – your PhD will follow a similarly iterative process. This means that your work will go through regular feedback and revision cycles. This is the path to excellence. Don't be frightened of this or interpret it as a sign of inadequacy. Your use of this book will also be an iterative process. When you first read it, you might be unconvinced by some of the techniques. Or you might try them once and find them too awkward. However, we urge you not to rush to judgement before you discard any of the tools. The expertise contained in the book will also be part of an iterative process for you as an individual. The initial investment of time in learning how to 'sharpening your saw' will pay dividends in the long run.

The other lesson of our collaboration on this book was a reminder of just how great it is to work with someone else. A PhD can be an isolating experience, but it is not and should not be an individual endeavour. We return to this throughout the coming chapters, and we hope that, by reading this book, you feel that we are in your corner with you. Our own PhD experiences aren't that long ago and the joys and the challenges are still fresh in our minds. We hope this comes through in the book.

Part 1

How to Make a Good Start

Part 1: How to Make a Good Start

Welcome to the start of your PhD adventure! The purpose of Part 1 of the book is to help you start like you mean to continue: your first chance to 'sharpen your saw'! These early weeks and months present an unrivalled opportunity to establish sound foundations for your work – plans, goals, working habits, supervision relationships, support networks – that will carry you through the rest of your PhD. Part 1 covers the main issues that PhD students ask us about in the very earliest days of their doctoral experiences, such as:

- How to get started on work when so much about your PhD is unknown
- How to find your feet in the new world of PhD study
- What to expect from your supervision relationships
- How to avoid the isolation trap.

Part 1 also gives you the first taste of the style of this book. Our aim, as described in the introduction, is to provide you with tools for everything you need for a successful PhD experience, other than the academic skills of research. Don't worry – this isn't 'all the things your supervisors don't tell you' clickbait! It is to help you have clearly in your own mind what you can do to take care of yourself, your research project and your future right from day one. Our focus is on practical, actionable techniques that we know from our experience with thousands of PhD students will make your PhD easier and more fulfilling. In the following chapters, you will find many prompts and activities to help you apply the content to your own life.

> **Already started?**
> If you are already further on in your PhD, you may find much to recognise in these chapters from your own early experiences. You can still use the tools to improve your PhD experience, at whatever stage.

Part 1 is also your chance to establish how you will use the book. The more you get into the habit of trying out the tools from the outset, the more you will get out of it.

- In Chapter 1, you gain an understanding of what to expect from a PhD and, in particular, what you might find puzzling or disorientating. This will mean that you are better able to deal with any culture shock you experience at the start of your PhD and instead make a smooth transition to your new status. You also learn how to respond positively to the challenging learning curve that will define your whole PhD.
- In Chapter 2, you identify your key personal and professional goals for your PhD. This clarity of purpose will help you to prioritise your research endeavours, ensure you allow time for valuable non-research activities, make the most of the opportunities that the PhD offers and set your direction towards your future career.
- In Chapter 3, you consider one of the most crucial elements of your PhD experience: the relationship you have with your supervisory team. You learn ways to make the most of supervision from the beginning and how to foster relationships that will take you through the PhD and beyond.
- In Chapter 4, you get started on your work, despite the many uncertainties you face. You create an initial plan for your PhD, which will map the main phases of work to give you short-term focus as well as a bigger-picture overview. You also learn fundamental principles of good planning that you will build on when you learn how to manage your research project in detail in Part 2.
- In Chapter 5, you learn how to establish good habits that will help you complete your PhD efficiently and reduce stress. You learn the principles of habit formation and consider how best to create useful habits at the start of your PhD that will support your work throughout.
- Finally, in Chapter 6, you take steps to create the support networks that will help you deal with the academic, professional and personal challenges of a PhD. You learn why social connection will improve your well-being and enhance your learning.

You are embarking on one of most challenging, most complex, most intense undertakings you will ever be involved in. Exciting, isn't it? Setting out like you mean to continue and establishing these solid foundations will enhance the quality of your experience, increase your enjoyment and ensure you make the very most of everything your PhD has to offer.

1 What to Expect

How to ... Stop worrying and start working

> Manage your expectations – Deal with the practicalities – Adjust to the new culture – Avoid imposter syndrome – Prepare for a steep learning curve – The conscious competence framework

What can you expect in the first weeks and months of your doctoral degree? Whatever your personal circumstances or the specifics of your PhD programme, you will experience a degree of culture shock. A PhD is like nothing else: part job and part study, but somehow not like either. Whether you're coming to your PhD straight from a Masters degree or from a job outside the academic world, the first weeks and months may be disorientating. It's not just the PhD study itself that presents a challenging transition. The culture of academic institutions is very different from other kinds of work organisations. You may find yourself slightly baffled by the way things operate.

The culture shock of PhD study is often underestimated by the staff involved in welcoming new PhD students. This is understandable: they are already familiar with the academic research culture. In this chapter, we want to take a moment to explain some of the particular characteristics of PhD study, and help you to adjust to this new lifestyle. By managing your expectations, we aim to smooth your transition to PhD study, reduce your anxieties and frustrations and help you make the most of the opportunities of these early days.

Focus on the practicalities first, worry about the research later.

All PhD students start their PhD in different circumstances that bring individual practical and personal demands. You may have just finished a Masters, or you may be returning to study after a period in employment. You might have just landed at a new university, in a new city or even in a new country. You may be a virtual student contacting your supervisors and fellow students remotely. You may be a full-time student or a part-time one juggling research with employment or family commitments. Your PhD topic could be your own choice or you may have been recruited into a large project to work on a closely defined research area. You might be starting your PhD at the age of 23, 43 or 73! Whatever the specifics of your personal circumstances, there are common experiences for all PhD students. Being prepared for some of those issues will help you to make a good start.

Along with feelings of excitement and enthusiasm, starting a PhD can be a time of disorientation, uncertainty and anxiety about the challenge. The early weeks can feel like a false start, with little 'research' being done. Many PhD students worry that they aren't making progress, or they feel frustrated. However, this impatience or anxiety can distract you from the very important early opportunities to lay the groundwork for a successful PhD. Try not to worry too much about the research at this point. Instead, in these early weeks, focus your energies on setting yourself up for future success in terms of your work practices, supervision arrangements, support networks and broad plans. Effort spent establishing these foundations now will pay great dividends in the future. It's a cliché to say that a PhD is a marathon not a sprint, but it doesn't make it any less true. In the early stages of your PhD, you haven't even started the race – you're just limbering up; in fact, you're still in training.

The early weeks of your PhD will be busy with administrative and practical matters that might not seem like they have much to do with your research. Remind yourself that this apparent lack of progress on your research isn't a lack of progress. It's simply a different kind of progress – and just as important.

- You will meet with your supervisors and get information about the processes and milestones that your institution puts in place.
- You may have administrative duties to address, such as matriculation and registration for online or campus services.
- You may have induction events, meeting other PhD students, exploring facilities such as labs or libraries, or learning about the researcher development support available to you.
- You may have personal matters to deal with, especially if you've moved to a new city or country, such as visas, bank accounts or accommodation.

Getting started

Create a checklist of the practical matters you need to address during the first few weeks of your PhD. This will make sure you get them done and it will also give you a reassuring sense of doing *something*, when progress on your substantive research may be lacking. For example:

Checklist examples	
Personal • Open bank account • Arrange accommodation • Get your visa • Register with doctor/dentist • Join gym	**PhD** • Induction meetings • First supervisory meeting • Research methods courses • Tours of campus • Library registration • Email account • PhD terms and conditions • Fee payments

✏ Activity: Getting started checklist

1. Create a checklist of all the practical tasks you need to do to get started on your PhD.
2. Tick them off when you have done them.

Personal		PhD	
Buy *The PhD Handbook* by Doyle and Robertson	☑		☐
	☐		☐
	☐		☐
	☐		☐

	☐		☐
	☐		☐
	☐		☐
	☐		☐
	☐		☐
	☐		☐

What will it be like?

As well as addressing practical matters, you will find that you need a period of orientation to the culture and experience of being a PhD student. The following pages discuss some of the characteristics of PhD life that may demand some adjustment.

> ➡ **Action: Accept uncertainty.**
>
> The uncertainty that characterises PhD research is a theme we will return to many times. Indeed, it is an inherent characteristic of academic research. If you knew for certain what you were going to find out, you wouldn't need to do the research!

At the start of your PhD, you don't know what to expect from a PhD and you don't know what is expected from you. This can become an obstacle to getting started on your work. Despite this, you do need to find a way to get started – not only because you need to do some work but because, for your own peace of mind, you need to feel like you're making progress. As such, uncertainty can't be a reason to avoid or procrastinate about work and it shouldn't be a reason to doubt your ability to do a PhD. You will increasingly develop strategies to work with uncertainty – and we will help you with this.

Chapter 4 will help you create a high-level plan to enable you to make progress on your work in spite of the uncertainty of the early stages of your PhD. Later, Chapter 11 provides tools to help you allow for the inherent uncertainty of research. For now, we just want to reassure you that uncertainty is a common state of affairs at all stages of a PhD.

> Chapter 11 shows you how to manage uncertainty and how to deal with problems before they happen.

> ➡ **Action: Adjust to the pace of PhD work.**
>
> Whether you've come straight from a taught Masters or from the workplace, you may find the work patterns and pace of a PhD different from previous experiences.

At the very start of the PhD, you have induction meetings and events, and the supervision meetings that form the backbone of your schedule. Despite this, your calendar might seem strangely empty compared with what you're used to. In the first few months, your calendar will start to fill up, for example with research-methods courses or research-group meetings. As you move into the later stages of your PhD, you might have more calendar commitments, such as teaching, interviews or field- or lab work. However, compared with a non-academic job or a taught Master's degree, you will almost certainly have much greater control over your schedule.

The long-term pacing of a PhD is also quite unusual. It's a long arc, stretching across at least three years, or five or six years if it is part-time. There are periodic, major deliverables, such as annual progression reports and, eventually, thesis submission, but few short-term, externally imposed demands. In the early days of your PhD, the only research-related item on your 'to do' list is likely to be: 'read'. What to read, and what to do with it, is broadly up to you – in consultation with your supervisors.

This change of pace can be a relief and a luxury at first. However, it can also leave you feeling high and dry, especially at the start. There are ways in which you can create a structure for your work that will ensure you make progress and generate your own momentum. Throughout the book, we provide suggestions to get you started and to maintain this progress, such as:

- Defining and regularising your working hours (Chapter 5)
- Creating your 'office space', so 'going to work' feels automatic (Chapter 5)
- Taking control of your agenda, and instigating short-term deadlines (Chapters 9 and 10)
- Setting time-based targets for work to get a sense of progress irrespective of deadlines or deliverables (Chapter 12).

> ➡ **Action: Take charge from the start.**
>
> Whatever your previous background, you are probably used to being told what to do, to a greater or lesser extent. Now it is *your* job, with supervisory guidance, to work out what needs doing and how to do it.

If you've come from employment, your job description defined your duties and responsibilities, and a line manager monitored your work. Maybe you had annual appraisals that would give feedback, set targets and check you were doing what you were paid for. You had agreed working hours and were expected to keep to them, explicitly having to request time off. Even for a CEO, systems exist to give accountability to colleagues, clients or shareholders.

If you were a Masters student, you had to turn up to regular classes, read from a designated reading list and undertake specified assignments. Your Master's dissertation came with more autonomy, but even this will have been undertaken within the parameters of your taught course. Plus, that only took a few months, not a few years.

It can come as a bit of a surprise that, even in the early days of your PhD, you have a lot of discretion about your work. Of course, there are regulations and procedures that you must follow. Your research topic may have been substantially specified by others as part of a research funding agreement. Your supervisors will guide you about content and process, but, broadly speaking, you're in charge. You will decide – and must justify – the research questions, theoretical context, methodology, and, eventually, the conclusions of your work. You will also have to decide how to organise and deliver your work. **You are responsible for the successful completion of your PhD**; with help, but, nonetheless, responsible.

Many new PhD students fall into the trap of waiting for instruction and guidance. You're not sure what you're supposed to be doing and you assume someone will explain it to you. You might be afraid of doing the wrong thing and expect to be told the right thing to do. Don't worry, you're not completely alone – your supervisors are there to support you through your doctoral experience. However, your supervisors' role is not to manage your PhD for you, or to teach you how to do a PhD – they are your guides and mentors. We go into the role of supervision at some length in the next chapter and give you some techniques to help you build good supervision relationships.

If, from the outset, you take charge of yourself and your research project, you will be making a good start. It helps for you be proactive and develop the habit of independence that is demanded by a PhD. Taking charge of your work from the start will help you to appreciate, and therefore take, responsibility for steering your PhD. It also means that you get used to creating the motivation and momentum to see it through yourself.

> Chapter 3 deals with the supervisory relationship.

> ➡ **Action: Avoid imposter syndrome.**
> This is easier said than done, but you have been accepted into a PhD position because you *are* capable of completing doctoral-level research.

Many PhD students we talk to admit to feelings of imposter syndrome. This is a particularly pernicious problem that means you suffer from a belief that you aren't good enough, and worse, that it is also your guilty secret. You live with the worry that you will be revealed as inadequate at any moment: a very stressful way to live! Unfortunately, a PhD can easily exacerbate imposter syndrome. A PhD is a difficult undertaking with high levels of uncertainty in both the process and the outcomes of the work. Let's not pretend that it doesn't demand a lot – not everyone has the ability to complete a PhD. As a PhD student, you may go for long periods with little close examination of your work. This can allow the belief to develop that your 'real' (low) ability is somehow going unnoticed and will only be revealed when you submit your progression report or face your Viva.

Unfortunately, imposter syndrome can become self-fulfilling, limiting your ability to engage with the learning process, take risks, face new challenges and embrace opportunities. It can mean that you aren't able to get the best out of yourself or your PhD experience. Worse, it means that your PhD will be far more stressful than it needs to be.

Imposter syndrome can dog you throughout your PhD, but it is at the start, when your confidence may be shaky, that it's more likely to take hold. Conversely, this is the point at which you can (mostly) dispel these doubts by understanding and embracing the necessary learning curve that is intrinsic to a PhD.

Even if you aren't suffering from imposter syndrome, understanding the learning curve of a PhD can help you to meet the challenges of the process. You have been awarded your PhD place because you have the *potential* to do a PhD. No one thinks you already have all the skills to complete this academic research. If you were expected to turn up at the start of your PhD as an oven-ready academic researcher, it would make the PhD process a waste of everyone's time and money! You are expected to learn the necessary skills *during* your PhD so that, *by the end of it*, you have developed your expertise as an academic researcher.

We've found that a simple learning model is a valuable and often reassuring tool to help you navigate the challenges of your PhD.

> See Chapter 18 for more information on how your mindset can help you overcome imposter syndrome.

The conscious competence framework

We have used the conscious competence framework to help hundreds of PhD students prepare for the steep learning curve of a PhD. Central to this model is the fact that acceptance of your *lack* of expertise is a prerequisite for developing that expertise. This is the first of many psychological tools we introduce in this book. These are designed to help you reflect, understand and, if necessary, adapt your *attitude* to your PhD. You may be surprised just how much these 'thinking tools' can help.

The conscious competence framework describes any learning process as a combination of two factors: consciousness and competence:

- **Consciousness**: the awareness you have of your abilities and knowledge. In the framework, you're either:
    - '**unconscious**' – unaware of your skill level or ability, or
    - '**conscious**' – aware of your skill level or ability.
- **Competence**: the expertise you have in a particular task or skill. In the framework, you're either:
    - '**competent**' – you have the necessary skill or ability, or
    - '**incompetent**' – you do not possess the necessary skill or ability.

In combination, these factors create a learning cycle with four phases.

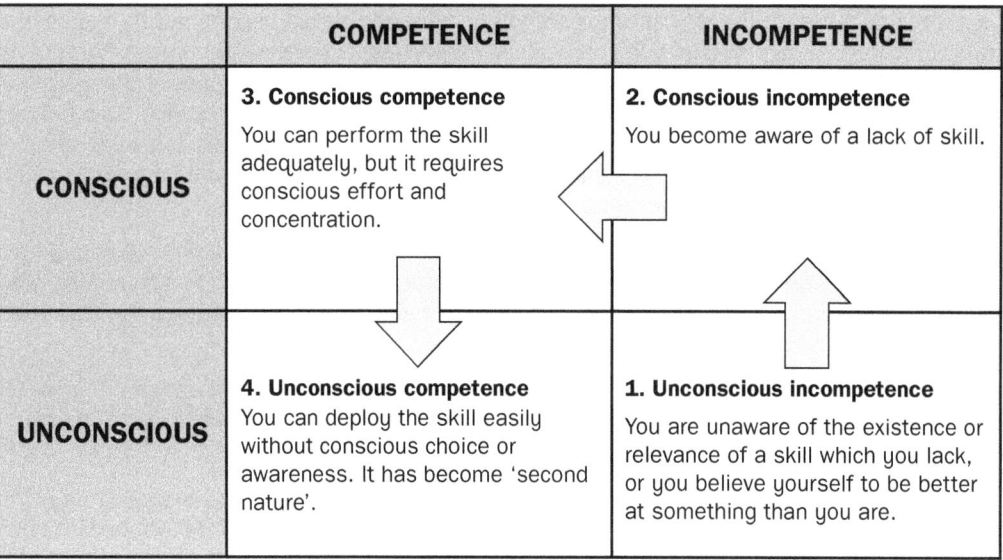

The conscious competence framework
Howell (1982) / © RDT&C

Remember that this kind of framework is designed help you make sense of your situation by simplifying things. In reality, the four stages are not discrete conditions – there are many grey areas between them. Let's look at how this model might play out for you at the start of your PhD.

1. Unconscious incompetence

At the start of your PhD, you won't have a clear idea of precisely what skills will be required and whether you have them. You might believe that you're pretty good at some of the things needed for a PhD. Perhaps you have just been awarded a distinction for your Masters thesis, or maybe your job has meant that you've written lots of reports, so you're pretty confident that you're a good writer, but, otherwise, you don't know all the skills you require and, even if you do, you don't know how to do them. You're in the unconscious incompetence phase (blissful ignorance!).

2. Conscious incompetence

At some point, something will happen that reveals your 'incompetence' to you. The most likely example at this stage is feedback from your supervisors, some of which might be critical. It turns out that you're not as good a writer as you thought, or apparently you don't know how to do a doctoral-level literature review. It might not only be supervisor feedback that reveals your lack of competence. Perhaps you try to do something and fail, or perhaps you discover that you're supposed to do something as part of your PhD that you have no understanding of: 'What on earth is a 'theoretical framework' anyway? I thought I would just send out some surveys!' You're in the conscious incompetence phase. You know you need to do something, but don't know how to do it – and it hurts. At this point, broadly speaking, you have two choices:

- You can run away! This doesn't mean you literally run away and leave your PhD. It could mean you avoid certain tasks and assume you'll never be all that good at some things. You'll stay in the painful limbo of conscious incompetence – which isn't good for your mental health or your PhD research.
- Or, you can knuckle down and acquire the necessary competence.

To move from conscious incompetence into conscious competence, you will have to put in time and effort to develop the necessary skill. You could, for example:

- Request additional feedback from your supervisors
- Seek advice from people who know better than you – such as students who are further in the PhD process or recent post-docs in the department
- Use 'trial and error'. Experiment with different ways of approaching the skill and see what works best for you
- Sign up for extra training
- Read textbooks or watch training videos
- Pool resources and set up a study group with some fellow PhD students struggling with the same skill.

Whatever strategies you use, the key message here is:

Practise, practise, practise!

During a PhD, you are developing research *skills*. It's not just a process of learning information or cramming for an exam. You are learning *how* to do something, not just engaging with *what* you're supposed to do. Understanding that a literature review includes critical evaluation of a range of relevant literature sources is a long way from being able to find and select the relevant literature, read it and critically evaluate its methodology and findings. If you've ever learnt to play a musical instrument, tried to pass a driving test or taken up a new sport, you know this from your own experience: new skills take practice.

Activity: Develop your competence

1. List the skill/s that are in your conscious incompetence phase.
2. Decide what you will do to improve the skill/s.

Skills at conscious incompetence	How to develop the skills into conscious competence
e.g. Academic writing	e.g. Rewrite anything I submit to my supervisors using their feedback. Take the university course on academic writing.

3. Conscious competence

Assuming you choose to stick at it rather than run away, you will make your way into the conscious competence phase. You now know how to perform this skill, and, eventually you can do it to, or almost to, the required standard, but it takes conscious effort and concentration. The conscious competence phase is hard work, and you might find yourself frustrated or discouraged: 'It took me two hours to read just one journal article. It's taking for ever.' Be patient – things will get easier.

➡ Action: Keep track of your conscious competence.

It is reassuring to note new skills that you have moved from conscious incompetence into conscious competence.

Not only does this show you that you are making progress, especially at the start of your PhD when you might feel that things are going slowly, but it will also remind you not to worry if this skill is still difficult.

It's part of a normal learning curve. Keep doing this throughout your PhD, not just at the start. You will continue to learn new skills until the very end.

Also keep track of the ways in which you improved this skill, for example through using feedback from supervisors, practice, training, peer support. This will suggest ideas to help you improve all the new skills that land in conscious incompetence in future. Do what has already worked for you!

> **✎ Activity: New conscious competence skills**
>
> Note any new PhD skills that are already in conscious competence.
> Reflect on what you did to improve your skill level.
>
> | Skill | How it was improved |
> |---|---|
> | | |

4. Unconscious competence

Over time, and through your sustained efforts, you will reach the final phase: unconscious competence. This is the point at which you can not only use the skill, but without thinking about it. It has become second nature. You can zip through a journal article without having a dictionary open; you can easily construct a keyword search of the relevant publication database, confident that your results are reliable; you can articulately discuss your 'theoretical framework'. You can use the required skills, and they now take less time and conscious effort.

Sadly, you often won't even realise that you've attained the much-longed-for phase of unconscious competence precisely because it's unconscious. You've forgotten that you ever found these things difficult. You will probably already be distracted by the next thing that has landed in your conscious incompetence phase: 'How do I do qualitative interviews …? How do I code using this software …?' And you're off again.

Understanding the process of learning as this combination of 'consciousness' and 'competence' can help you to handle the demands and setbacks of a PhD. A phase of incompetence is not only inevitable, but is a sign that you are involved in the learning that will ensure your success. The conscious competence framework can also protect you from imposter syndrome because it reminds you that:

> A lack of skill isn't something that needs to be hidden like a guilty secret: it is your path to learning.

> **✏ Activity: Manage and track your learning using the conscious competence framework**
>
> Use the template on page 13 to track your learning and development.
>
> 1. Every time a skill enters the conscious incompetence phase, note it in that box.
> 2. As you get better at the skill, move it into the conscious competence box, and then, over time, into the unconscious competence box.
> 3. Whenever you are struggling with a new concept or suffering from imposter syndrome, look at the table and remind yourself of all the skills you have developed during your PhD and that this process is a part of a PhD that you have successfully navigated for other skills.

This record of your skills development will also be useful when you need to demonstrate your expertise in the job market (see Chapter 23).

What to Expect

Template: Conscious competence framework

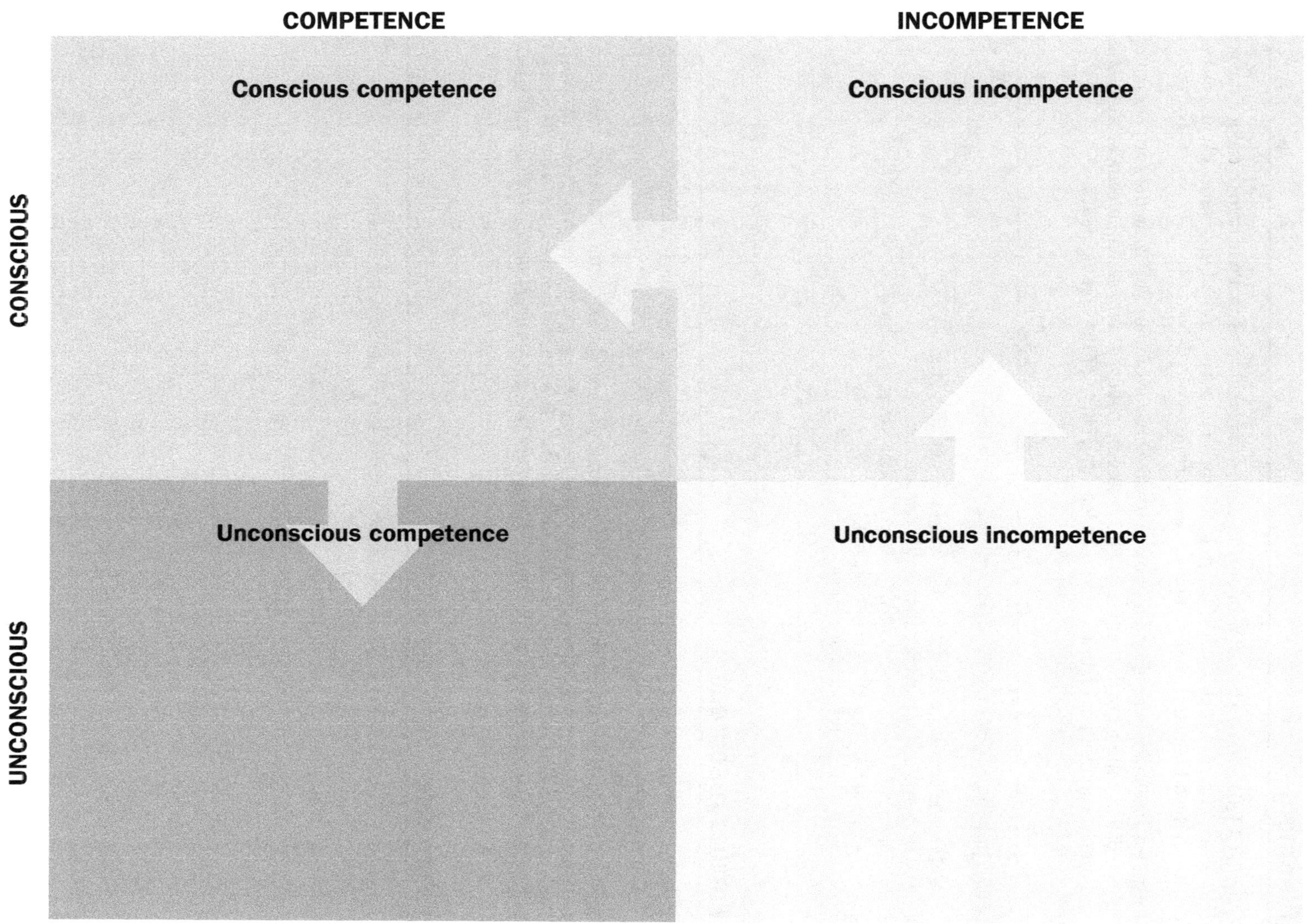

	CONSCIOUS	UNCONSCIOUS
INCOMPETENCE	Conscious incompetence	Unconscious incompetence
COMPETENCE	Conscious competence	Unconscious competence

Summary

Starting a PhD can be a big adjustment, and knowing what to expect will help to reduce the stress of the first weeks. Don't expect to make much progress on your research at this stage. It's just as important to deal with the administrative practicalities of starting out.

Despite all the unknowns, do what you can to take charge of your PhD from the very beginning. Use this time to orient yourself to the culture of PhD research, get used to the inevitable uncertainties of research, and prepare yourself to embrace the steep learning curve of the coming years.

Key points
- Manage your expectations for the first weeks of your PhD.
- Use this time for familiarisation and preparation.
- Take time to understand and adjust to your new working culture.
- Be ready for the inevitable uncertainty.
- Prepare for a steep learning curve.

Further resources

Back, L. (2007) *The Art of Listening.* London: Bloomsbury (Chapter: Epilogue – The Craft).
Bell, J. and Waters, S. (2018) *Doing Your Research Project: A Guide for First-time Researchers,* 7th edn. London: Open University Press.
Brown, G. (2021) *How to Get a PhD: A Handbook for the Journey.* Oxford: Oxford University Press.
Iornem, K.S. (2021) *A Social Science Student's Guide to Surviving your PhD.* London: Open University Press.
Petre, M. and Rugg, G. (2020) *The Unwritten Rules of PhD Research*, 3rd edn. London: Open University Press.
Phillips, E.M. and Johnson, C.G. (2022) *How to Get a PhD*, 7th edn. Maidenhead: Open University Press.

Reference

Howell, W.S. (1982) *The Empathic Communicator.* Minnesota: Wadsworth Publishing.

2 Clarify Your Personal Goals

How to ... Find your direction even when you don't know where you're going

Set academic, professional and personal goals – Visualise your future – Take action to achieve your goals – Goal-setting planner

The early days of your PhD are the perfect time to ask yourself: 'Why am I doing a PhD?' An obvious question perhaps – you want a PhD; you want to be able to call yourself 'Dr'. Clearly, the aim of a PhD is to get a PhD. You want to complete an original piece of academic research and present it as a thesis to a standard that warrants the award of Doctor of Philosophy or equivalent. A successful PhD, however, can be – and should be – so much more than the award itself.

A PhD is more than a research project, a completed thesis and a new professional title. You will learn research skills, such as detailed literature reviews and research design, technical skills linked to experimentation, software development, interviewing methods and data analysis. You will develop a deep knowledge of an intellectual field. You will learn how to write articles and to present conference papers. You might develop teaching skills. The research setting may mean that you connect with new professions and industries, which may fuel your career ambitions. Through your PhD work, you will also develop transferable skills that you will be able to utilise in different ways in your career, whether inside academia or elsewhere, such as project management, critical thinking, professional writing, constructing an evidence-based argument and public speaking. Your PhD is also an opportunity for personal development. Perhaps you want to overcome your shyness and learn how to assert yourself with other people, or increase your resilience to setbacks, or finally overcome your tendency to procrastinate.

> **It's never too late to set goals!**
> If you're reading this in the later stages of your PhD, it is still a useful exercise to set your goals and give a firm direction to whatever time you have left.
>
> We recommend that everyone reviews and refines their goals throughout their PhD, as they may change. (There is more on this in Chapter 16)

You also have a life outside your PhD. Maybe you have a job, with its own set of demands and goals. Perhaps you have important family commitments alongside your PhD. Maybe you are pursuing a significant personal goal at the same time as your PhD – such as completing a marathon or getting married!

Finally, you have your own hopes and plans for your life *beyond* your PhD. Do you hope to continue as an academic staff member, or do you wish to pursue a career in industry? Are you seeking promotion in your existing employment? Are you intending to make a career change and break into another sector? Are you aiming to launch your own business?

All these considerations affect your priorities during your PhD. Every PhD student shares the same aim of successfully achieving the award, but your PhD is also the pathway to your future. What that future will look like is different for everyone. Every PhD student will have different priorities and different aims. You have the chance to design your PhD experience so that it matches your individual priorities and delivers the future you want.

In this chapter, we encourage you to think about your wider goals for your PhD, however unformed they may be at this stage. By visualising your future in a positive and inspiring way, you can think in practical terms about how these future goals can influence your priorities during your PhD.

What next? Life after your PhD

In order to decide on your priorities during your PhD, it helps to have some sense of where you want your PhD to take you. What are your future goals – research, career and personal? Once you have some clarity about your goals, you can then make informed decisions about your choices during the course.

Why are we asking you to think about your future when you've only just started? Something that is at least three years away may not seem like much of a priority when you're still trying to navigate the immediate challenges of embarking on a PhD. You may not have a clue what you want for your future anyway, or you may be thinking: 'Obviously I'm going to be an academic, so there's nothing to consider.' However, the reason we're recommending that you spend some time thinking ahead to your future goals isn't to set them in stone, but rather to get some sense of direction. The sooner you start doing this, the easier it will be to make the necessary choices that your PhD will demand of you.

More importantly, it will mean that you don't miss useful opportunities that come up during your PhD, or 'waste' time on activities that might seem interesting but contribute little to your ultimate goals. You may not be in a position to state that you want to find a post-doc position researching the role of Argonaute proteins in vaccination, but you might know that you want to pursue a career in academic research. You might not know which company you want to work for, but you know you want a senior position in a FTSE 100 company. You might know you want to start your own business abroad, even if you're not sure exactly what that will be and where. Alternatively, you could have a very clear picture of what you want: you have held a passion for astronomy from a very early age and completing a PhD in astrophysics will take you a step closer to your dream role with one of the national space agencies. Maybe you're undertaking research into kidney transplantation because gaining a PhD is the next stage in the career ladder to becoming a consultant surgeon.

Thinking about your goals, even if at this stage they are only tentative or vague, will help you set a direction for the duration of your PhD. A PhD is a process of making choices. In your research planning, you have to narrow your research focus in order to formulate clear, specific research questions that can be adequately answered through your research design. Your research questions will then help you to maintain focus when setting parameters for your literature review and data analysis. No PhD student can read all the literature that might be relevant to their topic, nor analyse all the data. You have to make choices about the literature and data analysis that is most relevant to your research questions.

It's the same for all the other aspects of your PhD. Your PhD will bring you many, many opportunities: from teaching, to conference attendance, networking and training. It can be hard to know what to say Yes to and when to say No. What you can be sure of is that you won't be able to do *everything*. By getting a sense of your own priorities, it will be easier to make these choices. Knowing your goals will also prompt you to seek out the opportunities that will help you achieve them.

> ✎ **Activity: Reflect on your reasons for doing a PhD**
> Don't worry that this is a very vague instruction! We will revisit this in a few pages with greater direction, but beginning the thought process now will put you in a better position to complete the later activity.

Walking in fog

Pursuing a PhD, with all its uncertainties and myriad opportunities, can sometimes feel like walking through fog. How can you guide yourself through that fog? Well, what would be really useful if you actually were in real fog is a faint glimmer of light indicating the end of the journey – just a pinprick of light that you could steer towards and which would, hopefully, get a little bit brighter and clearer each time you move forwards. Determining your goals is a little bit like setting your compass in the direction of this glimmer of light. Because of the fog you might lose sight of the light now and then, but, as long as you follow your compass setting, you know you're on more or less the right track. When hiking through the fog, if you come to a fork in the path, which branch would you follow? Clearly, the one that aligns most closely with the direction indicated by your compass. It's the same in your PhD:

> **Everything you do should contribute to getting you closer to your goals.**

This sense of direction will help you use your time effectively, because you will be better equipped to focus on those things most important *to you*. It will help you to be assertive with your choices because you will know why you are making them. PhD students who aren't clear on their personal goals are more vulnerable to being influenced by other people's choices, whether from your supervisors, your fellow PhD students or your friends or family. Spending time considering your goals will *reinforce your confidence* in your choices.

Being clear about your personal goals will also motivate you to keep going in your PhD studies, even when things get tough. There will be times when you lose sight of the reasons for doing the hard graft of a PhD. Perhaps you feel discouraged by your progress or burdened by the work. Being able to step back and remember the ultimate purpose of your PhD will be a powerful means of connecting with your motivation.

The following series of activities will help you to gain some clarity about your personal goals. At this early stage, don't worry if you don't have any definite long-term aims, other than 'get a PhD'. You will firm up your goals as you go along, and they may even change altogether. If you are part-way through your research degree you can still use these activities to clarify your goals as they stand. Like many ideas in this book, it's an iterative process: you will revisit and adjust many things during your PhD, including your goals. Like the glimmer of light ahead of you in the fog, you may just be steering towards it, but things will become clearer the closer you get. A PhD should be a remarkable voyage of discovery, so it would be counterproductive to ask you to nail things down too firmly at this point. Who knows what you will learn about yourself and your opportunities and how this might affect your aspirations for the future? We will explicitly invite you to review your goals at points through the book, as you progress through your PhD and your thinking develops. So don't worry that we are asking you to commit to these goals for ever. This is just the starting point.

> **➡ Action: Visualise your future.**
>
> Start the process of considering your goals by harnessing the power of your imagination and your aspirations by using a visualisation technique. Spend a few minutes picturing what you would like your life to look like three years after graduating from your PhD. The purpose is just to stimulate your ideas. At this stage, it doesn't matter whether they're realistic; this is just to get the process started. If it helps, close your eyes.

To help you build the picture, here are a few questions that might help you imagine your desired future:

- **Imagine your job.**
    - What type of work are you doing?
    - How do you spend your time at work?
    - What is the impact of your work on others?
    - What type of organisation or company are you working in?
    - Where is it located – what country, what city, or is it in a rural setting?
    - How much are you paid?
    - Are you working full-time or part-time?
    - What are your colleagues like?
- **Imagine your skills and attributes.**
    - What expertise do you use in your work? What are you good at?
    - What do you enjoy doing?
    - What makes you proud of yourself?
- **Imagine your home and personal life**.
    - Where do you live and with whom?
    - Who do you spend your time with?
    - What do you do in your free time?

> 💬 One PhD student we met, who had just completed her PhD, admitted that one of her goals was to get a Nobel Prize! Another student was motivated by her childhood experiences of suffering discrimination because of her cultural heritage. Her goal was to use her research to reduce educational discrimination for marginalised groups. Another student simply wanted to be able to find an interesting job of a higher status.

Chapter 22 explains how to use visualisation to help you prepare for a successful Viva.

> **✏ Activity: Your vision of your future**
> Note down some of the details of your vision.

The purpose of this kind of visualisation exercise is to circumvent your rational mind and instead use your imagination to tap into personal desires and preferences that you might otherwise discount because they're not 'reasonable'. By doing this, you can uncover what you truly want and also stimulate your desire to achieve it. Research indicates that merely vividly imagining your desired future state can prime your brain to notice the opportunities that will help you achieve that future.

Set your goals and identify actions to achieve your goals

Simply imagining your desired future will not be enough to get you there, sadly! Instead, using that vision as a starting point, spend time considering what you could do during your PhD to set the wheels in motion towards achieving your vision. This is the point at which you will start defining some practical goals – and some actions – that will set you off in the right direction. Record your goals and actions on the Goal-setting planner template on page 22.

Step 1: Identify your goals

The template provides some general headings to reflect the type of goals you might pursue during your PhD:

- Research goals, such as the impact of your research, research skills
- Career goals, for example a future job, promotion prospects
- Personal development goals, such as time management, confidence
- Personal life goals, for example leisure, family, finance.

> **Vision board**
> If you like this kind of visualisation exercise, take it further by creating a vision board to reinforce the influence your vision will have on your subconscious.
>
> Create a collage or Pinterest board with images and words and phrases that represent your vision of your future. Keep it in sight – pin it above your desk or make it your screensaver – to remind you of your desired direction and to prime your unconscious to be alert for relevant information and opportunities.

> 'In a previous life as a salesman, we were encouraged to use the "vision board" technique to keep us motivated to make a sale – I had a picture of a red BMW 3 Series (I was 21!)'

Remember, we're not asking you to fix your goals (unless of course you do know exactly where you want to end up – which is fine). We want you to start the process. Within each category on the planner, identify goals that you want to achieve during your PhD. You may not have a clue yet what to do about these goals. The important thing for now is starting to get a sense of the direction you want to take – that glimmer of light in the distance. See the following example.

Date:	My goal/s	Actions to achieve my goal/s	Done ✓
Research	Ensure my research makes an impact on wildlife conservation in the UK.		
Career	Find work as a wildlife conservation consultant, specialising in rewilding projects in the UK.		

Personal development	Learn how to manage projects. Be more confident making presentations.		
Personal life	Compete in a triathlon.		

Goal-setting planner: example goals

Step 2: Identify actions to take you towards your goals

> 💬 A PhD student attended one of our communication skills courses because they were very nervous about making presentations, and knew it would limit them professionally. After building their confidence during the course, they took this further by joining the Toastmasters Club, an international association that develops public-speaking skills.
>
> Toastmasters has nothing to do with universities. It was something this student sought out because one of their personal goals was to improve their public speaking.

Once you have identified some goals, think about any actions you could take that would help you move towards your goal. Come back to this regularly, as other possible actions will emerge as you move through your PhD and discover the opportunities it presents. For example:

Date:	**My goal/s**	**Actions to achieve my goal/s**	**Done** ✓
Research	Ensure my research makes an impact on wildlife conservation in the UK.	• Identify the most endangered species in the UK. • Identify current policies on wildlife conservation.	
Career	Find work as a wildlife conservation consultant, specialising in rewilding projects in the UK.	• Use social media to connect to key figures in conservation and rewilding. • Attend the Big Picture – Rewilding Britain conference.	
Personal development	Learn how to manage projects. Be more confident making presentations.	• Go on a project management course. • Offer to present my interim results at the PhD Summer Symposium.	
Personal life	Compete in a triathlon.	• Start wild swimming.	

Goal-setting planner: example actions

➡ Action: Review your goals.

Regularly review your goals and actions during your PhD in order to amend and add to them as necessary and to identify more actions to take you to your goals.

> 💬 'I embarked upon a PhD in order to improve my professional prospects in a non-academic career. However, when I become part of a university department, I become absorbed in the world of academia, and found myself increasingly considering a future as an academic.
>
> Two-thirds of the way through my PhD I reconnected with my original purpose and adjusted my priorities accordingly. As a result, I made the choice to resign from my teaching role at the university and to complete my PhD alongside employment in training.'

Part 2 returns to the subject of setting goals for your research and identifying the deliverables that will ensure you achieve your goals. In these chapters, we provide you with some specific techniques to create well-founded goals and practical deliverables. You can apply these techniques to any kind of goal: research, career or personal.

In Chapter 16, we'll remind you to review your goals in the light of your progress in your PhD and incorporate any amended goals into your schedule.

> **Activity: Set your goals.**
>
> Use the template on page 22.
>
> 1 Choose some goals you want to achieve in each area: Research, Career, Personal development and Personal life.
> 2 Decide what you are going to do to move towards your goals.
> 3 Tick off the actions when you have done them.
> 4 Remember to review and update your goals regularly. They will change and develop as you make progress through your PhD.

Template: Goal-setting planner

Date:	My goal/s	Actions to achieve my goal/s	Done ✓
Research			
Career			
Personal development			
Personal life			

Summary

Use your PhD as a chance to make progress towards your *life goals*, not just research goals. Identifying your goals at the beginning will help you to make the most of the opportunities provided by your PhD and to spend your time and energy wisely, pursuing your own priorities. Create a strong vision of your future to guide you in the early stages, and then review and adjust your goals as necessary during your PhD.

Key points

- All PhD students will have different goals for their PhD.
- Identify your *personal* goals for your PhD. This will help you to set your priorities and find your motivation.
- Be proactive in taking steps towards your goals from the start.
- Review your goals as you progress through your PhD.

Further resources

Brann, A. (2013) *Make Your Brain Work*. London: Kogan Page.
Ditzler, J. (2006) *Your Best Year Yet!* London: Harper Element.
Hyatt, M. (2018) *Your Best Year Ever*. Grand Rapids, MI: Baker Books.
Miller, C.A. and Frisch, M.B. (2021) *Creating Your Best Life*. New York: Sterling.
Murphy, M. (2011) *Hard Goals*. New York: McGraw-Hill.

3 Establish Supervisory Relationships

How to ... Actively shape a positive supervision partnership

> What can you expect? – Be an active partner – Identify your supervision needs – Set ground rules – Conscious competence framework revisited

Whatever your personal goals, the relationship you have with your supervision team is likely to be the most important factor in shaping your PhD experience and achieving your goals. Supervisors offer you their support, intellect, experience and wisdom with the purpose of helping you successfully complete your PhD. They can become colleagues and even remain friends long after your doctoral journey is complete. Having said that, like all relationships, they don't always go smoothly. Problematic supervision relationships won't necessarily cause you to fail, but they will make the whole process more difficult and unpleasant. This chapter helps you to establish a fruitful, positive relationship rather than an obstacle to good work.

A global survey of PhD students (Woolston, 2019) reported that the majority (67 per cent) of PhD students were happy with their supervision relationship. The reasons for dissatisfaction were mainly a result of mistaken or unfulfilled expectations and poor communication. Most of the problems could easily have been avoided if care had been taken from the outset to create and communicate clear expectations of the supervision process. The early phase of your PhD is the right time to lay the foundations for your supervision relationships and avoid problems down the line.

> If you are further through your PhD, you can also use this chapter to reinvigorate and reposition your supervisory relationships for the remainder of your doctoral experience to ensure you get the best out of supervision and, if necessary, address any problems.

The formal procedures of supervision will be prescribed to a greater or lesser extent by your institution, such as the number of meetings, record-keeping and so on. There will be some kind of official Code of Practice, explaining the role and responsibilities of supervisors and the 'supervised' (you). During your PhD induction period, you should be told about these formal processes, but they don't tell the whole story. What is supervision? What can you expect from it? And, more to the point, how can you make it work well?

➡ Action: Read the code.

Find and read your key university doctoral degree guidelines (if you haven't already). Ask for clarification, if necessary, from your supervisors.

What is the supervision relationship?

The purpose of supervision is to provide you with guidance, assistance and support from two or more experienced research academics who know what is required to successfully complete a PhD. Understanding something about the nature of the supervision relationship will help you be realistic about your expectations and clear about your own role and responsibilities. We've identified six important characteristics of the supervision relationship that you need to understand in order to make the most of the supervision process.

The supervision relationship is:

1. A partnership
2. Purposeful
3. An apprenticeship
4. Individual
5. Not exclusive
6. Changing.

1. A partnership

Supervision is a partnership between you and your supervisors. It's not an equal partnership in terms of status and power, but, nonetheless, it's a partnership in which all the partners have a responsibility to make it work. The partners have different roles and responsibilities in terms of the work. For example, your supervisors are required to give you useful feedback on your submitted work, while you're expected to do the work in the first place. All the partners have a role in making the supervision process a success. As a PhD student, you have the responsibility and the opportunity to be more than a passive bystander. This means speaking up about what you need, being conscientious about fulfilling your commitments and facing problems when they arise. It means you can expect (and if necessary, ask) your supervisors to do the same.

➡ **Action: Be an active partner.**

Take responsibility and speak up when you need to.

2. Purposeful

The supervision process has one primary purpose: to ensure that you complete PhD-level research of sufficient quality within required timescales. There are other very valuable ancillary outcomes from the partnership, such as skills development, innovation and new knowledge, career development and publication. However, the bottom line is that your supervision should ensure that you achieve your 'Dr'. Make sure that you, and your supervisors, maintain the necessary focus. This might seem like stating the obvious, especially at the beginning. However, once you are deeper into your PhD, all the many opportunities and demands you encounter can distract you from the main goal of supervision.

➡ **Action**

Stay focused on the key purpose of supervision.

3. An apprenticeship

The supervision relationship is an unusual partnership. There is an obvious power differential in terms of relative status, but it's not a line management relationship. It is designed to support a professional undertaking, yet is often concerned with personal and psychological challenges. If you've come to your PhD after working in industry, you might be expecting a managerial relationship with clear lines of authority and find it hard to navigate the imprecision of supervision relationships. If you've come to your PhD straight from a taught Masters degree, you might struggle to get beyond a teacher–pupil relationship and the shift to the independent thinking that is demanded by academic research.

We think it's useful to think of supervision as an *apprenticeship*. Apprenticeships are more associated with trades or crafts, like plumbing or carpentry, rather than in relation to something as intellectual as research, but the concept of an apprenticeship accurately reflects the fact that, in a PhD, you are learning at the hands (or minds) of people who have experience doing the work. You'll learn as much from watching and listening to the experts in action as you will from their instructions. Pay attention!

> **Get your priorities straight**
>
> Be careful before accepting additional responsibilities from your supervisor or department. Teaching, data-inputting, proofreading or conference administration (all of which we were asked to do during our PhDs) may be good experience, a source of extra income or a way of creating goodwill with your supervisors, but not at the cost of submitting your thesis on time!

➡ **Action: Be prepared to learn from every expert you encounter.**

(This is a life lesson, not just PhD advice!)

4. Individual

Your supervision will be defined by the individual preferences and characters of the people involved. There is no blueprint for supervision beyond the procedural dimensions because each combination of supervisors and student will be different. The experience, knowledge and style of your supervisors will influence the kind of supervision they give you. Similarly, your experience, knowledge and personality will dictate the kind of supervision you require. This is why it is so important at the start of supervision to think about your needs. We will help you to do that later in this chapter.

Often, the match between supervisor style and student needs is comfortable and well aligned. Sometimes it takes a bit more compromise. That's all right. Unless there are serious, ongoing, professional deficits, you need to accept this and be realistic. It's like *any* professional relationship: you don't have to be best friends, you just need to be able to work together.

> **Credit where it's due**
>
> It might sound obvious, but don't forget to include your supervisors' relevant publications in your literature review.

> **Ask around**
>
> Get to know other PhD students who share the same supervisor and are further along in their PhD. Ask their advice on how to get the best out of the relationship with this supervisor.

➡ **Action**

Keep in mind (and accept) that the individuals involved will influence the nature of the supervision relationships.

5. Not exclusive

Supervision relationships are so important to PhD students that it's easy to become overly reliant on supervisors. It's often the PhD students who have the best supervision relationships that fall into this trap. Their supervision is so helpful and rewarding that they don't think to look elsewhere for information and support. They can even start to believe that going elsewhere can seem 'disloyal'. Being overly reliant on your supervisors can reduce the quality of your research because you don't have access to alternative viewpoints or wider expertise. It can cause also cause problems if things change. What if one of your supervisors leaves the institution or has a strong objection to the direction of your work?

Without undermining your supervision relationships, and always keeping your supervisors informed, make sure that you actively seek out additional contact with other people: academics, technical staff and other PhD students. There is more advice about creating the right professional support networks in Chapter 6.

➡ Action

Speak to others about your research and listen to different ideas and opinions.

6. Changing

This chapter emphasises how important it is to establish foundations for good supervision relationships from the very start of your PhD. However, we're not asking you to define what you will need from your supervision for the next few years. How can you possibly know?

Your needs will change over time. They *should* change over time if the supervision process is working. At first, you will need a lot of guidance about the nuts and bolts of research and the processes of doing a PhD. Your subject knowledge will be inferior to your supervisors' and you may feel very aware of your inexperience. As your knowledge increases and your confidence develops, you will need more challenge and debate from your supervisors, so you can test your position and learn how to argue your case. Then, towards the end of your PhD, you might need more help with establishing your future career.

At the start of your PhD, focus on creating supervision relationships that will allow for change and flexibility. How will you do that? Well, that's what the rest of the chapter is about.

> **Be transparent**
>
> If you're thinking of contacting other academic staff, at your university or elsewhere, always keep your supervisors informed. Explain who you might contact and why.
>
> Similarly, if you find yourself speaking at length to other academics at conferences, mention it to your supervisors. Academia is a small world and personal relationships are very important. It's professional courtesy to your supervisors and it may also create opportunities for further collaboration for all of you.

➡ Action

Be adaptable and prepared to change what you seek from your supervision as your research progresses.

If it goes really wrong

There's no such thing as a perfect supervision relationship. There will be frustrations and ups and downs during your PhD. However, if you feel that your supervision doesn't meet required standards, whether because of neglect, negligence or unacceptable behaviour, it is important to deal with it sooner rather than later. Many PhD students change one or more supervisors during their PhD. It doesn't have to be a damaging option.

- If you are unsure whether your supervision falls below acceptable standards, check with other PhD students. How is their supervision? What are their experiences? What should you reasonably expect? It can be hard to know what is reasonable and unreasonable. Specifically seek out other students who have your supervisor to identify if your relationship is typical.
- Check your university's Code of Practice. It will describe the roles and responsibilities of supervisors and provide information about what to do if you have a complaint.
- Raise your dissatisfaction directly with your supervisor, if you feel able. Difficulties are sometimes a result of poor communication or mismatched expectations. Don't just express your dissatisfactions. Suggest possible solutions for the problem.
- Speak in confidence to your research coordinator or doctoral college/graduate school about your concerns. Don't suffer in silence. The university is there to support you and wants you to complete your PhD successfully.

Don't forget ...

Your supervisors are very busy people

You are only one of the many demands on your supervisors' time. They will have other PhD students, teaching, meetings to attend and their own research projects. Being realistic about your status in your supervisors' lives will prevent unrealistic expectations about the amount of their time you can expect to have and how quickly they are likely to respond to requests.

You are responsible for your research

Your supervisors are there to provide guidance. They are *not* responsible for your work. They have a responsibility to oversee the progress of your PhD, keep you on track and follow necessary procedures. They should give guidance about research skills and subject knowledge and provide feedback that can help you to improve the quality of your work. They are not there to make sure you do your work or to take decisions for you.

You have more power than you think

In our contact with PhD students, we notice that the majority of them, irrespective of their PhD stage, underestimate their power in the supervision relationship. They don't see beyond the hierarchy of status and experience. Remember, supervision relationships are *partnerships* and, as one of the partners, you can have a significant influence on the quality and characteristics of the partnership through your attitude to it and your behaviours: irrespective of differences in experience, status or age.

They want you to succeed

Remember that your supervisors want you to succeed. They will invest a lot of time and effort, and don't want this to be wasted. Even when supervisors seem critical or harsh, they are trying to get the best out of you (and this is also part of academic discourse, so you will have to get used to it). Don't take it personally. Start with the assumption that your supervision team is there to help you succeed and you will be more confident and constructive in your dealings with them.

How to get what you need from supervision

The first step in ensuring you get what you need from supervision is to identify what you need! Taking time to consider your needs at the outset can help you to:

- Understand your personal priorities
- Communicate your priorities clearly
- Establish yourself as an active partner in the relationship
- Understand when to go outside the supervisory relationship to fulfill some needs
- Monitor your progress as your needs change.

What can you legitimately expect from your supervisors when it comes to your needs? First, refer to your university's Code of Practice, which should lay out the supervisory role and responsibilities. Research published by the UK Council for Graduate Education (2021) provides a useful insight into how research supervisors in the UK see their role and the guidance they can and should provide to PhD students. This can be divided into four main categories:

- **Managerial/administrative**, such as research management, procedures and administration, grants and funding, visas and travel
- **Intellectual**, for example methodology, critical thinking, academic writing, ethics and integrity, topic-related knowledge
- **Technical**, such as equipment / software, lab skills, research skills, referencing, information management, publishing and copyright
- **Personal**, such as well-being, work-life balance, confidence-building, motivation, career-development and networking.

Supervision needs analysis

At any stage in a PhD, but particularly at an early stage, it can be hard to identify your needs conclusively as you may have little understanding of the demands of the PhD. At least considering them in these early days, however, means you are establishing it as a *behavioural norm* – the habitual ways we behave in certain social situations. Your actions will cement your role as an active partner in the relationship.

Your needs will change at every stage in your PhD. If you are already further into your PhD, simply consider your needs as they currently stand.

✎ Activity: supervision needs analysis

Using the template on page 31:

1. Think of your current needs in terms of the demands of your PhD.
2. Identify how your supervisors can help you with your particular needs.
3. Decide what else you can do to make this happen.

Don't worry too much about which of your needs go into which category. The categories are simply there to prompt your thoughts about your different requirements. To help, we have provided an example of a completed template.

Example supervision needs analysis

Type of support	1. My current needs	2. How to get what I need from my supervisors	3. What else I can do to make this happen
Managerial/administrative e.g. research management, procedures/administration, grants and funding, visas and travel	I've worked internationally before and I want to do some of my fieldwork abroad. I need to know whether this is possible financially and practically.	I will ask for suggestions of potential funding and how best to include this in the timeline of my research.	I will contact the organisations I already have links with to ask about possible internships or visits.
Intellectual e.g. methodology, critical thinking, academic writing, ethics and integrity, topic knowledge	I haven't done any academic work for over 10 years. I am not sure about academic writing style and proper referencing.	I will ask my supervisors to look at a very early draft of my literature review and ask for particular feedback on my writing and referencing.	I will create or join a 'writing group' with other PhD students, so we can critique each other's writing.
Technical e.g. equipment/software, lab skills, research skills, referencing, information management, publishing and copyright	Some of the testing equipment is difficult to access and the rest of research team want to use the same equipment. I'm worried I won't be able to get enough access to do my research in time.	I will ask if there are any other available test rigs in the university that I could use, or if there is any funding for more equipment.	I could liaise with the technicians to set up a rota with other research students and post-docs, so that we have equal access to the equipment.
Personal e.g. well-being, work-life balance, confidence-building, motivation, career-development and networking	I struggle with my time management, especially long-term deadlines. I'm worried I will leave things to the last minute and end up rushing.	I will agree with them to submit my supervision reports a minimum of 7 days before each meeting.	I will go on the time management course offered by the Researcher Development Department and make sure I read Chapter 12 of this book.

Template: Supervision needs analysis

Type of support	1. My current needs	2. How to get what I need from my supervisors	3. What else I can do to make this happen
Managerial/administrative e.g. research management, procedures/administration, grants and funding, visas and travel			
Intellectual e.g. methodology, critical thinking, academic writing, ethics and integrity, topic knowledge			
Technical e.g. equipment/software, lab skills, research skills, referencing, information management, publishing and copyright			
Personal e.g. well-being, work-life balance, confidence-building, motivation, career-development and networking			

Establish Supervisory Relationships **31**

In an exercise designed to help you identify your supervision needs, it might seem curious that we're asking you to come up with ideas of things you can do yourself. It's because it's unlikely that your supervisors alone will be able to fulfill all your needs and, equally as importantly, you need to get into the habit of taking charge of your PhD research rather than passively relying on your supervisors.

Set ground rules

Use the early meetings with your supervisors to create ground rules for the way your contact with supervisors will proceed. Ground rules are simple 'rules of conduct', that are mutually agreed, to manage collaboration. You can do this both:

- **Explicitly**, by discussing things like meeting arrangements
- **Implicitly**, by establishing norms of behaviour, in the way that you interact with your supervision team.

Some institutions have very prescriptive arrangements for the frequency and duration of supervision contact and the practices around supervisory meetings. Many do not, however, and leave it to the supervisors and students. In either case, you can take an active role in agreeing the standard arrangements for your supervision meetings while, obviously, being respectful and accommodating of your supervisors' preferences.

Your ground rules for meetings, for example, might cover:

- Frequency*
- Usual duration
- Location/s
- Joint or individual supervisor meetings*
- Preparation and circulation of an agenda; standard items for the agenda
- Submission in advance of student work for discussion, such as method and timescales
- Note-taking/recording of decisions/minutes*
- Cancellation of meetings.

Your ground rules don't have to limit themselves to the conduct of meetings. You could also determine items such as:

- Holidays*
- Working hours*
- Email contact between meetings
- Preferred method of contact (email, phone, social media, knock on door)
- How quickly to expect a response
- What to do if problems arise in between meetings.

*These elements are often specified by your university.

> **Transferable skills**
>
> Ground rules are a great technique, in all sorts of situations, when you want to optimise collaboration. They are often used to establish agreements about behaviour in regular meetings.
>
> We often use them at the start of training courses and recommend them as a team-building activity for any kind of work team.
>
> The key point is that the rules have to be agreed to by everyone and, ideally, the rules are proposed by the team members rather than being imposed.
>
> The group discussion and agreement of the rules helps people get to know each other. It also means that you can create a group environment that people feel more comfortable with: respectful communication.
>
> The fact that everyone buys in to the 'rules' also makes it more likely that people will follow them (such as punctuality or no mobile phones in meetings).

There are a number of benefits from actively participating in the agreement of ground rules for your supervision arrangements:

- You have an influence on what is agreed and are more likely to get what you want.
- It ensures that (mutual) expectations are clear and explicit.
- It establishes you as an active partner in the relationship.
- It gives you practice in 'speaking up for yourself' early in the relationship on an uncontroversial issue (rather than only when you need to address something more contentious later on).

Deal or no deal

Get into the habit of verbally double-checking any agreements in your supervision meetings. Don't just assume that you know what's been agreed. Check *your* understanding against *your supervisors'* understanding by quickly summarising the agreements, either immediately after they've been agreed or at the end of the meeting as a summary, even if you're going to follow up in writing. It resolves misunderstandings early and also helps you to practise speaking up.

'I did this at the start of my PhD and it made a massive difference. I didn't call them "ground rules" (I thought that sounded a bit formal!), but we all discussed how the supervisory team meetings, and supervision in general, would run. It worked really well, as it established my expectations and needs with my supervisors, but also clarified their expectations of me as their student. We were all on the same page.'

Activity: Set your ground rules

1. Select some supervision issues that would benefit from ground rules, such as how often meetings will be, or what reports you will submit and when.
2. Then discuss and agree ground rules with your supervisors.
3. Use the template on page 34 to record your ground rules.

Template: Supervision ground rules

	Ground rules
Meetings	
Frequency	
Usual duration	
Location/s	
Joint/individual supervisor meetings	
Preparation and circulation of an agenda	
Standard items for the agenda	
Advance submission of student work, e.g. method, timescales	
Note-taking/recording of decisions	
Cancellation of meetings	
Other arrangements	
Holidays	
Working hours	
Preferred method of contact between meetings (email, phone ...)	
How quickly to expect a response	
What to do if there are problems between meetings	
Other issues:	

Conscious competence revisited

You can use the conscious competence framework introduced in Chapter 1 as a guide to help you get the most out of your supervision relationships. Remember, the framework describes how your route to expertise must inevitably go via the 'conscious incompetence' phase, progressing through 'conscious competence' before finally reaching 'unconscious competence'. Understanding this process as it applies to supervision means that you can:

- **Embrace your novice status**. You are not expected to know how to do everything at the start of your PhD, so don't pretend that you do.

➡ **Action**

Ask questions when you don't understand and seek advice on how to improve the skills you know you lack.

- **Push your limits**. Actively use your supervision to move things into the conscious incompetence stage, understanding that this a necessary path to improvement.

➡ **Action**

Take on work that tests the limits of your skill or knowledge, rather than avoiding it until you have no choice. For example, offer to present an early draft of your literature review chapter, before your supervisors have requested it.

- **Don't fear mistakes**. Getting things wrong is the path to doing them well. Accept and act upon the critical feedback from your supervisors.

➡ **Action**

When you make a mistake, repeat the task, incorporating the feedback, and see what difference it makes.

- **Access your supervisors' unconscious competence**. Even the best supervisors sometimes forget just how much 'unconscious competence' they have. They won't necessarily think to explain something to you. Ask what may feel like the 'stupid' question. You're a novice, remember!

➡ **Action**

If you don't understand something, ask.

✏ **Activity: Develop your competence**
1 Choose a research skill or task that is currently in your 'conscious incompetence' phase.

> 2 Decide how you will use your supervision team to help you move the skill or task into 'conscious competence'.

Summary

Your supervision relationships can make or break your PhD experience. As such, it is worth investing effort at the start to create the foundations for a good experience. Understanding the nature of supervision can help you to be realistic about what you can expect from it and ensure you make the most of it. Supervision is a partnership in which you have more power than you might think. Participate in the creation of behavioural norms at the start of the relationship to ensure that your supervision is flexible and constructive and meets your needs.

> **Key points**
> - Understand what you can and can't expect from your supervision team.
> - Take the time to create a solid foundation for your supervision relationships.
> - Establish yourself as an active partner in your supervision relationships from the start.
> - Identify your supervision needs and do what you can to obtain the right support at every stage.
> - Ask questions and learn everything you can from your supervisors.

Further resources

Badiru, A., Rusnock, C.F. and Valencia, V.V. (2021) *Project Management for Research: A Guide for Graduate Students.* Boca Raton, Fl: CRC Press.

Phillips, E.M. and Johnson, C.G. (2022) *How to Get a PhD*, 7th edn. Maidenhead: Open University Press.

Rugg, G. and Petre, M. (2020) *The Unwritten Rules of PhD Research*, 3rd edn. Maidenhead: Open University Press.

References

UK Council for Graduate Education (2021) *UK Research Supervision Survey 2021 Report.* London.

Woolston, C. (2019) Just a minute ... PhD students voice concerns on mentoring, *Nature*, **575**: 551–552.

4 Plot Your Course

How to ... Create a useful plan when you don't know what you're doing

> Unknown unknowns – The purpose of planning – What makes a good plan – Only plan what you can plan – High-level timeline

At a news briefing in 2002 (Department of Defense, 2002), the then US Secretary of State for Defense, Donald Rumsfeld, stated:

> As we know, there are known knowns – there are things we know we know. We also know there are known unknowns. That is to say, we know there are some things we do not know. But there are also unknown unknowns – the ones we don't know we don't know.

There was much critical commentary on this quote at the time, however it makes a lot of sense when discussing planning and applies very well to planning a PhD.

Known knowns: Events that you know will happen, work you know you need to complete and knowledge you know you already have. Your known knowns will make up the basis of your initial plan and inform how you will 'manage' your work. You *know* what they are, *know* they need to be done and *know* how to do them.

Examples: Known knowns

- Similar tasks you've done as part of your Masters dissertation, such as literature review and primary research
- Software you know how to use
- A theoretical model you're familiar with

Known unknowns: Events, problems or opportunities you *know could* happen but it is *unknown* whether they actually will. For example, you *know* that your supervisor could have time off sick, but it is *unknown* whether they will until it happens. It also covers things you *know* that you need to do but, at the moment, you *don't know* how to do them, such as skills you know you will need to learn and develop.

Examples: Known unknowns

- Research tasks you know you will need to perform but haven't done before, such as a particular research method or type of data analysis
- Theoretical models you know you need to learn
- A body of literature you're aware of but not familiar with

Unknown unknowns: Events or problems that are completely unexpected; things that you *don't even know* that you *don't know*. You can't predict if or when they will happen. They may also be skills or knowledge you need to acquire, but are as yet unaware of, in your 'unconscious incompetence'.

> **Examples: Unknown unknowns**
>
> There should be no examples here because you genuinely don't know these things yet! However, examples from other PhD students include:
>
> - The university unexpectedly cancelling its licence for the data-management software you use
> - A global pandemic meaning qualitative data has to be collected through one-to-one video interviews instead of face-to-face focus groups.

At the beginning of your PhD, you have a large number of unknown unknowns. It's not a comfortable position, but it's how all PhDs begin and is part of the interest and challenge of postgraduate research. It does mean, however, that you need to find a way of starting something as daunting as a PhD despite the many unknown unknowns.

This chapter takes you through three aspects of initial planning that will help you to make a start on your PhD:

- The purpose of PhD planning
- Knowing what makes a 'good' plan for you
- Creating your high-level PhD timeline.

By the end of the chapter, you'll have created a plan that indicates the key phases of a PhD. This will give you a sense of where you roughly expect to be during the lifetime of your research and help you to identify what you should be getting on with at what time. You will focus on using your known knowns as your initial foundation. When things become clearer as your PhD progresses, you will then build on this foundation to create detailed plans for the specific pieces of work required to complete the research successfully. We cover the creation of these detailed plans in Part 2: How to Get Going. For now, we hope that this chapter reassures you that, even though everything is a little hazy right now, it will all be achievable.

The purpose of PhD planning

Does anything ever go exactly according to plan? Rarely. If you accept this, you should also agree that your plan is almost always going to be wrong! Or at least it won't perfectly reflect the 'real world'. Once you accept this, it's wonderfully liberating.

If a plan is going to be wrong, then what is the point of it? The purpose of a plan, especially for a research project, is not to precisely map reality. Its purpose is to act as a guide to steer you through your work. It gives a reference point against which decisions can be made and progress can be assessed. A plan allows you to answer three questions:

1 Are you roughly where you want to be?
2 If so, are you happy to continue down this path?
3 If not, what do you need to change?

These three questions allow you to check at any time whether your PhD is going, quite literally, according to plan. If it is, then fantastic. Keep going. If not, you have the opportunity to adjust what you're doing before it's too late. It's only when you know you have a problem that you can fix it. Your plan helps you to see the problems and address them early on. We should also emphasise that:

The process you go through when planning is infinitely more important than the final plan itself.

US President Dwight D. Eisenhower famously said, 'Plans are worthless; planning is everything' (National Archives and Records Service, 1958), which is perhaps a contentious thing to quote in a chapter on creating a PhD plan! However, the point Eisenhower made was that, by definition, when something unexpected occurs, it simply means the work is not going to proceed in exactly the way you intended. We've already established that many things will happen in your PhD that are unforeseen and can't be anticipated. However, this is not a bad thing – it's just a reflection of the situation you find yourself in. Change is bound to occur and, by referencing your plan, you can see clearly what has changed, assess why and take back control by deciding what to do next. There are two main reasons why planning is useful:

1. The *process* of planning generates helpful information. The wealth of data you harvest about your PhD in the planning phases is extremely valuable. Planning requires a full, thorough, holistic understanding of the work and everything involved in completing it successfully. Through planning, you begin to think about a whole range of issues. It's not simply a process of deciding what task to do when. You consider the purpose, goals and objectives of the project, and the people involved and their differing expectations. You identify threats and opportunities; establish sound, professional relationships; understand your strengths and areas you need to develop. You think about your personal reasons for engagement and commitment. The process of planning produces useful information such as: how many hours you need to spend on a piece of work; how long it will be before it is finished; the people/facilities/software you will need and when. Planning means you achieve a level of detail that allows you to make better estimates, be more accurate in your predictions of resources and have a clearer understanding of where potential problems may lie. This allows you to manage your workload more easily and set realistic and achievable milestones, which in turn reduces your stress and worry.
2. The second major reason for planning is that it reduces the chance that you will miss something important. This can be a particular risk in a PhD when you are often completing complicated tasks for the first time. Planning will help you to identify the things you might otherwise overlook.

There is an important point that is crucial when you approach planning for your PhD. We can't emphasise this strongly enough:

A good plan is the plan that *works for you*.

The level of detail you need for your plan is the level of detail you need to *successfully do your work* with minimum stress. No more, no less.

This might seem obvious, but, too often, people spend time making plans that don't help them to do their work. At too high a level, there's no point in doing it: you're wasting your time *pretending* to plan; too detailed and you'll spend all your time updating your plan as things change. The rest of this chapter provides a method of producing a high-level plan appropriate to the beginning of your PhD. In Part 2, you learn how to increase the level of detail in a way that will be helpful in managing and completing your day-to-day research.

What is a 'good' plan for you?

How do you plan an entire PhD? The simple answer is, you can't – or at least not in very much detail. You don't know what you're going to be doing day by day, week by week or even month by month for the next three or so years. However, we've met many PhD students who have been asked to do this by their universities or supervisors: 'Give me a detailed timeline for the next three years of your research.' They do it, submit it, and then never look at it again because it was all make-believe!

To plan a project where the end point lacks clarity, such as a PhD, you plan it in the same way that you would go about eating an elephant: *one bite at a time*! If something is too big to manage as a whole, break it down into smaller, more manageable, bite-sized pieces and deal with each 'bite' as you get to it. This is one of the fundamental tenets of planning:

Only ever plan what you *can* plan.

If you cannot see clearly more than three months into the future, then only plan in detail for those next three months. There is no point in 'guessing' for the remainder, as you're just making things up. During those three months, you'll learn more about your work, your ideas will mature and you may develop new skills. By the end of the three months, you will be ready to plan for the next few months. Go through your project by planning each 'bite' as you get to it.

Remember, although the *output* of every PhD is unique, the *process* to get to that output is not. As such, almost all PhDs (regardless of subject area or topic) follow similar, predictable, and necessary, phases. At the very start, you can produce a high-level timeline based on these standard phases. Maybe not week by week, but even on the first day of your PhD, you can look at what other people have done and map your research by quarter (in three-month periods). As you arrive at each 'bite', plan it in detail, as you will know much more about that phase of your project now than you did at the very beginning.

So, back to the question, how do you plan your PhD? The level of detail to which you can plan will depend very heavily on your understanding of your topic, the clarity of the research objectives and how well-defined your PhD is. For example, you may be contributing to a bigger research project, in which case, on day one, your supervisor might be able to give you quite detailed instructions of the work you'll be expected to complete. Conversely, you could be taking a grounded theory approach, where the later tasks might only begin to emerge after you complete and begin to analyse the data, or you may be iteratively developing and testing an algorithm or model where you don't know what will work, so constant trial and error loops make it very difficult to plan.

Let's assume for the moment that, regardless of your particular topic or methodology, you have a lot of unknown unknowns. Try to establish what you do know and, therefore, what you can realistically get a handle on. Although you don't know what your unique PhD outputs look like, the process you'll go through to get to them is not unique. You *will* have to:

- Write a literature review
- Design your research (philosophy, approach, methods, experiments and so on)
- Collect data (experimentation, fieldwork, collation of sources, modelling, interviews, focus groups, questionnaires)
- Analyse your data
- Draw conclusions from your data
- Write up your thesis
- Prepare for your Viva

Regardless of your discipline, these are phases you have to complete as part of your PhD. You may already know about additional phases specific to your research, depending on your topic or methodology, for example:

- Social science researchers might conduct a pilot study to test the robustness of their intended research method.
- Some PhD students might not need to undertake the detailed research design because their supervisor has done it as part of the wider research proposal.

- A PhD that is contributing to a bigger research project and/or industry collaboration might need integration or additional feedback loops.
- There may be several iterative and overlapping 'hypothesise-experiment-evaluate' phases.

> **Learn from others**
>
> Speak to your supervisors, talk to colleagues who are further through the process than you, or chat to some recent post-docs in your research group or department. (People love to talk about their own work, especially if you buy them a coffee.) Look at recent theses submitted by other PhDs in your department, as, often, the rough phases of a PhD will map to the chapters of the final body of work.

> **Activity: Identify the main phases of your PhD**
>
> 1. Speak to others and skim through recent theses to give yourself an idea of the general phases of work that will make up your PhD.
> 2. Note down the phases.

At this point, you won't know much about the detail of these phases, but, for now, that doesn't matter. What is important is that you have a broad sense of the stages of your PhD. Identifying these phases allows you to create the high-level timeline that is the first stage of planning your PhD.

Creating a high-level PhD plan

This planning is a step-by-step process. By the end of it, you will have a high-level timeline, sometimes called a Gantt chart, that will:

- Allow you to see your entire PhD taking shape and, hopefully, give you some confidence that there is (although very far away) light at the end of the tunnel
- Act as a reference point and help you to understand the impact that changes may have on your PhD
- Allow you to ring-fence personal commitments by planning for, then taking, time off, holidays and so on.

> If you are already further on in your PhD, don't re-plan your research from the beginning, but follow the steps to map out the high-level phases for the remainder of your research project.

Step 1: Enter time axis and phases

A timeline is simply a table with two axes.

- Along the top, plot 'Time'. At this early stage, think very approximately, in terms of months (and mark O for October, N for November …) and years.

- The left side shows the different high-level 'phases' or 'stages' of the PhD that you identified on page 41. Write each phase (for example 'Literature review', 'Detailed design') in the left column. These do not need to be in any particular order – just capture as many as you can. Remember, you can ask your supervisors and/or other students or read recently published theses for inspiration for your phases.

PhD Year	Year 1	Year 2	Year 3
Month	O N D J F M A M J J A S	O N D J F M A M J J A S	O N D J F M A M J J A S
Literature review			
Detailed research design			
Pilot study			
Update design			
Data collection I			
Data analysis I			
Data collection II			
Data analysis II			
Data collection III			
Data analysis III			
Write-up			
Submission			

Project timeline: phases and timescale

> **Activity: Plot time axis and phases**
>
> Using the template on page 47, create your high-level timeline. Add an appropriate timescale across the top and as many phases as you can identify.

Step 2: Enter approximate durations

The next step is to estimate timescales, which means guessing how long it will take to do things you've never done before! Don't worry, we consider estimating in more detail in Chapter 9. For now, all you need are indicative durations.

Again, talk to people who've been there before (supervisors, post-docs, PhD students ahead of you). You may face the answer, 'I can't tell you – every PhD is different,' but press on. All PhDs *are* different, but there *will* be an average time for people within your field to complete a literature review. There *will* be a typical time for completing the data collection. The main thing to remember is that this is still a very high-level timeline, giving a rough indication of where you'd expect to be during a normal PhD in your field. Don't be too concerned about the accuracy of the estimates right now. Of greater importance at the initial stages is understanding what the whole process is going to look like.

> **➔ Action**
>
> Ask people in the know about the approximate duration of each phase of your PhD.

> **How long?**
>
> In qualitative research, collecting data via research interviews may take only around three months. But you may then spend 18 months transcribing, coding and analysing your data. Alternatively, if your PhD

> is experimental, you might spend 18 to 24 months in the lab, running, analysing and re-running experiments, simulations or developing models.
>
> Accuracy isn't too important just now – it's about giving yourself a 'feel' for the project.

As you estimate these approximate durations, on the right of the table (under the timeline), try to judge **when you'll start** and **when you aim to finish** each phase. Colour the boxes between those points. It is unlikely that everything will be completely linear or sequential (one phase finishing, then the next phase starting). There will be overlap between activities; for example, you may not finish the literature review before you begin the detailed research design.

PhD Year	Year 1												Year 2												Year 3											
Month	O	N	D	J	F	M	A	M	J	J	A	S	O	N	D	J	F	M	A	M	J	J	A	S	O	N	D	J	F	M	A	M	J	J	A	S
Literature review	■	■	■	■	■	■																														
Detailed research design					■	■	■																													
Pilot study								■																												
Update design									■																											
Data collection I										■	■																									
Data analysis I												■	■																							
Data collection II														■	■																					
Data analysis II																■	■																			
Data collection III																									■	■										
Data analysis III																											■	■								
Write-up																			■			■											■			
Submission																																				■

Project timeline: phase durations

There may be some activities that continue throughout the whole PhD, such as reviewing the literature. You will write a major literature review early in your PhD, but you'll revisit it regularly (especially when writing up) to ensure that your sources are up to date and you have noted and referenced the most recent work in the field. So, in theory, the 'lit review' phase could run for your entire PhD. That is not very helpful to your planning, however, so, for the time being, just have one initial block of your timeline allocated to literature review.

> **Activity: Enter approximate duration of phases**
>
> Continue the template by entering approximate durations. Colour boxes on the right to indicate when you roughly expect to be doing these activities. Using different colours will make it easier to read.

Step 3: Enter fixed dates

The next step is to identify any fixed (or hard) dates: deadlines that are immovable, or any events that you know of already. For example, you may be able to calculate approximate dates for your progress reviews. These form the process through which the university checks that you are progressing satisfactorily. Usually towards the end of the first year, the progress review decides whether you can move on from your first to second year. Different universities deal with this in different ways: some have review meetings; some call it 'differentiation', others 'transition'. If you have a rough idea of when yours might be, include it in your timeline.

It's never too early to begin considering other events, perhaps those not directly related to the substantive research work:

- **Formal events**, such as an induction programme that you want to (or must) attend.
- **Training opportunities** you want to take advantage of in the early months. Many universities have extensive training programmes for doctoral researchers.
- **Conferences** related to your research. It's probably too early to be thinking about presenting at these, but most conferences are advertised many months (sometimes years) in advance, so search for ones relevant to your discipline that you might want to attend. Your supervisors can help, as can browsing journals and asking other researchers (as well as searching online).

Activity: Fixed events
Investigate set events that interest you and note down the details.

Event	Date

Add these to your timeline and differentiate fixed dates from your 'normal' PhD activities by using a different annotation. In the example here we use dots for 'hard' dates (using colours to distinguish different types of activities can be helpful too).

PhD Year	Year 1	Year 2	Year 3
Month	O N D J F M A M J J A S	O N D J F M A M J J A S	O N D J F M A M J J A S
Literature review			
Detailed research design			
Pilot study			
Update design			
Data collection I			
Data analysis I			
Data collection II			
Data analysis II			
Data collection III			
Data analysis III			
Write-up			
Submission			
Induction	●		
3-month review	●		
First-year report preparation			
First-year report submission	●		
Research methods course	●		
Statistics training	●		
Conference Dublin	●		
Conference San Francisco	●		
Conference Valencia	●		

Project timeline: fixed dates

> ✏ **Activity: Enter fixed dates into your timeline**
>
> Continue to fill in the template on page 47 by entering any set dates you know about. Indicate on the right of the table approximately when you expect these to occur. Again, colour-coding may be helpful.

Step 4: Enter non-research activities

The final events that you *must* include in your initial plan are your non-PhD activities. Ensuring that you have an effective work-life balance is vitally important when undertaking a PhD. Do things that make you happy! Cultivating positive emotions has been shown to increase your resilience, reduce stress and boost learning. Doing what you enjoy gives you a well-earned break from the PhD and can positively impact the time and energy you devote to your research.

> Chapter 14 includes tips to use happiness to decrease your stress and increase your resilience.

For the purposes of this timeline, you don't need to schedule your HIIT class for every Thursday or choir on a Tuesday. However, do include time for days off and annual leave, and try to protect them at all costs. You may feel pressured (and put yourself under pressure) not to take any time off, and one thing that's guaranteed is, if you don't plan it, it won't happen. You don't need exact dates at this point. Indicate roughly the weeks or months where you want these things to happen.

PhD Year	Year 1												Year 2												Year 3											
Month	O	N	D	J	F	M	A	M	J	J	A	S	O	N	D	J	F	M	A	M	J	J	A	S	O	N	D	J	F	M	A	M	J	J	A	S
Literature review	■	■	■	■	■	■																														
Detailed research design					■	■	■																													
Pilot study							■	■																												
Update design									■																											
Data collection I										■	■	■	■																							
Data analysis I													■	■																						
Data collection II															■	■	■																			
Data analysis II																		■	■																	
Data collection III																				■	■	■														
Data analysis III																							■	■												
Write-up																	■	■					■	■	■	■			■	■	■	■	■	■		
Submission																																				●
Induction	●																																			
3-month review			●																																	
First-year report preparation							■	■																												
First-year report submission												●																								
Research methods course					●																															
Statistics training							●																													
Conference Dublin													●																							
Conference San Francisco														●																						
Conference Valencia																							●													
Holidays (Christmas, Easter etc)			■				■								■				■								■				■					
Visit family								■														■														
Barney's wedding																						●														
Vacation time		■							■	■											■	■											■	■		

Project timeline: non-PhD activities

We also recommend including public holidays when the university is closed because, during these times, access to people (your supervisor needs a break too) and facilities, such as the lab, might be limited. Again, you may want to indicate this type of activity with a different colour on your chart.

> **Activity: Non-research activities**
>
> Think about activities outside your research and list them here.

> **Activity: Enter non-research activities into your timeline**
>
> Continue to complete your timeline by including notable non-research activities. Indicate on the main body of the table approximately when you expect these to occur. Again, colour-coding may be helpful.

Congratulations! You have now created a high-level timeline for your PhD. Despite all those unknown unknowns, you have succeeded in beginning a plan that gives you an approximate, visual indication of where you hope to be at different points over the next few years. As you progress through the course, this will necessarily change, but you have a foundation to work from.

Template: High-level PhD timeline

Years	Months	PhD phases

Summary

At the start of your PhD, you face many unknowns. However, you can create a high-level plan to guide you, in spite of the uncertainties, by building on what you *do* know and planning in bite-sized pieces. A plan is not supposed to be perfect, but indicative. The act of planning provides you with lots of useful information about your project, not just the plan itself. All PhDs follow similar predictable and necessary phases, and you can use this to create a high-level overview for your whole PhD. For now, concentrate any detailed planning just on the next phase of your PhD: only plan what you can plan.

Key points
- Planning is possible despite uncertainties and unknowns.
- The process of planning is as valuable as the plan it produces.
- Create a plan that matches the current stage of your knowledge – whatever that is.
- Structure a high-level timeline for the standard key phases of your PhD.
- Implement a planning process that evolves with your PhD.

Further resources

Badiru, A., Rusnock, C. and Valencia, V.V. (2021) *Project Management for Research: A Guide for Graduate Students*. Boca Raton, Fl: CRC Press.
Heagney, J. (2022) *Fundamentals of Project Management*, 6th edn. London: Harper Collins.
Portnoy, J.L. and Portnoy, S.L. (2022) *Project Management for Dummies*, 6th edn. Hoboken, NJ: Wiley & Sons.
Wysocki, R.K. (2019) *Effective Project Management – Traditional, Agile, Extreme, Hybrid*. Indianapolis: Wiley.

References

National Archives and Records Service (1958) *Public Papers of the Presidents of the United States, Dwight D. Eisenhower, 1957, Containing the Public Messages, Speeches, and Statements of the President, Remarks at the National Defense Executive Reserve Conference, Date: November 14, 1957*, p 818. Available at: babel.hathitrust.org/cgi/pt?id=miua.4728417.1957.001&view=1up&seq=858 [accessed 23 January 2023].
US Department of Defense (2002) DoD News Briefing – Secretary Rumsfeld and Gen. Myers Rumsfeld, February 12, 2002 11:30 AM EDT. Available at: https://archive.ph/20180320091111/http://archive.defense.gov/Transcripts/Transcript.aspx?TranscriptID=2636 [accessed 23 January 2023].

5 Create Good Habits

How to ... Start as you mean to go on

> Habit formation – Save time and effort later – Regularise the working day – Set out your workspace – Show up to the page – Get the writing habit – Information management systems

Creating a high-level plan will guide you through your PhD and indicate the types of activities you should be working on and when, but it doesn't always help you to get on with the work. In this chapter, we encourage you to use the early stages of your PhD to establish working practices that will help you to be productive from the start of your PhD and make it easier for you to sustain your work output throughout. To do this, we discuss how you can harness the power of habit. In Chapter 3, we explained how to establish productive behavioural norms for your supervision relationships. Here, we suggest how you can create productive behavioural norms for your own work, by establishing helpful routines and habits.

For many PhD students, the absence of imminent deadlines and the personal autonomy around working hours can be both a blessing and a curse. The flexibility can be one of the joys of PhD work, but it can easily backfire if you get into a habit of not putting in a full day's work because you don't 'have to'. Not only will your output suffer, but the knowledge that you're not getting much done and falling behind can undermine your mental well-being.

You may have a strict regime of office hours set by your supervisors or the wider research group. Even if you aren't subject to explicit rules, there will be guidance around expected working hours in your university's doctoral Code of Conduct. However, this rarely translates into someone watching over you, insisting that you get on with your work at certain times or in certain places. As a PhD student, you are assessed by *results*, and it's very much down to you to make sure you put in the hours to achieve them.

As we've already emphasised, in the early weeks of a PhD, you should focus on familiarisation, rather than concerning yourself too much with substantive research outputs. There is a risk, however, that you let the early stages engender bad habits that you may struggle to shake off when the pressure ramps up. In Part 2, we show how to use planning and time-management techniques to improve productivity. In this chapter, we focus on how to form habits that will support productivity. We explain the process of habit formation and why good working habits, while requiring self-discipline to establish, will save you effort in the longer term.

Your PhD is your job

Most jobs have set hours, or at least broadly specified hours. You go to your place of work, whether office, shop, restaurant or your kitchen table, and begin work. Even if you don't feel like it, you have to go, and, once you start, you might be more or less productive, but you would get *something* done. You may have set office hours for your PhD work, required by your supervisors or the terms of your research place, or you may be left with great discretion about when and where you work and have to rely on your own motivation and self-discipline to put in the hours.

Uncertainty and a lack of short-term deadlines at the start of your PhD can also make it difficult to get down to work. So, get into the habit doing *something*: of putting in time or effort. Don't worry about finishing things or delivering outputs at this stage. Focus on the goal of forming the habit of working. This will sustain your work irrespective of other circumstances, such as the lack of deadlines, increased stress, uncertainty or other distractions.

In her best-selling book, *The Artist's Way*, Julia Cameron coined the concept of 'showing up to the page'. She maintained that artists shouldn't wait for inspiration to prompt them to write or paint or sculpt. Instead, they should diligently show up and do some work anyway. This is excellent advice if you need to find the motivation to make progress on anything without an imminent deadline or clearly defined goal, as in the early days of PhD research. Show up to your 'page' and do some work. Not only will you get something done – which is clearly a good thing, and you'll feel better for it – but, just as importantly in the early stages, you will be creating the habit of working that will carry you through the demands of a PhD.

> **But I'm not at the start**
>
> Even if you are further through your PhD, you can still develop the habit of 'showing up to the page' at any point in your research journey. It can also reduce procrastination (see Chapter 15) or help you work through writer's block (Chapter 21).

The secrets of habit formation

A **habit** is simply something we do routinely, without consciously choosing to do it. It's a behavioural shortcut that reduces the amount of conscious thought needed to function on a day-to-day basis. It's neurological efficiency. Far better to save our brain-power for things like decisions, creativity, planning, taking advantage of new opportunities, or conducting PhD research, than having to think constantly about every little thing we do. We all use habits to function efficiently on a daily basis, for example:

- Automatically grabbing our keys and closing the door behind us when we leave the house
- Pausing at the kerb and checking for oncoming traffic before crossing a road
- When driving, we automatically engage the clutch before we change gear
- Before heading to bed, we clean our teeth.

These may seem like minor activities, but they illustrate the important things we do repeatedly on a daily basis without needing to think much about them. These little habits save a lot of brain energy. What establishes behaviour as a habit are:

- **Repetition** – doing something regularly and repeatedly
- **Cues** – external circumstances that trigger the behaviour.

For example, if you're a new driver, you have to think carefully about depressing the clutch pedal before you change gear, until the repetition of the task means you come to do it automatically.

As well as repetition, the presence of an external cue that prompts the behaviour is a key part of habit formation. Teeth cleaning is based on a regular routine, but there's also a visual clue. Toothbrushes are typically kept in the bathroom, a place where you normally start and end the day, so seeing the toothbrush triggers the habit. Think how much more effort it would be to get into a habit if toothbrushing happened elsewhere than the bathroom.

By understanding the principles of habit formation – repetition plus cues – you can create good habits for your PhD. Establishing these habits may take effort and self-discipline at first; however, once established, they will be easier to sustain.

Establish good habits for your PhD

There are four areas in which you can easily begin to form habits in the early stage of your PhD:

- Your working day
- Your workspace
- Writing
- Information management.

> **It's never too late to get into good habits!**
> If you are already at a later stage in your PhD, and have fallen into some bad habits, take this chance to do something about it.

These are actions that you can start today to establish habits in each of these areas, which will make your life easier and more productive for the duration of your research.

Regularise your working day

If your supervisors or research team don't insist on a regime of regular office hours, implement your own 'office hours' routine.

➡ Action

Establish regular times when you are 'at work'.

Your 'working day' doesn't have to be 9 to 5, unless that is demanded by your PhD contract or supervisors. The specific timing can depend on your personal preferences and other commitments. It doesn't matter if you start at 7 or 11; what's important is creating the habit of being at work at certain times, staying there and working for a reasonable period.

➡ Action

Work when you are at your best.

All humans have biologically inbuilt patterns of alertness. (There is more detail on this in Chapter 12.) We are most mentally alert in the morning. Establish work patterns that mean you are devoting at least some of your 'alert time' to your PhD. Many PhD students admit that they don't begin work early, and instead work later into the evening. The danger in this kind of routine is that you miss out on the natural period when you are at your best. If your schedule and other commitments allow, try to establish a habit of starting work on your PhD early in the day.

➡ Action

Focus on quantity not quality (for now).

Your tangible work outputs during the early stages of your PhD are likely to be modest, and the early weeks, when the stakes are relatively low, are the ideal time to focus on quantity rather than quality. We recommend that you concentrate on spending *time* working, rather than focusing on how much you achieve.

- If you are more of a 'target' person, set a target for yourself of hours per day or week.
- If you are a 'routine' person, set yourself a timetable to follow for when you are 'at work'.

Don't judge your work output at this stage, for example how many journal articles you read in a day. Much of your work will be in the 'conscious incompetence' phase (see Chapter 1), and the last thing you need is to be disappointed by a lack of progress. Measure success based on the fact that you have put *time* into your work. The moment for quality will come later.

> **Activity: Establish your work schedule**
>
> 1. Decide on a work schedule that will:
>   - Suit your personal preferences
>   - Fit into your other commitments (other work, family, hobbies, etc.)
>   - Utilise your 'alert time'.
> 2. Commit to using this schedule for four weeks.
>
> **Work schedule**
>
> | Day | Hours |
> |---|---|
> | Monday | |
> | Tuesday | |
> | Wednesday | |
> | Thursday | |
> | Friday | |
> | Saturday | |
> | Sunday | |
>
> 3. Note to what degree you were able to follow your schedule. If you weren't, what prevented you, e.g. internal factors (procrastination or tiredness) or external factors (other demands, unexpected problems).
>
> | Week | Observations |
> |---|---|
> | Week 1 | |
> | Week 2 | |
> | Week 3 | |
> | Week 4 | |
>
> 4. Review and adjust your schedule as necessary.
>
> | Day | Hours |
> |---|---|
> | Monday | |
> | Tuesday | |
> | Wednesday | |
> | Thursday | |
> | Friday | |
> | Saturday | |
> | Sunday | |

Establish your workspace

Some PhD students have a designated location in which to work, perhaps lab or office, but many have freedom to work where they want. If you do a lot of work from home, whether through personal preference or necessity, you can also use location and objects to provide signals to your unconscious brain that mean 'work'. The association between the cue and the habit can be strengthened through conscious repetition – like the toothbrush in the bathroom. There are no specific rules for this, but the following are some ideas to get you started.

➡ Action

Decide where your 'office' is.

One of the pleasures of PhD life is the freedom to work in different places – lab, office, café, library and so on. However, to build a good working habit, there is a value in having one place you primarily associate with work, whether that's a spot in the library, your kitchen table, a nook under the stairs or a desk in an office. Again, it's about building up associations that unconsciously trigger the state of 'work'. It doesn't preclude having a change of scene now and then, but, if you keep to your designated work location for most of the time, the location itself will be a cue for productivity.

➡ Action

Set up your workspace.

If you don't have a dedicated desk, but have to use a work surface at home that is used for other things, such as the kitchen table, or if you have to 'hot-desk' on campus, find a way of setting it up with a work mode that differentiates it from its other uses. Clear the space and place a set of work objects that signal 'work' to your unconscious brain: items that you can store easily in a box or bag and bring out when it's time to work. For example, as well as your laptop, lay out pens, a notepad and a special coffee mug in your temporary working space. You can also use your other senses to create cues, for example a special playlist or radio station or a scented candle.

➡ Action

When you are at your desk, work.

When you are at your workspace, do something connected to your PhD. Don't allow being 'at your desk' to become associated in your unconscious brain with distractions such as browsing social media, online shopping or gaming. If your subconscious brain associates your desk with work, it will be easier to get on with it. If your subconscious brain associates your desk with social media or online shopping, you will always be fighting that impulse.

> 💬 Completing this book alongside a full-time job meant it was very tempting to write at the same desk where we design our training courses and deliver webinars. However, we both set up a separate writing area to mentally distinguish between our two different 'jobs'.
>
> No writing gets done at the training desk and vice versa – we trained our subconscious brains to focus.

➡ Action

Decide on your work 'uniform'.

How we dress is another source of subtle signals to our unconscious. This can be an issue if you do work from home a lot. Self-awareness and honesty are key: if you work well in your pyjamas, then fine. However, if you know that you would be more productive sitting at a desk in 'work' clothes, then wear them. You can even change some aspects of your dress to signify being 'at work' even though you are still at home. It could be as simple as putting on shoes instead of slippers.

> **✏ Activity: Establish your workspace**
>
> 1 Identify your primary workspace/s: campus office, home desk, library, kitchen table, etc.
>
>
> 2 Identify what items will signify work, e.g. equipment, favourite mug, favourite pen, folders.
>
>
> 3 Identify some personal habits that will signify work (particularly if working from home): clothing, shoes, etc.

Establish a writing habit

Why mention 'writing' in a chapter about the early days of your PhD? Surely you don't have to concern yourself with this until later? We believe it's unhelpful that the PhD process ends with a phase called 'writing up'. Writing is one of the core research skills that you, as an apprentice academic researcher, will need to develop throughout your PhD. Writing is just as important as critical thinking, research design, data analysis and all the other research skills you will acquire. Even if your research is excellent in terms of methodology or data (whether in a thesis, journal article or grant application), you will struggle to get due credit for your work unless you can present it effectively in writing.

One of the difficulties of PhD study is a tendency to think about *doing* the research without understanding that *writing about* the research is just as important and just as time consuming as the research itself. This underestimation of the importance, and potential difficulty, of the skill of writing means that you can be unprepared for the challenge, and may neglect to develop the skills needed to do it well. Furthermore, the task students procrastinate about most is writing. This becomes even more acute for final-year students. Their fear and struggle with writing can be a real obstacle to progress at the point when they need to be firing on all cylinders to get their thesis finished.

> Chapter 21 includes more writing tips and techniques for the writing-up phase.

We recommend that you start writing up your research *from the very beginning* and maintain a regular writing habit. The more you've practised writing during your PhD, the easier the final stages of writing up will be, practically and psychologically. This means writing about your research even when you're not producing something to submit. Your aim is to write to develop a writing habit and to practise the skill of writing itself.

Establishing writing as a habit, will:

- **Reduce fear and resistance** – helping to prevent procrastination about writing in the later stages
- **Increase writing skill and fluency** – developing your competence
- **Provide substantive research benefits** – writing about your research is *thinking* about your research.

> 💬 'A fantastic tip I learned is to always write in full sentences rather than truncated bullet points, even when just making notes for my own use. Writing in full sentences forces me to 'finish the thought' and I find I get a much greater intellectual value from my writing.'

Academic writing is a particular kind of writing, with strict standards for style and accuracy. Even if you are comfortable at writing, you may struggle. Most universities provide academic writing workshops, so, especially if you are writing in a language other than your native one, consider taking these extra classes sooner rather than later. Don't wait until you are in the writing-up phase to battle with your writing skills. Try the following tips to establish a writing habit for your PhD:

➡ Action

Write every day.

Start by writing every working day for a *short* period – such as 15 minutes, and no more than 30 minutes – even if you think you don't have much to write about. In the early days of your PhD, the point of writing every day is as much about establishing the habit of writing than noting down any vital observations. If you can't think of anything to write, try using these questions as prompts:

- What do I find interesting in my reading?
- What have I discovered about my research?
- What are the key things I have learned recently?
- What questions do I have?
- What problems am I facing?
- What am I enjoying about my research?
- What am I finding difficult in my research?
- What are my next steps?

> You can also use the 'freewriting' technique on page 287 to get writing.

➡ Action

Start a personal research journal.

You might be advised to maintain a formal research journal by your supervisors, for example a lab book or a research log. However, an informal, private journal can be a place to develop your thinking and your writing habit.

➡ Action

Write *about* your research.

Rather than just making notes from your research to record facts, write fully about what are you doing and reading and what you *think about it*.

➡ Action

Keep your writing in one place.

Electronic documents have the advantage of searchability, however many people enjoy the feel of a real pen on paper and find it stimulates their thinking in a way that typing doesn't. A paper notebook or journal also has the advantage of portability, although has no back-up if lost. Experiment a little and decide what works best for you.

➡ Action

Just keep swimming. Just keep swimming!

Don't get too hung up on systems or methods. Just write and keep writing!

✎ Activity: Establish a writing habit
1 What will you do to form your writing habit?
2 What will you do to improve your academic writing?

Establish good information-management habits

Your PhD research will generate large quantities of material, such as literature notes, data, analysis and text, for which you will be personally responsible. Like any large project, there will also be all the ancillary information from the management of your PhD, such as emails, documents and so on. You need proper systems to keep everything organised and accessible, whether that's your literature notes or email addresses for interviewees. From a research practice perspective, it's vital that you can track back through the data and literature upon which you base your conclusions. Mistakes and omissions can destroy the credibility and even the validity of your work.

Having a system is not the same as *using* it. Getting into record-keeping habits from the start is an important foundation for your PhD that will save you a lot of time, effort and heartache later on. At the beginning of your PhD, you won't necessarily know what kind of systems you will need in order to manage your research data, unless they are specified as part of your research project. You may not be aware of the ethical, statutory or legislative regulations with which you must comply. However, as a minimum, you can initiate systems to record and access your literature notes, which will be the main priority in the early phase of your PhD. Revisit your information-management requirements regularly as you embark on the different phases of your research work to update, adjust and amend your systems as necessary.

➡ Action

Ask for advice from your supervisors.

Supervisors know what you need in terms of data management. They should be able to advise you on any ethical dimensions of your data management and research practice in terms of plagiarism and so on.

➡ Action

Find out what information management software your university provides.

For example, do you have access to reference-management software, or statistical- or qualitative-analysis software? If so, use it from the start. This will help you in terms of IT support, backing-up and so on. If something is widely used and/or recommended by your institution, use it.

➡ Action

Ask other students.

Ask other PhD students who are using similar research methods how they go about managing their data and records. It can be especially helpful to ask students who are further along in their PhD. They can tell you not only what they do, but what they wish they had done. Keep things simple.

➡ Action

Give it a decent shot.

If you start using a system, such as a particular reference-management software, stick to it unless it really isn't fit for your purposes. You have to develop your 'competence' in using it, in the same way that you will be developing competence in all manner of research skills. What feels awkward at the start may just be in the 'conscious competence' phase. Keep at it.

➡ Action

Get into the habit of using any system you implement regularly.

Little and often is key here. Like any habit, regular routines that are easy to sustain are far more productive than periodic attempts to catch up. These moments of self-discipline, when you force yourself to enter your journal article reference in your citation software every time you finish a paper so it becomes automatic, will pay off later.

➡ Action

Establish good habits when to annotating your literature notes.

Establish simple personal codes to use in your notes and use these consistently, for example identifying direct quotes with quotation marks, always putting your own ideas and comments in square brackets or a different colour and always paraphrasing when making notes of ideas from the literature. Consistent annotation is good academic practice, and establishing it as an automatic habit will make it easier to sustain.

✏ Activity: Form information-management systems and habits

1. What kinds of information do you need to store and manage at the start of your PhD, e.g. literature notes, references, supervision meeting notes?

2. How will you find out about best practice for this kind of information management, e.g. who will you ask?

3. What systems and habits will you establish and how?

Summary

The degree of autonomy you have over your PhD work can be a blessing and a curse. It's your responsibility to manage your workload. From the outset, establish habits that will help you with your work throughout your research studies. Habits take effort and self-discipline to establish, but save time and effort in the long term. Use routines and environmental cues to form habits. Consider creating habits to help you get to work and stay there; establish a writing habit from the start of your PhD; and set up the information-management systems you will need to keep on top of your research work.

Once you understand the value of habits and the process of establishing them, you can utilise habit formation as a tool throughout your PhD. It's never too late to update your working habits, and you will probably need to adjust your habits as you meet new challenges during your PhD. If you've already started your research, you can choose to introduce some useful habits from now on.

> **Key points**
> - From the very start of your PhD, establish good habits that will support your work throughout the whole doctoral experience.
> - Good habits take work to establish, but will save you time and effort later.
> - If you've developed bad habits, it's never too late to establish better ones.
> - Create triggers and cues in your environment that support good working habits.
> - Set up key information-management systems and get into the habit of using them.
> - Develop a writing habit from the very start of your PhD.

Further resources

Bell, J. and Waters, S. (2018) *Doing Your Research Project: A Guide for First-time Researchers*, 7th edn. London: Open University Press.
Brann, A. (2013) *Make Your Brain Work*. London: Kogan Page.
Clear, J. (2018) *Atomic Habits*. London: Random House.
Duhigg, C. (2013) *The Power of Habit*. London: Random House.
Hills, J. (2016) *Brain-Savvy Business*. London: Head, Heart & Brain.

Reference

Cameron, J. (2020) *The Artist's Way*. London: Souvenir Press.

6 Build Support Networks

How to ... Surround yourself with the people you need

> Social networks and your PhD – Evolution and social contact – Social biome – Get out and about – Prune your social networks – Community of practice – Build academic networks

Although ultimate responsibility for your PhD lies with you, a PhD is not an individual undertaking. All successful PhDs rely on the contributions of a range of different people, often including supervisors, colleagues, research subjects and funders. These contributors are stakeholders in your research and will have a significant influence on the direction and content of your PhD. (This is explored further in Chapters 7, 8 and 11.)

Your support networks are groups of people who can provide you with academic, technical, professional as well as emotional support, throughout your PhD experience. The importance of support networks isn't unique to being a PhD student. We all need people in our lives with whom to share our experiences and who will help us deal with our problems. However, embarking on doctoral study may mean that you need new and different support networks. In this chapter, we explain why robust support networks will help you complete and make the most of your PhD and make the whole experience easier and less stressful, and we show you ways to establish the support you need.

Why support networks are vital for your PhD

A PhD can be an isolating experience. You may find yourself working alone a lot. You may have moved away from home to study, or, conversely, you may be completing your PhD via distance learning, rarely visiting your university in person. The steep learning curve of your PhD, discussed in Chapter 1, can challenge your self-confidence. It will test your abilities too, and require stamina and resilience. To deal with the demands of your PhD, you need the support of friends, family and colleagues. Having people around whom you can rely on will be a key factor in your PhD success. Research has shown that PhD students with higher levels of social support have more positive outcomes and better mental health (Milicev et al, 2021).

A PhD also offers opportunities to learn, develop, experience new things and, not least, embark on the pathway to your future career. You will benefit from support networks of people who can provide relevant academic advice and expertise – supervisors, other academics and other PhD students. These professional support networks will help you along the stepping stones towards your career beyond your PhD. (We return to the topic of building your networks in line with your future career aspirations in Chapter 17.)

Your social and professional support networks are another example of the foundations of a successful PhD that you should take the time to establish in the early stages. They will, like everything else, require maintenance and development as your PhD progresses, but, by taking steps to consolidate your existing support networks, expanding them in line with the demands of a PhD and establishing the *habit* of maintaining and interacting with them, you will have a resource that you can rely on throughout your PhD.

The importance of social connection for humans

It's accepted that one of the reasons our species survived and became so successful is the evolution of our social groups and our ability to collaborate. Many animals live in groups. However, for Homo sapiens, our superb abilities to communicate and act collectively meant that we could be more effective at finding food, shelter and rearing offspring. Imagine trying to chase down a mammoth on your own! This ability to collaborate resulted not only in the survival of our species, but, over time, our capabilities for innovation and exploration – inventing tools, controlling fire and expanding around the globe. Our collaboration led to permanent settlements, agriculture and the birth of civilisation. It's no wonder that being part of a social group is important to human beings, even to those who think of themselves as loners. It's not just chasing down mammoths in the distant past that lends itself to teamwork. The modern world of work, including PhD research, is built on collaboration.

Social connection is so important to humans that its impact on well-being can be seen in brain activity. Positive social contact has been observed to fire up the pleasure sensors of the brain and reduce stress hormones. Meanwhile social threats, such as rejection or isolation, increase stress. The social pain of rejection has been shown to trigger some of the same responses in the brain as those caused by physical pain. In the past, isolation from our social groups would have led to a certain, lonely death through starvation or predation, so, we are hardwired to seek out social connection. Social connection is associated with better levels of well-being – reduced anxiety, enhanced immune-system functioning and even longevity.

Social support networks

Your social support networks are, essentially, people you like to spend time with and with whom you have something in common. As a PhD student facing the stresses and demands of doctoral study, make sure that you have access to networks that provide personal support and improve your well-being. You have more time early in your PhD to do the work (and it is work!) of finding new social contacts. There are also likely to be opportunities to make new social connections at the start of your PhD, through orientation events organised by your institution, and other PhD students, like you, will be open to making new connections. These efforts will pay dividends later when you really need support but may not have the spare time to establish new connections. As you get deeper into your PhD work, it can be very easy to neglect social contact with friends and family. You may feel that your PhD work is so important that you can't justify time with them. However, time spent with people who make you feel good isn't just relaxation, it's a vital investment in your well-being.

If you moved away from home to begin your studies, it is particularly important to put some effort into establishing some new social connections at the start of your PhD. Even if you've stayed close to home and still have easy access to your existing social circles, it's important to make new social connections with people who understand what it's like to undertake a PhD. In other words, other doctoral students.

> 'Your PhD peers are your support group. I wish I hadn't been so isolated at the start [because of the Covid lockdown]. I had problems with my supervisor, but I didn't know what was reasonable to expect because I didn't have any other PhD students to compare notes with.'

Establishing and maintaining social support networks

The early days of your PhD are a good time to establish the support networks you will need to help you face the challenges of doctoral research, not least because your university will help with mixer events and activities for new students. Once established take steps (develop more habits!) to maintain the social support networks through regular contact. Here are some ways you can build your social support networks at the start and throughout your PhD.

> **But I'm not at the start**
> It's not only at the start of your PhD that you can make new social connections. It's never too late to join a club or attend events held by researcher development, your doctoral college or student union. In our experience, most PhDs and post-docs are very keen to meet people who understand what they are (or have been) going through.

Your social biome

Research suggests that our regular social interactions create a social biome: the ecosystem of our relationships and interactions (Hall and Merolla, 2020). Like our gut microbiome, our social biome can be healthy or less healthy depending on our lifestyle. The researchers found that a healthy social biome depends on frequent social interactions, as well as close relationships. People with the most regular social interactions reported higher levels of well-being, and this included quite superficial or short interactions. So, make sure you are in the habit of getting away from your desk and interacting with other human beings. It was also accepted, however, that the social interaction required depends on your personality and should be balanced with an appropriate level of solitude to align with your preferences and needs. You don't have to force yourself to be a social butterfly.

➡ Action

Get out and about.

Hall and Merolla (2020) identified the following four types of interaction that contribute to a healthy 'social biome'. See if you can get into the habit of having all four at different times in your week.

- **Meaningful talk**: Talk about personal experiences or inner life with intimate friends; serious discussions about topics that are important to us, such as politics, philosophy and so on.
- **Affectionate communication**: Exchanges with people we care for and who care for us
- **Catching up**: Exchanging personal news with people we know.
- **Joking around**: Banter with mates or superficial humorous interactions with strangers (in the UK, often based on the weather).

At first, it might seem strange to 'schedule' or 'formalise' these interactions, but it's helpful until this type of social contact becomes a habit.

Activity: Create a healthy social biome

Identify what you can do and who you can see to tend to your 'social biome' on a regular basis by integrating the four valuable dimensions of social contact into your daily/weekly schedule.

Meaningful talk	
Affectionate communication	
Catching up	
Joking around	

University events

Use every opportunity you can to attend events organised by the university to put PhD students in touch with each other. Most universities provide induction opportunities, such as events and training sessions, to help you meet up with other students and academics. View these not only as chances to learn something, but as opportunities to build your social support networks.

> **Being remote**
>
> If you are studying remotely, you will not be able to attend the face-to-face events organised by the university. Instead, find ways of creating contacts virtually through online events, such as webinars and meetings, as they are a vital means of developing your social support networks linked to the university.

➡ Action: Get out there.

Attend everything you can.

✏ Activity: University events schedule

Identify some events organised by the university that you can attend in order to meet new people. Then add details of people to include in your networks.

Event details	Date	New contacts to follow up

Social media

All PhD students can make the most of social media to develop virtual social support networks. This can afford you access to a wider support network than might be available at your institution or if you are studying remotely. Search out relevant formal online communities, such as membership groups or message boards, or ask for recommendations from other PhD students. Alternatively, participate in informal groups on social media through relevant hashtags. Despite being informal and virtual, social-media contact can create a reassuring sense of community with fellow travellers on the PhD path and can be a source of useful advice and information.

➡ Action

Get online.

💬 'I completed my PhD away from my home town and so had less contact with my existing social networks. I was also a mature student in a group of PhD students who were much younger than me. Most of the other PhD students in my department were doing very different kinds of research – quantitative economics and marketing studies, compared with my qualitative social-science-based work. As a result, I felt lonely and isolated in the early weeks of my PhD.

I attended a course on research methods run for the wider faculty and met a couple of other mature students who became friends. Not only were they a similar age and facing some of the same challenges of mid-life study, but they were doing qualitative research. Although they were researching in different disciplines, we had enough in common that we were able to support each other through our PhDs. In fact, we're still good friends five years later.'

Maintain your existing support networks

Don't forget about the social support networks you already have. It's easy to become so involved in your PhD that you neglect the people already in your life. While family and friends may accept being lower in your priorities during your PhD, don't sacrifice the well-being-enhancing benefits of positive social interaction. Plan for interaction – in person or remotely – with family members and existing friends. Even if you are away from home, these relationships can still provide comfort, so it's even more important that you keep in touch with them via whatever method you can. It is one of the main reasons we recommend including personal events in your timeline in Chapter 4.

> **It's not all about work**
> Not all social connections have to be linked to your PhD. There are also opportunities to expand your networks through shared common interests. Take advantage of the university societies or non-university clubs that will bring you contact with new people, for example, music or drama, language clubs, crafts, gaming or sports.

➜ **Action**

Keep in touch.

Make good connections

The *quality* of your social connections is important. While social contact is good for you, some connections can be negative or stressful. Embarking on a PhD might be a good time to have a social 'clear out'. You need to devote as much of your personal resources as possible to your PhD and there may be people in your life that demand more of you than they give back. It could be the 'friend' who only ever talks about their problems and never listens to you, the colleague who frequently interrupts your work with questions, or the sibling who is critical about your life choices. Consider whether you can limit your exposure to them. We are not recommending radical life changes, but some subtle pruning of your social network might be positive.

➜ **Action**

Focus on quality not quantity.

Use the template on page 65 to take stock of your social-support needs and plan how you are going to expand, maintain and, if necessary, trim your social network. You might feel uncomfortable thinking so instrumentally about social connection. Perhaps it seems slightly exploitative to plan how to create a social network as a resource to help you with your PhD. However, we are not proposing that you conduct your whole social life according to a strict plan. Rather, we want to emphasise the importance of social support during your PhD and encourage you to invest time, thought and energy into ensuring that you have the social environment you need.

> ✎ **Activity: Plan the development of your social support network**
> Use the template on page 65 to create a plan for developing and maintaining good social support networks during your PhD.

📄 Template: Social support network development planner

1 Identify the important people you currently have in your social networks and how you will keep in touch with them.	
Important people in my life	**Activities to keep in touch**
e.g. partner, parents, siblings, close friends	e.g. Zoom with X once a week; create a family WhatsApp group; meet Y for coffee once a week

2 Identify the gaps in your social support network and how you will fill them.	
Who's missing from my social support network?	**Activities to build my social network**
e.g. friends local to the uni, PhD students in my discipline, people my age	e.g. Join a society; spend time in the common room or canteen; introduce myself to people at …

3 Identify the people in your current social network who have a negative impact on you and consider how you can minimise their influence on you.	
Who causes me problems?	**How I will reduce their negative impact**
e.g. difficult friend, over-demanding relation	e.g. Only meet them occasionally and in a group, explain how busy I am in my PhD studies

© RDT&C

Professional support networks

Your *social* support networks will play a major role in sustaining your emotional well-being and bolstering your resilience throughout your doctoral studies. The start of your PhD is also a good time to establish *professional* support networks that will help you develop the skills and knowledge required to complete your PhD successfully. It's important to review and update these networks throughout your degree, as your needs will change. If you're already further along in your PhD journey, you can develop the professional networks that meet your current needs.

> Read more about how to enhance your resilience in Chapter 14.

Remember, a PhD is a professional apprenticeship; it's not the equivalent of an academic course. You will learn a great deal through your exposure to expert professionals – you're not just learning *about*, you are learning *how*. This is why your professional support networks are a key element in your development. Taking steps to build and maintain professional support networks that will help you develop your skills provides a solid foundation for your PhD. It also ensures that you achieve your career goals beyond your PhD. (We return to this in Chapter 17.)

> Learn more about achieving your career goals in Chapter 17.

Build your community of practice

One way to think of your professional support network is as a community of practice (CoP) (Lave and Wenger, 1991). A CoP is a group of individuals who:

- Have interests, roles and knowledge in common
- Are in regular contact with each other (a community)
- Work alongside each other and share skills (their practice).

Exposure to expert practitioners in a CoP as they actively deploy their skills is a more effective way of learning than formal instruction alone. We learn by interacting with experts and peers because a lot of expertise is based on 'unconscious competence', as discussed in Chapter 1. Experts may not even realise what it is that they do that makes them experts, but, by spending time with them as they use their skills – whether it's your supervisors interrogating your literature, a subject librarian constructing a database search, or a lab technician setting up equipment for an experiment – you will learn through observation. Rather than asking someone to *tell* you how something is done, consider asking them to *show* you.

> **Learn from others' mistakes**
> You can learn just as much from other people's mistakes as their successes. Ask them what went wrong or what they wish they'd done differently so you can avoid making the same mistakes yourself.

The kinds of skills and knowledge you are likely to need to develop during your PhD are:

Academic and research practice	e.g. methodological issues, research design, plagiarism and referencing, data management, ethics
Subject knowledge	e.g. literature, current debates and controversies
Intellectual skills	e.g. critical thinking, data analysis, academic writing
Personal development	e.g. self-presentation, communication, teamworking
Technical skills	e.g. software use, equipment use, lab procedures, information management
Administration	e.g. university procedures, grant applications, submission procedures
Career development	e.g. networking, CV-building

Your supervision team is your ready-made CoP, but look to expand your access to other CoPs by building additional connections with:

- Other research academics in your field
- Other doctoral students –
   - Sharing your subject area or methodological approach
   - At the same stage as you in the PhD process, even if they don't share your field
   - Further ahead in the process, to learn from their experiences – successes and failures!
   - Who share other features with you, perhaps as mature students or international students
- Researcher development staff
- Technicians / lab assistants
- Subject librarians
- Administrative staff
- Industry professionals.

> 'Our lab group were really intertwined. We worked together and socialised together. Even during the lockdown of 2020, we would have lunch together online.'

To get the best out of your communities of practice:

➡ Action

Be proactive.

Seek out people from whom you can learn the skills you need.

➡ Action

Maintain contact and exposure.

It's not just about keeping in touch through the odd email or message – you need to *spend time with these people* while they are doing their work, ideally face to face.

➡ Action

Ask questions.

As well as absorbing and observing expertise, be ready to ask *how* or *why*. This helps you to grasp the 'unconscious competence' dimension of the skills, which might be otherwise invisible.

For example, a skilled lab technician may adjust their methods in response to subtle clues from the equipment; an expert qualitative interviewer may develop rapport with their subjects through the use of eye contact. They may not even be aware themselves of the nuances of their practice until you ask them to reflect on it through your questions.

➜ Action

Be interactive.

Community-building is not a one-way street – find ways to be an active participant. Be generous with your own expertise and insights. These reciprocal connections will strengthen your bonds in the CoP, for example:

- Rosie used her professional expertise in event organisation to help her supervisor arrange an international seminar.
- Fraser used his project-management expertise to deliver seminars during inductions for new PhD students.

➜ Action

Keep in contact.

A CoP is a *community*, and you need to *nurture and sustain the connections through regular contact*. This can be casual and informal: bumping into people in the office, library or canteen will cement relations. A lot of learning takes place through these informal 'water-cooler moments'. By having a coffee with a fellow PhD student, you might hear how they successfully navigated their recent Ethics Committee submission; chatting to a member of administrative staff in the lift may mean you hear about a new fund for international conference visits. Checking in with your CoP can also be part of your 'social biome' maintenance, as the pressures of a PhD may keep you chained to your desk unless you make a special effort to get out and about.

➜ Action

Build informal online contact.

In situations where contact with your CoP is only online, it can be hard to replicate the casual contact available on site. However, you can *engineer* some informal contact, for example scheduling an online coffee break or lunch date (rather than 'meetings') and using casual contact through social media.

✏ Activity: Plan the development of your professional support network

Use the template on page 69 to plan how you are going to develop and maintain your professional support networks from the start of your PhD.

- Be strategic about it. Identify your current needs: proactively building a support network to fulfill these needs.
- Regularly review your needs and expand your support networks as required.
- As with so much we are recommending in this section of the book, establishing a *habit* of seeking out contact with your professional support network is the big win at this stage.

📄 Template: Community of practice development planner

	1. What do I need to learn at the moment?	2. Who can I learn from?	3. How will I learn from them?
Academic and research practice			
Subject knowledge			
Intellectual skills			
Personal development			
Technical skills			
Administration and procedures			
Career development			

© RDT&C

Summary

Your PhD isn't an individual undertaking. As well as the stakeholders involved in the delivery of your PhD, you will rely on academic, professional and emotional support from other people. Social support is a fundamental part of human well-being and yours will help you to deal with the challenges of PhD life and thrive as a PhD student. Academic and professional support networks will help you to develop the skills and expertise you need to complete an excellent PhD research project and take the next steps in your career.

Consider your support networks as one of the essential building blocks of a successful PhD, not a luxury. Use the early stage of your PhD to make the most of opportunities to create new social and academic connections related to your new status. Throughout your PhD, pay attention to regular social contact as a means of enhancing your well-being. Develop and spend time with a wide community of practice to gain exposure to the experts from whom you can learn the necessary skills to complete your PhD. The better you get to know the members of your CoP over time, the more rewarding it will be.

> **Key points**
> - Your support networks will play a vital role in your success as a PhD student.
> - Appreciate the importance of different kinds of support networks – social and professional.
> - Develop new, relevant support networks that meet your needs as a PhD student.
> - Don't neglect your existing support networks – but, if necessary, reduce contact with people who hinder rather than help.
> - Take steps to maintain connections – keep in touch.

Further resources

D'Souza, S. (2011) *Brilliant Networking*, 2nd edn. Harlow: Pearson.
Ferrazzi, K. and Raz, T. (2014) *Never Eat Alone: And Other Secrets to Success, One Relationship at a Time*. London: Penguin.
Hills, J. (2016) *Brain-Savvy Business*. London: Head, Heart & Brain.
Lieberman, M.D. (2015) *Social: Why Our Brains Are Wired to Connect*. Oxford: Oxford University Press.

References

Hall, J.A. and Merolla, A.J. (2020) Connecting Everyday Talk and Time Alone to Global Well-being, *Human Communication Research*, **46**: 86–111.
Lave. J. and Wenger, E. (1991) *Situated Learning: Legitimate Peripheral Participation*. New York and Cambridge: Cambridge University Press.
Milicev, J., McCann, M., Simpson, S.A. et al (2021) Evaluating Mental Health and Wellbeing of Postgraduate Researchers: Prevalence and Contributing Factors, *Current Psychology*. Available at: link.springer.com/article/10.1007/s12144-021-02309-y#article-info [accessed 28 December 2022].

Part 2

How to Get Going

Part 2: How to Get Going

In Part 1 of the book, we ensured that you made a good start on your PhD, giving you a sense of direction, the confidence to take charge of your research and good foundations for your work. In Part 2, we give you the tools to really get moving on your PhD and start to make progress on the substantive research itself.

Here we address the main problems that PhD students encounter when trying to make a start on the real work of their PhD, such as:

- How to work out what a successful PhD looks like
- How to know what to do in the short and mid-term to make progress on such a lengthy, uncertain project
- How to create a structure for their work
- How to manage their time and get the best out of themselves
- How to ensure they have the support they need to make progress on their PhD.

The centrepiece of Part 2, in Chapters 7 to 11, is effectively a foundation course in research project management that you can use to plan and replan your work throughout your PhD. It takes you through the steps to create an accurate, comprehensive, useful plan for your work, providing techniques for each stage of the process. By following these steps now, and repeatedly throughout your PhD, you will be equipped to manage your research effectively and to complete your PhD efficiently and with the minimum stress. The planning process ensures that you know exactly what you must do to satisfy everyone with an investment in your research. It helps you to specify and schedule your work so that you can make sustained progress in the right direction. It also helps you to avoid the negative impact of unexpected problems.

72   Part 2 – How to Get Going

You could, in theory, apply the planning methods to your whole PhD at once. However, because of all the unknowns involved in research, it will be more accurate, and therefore more useful, if you do it for *each phase*. As such, the planning methods in Part 2 will be something you revisit throughout the research process, each time you start a new phase of work.

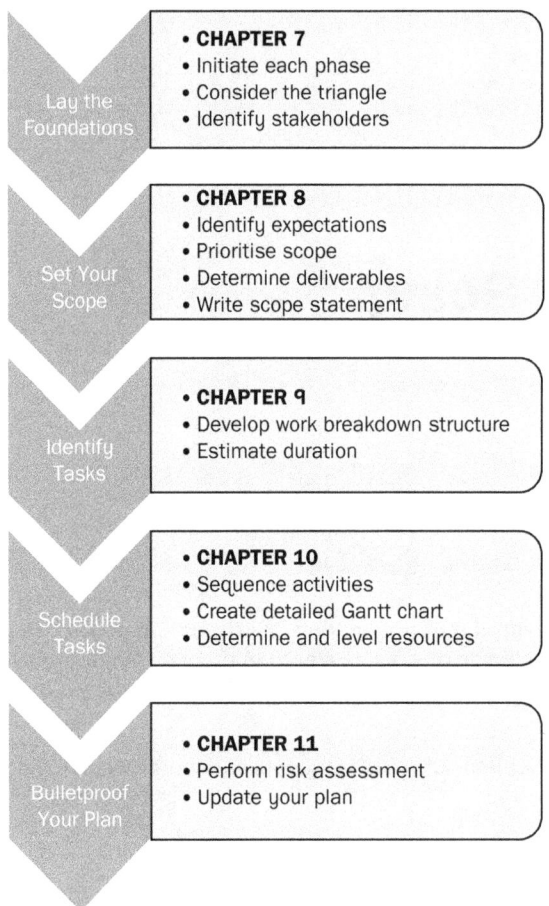

The planning process

- In Chapter 7, you learn the foundations you need to put in place to support your planning. The information from this initial stage will underpin the entire planning process. Remember: we don't recommend trying to create a detailed plan for your whole PhD at once. You will come back to these foundations time and again as you plan future phases of your research.
- In Chapter 8, you establish exactly what must be delivered for a successful PhD, and learn how to set priorities to provide a clear focus for every stage of the research. This chapter provides the tools you need to establish boundaries for your work so you can effectively plan and deliver the necessary outputs.
- In Chapter 9, you work out what exactly you need to do and how long it will take. This detailed information will allow you to manage your workload and feel in control of your work, in spite of the inherent uncertainties of PhD research.
- The final piece of the planning process is addressed in Chapter 10 – the scheduling of your work. Scheduling is the element of the process that many people think of as 'the planning'. Without the

previous steps, however, your timeline would be inaccurate and meaningless. By following the planning process, you can be confident that your schedule is well-founded.
- However good your planning is, there are inevitably surprises and unforeseen problems that disrupt the best formulated plans – that's just life. In Chapter 11, you learn how to reduce the likelihood of unforeseen problems derailing your PhD through a risk assessment process.

It might look as though there is a lot of planning to do – and there is – but you are undertaking a very complex project. Everything we suggest here will take time, particularly on the first occasion you do it. However, as explained in Part 1, the time you invest early in your PhD setting yourself up for your work will pay huge dividends in terms of efficiency and save you time later. This is another example of 'sharpening your saw'. The first time you do this – creating the foundations and learning the techniques of good planning – will take time and effort. Once you have laid these foundations, however, the subsequent iterations of planning will be easier and quicker.

At the end of this part, we provide skills that will help you to deliver the plans you have made.

- Chapter 12 introduces a range of time-management techniques so you can make the most of your time.
- Chapter 13 includes communication techniques that you can use to engage other people in helping you deliver your project goals.

> **Transferable skills**
>
> Project management skills are highly sought after by employers. By learning how to use these planning tools, you will make your PhD easier and more successful, and you are building up a valuable set of transferable skills.

Every PhD is different. In Part 2, we are not prescribing a set of rules, but rather providing advice and guidelines on techniques that we know from experience will help you complete your PhD. However, this is *your* PhD. Complete it in any way that you see fit. If you want to adapt the methods we provide here so they suit your needs, do so. Having said that, all our recommendations are based on supporting thousands of students going through a similar experience. We know this works, so try it our way first, and only once you are familiar with the techniques and principles, adapt them if you need to so that they work for you.

7 Lay the Foundations

How to ... Create the underpinnings of a successful PhD plan

> The building blocks of successful planning – Plan before you do – Project initiation – The project triangle: scope, cost, time – Project stakeholders – Stakeholder diagram – Mind maps – Planning review schedule

In this chapter, we introduce the three tools that constitute the building blocks of all future planning activities:

- **Initiation**
- **The project triangle**
- **Stakeholder identification.**

Whether you're on day one of your PhD or have come across this book in year two or three, building your project plan on these foundations ensures that they are accurate and useful. These building blocks are a vital first step in the detailed planning of the first phase of your PhD work. The information they produce will also continue to be useful throughout the planning and delivery of your PhD.

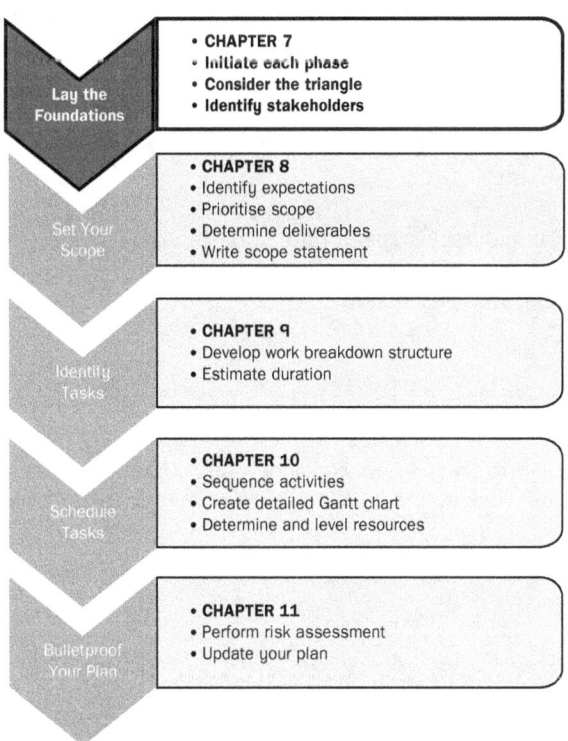

The planning process

Initiation

In Chapter 4, you created a high-level timeline to indicate roughly where you want to be and when for the whole of your PhD journey. It's only as you get to each phase or 'bite of the elephant' that you should create a much more detailed work plan. If all you can see clearly is the next month, then that's all you should plan for *in detail*. Remember:

> Only ever plan what you *can* plan.

The first building block of your detailed plan is initiation. Put simply this means: *plan before you start doing*. Spend a little time determining *what* you're meant to be doing and *how* you're going to do it *before* you actually start doing it.

This might sound obvious, but too often it's not done well or at all. There are many reasons why people overlook initiation: 'I don't have time'; 'I don't know enough so it's too difficult'; 'There's no point as things will change anyway'; 'I've already started the work.' However, investing a small amount of effort in this initial activity will pay great dividends further down the line. Where do you want to invest your energy: extending the planning of your work by a few hours, or extending the duration of the work by the weeks or months it will take you to recover when unexpected things happen?

The amount of time you need to spend on initiation will change depending on the scale of work.

- It could simply be sitting down with a cup of coffee for ten minutes and reviewing your 'to do' list for the week.
- It could be an hour or two mapping out the next six weeks of activity.
- It could be half a day spent creating a PhD work plan for the next three to six months.

For every piece of work you undertake, spend time initiating it. Think of initiation as taking a deep breath before you start. It's a moment of calm reflection on what lies ahead.

> **But I'm not at the start**
>
> If you are reading this book part-way through your PhD, you may have missed the initial planning phase of the project. Don't worry – it's not too late to catch up! Every bit of work you do should be initiated, and a lot of the work *we* do is exactly this – helping people to 're-initiate' their projects. If you are halfway through your PhD, for example, planning is basically asking three questions:
>
> - How much *longer* is remaining?
> - How many hours can I *spend* working?
> - Therefore, what is *actually* achievable?
>
> The tools and techniques in Part 2 allow you to answer these questions.

> ✎ **Activity: Project initiation**
>
> For the next phase of work you're going to do, consider roughly how long to spend planning it. You don't need to be exact, but will you measure the time in minutes, hours or days? Make notes here.

The project triangle

The primary aim of the initiation phase is to be able to apply a very simple, yet powerful, model to your PhD project: the project triangle. This is your second planning building block.

When you initiate work of any size or complexity, the key is to establish three main elements:

- **Scope** – What it is you're actually doing, for example tasks, outputs, requirements or expectations
- **Cost** – How many hours you will have to spend doing it, for example 16 hours
- **Time** – The overall duration or *length of time* it will take you to complete it, such as 2 days (16 hours working 8 hours per day) or 4 days (16 hours if you only work 4 hours a day).

For your PhD, cost represents the number of hours you must *spend* to complete a piece of work. In project management more generally, cost also represents the financial resources you have for a project. It's unlikely that you have a large project budget to manage, so, in this book, we equate cost with *effort*: the hours you have to invest in your work.

Identifying these three key elements – scope, cost and time – allows you to draw the most important project management diagram you will find in this book: the project triangle. We will refer back to it regularly.

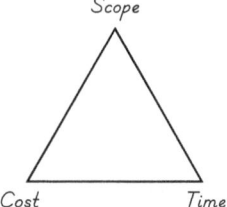

The project triangle

This very simple model underpins your entire PhD plan. For every phase of work, you need to determine what it is you're doing (scope) in enough detail that you can estimate how many hours you will need to spend doing it (cost) before considering how many days it will take to complete it (time). The key to project-managing your PhD is very, very simple:

Join the corners of the project triangle. Never let it become disconnected.

As explained in Chapter 4, the only thing that is guaranteed to happen during your PhD is change. Something *will* change. The project triangle means that you can more easily accommodate change.

You want to do more? No problem, but you'll either have to work more hours each day or everything will take longer.

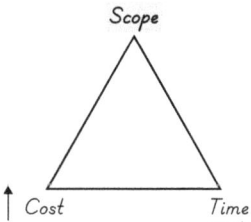

Project triangle: impact of increasing scope

78   Part 2 – How to Get Going

You want to finish things sooner? Ok, you'll need to work more hours per day otherwise you'll get less work completed or the quality of the work won't be as good.

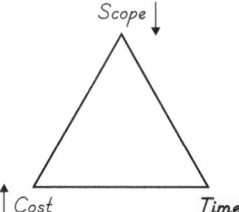

Project triangle: impact of reducing time

You want to cut back on the hours you work per day? Fine, but either you will miss your deadline, you will complete less work in total or the quality of the work will be reduced.

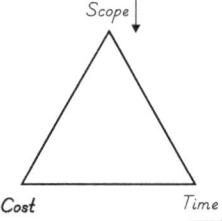

Project triangle: impact of reducing cost

This triangle is a very simple device that always gives you three choices. If one element changes, what will be the impact be on the other two elements? You can use the model to understand the impact of any change on your current workload. It is useful for managing yourself, and is a powerful method of explaining to other people (perhaps your supervisors) why you can't 'do more' or 'work faster'. It makes your explanation *objective* rather than *subjective*.

> ### ✎ Activity: Project triangle
>
> Identify whether any points of the triangle are 'fixed' during your PhD. Do you have a set deadline (maybe when funding expires)? Are you doing it part-time so have a set number of hours per week to dedicate? Note your fixed points here.

As you move through the planning process, you will learn various practical uses for the triangle. But for now, you just need to remember that the creation of a plan is a process of identifying the key elements: scope, cost and time. The next few chapters will examine different ways of establishing the three corners of your triangle.

Stakeholder identification

The third and final planning building block is to consider your project stakeholders – the people who influence the success or failure of your PhD. At times, a PhD can seem to be quite an individual, even isolating, experience – 'just me on my own' – but, stakeholder identification helps you to appreciate that you are not alone; that, in fact, there is a large number of people who can potentially impact upon or be impacted by your PhD.

The activities you do during your PhD and the way you do them will be shaped by a wide range of influences and influencers. Failure to consider these means that you run the risk of heading in the wrong direction, producing outputs of little value or delivering work that is less successful than it should be. Identifying and understanding these stakeholders will help you to develop your understanding of the key elements of your work and determine the direction it should take.

A stakeholder is any person, team, organisation or collaborative partner who is involved in your project, can affect your project (positively or negatively), can influence your project (positively or negatively) or may benefit from it; they may be anyone who could potentially touch on (or 'make or break') your project. Stakeholders can be:

- **Advantageous** – positive about your PhD or will benefit from it
- **Adverse** – negative about your PhD or likely to cause it problems (even unintentionally).

You won't (and don't need to) know all your stakeholders at the start of your PhD. Your understanding will grow and expand over time. There are, however, stakeholders common to most PhDs and whom you can easily identify:

- You (an important stakeholder!)
- Your supervisors
- Examiners
- The university
- The research community and current researchers
- The library and subject librarian
- The sources of your data, including:
    - The laboratory – technician, lab manager, other users, suppliers of equipment and material
    - Fieldwork – transport providers, equipment suppliers, people who grant permissions/access
    - Interviews – participants, ethics committee
    - Analyses of secondary data – your sources (or the gatekeepers to the sources).

Another important set of stakeholders, and one that is often overlooked, are the users of your research – any stakeholder who will ultimately *use* the output of your PhD. For example:

- Every thesis must provide a unique contribution to knowledge, so the research community is one such stakeholder.
- If you're investigating the inequalities in access to higher education, for example, your PhD is aimed at informing policy. As well as the lawmakers themselves, who else will ultimately be affected by a change in policy – teachers, pupils?
- If your PhD is focused on developing a new and tangible product (for example, a drug delivery method, composite material, modelling algorithm, hybrid crops), who could be using this in the future and what are their needs? This may influence the direction of your study.

80 Part 2 – How to Get Going

- If your focus is on 18th-century French history or the ontology of photography, who will be informed by your study and why should they be interested?

> You will revisit your stakeholder diagram in Chapters 8, 11, 16 and 20 – throughout the lifetime of your PhD!

Identify your stakeholders through the process of creating a stakeholder diagram – a mind map of the stakeholders linked to your PhD. This diagram, and the thinking that you go through by creating it, will form the basis of your PhD plan. Its use might not be immediately apparent to you as you create the stakeholder diagram, but the information it provides will determine the direction your PhD will take. You will use the information repeatedly in the planning techniques in the following chapters.

Create your stakeholder diagram

Step 1: Identify your first-level stakeholders

The first step on your stakeholder diagram is to identify as many stakeholders as you can who are directly involved or connected to your project. These are 'first level' stakeholders (and some were discussed earlier, on page 79).

Use a mind map to help identify your stakeholders. Place your PhD in the centre and add different branches to represent all the potential stakeholders. How you structure it in terms of grouping is completely up to you. Do whatever makes most sense for your PhD.

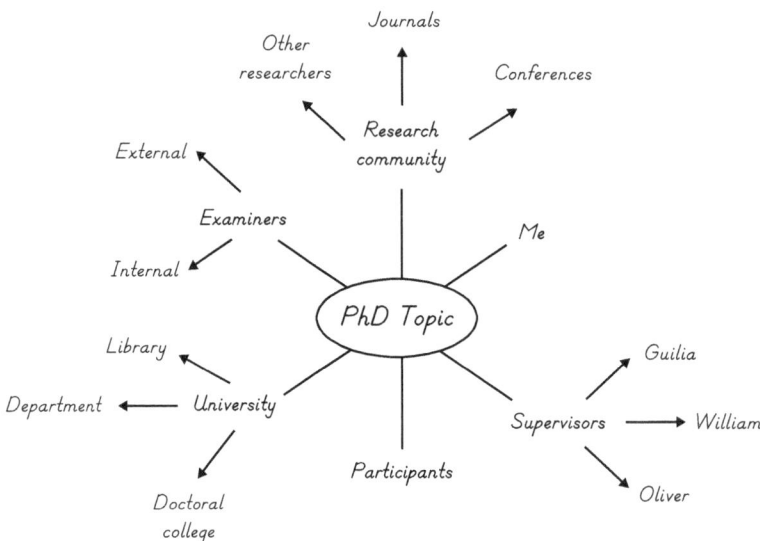

First-level PhD stakeholders

To help identify stakeholders, ask the following questions (also included in the template on page 82). Then, as you identify new stakeholders, add them to your diagram. Some stakeholders may appear as answers to more than one question.

Stakeholder identification questions

Who will be involved in your PhD?	e.g. you, supervisors, examiners, research group, collaborative partners
Where does your data come from?	e.g. participants, archives, laboratory, secondary sources, fieldwork
What administration is involved?	e.g. doctoral college, grad school; departmental admin, researcher development, Centre for Doctoral Training, funder
Who can help you?	e.g. lab technician, post-docs
Who will use or be interested in your PhD outputs?	e.g. research community, 'end users' (such as patients or policy makers in a medical research project)
Who will be affected by your work during the PhD?	e.g. family, friends, social activities, colleagues/employer
Who will be affected by your work post-PhD?	e.g. research community, future employers

Try to get as much detail as is reasonably possible when you are doing this: the more information the better when you start using it to inform your plan. For example, rather than simply having a generic 'supervisors' stakeholder, add individual names (in the example here, Guilia, William and Oliver). Among other things, you will use this information to understand differences in expectations, which is much easier to think about for 'William' (based on their *individual* research experience and particular field of interest) than considering supervisors as a whole.

> **Activity: Stakeholder diagram: add first-level stakeholders**
>
> 1 Answer the questions on the stakeholder identification template on page 82, noting as many stakeholders as you can.
> 2 Take a blank piece of paper and, using the information captured in the template, begin to create a stakeholder diagram mind map.
> 3 Write your PhD topic or working title in a circle in the middle of your mind map.
> 4 Try to identify all of the stakeholders directly connected to your PhD (you, your supervisors, research participants, lab technician, etc.).
> 5 Use the questions in the template to prompt you.

Template: Stakeholder identification

Who will be involved in my PhD?	
Where does my data come from?	
What administration is involved?	
Who can help me?	
Who will use or be interested in my PhD outputs?	
Who will be affected by my work during the PhD?	
Who will be affected by my work post-PhD?	

Step 2: Identify second- and third-level stakeholders

You will also have second-level and third-level stakeholders where the link to your PhD is not so immediate. These stakeholders are not necessarily directly connected to your PhD, but can potentially impact it through their connection to a first-level stakeholder. For instance, other PhD students that Oliver is supporting could be regarded as potentially adverse stakeholders. They are not directly connected to your work, but they are stakeholders in your PhD because the time Oliver spends with them is time that he is unavailable to you. They are not intentionally adverse, but could potentially cause you a problem if Oliver isn't available when you need him. It's wise to consider the effects that these second- (or third-) level stakeholders could have on your work.

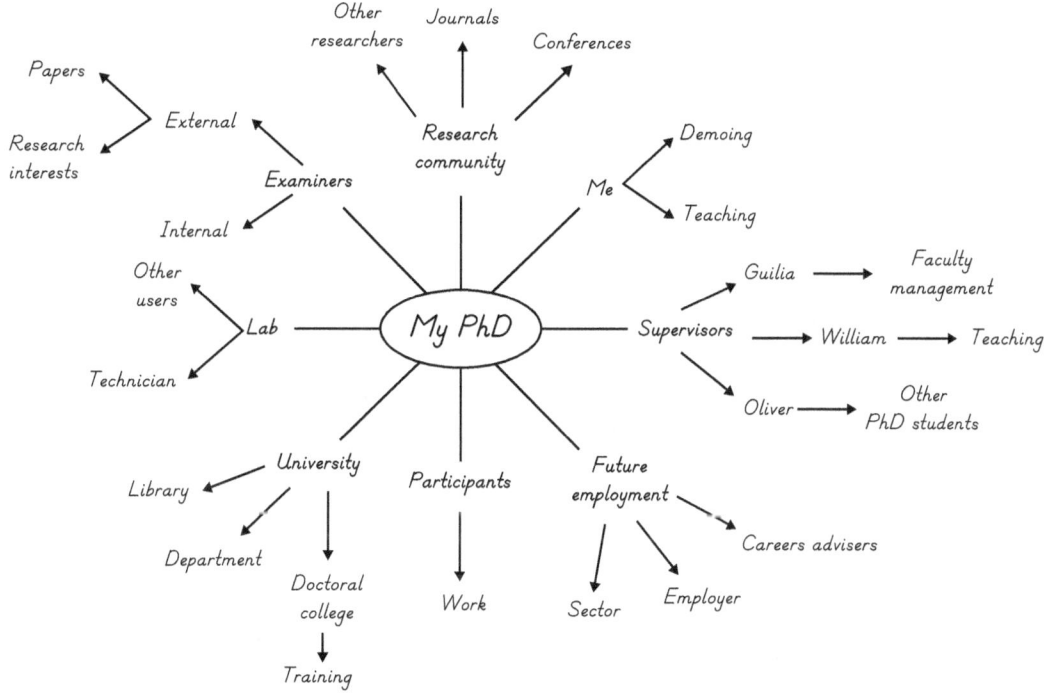

Second- and third-level PhD stakeholders

Revisit the goals you identified in Chapter 2 to identify any additional stakeholders that are connected to your wider PhD goals. Do you have stakeholders that could influence, impact upon or affect your future goals, for example potential future employers? If so, make sure to note them, as aligning to their expectations is important for you in achieving your personal goals.

> ✏ **Activity: Stakeholder diagram: add second- and third-level stakeholders**
>
> Identify any second- or third-level stakeholders in your project and note them on your mind map.

Identification of stakeholders will allow you to begin to assess three fundamental considerations within your PhD, which we address in the coming chapters:

- **Expectations** (Chapter 8) – wants, needs, desires and expectations that inform your project outputs
- **Impact** (Chapter 8) – research impact, the difference you're making
- **Risks** (Chapter 11) – opportunities and threats that may be present in your PhD.

The stakeholder diagram is the basis for a wealth of information that will guide your plan. This is an *iterative* process that you will keep revisiting throughout your PhD as you develop personally as a researcher and understand more about the PhD process, and as your research idea matures overtime. For now, focus on identifying as many stakeholders as possible *at this point in time*.

Capturing and revisiting your stakeholder diagram

Although you can create these diagrams using software, we believe the first time you try this, it's best to do it with a pen and paper so you're focusing on the task not the computer. However, it makes sense to convert it into an electronic format that can be easily saved, updated and circulated. This is really important because you will want to refer to it during your PhD as your research, your understanding and even your scope changes. Over time, new stakeholders will become apparent. Some who have been important in the early stages take on decreased significance, and others may become more important in the later stages of your research. Frequently reviewing your stakeholder diagram allows you to take stock of the current situation of your PhD – which will be different from how it looked at the start.

> **Software options?**
>
> There are many different programs in which you can create stakeholder diagrams or mind maps. Many universities have licensed software you can use, but there are also some decent open-source options available.

If you are creating a stakeholder diagram for the first time in the middle or towards the end of your PhD, it can also help the process of focusing on who you need to prioritise and communicate with in order to successfully complete on time.

🔧 Transferable skills

Mind maps are a very useful tool when you want to scope out different elements, connections or ideas. They allow you to drill down into increasing detail and create a simple, visual overview of the object under consideration (in this case, PhD stakeholders).

Some students even use a mind-mapping technique to 'draw a picture' of the literature (see Chapter 22).

When we suggest reviewing your stakeholder diagram, we don't mean spending hours re-performing the same exercise. It's about spending just five minutes contemplating whether anything has changed. (This is discussed in more detail in Chapter 16.)

> In Chapter 17 we recommend using mind mapping to map your professional networks.

| 0–9 months: revisit and update every month | Middle stages: review once every 6 months | End of write-up and before submission: reperform the exercise from a research perspective being directed by your findings and results |

Stakeholder review schedule

- In the early stages of your PhD, revisit your stakeholder diagram at least once a month for the first nine months. It only takes five minutes or so each time, but your learning curve is so steep in the early days of a PhD, you will find it changes a lot as you understand more about your research and the research process.
- Throughout the mid-stages of your PhD, review the stakeholder diagram approximately once every six months. Again, this should mean about five to ten minutes of effort.
- Towards the end of the write-up phase and before submission, review more deeply, perhaps for 30 minutes or more. An important part of this review will be to consider the stakeholder impact and expectations for the next steps in your research and your career.

➡ **Action: Review your stakeholders.**

In your calendar, schedule times to review your stakeholder diagram in the coming months. Choose a frequency and duration appropriate to the stage of your course.

Summary

Successful planning for your PhD must rest on sound foundations. The building blocks of these foundations, considered at the very start and throughout the planning process, are an initiation phase, the three dimensions of the project triangle and stakeholder identification. Investing time on these building blocks will provide the information necessary to create accurate and reliable plans that will save you time down the line. The initiation phase of planning is a 'stop and think' moment, to assess key information and factors that will affect the viability of your plans. Considering the three corners of the project triangle – scope, cost and time – produces stable dimensions for your plans that allow you to plan effectively and respond to inevitable future changes without destabilising your project. Identification of all your stakeholders generates a wealth of information that will be used to establish the direction of your work, prioritise the key indicators of success and identify and avoid potential risks for your project during all phases of research.

> **Key points**
> - Only ever plan what you can plan.
> - Plan 'bites of the elephant' – only short phases of work should be planned in detail.
> - Always *plan* before you *do*.
> - Join the three corners of the project triangle and always keep them connected.
> - Identify as many PhD stakeholders as you can.
> - Review your stakeholder diagram regularly.

Further resources

Giangregorio, E. (2017) *Practical Project Stakeholder Management: Methods, Tools and Templates for Comprehensive Stakeholder Management*, 2nd edn. Self-published.

Heagney, J. (2022) *Fundamentals of Project Management*, 6th edn. London: Harper Collins.

Portnoy, J.L. and Portnoy, S.L. (2022) *Project Management for Dummies*, 6th edn. Hoboken NJ: Wiley & Sons.

Wysocki, R.K. (2019) *Effective Project Management: Traditional, Agile, Extreme, Hybrid.* Indianapolis: Wiley.

8 Set Your Scope

How to ... Figure out what you need to do

Set project boundaries – Stakeholder expectations – Determine project priorities – Must-haves, nice-to-haves, bells-and-whistles – The convergence method – SMART deliverables – Scope statement

By defining the scope of your work, you are beginning to identify in detail what it is you're doing for each phase of your PhD. If this isn't done well, then how do you know:

- The tasks you need to perform?
- Whether you've finished completely?
- Whether you've done it successfully?

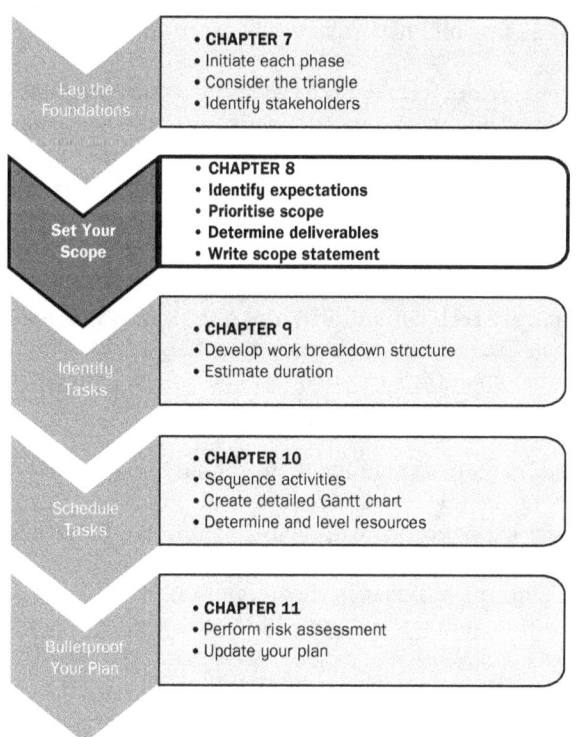

The planning process

Without a clear understanding of your scope and end point, planning of any kind is virtually impossible. This is particularly problematic in a PhD because of the inherent uncertainty of research. In the early days especially, your end point is often quite vague and poorly defined, but there are ways to clarify the scope of your PhD and create a plan to deliver it.

This chapter shows you how to begin to use the information gathered in your stakeholder diagram to understand the expectations and needs of your stakeholders. This informs the direction your PhD should take and the outputs it should produce. By understanding your stakeholder needs, you will be able to prioritise the most important outputs. Finally, you will create a scope statement that clarifies these expectations, aims and outputs for each stage of your PhD, allowing you to satisfy both yourself and others that the work has been completed as required and to the agreed standard.

Identify stakeholder expectations

Through your stakeholder diagram, you have identified the different stakeholders for your PhD. Each one of these will have slightly different expectations of your PhD, and you should interrogate the differing opinions they may hold about your research.

Expectations are the ideas that people have about the focus of your work, the outputs you should produce, the approach you should take and where your priorities should lie. Every stakeholder has wants and needs that are individual to them. It is incredibly important to try to unearth these as early as you can because they will strongly influence the direction of your work.

Each PhD will have different stakeholders with their own unique expectations, but the following are the key categories of stakeholders that all PhD projects will share, and their possible expectations:

- **The university** – There are doctoral degree regulations you have to follow, such as thesis assessment criteria, rules around advancement from one year to the next, and the evidence you need for each stage. You have no choice about these and they must inform your plan.
- **Your supervisors** – Each has their own particular areas of interest and expertise, which impact on the direction your research takes. They may be very keen for you to investigate something that holds little interest to you personally. Clearly, it is your PhD, so it is your decision, but ignoring supervisory advice is a sure-fire way to create an adverse stakeholder!
- **The extant research, research community and ongoing developments** – Other researchers in your field play a role in forming and reshaping your PhD all the way through to submission. You must build your research upon their existing literature. New publications throughout the lifetime of your PhD may necessitate adjustments in your work.

In order to avoid disappointing your stakeholders, you should manage expectations by agreeing with them what can realistically be achieved over the course of your PhD. Recognising, and subsequently managing, these stakeholder expectations will have a significant influence on the perceived quality of your research. Almost regardless of how well you complete your work, if a stakeholder believes it should have been done slightly differently, for example if they have a different expectation of the method or output, then they might view your PhD as being less successful than it really is. For example:

- If your PhD is part of a wider research project, there may be funding deliverables that are a priority and which could seem at odds with your own personal ambitions.
- Industry partners may prioritise commercial applications over scientific innovation.

- You may be aiming for a career in industry, but your supervisor is keen on multiple journal publications.
- It might just be that your supervisor would prefer you to focus on one particular aspect of your research while your real interest lies in a slightly different area.

If possible, speak to stakeholders about your work and elicit their opinions on:

- The direction your research should take
- Key outcomes
- Other useful outcomes
- Particular areas of interest

Ask questions such as:

- What outputs would they expect or like to see from your PhD?
- What would be really useful or helpful or would make a difference to them?
- What would really excite them and make them engage with my work?

And maybe even:

- What would they hate this project to look like?

> **Supervisory expectations**
>
> Hopefully, the expectations of your PhD for you and your supervisor are fairly closely aligned. They will not be identical, however. You might have aspirations of moving out of academia post-PhD; your supervisor may be interested in enhancing their own research credentials and, as a result, has a greater focus on getting published than you. Maybe your PhD is part of a larger research project – your primary focus is completing the work required to pass your doctoral degree, while your supervisor might be more interested in the contribution to the bigger picture. We look at ways of confronting these tensions in Chapter 19.

> **But I can't meet people!**
>
> It's not always possible to get in front of these 'key' stakeholders, especially if they are several levels of abstraction away from your PhD. So, on your own, go through this process by putting yourself in their shoes. Attempt to see *your* PhD from *their* point of view.

➡ Action: Consider the expectations of your stakeholders.

Review your stakeholder diagram and consider the expectations that these stakeholders may have of your PhD.

Although it is *your* PhD, and you will repeatedly be reminded to take ownership, ultimately its success will be built on a *compromise* between the needs and expectations of several key stakeholders. This early part of your PhD offers you the opportunity to identify all these expectations in order to avoid major, but potentially necessary, deviations and changes of direction later on.

> **Don't forget about number one**
>
> Remember that your own PhD expectations are a very important. You don't want to compromise on your reasons for starting a research degree. Make sure that your personal goals, developed in Chapter 2, are included when you use the convergence method that follows.

Your research impact

We explained in Chapter 7 how the potential 'users' of your research are stakeholders in your PhD. Many of these stakeholders won't even be aware of your PhD research, but it is valuable to reflect on what their expectations might be if they did know about it. For example, your PhD might be focused on the improvement of energy-storage systems for Formula 1 racing cars. The direct impact of your research is on F1 car performance. However, from the user perspective, developing new storage systems may have secondary benefits to the wider automotive industry, particularly hybrid road-car technology and more environmentally friendly public transport.

The identification of the way users could benefit from your research is called your research 'impact'. The focus on impact forces you to consider:

> 'Considering the impact also allowed me to better explain my recommendations for future study. Being able to articulate this was the primary reason I got my post-doc grant proposal approved!'

- Who will be affected by this (however tenuously)?
- What will the benefit be to them?
- What will my PhD change?

Identifying research impact is part of effective planning, and it will become a key asset in the way you demonstrate the value of your research.

> **➡ Action: Consider what your 'users' might expect from your research.**
>
> Revisit and update, if necessary, your stakeholder diagram, identifying new 'users'. Consider what they would like your research to cover. This can guide you to adjust the direction and focus of your research to generate maximum benefits.

The convergence method

Once you have identified your stakeholders' expectations, use a technique called the convergence method to find a way of prioritising the expectations of your PhD. This technique uses the expectations of key stakeholders to develop a comprehensive understanding of the direction your work must take. It allows you to identify where similar expectations exist so that you can concentrate on them. It can also highlight differences in opinion that – using the techniques coming later in this chapter – you can address sooner rather than later. It's important to remember that this is an iterative process: you should revisit this exercise throughout your PhD as the maturity of your idea evolves and your maturity as an independent researcher develops.

> 'The first time I used the convergence method it was really helpful. I had nothing in the column under 'Supervisor', which highlighted that I had no idea what their expectations were for my PhD. I realised I had better find out pretty quickly!'

Step 1: Identify your key stakeholders

In an ideal world, you would be able to satisfy every stakeholder desire, but that is unrealistic – there are simply too many. Instead, assess which stakeholders are the most important to the success of your PhD, and focus on them. Identify your key stakeholders based on:

- How closely involved they are with your project
- How significantly they can be impacted by it
- How greatly you value their opinion.

Step 2: Create a convergence table

Write your key stakeholders as column headings in a table. Under each name, note down the expectations you have discovered through your conversations with stakeholders, or, for those you haven't met, potential expectations that they might have. Include your own personal goals, then use the questions on page 89 for guidance on other stakeholders. *Write down anything that springs to mind – you can always cross it out later!* For example:

You	Supervisor 1	Supervisor 2	Funder
PhD	Quality thesis	Pass	Publish in prestigious journals
Two papers	3–4 papers in *Nature*	Papers in *Nature*	Conference presentations
Lab-based	Lab-based	Research group outputs	Data-management plan
Make compound	Make strong compound	Make additional compound	Quarterly reports
Conference (travel!)	Conference speaking and attendance	Book chapters	Gantt chart
Continued professional development	Data-management plan	Future grant applications	
Full-time job	Future grant applications		
Nobel Prize			

Convergence Table: Stakeholder Expectations

Step 3: Identify and focus on similarities

Having identified each of these key stakeholders' expectations you can now identify where similarities exist. The similarities are easy to deal with: as long as they are relevant to your PhD, make sure you achieve them! Be aware when you check for similarities that sometimes stakeholders use different words to refer to essentially the same thing, such as 'PhD', 'thesis' and 'pass'.

You	Supervisor 1	Supervisor 2	Funder
PhD	Quality Thesis	Pass	Publish in Prestigious Journals
2 Papers	3-4 Papers in "Nature"	Papers in "Nature"	Conference Presentations
Lab-Based	Lab-Based	Research Group Outputs	Data Management Plan
Make Compound	Make Strong Compound	Make Different Compound	Quarterly Reports
Conference (travel!)	Conference Speaking & Attendance	Book Chapters	Gantt chart
Continued Professional Development	Data Management Plan	Future Grant Applications	
Full Time Job	Future Grant Applications		
Nobel Prize			

Convergence table: identify similarities

Step 4: Identify and manage differences

Where expectations diverge (which we'll address with Prioritisation and the Scope statement), it becomes slightly trickier. However, by using the convergence method to identify potentially conflicting stakeholder expectations in the early stages of your PhD, you have the chance to determine how to address them. This is infinitely better than only discovering these different expectations later in your project when it might be too late to fulfill them.

The convergence method allows you to develop a clear picture of the expectations common to your key stakeholders and those that differ. This means you are in a position to establish your priorities and define the scope of your PhD research.

You	Supervisor1	Supervisor2	Funder
PhD	Quality Thesis	Pass	Publish in Prestigious Journals
2 Papers	3-4 Papers in "Nature"	Papers in "Nature"	Conference Presentations
Lab-Based	Lab-Based	Research Group Outputs	Data Management Plan
Make Compound	Make Strong Compound	**Make Different Compound**	**Quarterly Reports**
Conference (travel!)	Conference Speaking & Attendance	**Book Chapters**	**Gantt chart**
Continued Professional Development	Data Management Plan	Future Grant Applications	
Full Time Job	Future Grant Applications		
Nobel Prize			

Convergence table: identify differences

✏ Activity: The convergence method

Use the convergence table template on page 93.

1. Look at your stakeholder diagram and identify your key stakeholders. Put them in the column headings, for example: you, 'Supervisor 1', 'Supervisor 2', industry partners, research users.
2. Identify your key stakeholders' expectations, writing them in their columns.
   - If possible, speak to the stakeholders and try to identify their expectations of your PhD (the questions suggested earlier can guide your conversation).
   - If you can't speak to stakeholders, consider on your own the expectations that these stakeholders might have of your PhD.
3. Identify similarities between the expectations.
4. Highlight any significant differences between the expectations.

Set Your Scope **93**

Template: Convergence table

Stakeholders	Stakeholder expectations												

Prioritise scope

Having used the convergence method, you will inevitably discover that there are too many expectations to meet. So, which expectations should you meet? How can you prioritise them? Imagine, for example, that during convergence you identify 20 different things that, ideally, you would deliver over the course of your PhD. You could try to rank them in order of importance from 1 to 20. That is difficult and would take you a long time. If you then asked your supervisors to review your ranking, they would almost certainly have a slightly different order and you'd end up debating whether an item should be position 12 or 15 on the list. In this case, *numeric prioritisation* is difficult and inefficient. A better method is *categorisation*. Rank the items within three different groups.

Scope prioritisation categories

	Explanation	Examples
Must-haves	• Absolute essentials, non-negotiable. • You must do this or you will not get your PhD.	• Unique contribution to knowledge (i.e. established within the relevant, extant literature). • Your own work. • Conduct X experiment. • Interview 5 participants.
Nice-to-haves	• Very valuable but not essential. • The expectations of both you and your supervisors often fall into this category.	• Conduct Y and Z experiments (X is enough to write up). • Interview 12 participants (5 is sufficient for the study). • Present at conference.
Bells-and-whistles	• Add-ons, personal interest, aesthetics. • Fun and interesting but probably not *that* important in terms of getting a PhD.	• Create pen portraits / vignettes for each participant. • Enter 3-Minute Thesis competition.

Categorisation is much quicker and straightforward than numeric prioritisation. It is also much easier to get agreement with other people using this approach. Generally speaking, the only argument you will have is whether or not an idea is a nice-to-have or a bells-and-whistle, because the must-haves are easy to identify. If you don't do those, you won't get a PhD.

> 'My supervisors often told me that I was working at too high a level, that I wanted to do everything and there simply wasn't time (and it wasn't necessary!) to do it all. Basically, I needed focus and I found this technique really helpful in allowing me to do that.'

You might categorise the common expectations identified during the previous convergence example as follows.

Must-haves	• PhD thesis of doctoral quality • Continued professional development (need for job) • Lab-based (want a laboratory job) • Quarterly reports and Gantt chart (no funding without it!)
Nice-to-haves	• Make compound • Publish in *Nature* • Conference presentations • Future grant applications (will help secure job) • Data-management plan • Research group outputs (will help secure job)

Bells-and-whistles	• Book chapters • Make different compound • Nobel prize

Example categorisation of scope priorities

If you find that every item on your list is a must-have, it probably indicates that you are considering your workload at *too high a level* – the items are too large. You will find more distinction comes with greater detail. Break down the high-level items into smaller blocks. For example, 'Continued professional development' could be broken down into: industry-related technical skills and personal effectiveness skills (we have a technique – the work breakdown structure – in Chapter 9, that can help you to break this down).

Mapping the outputs from convergence into must-haves, nice-to-haves and bells-and-whistles will allow you to take stock of your personal goals and your stakeholders' research expectations. As a technique, it becomes even more valuable when you apply it to each 'bite of your elephant', so repeat it for every phase of the project as you progress through your PhD. For example, your priorities for the first 'bite' (the first three months of your PhD, say) might look like this:

Literature review: What *must* you cover in order to position, contextualise and justify the need for your research?

Items of scope	Must-haves	Nice-to-haves	Bells-and-whistles
Review of 'value perception' literature within training	☑	☐	☐
Review of 'management' and 'management training' literature	☑	☐	☐
Review and appraise different management methodologies	☐	☐	☑
Review of 'evaluation' literature within training	☑	☐	☐
Review of generic 'evaluation' literature	☐	☑	☐
Review, comparison and critical appraisal of 'training evaluation frameworks' within extant literature	☑	☐	☐

Prioritisation of a later bite might look like this:

Data analysis: What analysis *must* you perform in order to demonstrate robust findings/conclusions?

Items of scope	Must-haves	Nice-to-haves	Bells-and-whistles
NVivo software training course	☐	☑	☐
Inductive (in vivo) interview data coding	☑	☐	☐
Axial interview data coding	☐	☑	☐
Create management training evaluation taxonomy	☐	☐	☑

It's likely that you have more things on your list than you can complete in the time allocated for this stage of your PhD. Looking at your list, if you think you'll struggle to achieve it all by the deadline indicated in your high-level timeline (Chapter 4), then you can start compromising on your bells-and-whistles. If you have time remaining towards the end of this phase, or beyond, you might get the chance to complete them. Don't delete them, or they might be forgotten, but leave them out of your focus for now, so you can concentrate on the more important elements. It's probable that you'll still feel uncomfortable with the amount of scope on your list, so you need to begin to omit some nice-to-haves. Again, if you have time remaining, you might be able to fit them in, but you should *focus on the essentials first*. If you seem to need to cross out must-haves, your project will not be successful. That's the very nature of a must-have: it *must* be there for you to get a PhD. If you find yourself in this situation, you need to revisit what you intend to do at a fundamental level or request an extension. Tackling everything on a list at 80 per cent will not get you through your Viva – completing the must-haves at 100 per cent will!

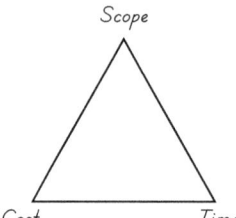

Remember the links in the project triangle.

✏ Activity: Prioritisation

1 Using the template on page 97, list down the left all of the items of scope identified during convergence. (Add anything to the list that you feel has been omitted.)
2 Using the definitions provided earlier, categorise your items as must-haves, nice-to-haves or bells-and-whistles in terms of *your* PhD.

Template: Prioritisation

Items of scope	Must-haves	Nice-to-haves	Bells-and-whistles
	☐	☐	☐
	☐	☐	☐
	☐	☐	☐
	☐	☐	☐
	☐	☐	☐
	☐	☐	☐
	☐	☐	☐
	☐	☐	☐
	☐	☐	☐
	☐	☐	☐
	☐	☐	☐
	☐	☐	☐
	☐	☐	☐

Determine your deliverables

If the goals you defined in Chapter 2 are the glimmer of light in the fog, your scope lays out what you need to complete in order to move closer to them. The outputs that you will produce to ensure the work satisfies its purpose are deliverables – things your project will deliver. The deliverables that you identify at the beginning of a project or a phase (a bite of your elephant) form a checklist for the work that needs completing during that phase. Knowing whether you have achieved everything simply becomes a matter of going through the list.

You might think that your deliverables are easy to define:

- Write a thesis
- Do this experiment
- Pass my Viva.

These are too high level, however. To use deliverables to plan your project, you require a little bit more detail. Deliverables need to be more than just descriptive: they need to specify precisely what you will deliver. For example: 'submit a journal article' doesn't give you enough detail about the deliverable to be able to plan how to deliver it. Which journal? What topic? Word count? Submission and review process?

Many organisations and funders ask for SMART deliverables (Doran, 1981) and, even if you're not required to do this, there is real value in using the SMART deliverables method when planning your PhD. The SMART acronym states that all deliverables should be:

- **Specific** – Uniquely identifiable and different from the other deliverables so you can demonstrate whether it has been completed or not
- **Measurable** – Understood in enough detail that it is possible to objectively assess whether or not it has been completed correctly
- **Achievable** – With verification that you have the time, skills, resources, ability and so on to complete this deliverable
- **Realistic** – Having checked that it is genuinely possible (for a PhD student researching geo-political leadership, personally interviewing the Secretary General of NATO may not be realistic, but using secondary sources of interview data might be)
- **Timebound** – With a definitive deadline for completion.

So, for example, rather than:

Start writing.

How about:

Document test results for new cultivar's aphid resistance by end of March.

Or:

Before Christmas, write up the meta-analysis of the literature pertaining to visual culture in 16th-century Reformation Germany.

Admittedly, this can be tough in a PhD, as you do not know exactly what you're going to produce. You can mitigate this by using objectively measurable terminology to specify your deliverables, rather than subjective, descriptive terminology. For example, rather than describing a deliverable as 'innovative', you could specify it as 'applying this technique to this field for the first time'. You can then demonstrate in your literature review that the technique hasn't been applied to your field previously and, therefore, prove you've done what you intended to do. 'Innovative' leaves you more open to debate, argument and disagreement because there is subjectivity associated with it.

The SMART technique has several benefits. In the planning stages:

> **Measure**
>
> We know that *measure* can be a value-laden word, particularly in qualitative research. However, all it means here is that you know roughly what the deliverable will look like, so you can assess whether or not it has been done correctly. As you'll see in our examples, you can do this even if your approach is grounded theory.

- It makes the work more tangible and therefore easier to plan
- It ensures that there is a single, shared expectation of an output for all stakeholders.

It also proves extremely valuable at the end, and at milestones throughout the project, because:

- It gives you confidence that you've completed something *as planned* (and completed it successfully)
- It allows you to demonstrate to others that you've completed something *as they were expecting* (and completed it successfully).

In defining your deliverables, you paint a picture of your project outputs. You are describing in advance what you intend them to look like. If you don't do this, it's very difficult to demonstrate successful completion, because everyone will have slightly different expectations of what is to be delivered.

You should also be careful not to subject your deliverables to influences that you cannot control, such as the results of your data. You don't know exactly what your study will find when you start off. You don't know what data you will collect, what the analysis will show, the findings you will discover or the conclusions you will draw, so don't base your success criteria on any of these. Instead try to identify the 'definites' in terms of the project.

Looking at the examples given earlier: 'Document test results for new cultivar's aphid resistance by end of March.' What are the test results? You have no idea because you haven't run the tests yet, but, as long as you document them by the end of March, you can tick the box that indicates this deliverable has been completed.

'Before Christmas, write up the meta-analysis of the literature pertaining to visual culture in 16th-century Reformation Germany.' You'll notice that this deliverable doesn't just say, 'complete meta-analysis' because what does 'completion' actually mean? Reading the literature? Entering the papers in your reference manager? Have a peer-reviewed paper accepted for publication? 'Completion' is subjective, however 'write up' gives you something tangible to demonstrate that you've done what you intended.

This can be difficult, particularly for a PhD, but the biggest reason for projects struggling is that people don't really know what they're meant to be doing. If you don't know what you're meant to be doing, how can you plan your work? Take time on these identifications for each 'bite of your elephant'. It will help you to understand the work and the outputs more deeply, it will make the subsequent planning activities much easier and it will, as a result, allow your work to run more smoothly.

Examples of SMART deliverables linked to a PhD

Deliverable	SMART deliverable
First year progress report	Present first year progress report to supervisor by end of Q1
Submit ethics	Submit required documentation to ethics committee in order to be considered at meeting on [date]
Organise focus groups	Arrange participants, venue and logistics for focus-group meetings during Aug and Sep, by end July
Fieldwork	Organise all travel, accommodation and equipment for fieldwork trip by 29 May (inc. H&S risk assessment)
Write up	Transcribe all interview data and codify all data in NVivo software by end Nov
Set up equipment	Order chemicals and bacteria stock for delivery no later than 17 July
Create model	Calculate fuel flow rates for Schnell turbo-compound engine by end Q2
Publish	Submit paper to International Journal of Heritage Studies at least once per calendar year throughout PhD

✏ Activity: Deliverables

Complete the template on page 101:

1. Considering the next phase of your project, identify all your deliverables.
2. Make them SMART.

Check them off when completed.

📄 Template: Deliverables

Project phase:		
Deliverable	**SMART deliverable**	**Delivered**
e.g. First year progress report	e.g. Present first year progress report to supervisor by end of April	☐
		☐
		☐
		☐
		☐
		☐
		☐
		☐
		☐
		☐
		☐
		☐
		☐

Write your statement of scope

You have used convergence to identify everything that you want or need to do, have categorised these as must-haves, nice-to-haves and bells-and-whistles to note your priorities, and, using SMART, have determined how they will be assessed. Now comes the *most important* part of managing expectations: a scope statement.

This is a technique you can use constantly throughout your work, regardless of the size or scale of the undertaking. A statement of scope can be a 500-plus-page detailed specification of everything a project must deliver, or it could be just a two-line email. Size is irrelevant as long as it covers two fundamental points:

- What you are going to do
- What you are *not* going to do.

This might sound strange. Why define what you are *not* doing? to plan the scope of your PhD you need to determine these two points. Project managers use the terms 'in scope' for the things you are going to do and 'out of scope' for those you choose to omit. Many research funders use a similar concept but refer to 'outputs' and 'exclusions'. In your thesis, you will write about the 'outcomes' and 'limitations' of your study. These terms all say the same thing: what you will do and what you will not do. You're establishing boundaries around your project.

In scope:

- You explicitly state what you're going to do for your PhD, or for this particular *stage* of your PhD.

Out of scope:

- Anything that you identified during convergence that you're not going to do. (Explicitly write down that it is 'out of scope'.)
- Any of the nice-to-haves or bells-and-whistles that you have contemplated but decided not to pursue. (Note them as 'out of scope'.)
- Anything that people could *reasonably* expect you to deliver within the context of the project, but you're not going to do. A key term here is 'reasonableness' because, otherwise, the list of 'out of scope' would go on for ever!

The convergence and categorisation processes will have helped you establish these elements.

The concept of 'in scope' and 'out of scope' should be applied at every level of your PhD, from managing the high-level expectations that your stakeholders may have of the ultimate outputs of your research, to when you are planning the day-to-day activity of conducting the research. For example, you could say that, as part of your PhD:

The scope of this book

We took a similar approach in the introduction of this book. We wanted to set your expectations from the outset, so, within the first few pages, we wrote 'What this book is' and 'What this book isn't'. It was a very deliberate attempt to get a common, shared understanding between us (the authors) and our key stakeholders (you!) about the purpose and scope of the book and to manage your expectations accordingly.

The PhD will	The PhD will not
Investigate the impact of social-media usage on the mood and body image of teenagers	Consider medical aspects of illnesses developed as a result of online pressure
Focus the study on teenagers aged 13–17	Investigate psychology of why online bullying occurs
Adopt a mixed-methods approach to the study, offering both quantitative and qualitative data	Pursue multiple publications
Apply to present at July conference in Vancouver	

You have established at a high level the main points that your PhD will address, and the major exclusions. It should be clear to anyone reading this where the boundaries of your project lie. Alternatively, you could say that, for your next supervisory meeting:

You will	You will not
Complete a draft of methodology chapter	Begin working on journal paper
Complete the analysis of experiment X	Move on to experiment Y
Review new literature published during last quarter	
Organise travel for July conference	

This clearly establishes the work to do before the next meeting, but it's also a reminder of what you've agreed to postpone for the time being. Put it in an email or write it in your meeting minutes, and, next time you meet with your supervisors, you will be able to show that you have completed exactly what was agreed. The danger of not writing this down is that we tend to have selective memories! It can be difficult to remember everything that has been discussed and agreed if they aren't written down – especially for your supervisors who have 1001 things on their plate. They will remember discussing a certain point with you, but may not remember that you jointly decided not to do it. This could create a tension with the potential to impact on the perceived success or completeness of your work and even make you doubt your own progress.

This technique works equally well for managing boundaries around your whole PhD as well as when you're planning discrete 'bites of the elephant'. The examples just given show that this doesn't need to be onerous – it would take just a couple of minutes to compose and send that email, but it could save you a whole lot of trouble.

✏ Activity: Scope statement

As you come to each phase of your project, using the template on page 104, list what you are going to do 'in scope' and what you are not going to do 'out of scope'.

Retain this list and refer to it at the end of each phase to demonstrate to yourself and others that everything has been completed as planned.

📄 Template: Scope statement

Project phase:	
In scope	**Out of scope**
e.g. • Transcribe interviews • Email transcription copy to participants	e.g. • Begin thematic line-by-line coding

Summary

When planning your PhD, defining the scope of your work is one of the most important things you can do. By understanding the expectations of your stakeholders, you can identify the key outputs for your research project. Once you recognise the expectations of your important stakeholders, you can manage them by focusing on the shared wants and finding a compromise between conflicting wants. This allows you to set priorities for your work and ensure that you deliver exactly what is required to be judged a success. Establish the parameters of your work by specifying what you will do and, just as importantly, what you will not do. These clear deliverables allow you to manage expectations and confidently demonstrate that you've successfully completed your work as intended.

> **Key points**
> - Set the scope of your PhD research by identifying the common and conflicting expectations of your stakeholders.
> - Managing your stakeholder expectations is the key to ensuring your work is judged to be successful.
> - You are an important stakeholder in your PhD!
> - Determine the deliverables you must achieve and how they will be assessed.
> - Set your priorities in line with stakeholder requirements – ensure you deliver the must-haves.
> - Articulate the scope of your work – what you will do, as well as what you will not.

Further resources

Giangregorio, E. (2017) *Practical Project Stakeholder Management: Methods, Tools and Templates for Comprehensive Stakeholder Management*, 2nd edn. Self-published.
Heagney, J. (2022) *Fundamentals of Project Management*, 6th edn. London: Harper Collins.
Obeng, E. (1994) *All Change! The Project Leader's Secret Handbook*. Harlow: Prentice Hall.
Portnoy, J.L. and Portnoy, S.L. (2022) *Project Management for Dummies*, 6th edn. Hoboken NJ: Wiley & Sons.

Reference

Doran, G.T. (1981) There's a S.M.A.R.T. Way to Write Management's Goals and Objectives, *Management Review*, **70**: 35–36.

Identify Tasks

How to ... Work out how to do what you need to do

Define tasks – Work breakdown structure – Necessary level of detail – The importance of verbs – Handle uncertainties – Estimate task durations – Comparative, parametric and three-point estimations

In the previous chapter, you identified *what* you need to do for the next phase of your PhD. This chapter helps you determine *how* you're going to achieve it.

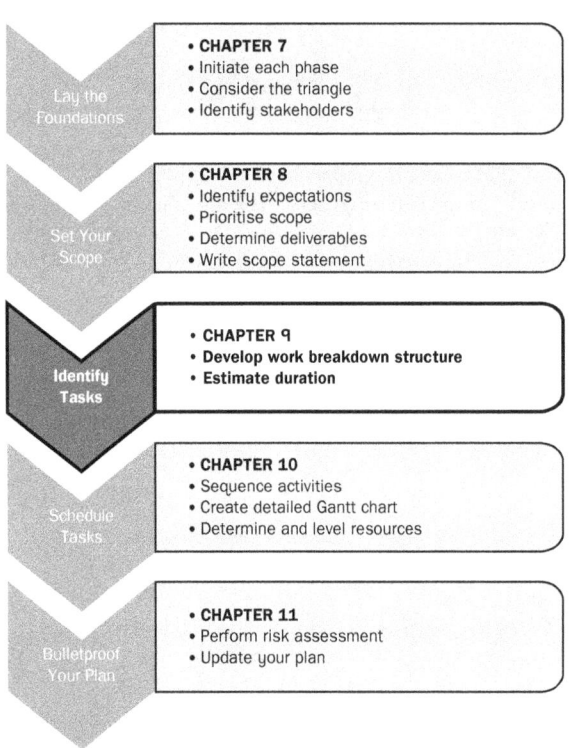

The planning process

You do this in two stages:

1 Identify all the different tasks or activities that must be performed (either by you or others) to complete your deliverables – using a tool called a work breakdown structure.
2 Estimate how long these tasks will take, using a range of estimation methods.

These two steps will prepare you to schedule your work (which you do in Chapter 10).

As with the earlier techniques, the following are most effective when applied to individual 'bites of the elephant'. Although you could try to use each technique to plan your entire PhD, it's difficult to achieve the necessary level of detail to do it well. These techniques will give you a *good grasp of your day-to-day work*.

The work breakdown structure

The work breakdown structure (WBS) is probably the *most 'transferable' project management technique* in this book. The WBS is, as the name indicates, a way of breaking down work into tasks. The WBS helps you to understand your work in detail by encouraging you to:

- Identify the phase of work (the 'bite of the elephant') that you want to plan
- Subdivide that work into the different deliverables to be completed during the phase
- Pinpoint all the different tasks (also called *activities* or *actions*) that you need to perform in order to complete your deliverables and finish the phase.

Create a work breakdown structure

We use the simple example here of 'building a wall' to illustrate the WBS method. You will apply the method to your own work later in the chapter.

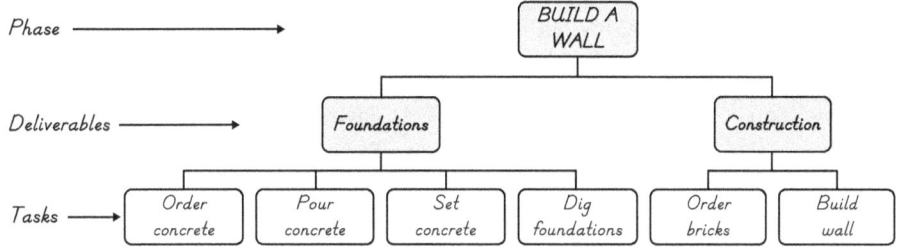

Example work breakdown structure: building a wall

1 At the top level of the WBS, you have the 'phase' of the house-building project that you're planning: building a wall.
2 You then consider the deliverables or sub-phases within that, in this case completing the 'foundations' that form the base of building and the 'construction' of the wall itself.
3 Finally, you identify all the different tasks needed in order to fulfill these deliverables ('order …', 'dig …' and so on).

It is these *final* tasks that you use as the basis for your plan. You estimate durations of the tasks and identify the different resources (you, equipment, other people and so on) that are needed to complete them. They will ultimately make up your timeline, so it is a very important step in planning.

Benefits of using a work breakdown structure

There are two primary reasons for using this technique. First, drilling down to task level *improves ease and accuracy of estimation*, something many PhD students tell us they struggle with. Trying to anticipate how long work will take is very difficult at the top level of a WBS (by just considering 'building a wall'). You will almost certainly underestimate how long things will take (most people tend to be optimistic estimators). This level of detail also helps you to clarify your resource needs (which we will address in Chapter 10), as well as identify potential risks (looked at in Chapter 11).

The second reason to use a work breakdown structure is to *ensure that you don't overlook anything*. You've almost certainly had the experience of realising halfway through a project that there was something you should have done at the beginning but you have overlooked, either because you forgot about it or weren't aware of it. The latter can be particularly prevalent in a PhD, when you are often completing complicated activities for the first time. The process of drilling down to individual tasks in the WBS allows you to identify all the tasks that you might otherwise miss.

There is a particular class of task that is often overlooked. These are what we call the passive tasks: those that require you to *wait* for something rather than *do* something. They need time to be set aside for them to happen in your schedule, but do not need your involvement. A very simple example of this would be repainting window frames: you need to paint the window frames (active task), wait for the paint to dry (passive task) before you rehang the curtains (active task).

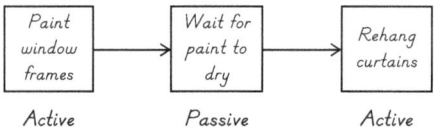

Task-planning example: active and passive tasks

Paint drying does not require you to *do* anything but it does take time so needs to be in your plan as a task. For your PhD, it might just be as simple as waiting for feedback from your supervisor: you are not actively involved in the task, but it will take time. It might also be the case that you cannot progress any further until it has been completed. Some other examples of passive tasks in your PhD could be:

- Number crunching
- Travel grant awards
- Running simulations
- Governmental permissions
- Running automated analyses
- Delivery times
- Waiting for cells/plants/crops/animals to grow or mature
- Data back-ups
- Ethics committee approvals

- Participant responses
- External transcription services
- Printing
- Software installations
- Agricultural seasonal cycles
- Visa approvals
- Waiting for organic materials to degrade
- Gestation times
- If you're an artist, you might literally have to wait for paint to dry!

It is crucial that these passive tasks are included in your WBS, as they take time to complete. This information can also help you to manage and distribute your PhD workload more effectively (as you will see in Chapter 10).

Using the WBS, this gradual subdividing of each phase of work into its deliverables, and then further into the tasks needed to complete those deliverables, will give you a clearer, more accurate understanding of all the work involved.

Level of detail

How far should you break down the work? How much detail do you need? Too high a level and you can't plan accurately; too detailed and you'll spend all of your time updating your plan as things change. As you complete the WBS, you'll find that you start using *verbs* to describe the tasks. As soon as you find verbs appearing, you've probably drilled down far enough. The task 'experimentation', for instance, is rather high level. It is a noun, not a verb. As a result, it is difficult to ascertain all the work involved, which, in turn, makes estimation and planning difficult. However, breaking it down into several task verbs linked to 'experimentation' makes the activities involved far easier to specify. For example:

1. *Centrifuge* flask
2. *Resuspend* in H_2O
3. *Pour* into solution
4. *Leave* for one week
5. *Test* ureolytic activity.

The WBS can also be an excellent communication tool. You could use the WBS to get input from your supervisors, for example by sharing a WBS for a phase of work and asking for feedback. It allows them to easily understand the upcoming work and offer comments such as, 'There are a couple of things over here that you've missed' and 'This task is unnecessary right now.' See the WBS as another way of sharing and understanding expectations.

The following examples are WBS diagrams created by PhD students for phases of their work.

> **Mind your language!**
>
> 'When I showed my supervisors my WBS, I didn't call it a work breakdown structure because sometimes people are uncomfortable with unfamiliar terminology! I asked them to have a look at my list instead.'
>
> Sometimes, people are sceptical about applying these techniques to a research environment. We know through years of experience that these tools can help, but, to combat any potential cynicism, you should always be careful with the language you use.
>
> Having said that, we are consciously providing the 'formal' language here so that you can discuss the process you've been through with future employers (particularly in industry) and demonstrate the valuable transferable skills you've developed throughout the PhD process.

Examples of PhD work breakdown structures

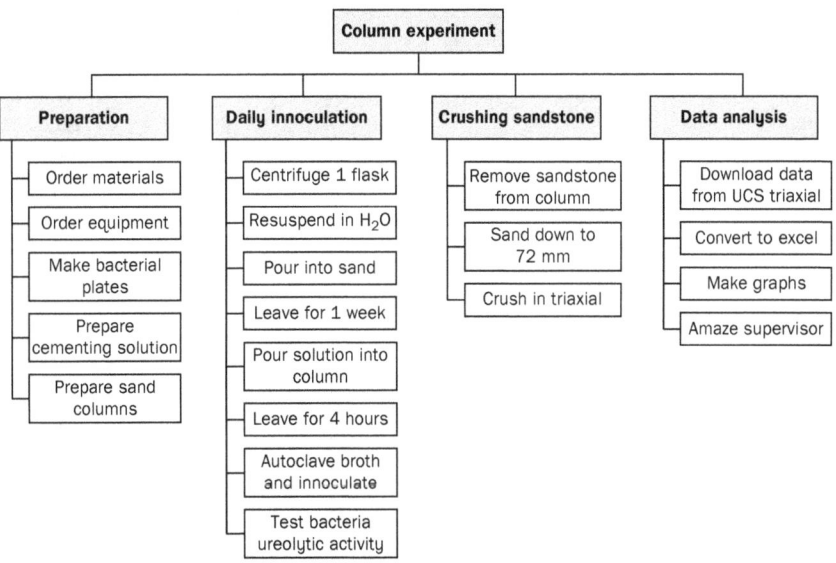

Five-week experiment

110 Part 2 – How to Get Going

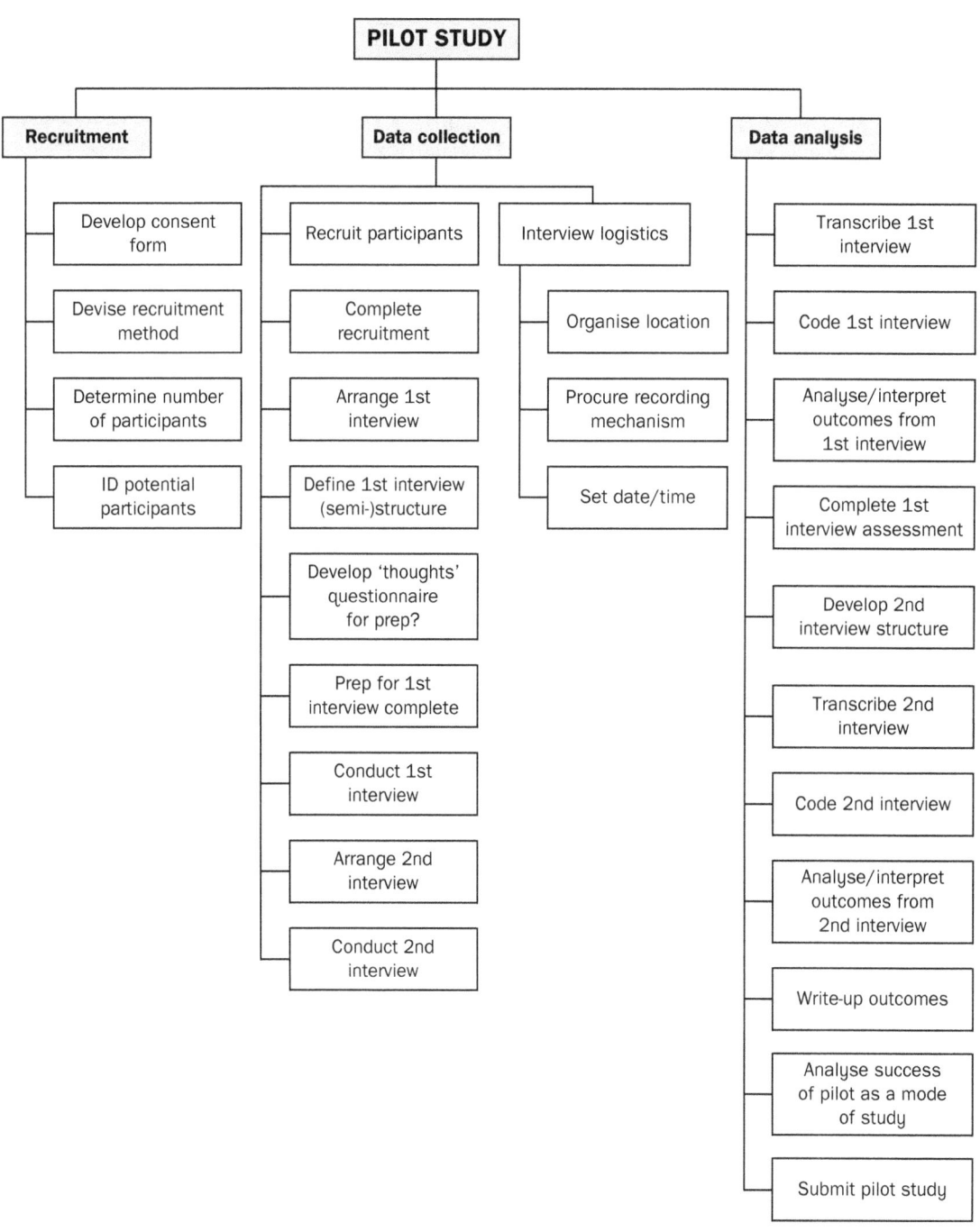

Three-month pilot study

> **✏ Activity: Create a work breakdown structure**
> 1. On a blank sheet of paper, draw a WBS for the next phase of your PhD.
> 2. Set the 'phase' as your top-level task.
> 3. The following level should be the deliverables you have identified using the template on page 101.
> 4. Finally, break all of the deliverables down into tasks.

Estimate task durations

Once you've used the WBS to identify the individual tasks, you can determine how long these activities will take. Estimation is difficult at the best of times, but, in a PhD setting, you are often trying to estimate how long it will take you to do things that you have never done before. It's difficult, but not impossible! The key principle in good estimating is not how *right* the estimate is, but how *wrong* you're comfortable with it being.

You will only know how good an estimate is when you've actually finished the work! It's rare for estimates to be spot on. For instance, you might schedule a task for completion at exactly 17:00 on Friday afternoon. In reality, it will probably be finished *roughly* around that time – maybe a few minutes before, or several minutes after. Can you be comfortable with that estimate? Do those few minutes either way matter?

Similarly, *don't confuse precision with accuracy*. A precise estimate isn't necessarily an accurate estimate. When we deliver training, we don't tell a class that the course will finish at 16:23 exactly. That figure is very *precise*, but not necessarily *accurate*. Just because something is precise does not mean that it will be accurate, and to be accurate, you do not necessarily need to be precise. We can't be so precise on training courses, despite having done them hundreds of times before, because there are simply too many unknowns. For example, we don't know:

- How interactive the class will be
- How long it will take attendees to complete exercises
- What questions will be asked or how long the answers will take.

These uncertainties mean we cannot be confident that the day will end at 16:23 precisely.

If precision is an unrealistic option, instead use a *range* for your estimate. For example, 'This course is due to finish between 16:00 and 16:30.' This estimate might seem vague, but there is a much higher chance of successfully hitting this new estimate than the precise estimate of 16:23. Does it matter if, rather than finishing at 16:23, the course ends between 16:00 and 16:30? Probably not. The 'vague' estimate is good enough. Incorporating 'vagueness' (a range) into an estimate also tells you there is uncertainty in the estimate. Recognising there is uncertainty means you can begin to address it as necessary (which we will in Chapter 11).

Putting an estimate in a range (such as somewhere between 16:00 and 16:30) allows you to plan. If you need to meet with your supervisor at 16:45, you can be confident of that subsequent, dependent activity beginning on time. A range gives the flexibility that you need in real life without having to compromise (finish early or start late) on either the current or subsequent activity.

> **But I need a single figure ...**
>
> You can't always plan in ranges. Sometimes you do need single figures. We'll revisit this idea later in this section, but, for now, accept that, when estimating, you should take into account the uncertainty of real life and build in flexibility.

In PhD research – where uncertainty is inherent – you can plan using ranges. The greater the unknowns, the bigger the range. As you progress in your PhD, you learn more about your work and the range will get narrower. For example, by lunchtime on a course, our new estimate might be to finish between 16:10 and 16:25. As we've learned more about the class, the uncertainty has begun to fade. So, a key to estimating is:

Where uncertainty exists, plan in ranges!

Estimation considerations

Even if you aim for ranges in your estimations, how do you identify the range? Estimating is not a matter of plucking a figure from thin air. There are many different factors to consider when estimating. The following checklist encourages you to take into account factors that might affect the duration of the task. As a result, the timeline you build with these estimates will be more realistic and, therefore, more achievable.

Estimation checklist

• How experienced are you in the task?	If you've done this before, you'll probably be able to do it quicker than if it's your first time.	Yes / No
• Do you need training/upskilling?	If training is required, it may take longer and you might need to add a 'training' task to your WBS.	Yes / No
• Are other people involved?	If you're working as part of larger research group, sometimes having more people can speed things up. But, the greater the number of people involved the more communication and coordination needs to be managed, so this should be accounted for.	Yes / No
• Are the other people available?	Are other resources available when you need them? If not, the task may take longer.	Yes / No
• Are you multi-tasking?	Multi-tasking is a great skill to have, but is said to add 20% to the duration of a single task because of the time it takes to get back up to speed when you restart an activity.	Yes / No
• Do you have other things on?	Other activities on in your life (e.g. teaching, writing papers or social events) could affect how long it takes to complete your work.	Yes / No
• Is the task active or passive?	If the task is active over 16 hours, it might take 2 days in duration (8 hrs/day). If it is passive, it could potentially run overnight and the duration might be 4p.m. to 8a.m.	Active / Passive
• Is everyone co-located?	If you are working remotely and need to speak to other people about the work, that will (usually) take longer than if you just ask a question across a shared work space.	Yes / No

➜ Action

Use this checklist when you're considering how long a task might take.

Estimation methods

The considerations here will affect the time needed to complete a task. To create an estimate, you need to identify the *duration* of a task: how long it will take to complete overall. Make the most accurate estimates of duration for the lowest task level of the WBS – where you have broken the work down into detailed tasks. There are many different estimation methods you can use for activity durations. The following are the three that we believe to be most appropriate for planning a PhD. All three methods take time, but using them to inform your plan will make it far more accurate and more achievable.

1. Comparative estimation

Comparative estimation is based on a comparison between the current task and the duration of similar tasks you've done before. You might have experience of completing a similar task during your Masters or earlier in your PhD. Use this experience to inform your estimate. If you personally haven't done the task before, there are almost certainly people in your department who have done similar things: your supervisors, other PhDs who are further along, or recent post-docs. Use their experience as a basis for your estimates. You could also obtain the extant data you are looking for by reading the methods and research design sections of academic papers. For example:

> 'Last time it took me a week to do this task, but this time it's twice as complicated. Is two weeks a reasonable estimate?'
> 'My supervisor says it takes them a day to do this, so maybe I should give myself a day and a half?'

Advantages of comparative estimation:

- This is one of the most accurate methods because you are estimating realistically at task level using past experience to inform the judgements.

Limitations of comparative estimation:

- Every person and every project are different, so exact comparisons can be difficult to make.
- Different people have different levels of proficiency and productivity, which can impact upon task duration.

So, *use comparative estimation*: when task-level estimates are possible (such as planning data-collection activities or write-up where the WBS is well defined).

Don't use comparative estimation: at task-level when the outputs of one task might influence how long the subsequent task will take. For example, when estimating your literature-review duration, it might take 30 minutes to read one paper, but that may spawn seven citations to follow up. In this case, draw comparisons at a higher level; perhaps your supervisor suggest that it usually takes around five months to complete the initial literature review in this field.

2. Parametric estimation

Parametric estimation uses simple maths to calculate a figure. If you do the same (or similar) task/s several times, you can estimate how long it takes to complete one, then multiply by the number of times you have to repeat. For example:

> 'It takes 1 hour to process a sample in the lab, meaning over an 8-hour day I could process 7 samples' (7×1 hour, with an hour off for lunch).

'The general rule for transcription is that it takes around 4 hours to transcribe 1 hour of audio. Therefore, if I have 5 interviews of 1½ hours each, it will take me around 30 hours in total to transcribe' (4 × 1½ × 5).

Advantages of parametric estimation:

- Excellent for very clear, well-defined activities, especially those that will be repeated over the project duration.

Limitations of parametric estimation:

- Sometimes 'rule of thumb' (such as it takes 4 hours to transcribe 1 hour of interview) can be misleading, as it clearly depends upon the person doing it.

Use parametric estimation: when estimating the duration of well-defined tasks (such as the examples here) of which you have reliable experience and know that a linear relationship between them exists. For example, if once takes 30 minutes, then four times will take 2 hours.

3. Three-point estimation

The technique of three-point estimation can be used in combination with the others to accommodate uncertainty. A word of warning: it does involve numbers! You might not be keen on maths, but please stick with it – it's a very powerful tool and many of our students credit it with changing their (PhD) life!

Let's walk through it step by step. First, think of an activity that you're familiar with at work or even something personal (such as driving to the airport). Now think: how long will that take? One of two things has just happened:

1. You've come up with a number – 'This normally takes X amount of time.'
2. You're not so sure – 'It depends. It'll take somewhere between Y and Z amount of time to finish. Let's go somewhere in the middle.'

Either way, you'll end up with a single figure. In reality, however, you also know that, if things go really well, you could finish a little quicker, but, if things go wrong, it could take a little longer. Unfortunately, when most people estimate they don't take this variability into account. Three-point estimation embraces this variability by asking three questions:

1. Under perfect conditions and if things go better than expected, how long will it take? This is the ***optimistic* estimate**.
2. Under normal conditions and where everything happens as per usual, how long will it take? This is the ***most-likely* estimate**.
3. If everything that could go wrong does go wrong, how long will it take? This is the ***pessimistic* estimate**.

This gives a range and, as we said earlier, vagueness is good. This method of estimation incorporates the potential impact of problems. Identifying these problems means that you have a chance to address them before they actually happen (see Chapter 11). If we put these three different estimates onto a timeline it will look very similar to the following example.

Three-point estimation: common distribution

You already know this intuitively: there is an amount of time a task will normally take (*most likely*), if things go really well it could be completed a little quicker (*optimistic*), but if things go wrong, they could go pretty badly wrong (*pessimistic*). The gap between *most likely* and *pessimistic* is *almost always* bigger, and, normally, substantially bigger, than the gap between *most likely* and *optimistic*. This will be the same for the vast majority of tasks in your PhD.

Three-point estimation uses a formula to calculate the most likely duration of a task, using these three estimates – optimistic, most likely and pessimistic.

The three-point estimation formula

$$e = (o + 4m + p)/6$$

where e = expected value, o = optimistic, m = most likely and p = pessimistic

This formula produces what is called a weighted average – an average weighted towards the *most likely*. This adds a little contingency into your plan.

> The calculation to produce the weighted average value is widely accepted. If you're interested in the statistical basis for it, it is explained in Clark, 1962. However, you don't need to know the background to be able to use it for your estimation.

Try this example. Ask your supervisor three questions:

> **Help is always available**
>
> If you're not too keen on numbers, don't be put off! We have produced a template available from the Open University Press website that can do the calculations for you.

1 'For this next task, how long does it normally take people?'

'It takes most people a couple of weeks.'

You have your first data point – your 'most likely' value:

$m = 10$ working days.

2 'Is there anything I can do to speed this up a bit?'

'Well, if you do a, b and c, it might save you a couple of days.'

You have a second data point, your 'optimistic' value:

$o = 8$ working days.

3 'And what problems could I encounter when I'm doing this?'

'OK ... x, y and, sometimes, z happen, and if they all do, it'll take you twice as long.'

You now have your third, 'pessimistic' estimate:

$p = 20$ working days.

You can now put the values into the formula to create your estimate:

$$e = (o + 4m + p)/6$$
$$= (8 + 40 + 20)/6$$
$$= 11.33$$

Your estimated duration for this task should be rounded to: *12 working days*.

You will see that the 12 days estimate is slightly above the 'most likely' value (10 days), which gives you a fighting chance of doing it on time. You may also notice that we have rounded up – always round up, as it gives you extra contingency.

Advantages of three-point estimation:

- It introduces a contingency allowance for uncertainty based on calculation, rather than randomly adding 10 per cent 'just in case'.
- It lets you consider actions that you could take to speed things up and, possibly more importantly, lets you identify potential problems early and so make allowances for these in your plan (see Chapter 11).

Limitations of three-point estimation:

- Even though you have a formula, it is still just an estimate and only as good as the numbers you put into the formula.
- Some people are intimidated by numbers and formulae. (If you are, download the spreadsheet from the OLC available at https://www.mheducation.co.uk/professionals/open-university-press/olc/doyle-robertson-the-phd-handbook, which will do the work for you.)

Use three-point estimation:

- When tasks include unknowns (any research project and, particularly, a PhD)
- For any task – it's an excellent estimation method.

✏ Activity: Estimation

1. Download the template from the Open University Press website or use the template on page 117.
2. Enter the tasks from your work breakdown structure.
3. Assess how long each task will take.

Template: Three-point estimation

Task from work breakdown structure	Optimistic estimate (o)	Most-likely estimate (m)	Pessimistic estimate (p)	Expected value $e = (o + 4m + p)/6$

You won't know how good your estimates are until you have finished the work, which, admittedly, doesn't sound very helpful when you're at the planning stage! Things rarely go exactly to plan, so your plan will never be perfect. However, using these techniques will help you to make better estimates and give you more realistic and achievable deadlines. You will find hitting milestones easier and work less stressful as a result of investing a little effort up front applying these ideas.

Discovering how exact your estimates are at the end of the task can also be a help going forward. Your initial estimates, whether fantastically accurate or miles off, will become your comparative data for the next phase of your project. You'll use these to inform your future planning and, over the period of your PhD, you will understand both yourself and your work a little better, allowing improvement in all aspects of completing a complex research project, including estimation. Little by little, you'll learn how to manage your research more effectively.

Summary

The work breakdown structure helps you to identify all the tasks necessary to achieve each deliverable, as a precursor to making a realistic schedule of work, and is best done for each phase of your PhD – your next 'bite of the elephant'. The detail you reach in the WBS will also reduce the risk that you miss something important, even if you haven't done the majority of these PhD tasks before. It will help you to define the level of detail you need to create a viable plan; one that guides action without becoming too unwieldy to update. The graphical nature of the WBS also allows key stakeholders (your supervisors) to quickly understand your approach and tasks, and affords an early opportunity to develop shared expectations or make changes accordingly. Once you have identified your tasks, you can use a range of reliable estimation methods to accurately assess how long each task will take. At this point, you can be confident of creating a reliable plan for your work.

> **Key points**
> - Use the WBS to split your deliverables into their component tasks in order to create an accurate plan.
> - Know when to stop – aim for a practical level of detail.
> - When it comes to estimating task duration, don't confuse precision with accuracy.
> - Estimate in ranges to account for uncertainty and unfamiliarity with the tasks.

Further resources

Buttrick, R. (2019) *The Ultimate Guide to Directing and Managing Business-Led Projects*, 5th edn. Abingdon: Routledge.
Heagney, J. (2022) *Fundamentals of Project Management*, 6th edn. London: Harper Collins.
Obeng, E. (1994) *All Change! The Project Leader's Secret Handbook*. Harlow: Prentice Hall.
Portnoy, J.L. and Portnoy, S.L. (2022) *Project Management for Dummies*, 6th edn. Hoboken NJ: Wiley & Sons.
Wysocki, R.K. (2019) *Effective Project Management: Traditional, Agile, Extreme, Hybrid*. Indianapolis: Wiley.

Reference

Clark, C.E. (1962) The PERT model for the distribution of an activity time, *Operations Research*, **10**: 405–406.

10 Schedule Tasks

How To ... Decide what to do when

Efficient scheduling – The network diagram – Task dependencies – Critical path – Slack – Using 'wriggle room' – Level workload – Gantt chart – Managing resources

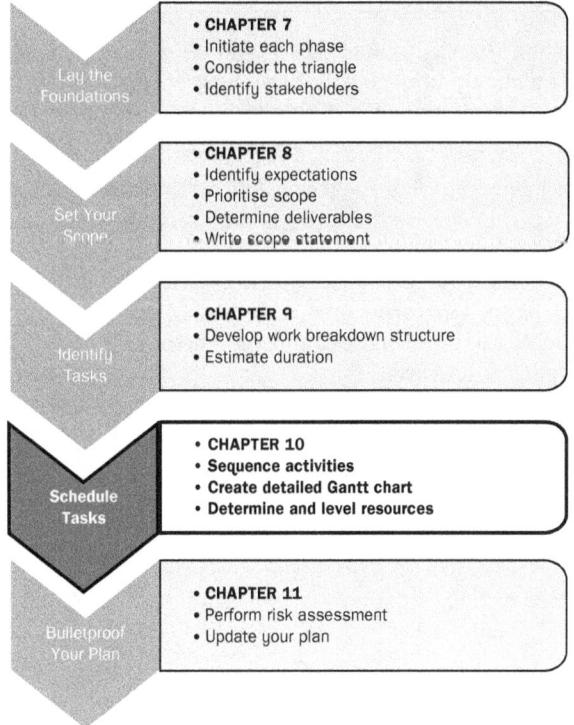

The planning process

A PhD is like a juggling act. You have to handle multiple activities at once. In complex projects such as a PhD, it can be hard to identify how different tasks relate to each other and the best order in which to do them. Many tasks are dependent on other tasks before they can be completed. For example, you cannot dispense drugs in a clinical trial until ethics approval has been granted and sufficient participants have been recruited; you cannot perform your new composition until the orchestral score has been completed. This connection between tasks is called a dependency. If you don't take account of the dependencies between tasks in your scheduling, you risk inefficient working, unnecessary frustration, stress and time delays.

Identifying the dependencies between your tasks is crucial in creating a detailed timeline that reflects when the work needs to be performed on a day-to-day basis. This timeline (or Gantt chart) will be your primary method of scheduling, tracking and controlling your PhD work.

In this chapter, you'll use a network diagram to determine the best order in which to complete your tasks and, as a result, manage your PhD workload in the most efficient and effective manner. This sequencing of tasks becomes the basis for creating a practical timeline (or Gantt chart) that takes account of the resources needed to do the task and their availability. By following this process, you create an efficient timeline to guide your work.

The network diagram

In Chapter 9, you established the tasks needed to complete deliverables and estimated how long you expect them to take. You should now consider the most efficient order in which to complete them. A network diagram helps you to determine the 'best' working order for the tasks identified in your work breakdown structure.

A network diagram is a very simple tool. It focuses *solely* on the concept of task dependency: the order in which your activities (or tasks) *can* be done (by understanding which tasks are *dependent* on each other). It asks you to consider:

- What activities *must* happen before other activities (for example, you can't make bacterial plates until the chemicals and bacteria have been delivered)
- What activities can be done simultaneously (you can draft your methodology chapter and formulate your interview questions while waiting for ethics approval).

> 'The network diagram is so valuable – if you can map your work in advance, you're already ten steps ahead.'

Create a network diagram

We'll demonstrate the process of creating a network diagram by continuing the example of 'building a wall' used in Chapter 9.

Step 1: Write out your tasks

- Use a whiteboard or put a sheet of flip-chart paper on a wall. One PhD student told us they had used decorator's lining paper to do this.
- Write each of the bottom-level tasks from your WBS on sticky notes. Sticky notes lend themselves extremely well to this because the tasks need to be movable: you need to be able to rearrange them to understand the dependencies and different methods of completing the work.

Schedule Tasks **121**

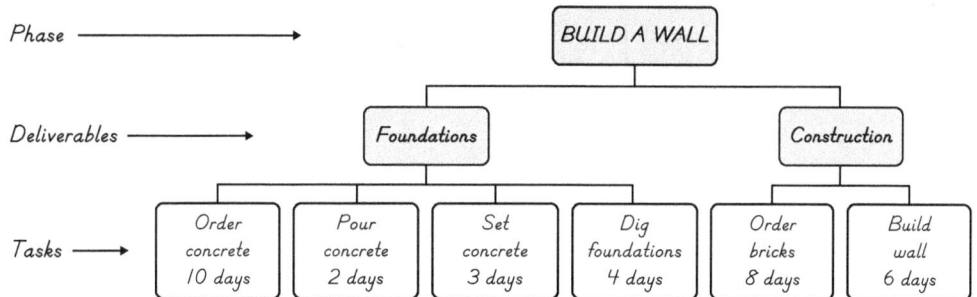

Work breakdown structure with tasks on sticky notes

Step 2: Add milestones and start arranging

- On the left of your paper, draw a diamond in which you write 'Start'. This is an important milestone!
- Look at all of your tasks and consider which tasks could, *in theory*, begin immediately – i.e. they have no tasks that have to happen before they can begin (no dependencies). Place them in a vertical line close to the 'Start' milestone.
- Connect them with a straight line to the 'Start' milestone to indicate that they can begin right at the start.

In this example, there is nothing to prevent the 'ordering' tasks from beginning immediately ('Order concrete' and 'Order bricks'), so, place them on the left and draw lines to connect them to the start. Similarly, 'Dig foundations' could begin straight away, so this is also placed on the left and connected to the Start diamond.

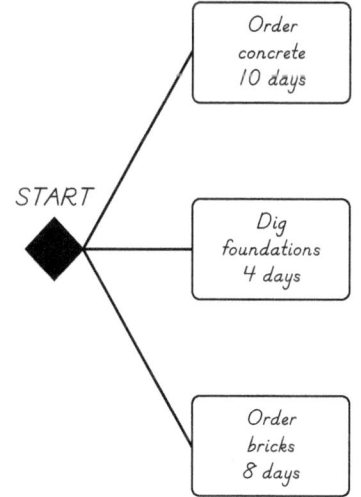

Network diagram: tasks with no dependencies

Step 3: Place tasks in order

Identify which tasks could begin *after* these first tasks have been completed. For example, to be able to 'Pour concrete' you need to *have* concrete, so it must come after the 'Order concrete' task. You must also have somewhere to pour it, so it has to come after 'Dig foundations'.

122 Part 2 – How to Get Going

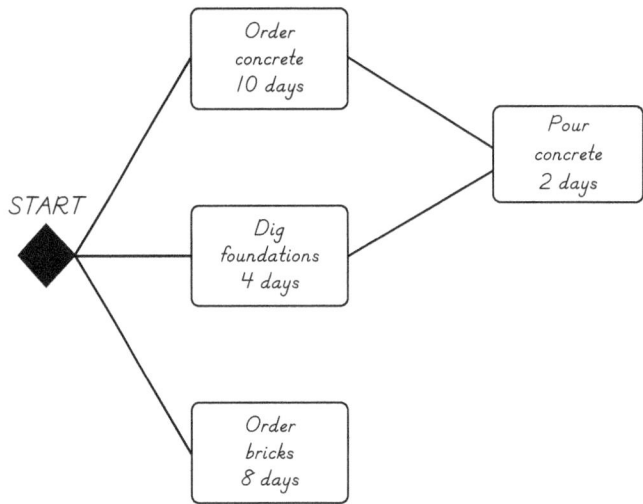

Network diagram: adding a dependent task

This sequence of consecutive tasks is called a *path*. Basically, you're asking yourself, 'What tasks must be completed for this task to be able commence?' If the answer is 'None', then the tasks can appear right at the start, otherwise they come after their prerequisite tasks.

Get in position

When creating a network diagram, don't draw the lines in pen until you have all your sticky-note tasks in position. Your diagram will be difficult to use if it's full of crossings-out!

Step 4: Connect to 'End'

Go through the remainder of the tasks, each time asking 'What must come before?' and 'What happens after?' until all the tasks have been assigned. For example, concrete cannot set until it has been poured, and to 'build wall' you need solid foundations (so *after* 'Set concrete') and bricks (*after* 'Order bricks').

Once everything is joined, add an 'End' milestone diamond on the right of your sheet and connect the final tasks to that.

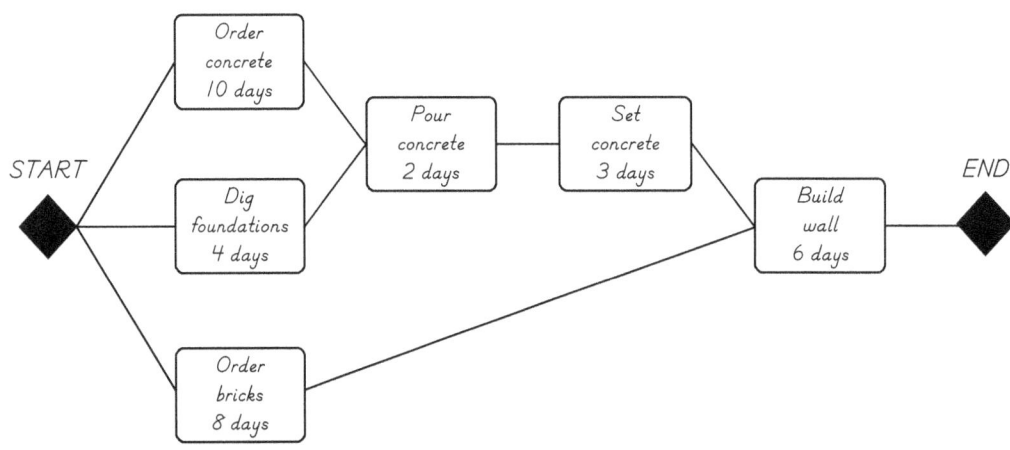

Completed network diagram

As with the other planning techniques, we don't recommend drawing a network diagram for an entire PhD. Use it to plan sub-projects or time-limited phases, for example a three-month pilot study, a complex run of experimentation, a fieldwork expedition, or interviewing participants. You can use it to plan the final write-up of your thesis (as we discuss in Chapter 20). There are no rules for the number of tasks required to justify using this technique. In our experience, it's been invaluable when planning any work that includes more than eight to ten tasks. Use it whenever you feel it will help.

> **Activity: Sequencing tasks**
> 1 Hang a large piece of paper on the wall; or use a whiteboard.
> 2 Write all of your bottom-level WBS tasks on individual sticky notes (task name and estimated duration).
> 3 Using the steps detailed in this section, create your network diagram.

Calculate total duration

Once you've identified the required order for the tasks, you need to work out how long everything will take. You've already used your estimating methods to calculate the duration of each task in the WBS. Now that you know how the tasks fit together (their dependencies), you can calculate how long the work will take in total. Software can do this for you, but we'll explain the step-by-step process so you understand how it's done. There are three steps to this process:

1 Mark the junctions.
2 Identify the critical path.
3 Calculate the slack.

Step 1: Mark the junctions

A junction is where two or more paths converge: multiple prerequisite tasks. In our example, before the task 'Pour concrete', there is a junction of the tasks: 'Order concrete' and 'Dig foundations'. To calculate the total duration of the project, you need to calculate first how long the project takes to reach a junction, by working out the duration of every path leading up to that junction. For example, looking at the following diagram:

- The top path ('Order concrete') will take ten days to complete.
- The bottom path ('Dig foundations') will only take four days to complete.

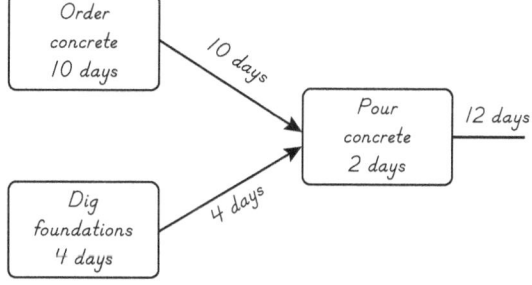

Critical path: marking the junctions

124 Part 2 – How to Get Going

You can't go past a junction until all the work before it has been completed. You always have to wait for the longest (or slowest) path to complete before you can move past a junction and begin the next task. You can't start to 'Pour concrete' until both the 'Order concrete' and 'Dig foundations' tasks have been done, so it will be at least ten days until you can begin to 'Pour concrete' because you need to wait for the concrete to be delivered. If it then takes a further two days to complete 'Pour concrete', this part of the network will take 12 days in total: the longest path (ten) plus the duration of 'Pour concrete' (two).

Step 2: Find the critical path

The *longest path of linked tasks* through the project is the critical path. In our example, this is 'Order concrete' and 'Pour concrete', which add up to 12 days.

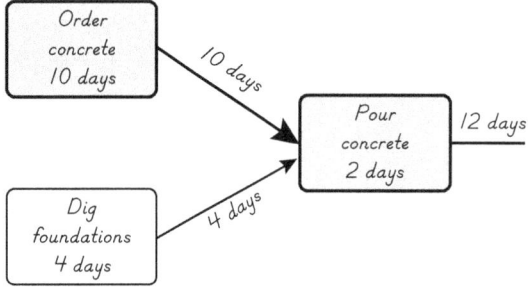

Marking the critical path

It is called the critical path because it is the sequence of activities that cannot be delayed without delaying your overall project and missing deadlines. These tasks are critical. It is extremely helpful to identify your *critical-path tasks* for several reasons:

- They become your *highest-priority* tasks – if they are delayed, your whole project will be delayed.
- If you're fortunate enough to be working with other people, this is where it's sensible to involve the *most experienced, most reliable people* to avoid delays that could risk your whole project.
- You can try to *proactively address risks* to these tasks to avoid problems that could delay your whole project.

The critical path shows you where to focus and where to invest time and effort. Tasks in this path become your number-one-priority tasks. Neither 'Order concrete' nor 'Pour concrete' can be delayed without impacting the whole timeline.

Step 3: Calculate the slack

Although your critical path can't be delayed, there will be other tasks where a delay isn't critical. This permissible delay is your slack. For example, 'Dig foundations' takes four days. The task after it, 'Pour concrete', has to wait until ten days have passed to begin because of ordering concrete. The difference between these two paths is six days (10 minus 4). So, 'Dig foundations' could:

- *Overrun or be extended* by 6 days (4 days effort + 6 days slack = 10 days)
- *Be delayed* in starting by 6 days (6 days slack + 4 days effort = 10 days).

Either option would cause no delay to the rest of the project.

For tasks with slack:

- They don't need to be a number-one priority because, if they're delayed slightly, it won't affect the rest of the project.
- If you have people who are reliably unreliable (for example, if your supervisor rarely gives you feedback when they say they're going to) assign them to these tasks because, again, if they're delayed by a small amount you don't need to worry as it won't affect the rest of the project.
- If there are potential problems or risks associated with these tasks, you can be more relaxed and may not need to address them at all.

> 'I created network diagrams and showed them to my supervisors. I didn't include numbers or critical paths; I just used it to show progress, identify where bottlenecks may appear [many paths colliding at a single junction], but, most helpfully, it let me show when I needed *them* to do things for me.'

In summary, your network diagram allows you to:

- Focus on the critical path because those are the tasks that cannot be delayed.
- Use slack to give a little bit of flexibility or wriggle room.

Activity: Calculate duration

Using the steps detailed, calculate the duration, critical path and slack for your network diagram.

Don't worry if you find this tough – your university will almost certainly have project-management software that can do the calculations for you.

126 Part 2 – How to Get Going

Examples of PhD network diagrams

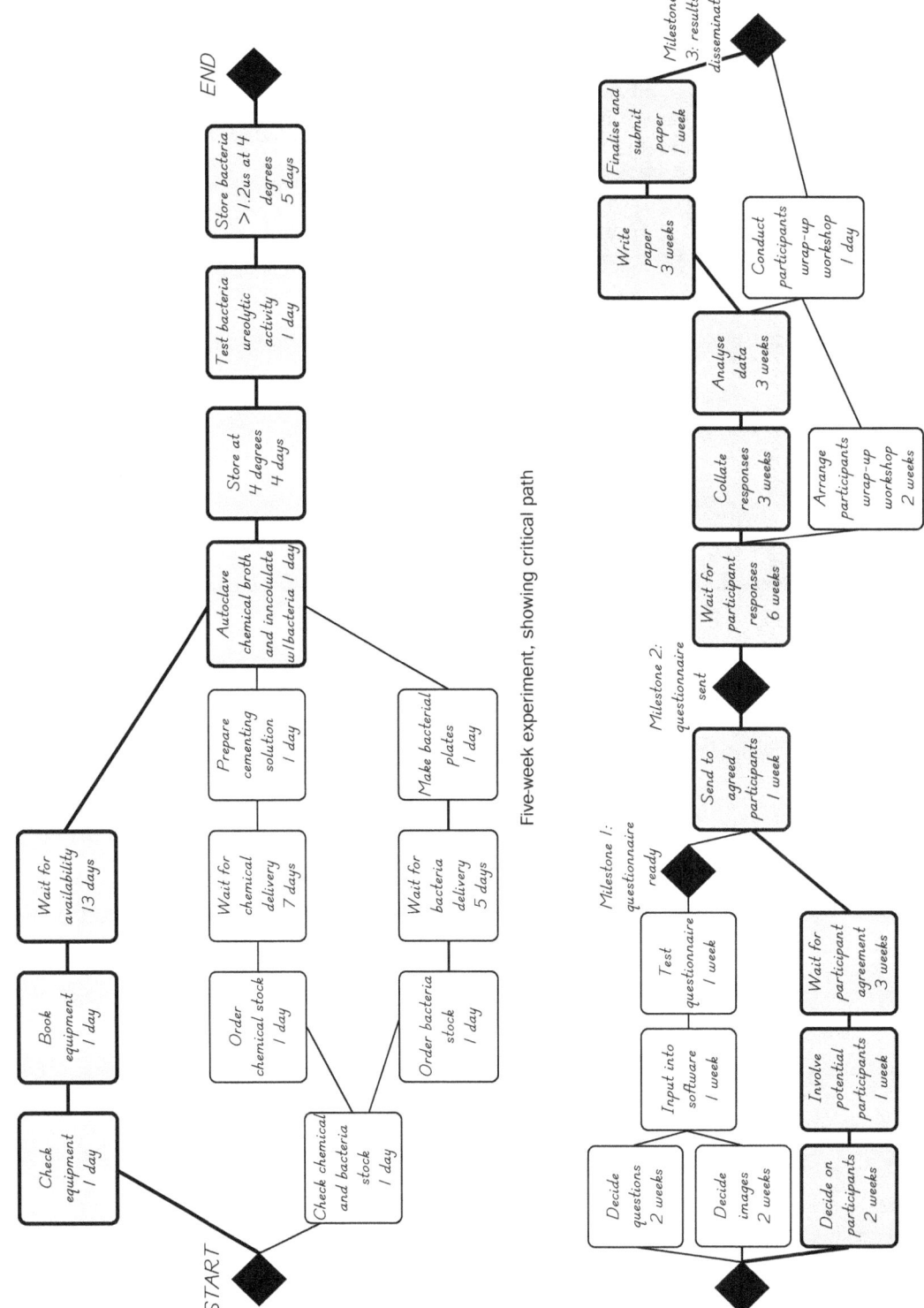

Five-week experiment, showing critical path

Three-month pilot study, showing critical path

The Gantt chart

You now know what it is you should be achieving; you've determined the tasks needed to do it and how long it will take; and you've set out the order in which to do the tasks. You now need to decide *when* you're going to do them. For this you need the last piece of the planning jigsaw: the famous Gantt chart.

We say 'famous' because it's the one project management tool that most people have heard of. You already created a high-level Gantt chart for your overall PhD in Chapter 4. It gave you an overview of your PhD and showed key phases of your research. Now you need to get into the detail and create more realistic day-to-day work plans. You'll use the Gantt chart to decide what to do when, and identify when you'll be busy and when you'll have slightly quieter times. You'll also use it to consider what resources you will need when, so that you can ask other people (supervisors, technicians, participants, archivists) to include you in their busy diaries. As you will see in Chapter 16, this is also going to be your primary device for tracking and reporting progress throughout your PhD. It makes up the main visual element of the plan.

> See Chapter 16 to use the Gantt chart for tracking, reporting and managing change.

Creating a Gantt chart

Drawing up a Gantt chart is simply a matter of converting the network diagram into a timeline. It's easy to do, as long as you have gone through all the steps discussed in the previous chapters. It summarises and displays the detail you've already identified. The process begins in a similar way to the creation of your high-level timeline in Chapter 4, but, to create a full Gantt chart, you expand the process to five steps:

1. Draw a table with tasks and timeline,
2. Enter the critical path tasks.
3. Enter non-critical path tasks.
4. Annotate the slack.
5. Add and level resources.

Step 1: Enter tasks and timeline

Take all the tasks from your network diagram and list them vertically down the left of the table.

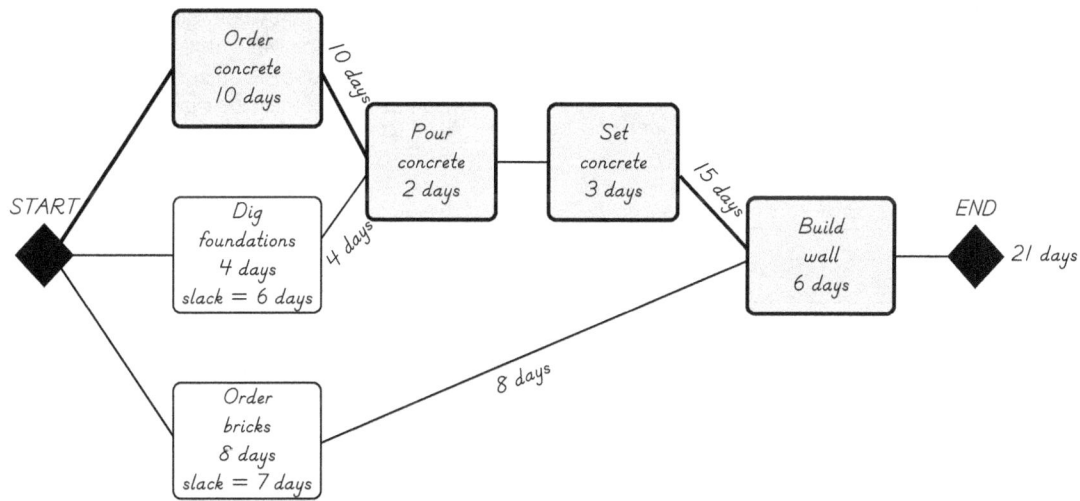

Network diagram with critical path and slack

Along the top add a time axis that allows you to schedule dates for individual activities. The network diagram gives you the *order*, but the Gantt chart actually tells you *when* the tasks will happen. Now that you're planning in detail, use days or weeks as an appropriate unit of time rather than the months of the high-level plan.

Tasks \ Days	1	2	3	4	5	6	7	8	9	10	11	12	13	14	15	16	17	18	19	20	21	22
START	◆																					
Order concrete																						
Pour concrete																						
Set concrete																						
Dig foundations																						
Order bricks																						
Build wall																						
END																						

Gantt chart: basic outline

In this example, the timeline is simply the numbered days of the project, but in real life (as in the examples later), you would use actual days, months and dates. Enter the start milestone as a black diamond on the day you want your plan to begin (in this case, at Day 1).

Step 2: Enter the critical path tasks

Next, enter the critical-path tasks. Choose a colour (usually red) for the boxes occupied by your critical path tasks. Reserve that colour for critical path activities so you can easily identify them in your plan – these are the tasks that cannot be delayed, so you want to make them noticeable.

In our wall-building example, the first task after Start on the critical path is 'Order concrete', which will take ten days. In the Gantt chart's 'Order concrete' row, colour the first ten boxes red to represent the ten days the task will take. Continuing along the critical path, the network diagram tells you that, once 'Order concrete' has finished, 'Pour concrete' can happen and will take two days. Colour in days 11 and 12 to indicate when 'Pour concrete' will happen. Repeat this until all the critical path tasks have been entered into your Gantt chart.

> **Gantt chart software**
>
> The easiest way to make a Gantt chart is to use software. Your university might have some you can use, or there are free programs and apps online. They are normally very simple and intuitive.
>
> Some PhD students ask about using Excel or similar but, as you'll see in Chapter 16, the benefit of using bespoke software is that when things change – as they inevitably will – it is very quick and easy to adjust your plan. In Excel, all adjustments must be made manually.

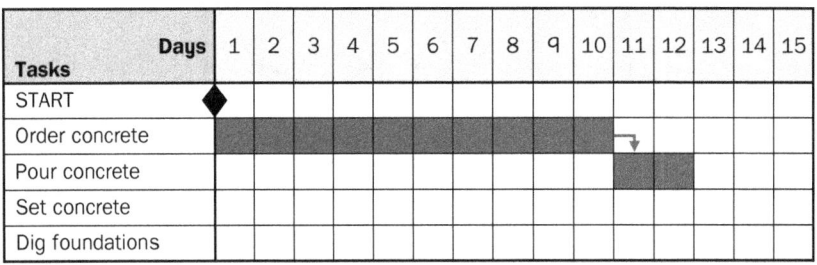

Gantt chart: critical path tasks

Creating a Gantt chart is genuinely that easy – it's colouring in boxes! You'll see in the example that we added arrows between the tasks to indicate dependencies (which tasks are joined together). This will help you to see the relationships between the activities more clearly.

> **Also available in technicolour ...**
>
> Although this book is in black and white, in most project plans the critical path will be in red, non-critical tasks in blue and slack indicated in green. However, as with everything, you should format your plan in the way that you find most helpful.

> **✎ Activity: Gantt chart Steps 1 and 2**
>
> 1. Choose a software program to create your Gantt chart.
>   - Your university may offer something like Microsoft Project, or there are many good, free packages available online.
>   - Speak to other PhD students to find what they use.
> 2. Enter your tasks and an appropriate timescale (days or weeks).
> 3. Enter the critical-path tasks in the order indicated in your network diagram.

Step 3: Enter non-critical tasks

The next step is to add the remaining tasks in the order they appear in the network diagram. For example, 'Dig foundations' could begin immediately and takes four days, so, colour in days 1 to 4 (differently from your critical tasks – blue is often used). 'Order bricks' could also begin straight away, and would take eight days, so, days 1 to 8 should be coloured.

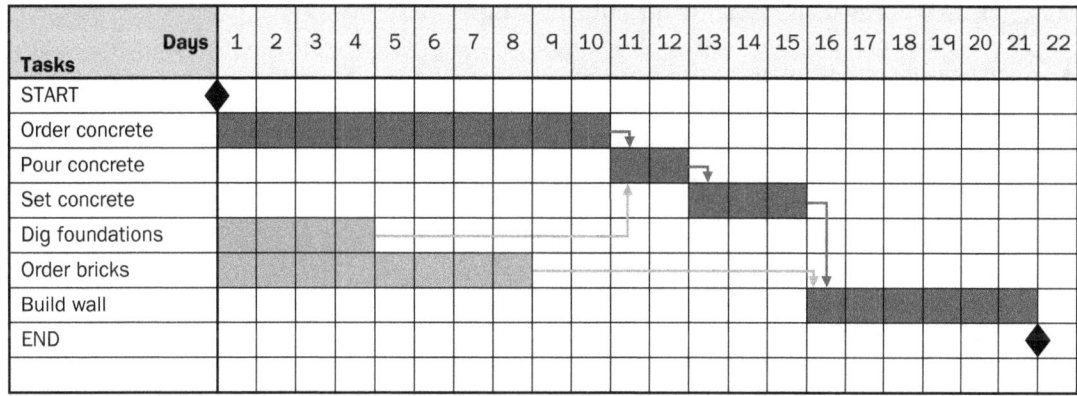

Gantt chart: non-critical tasks

Step 4: Annotate the slack

The only thing missing now is slack –the amount of time that a non-critical task could be delayed or overrun without delaying the whole project. It is drawn as a solid line (usually coloured green) at the end of the task. For example, the wall-building network diagram states that 'Dig foundations' has six days' slack, so draw a line six days long following the task.

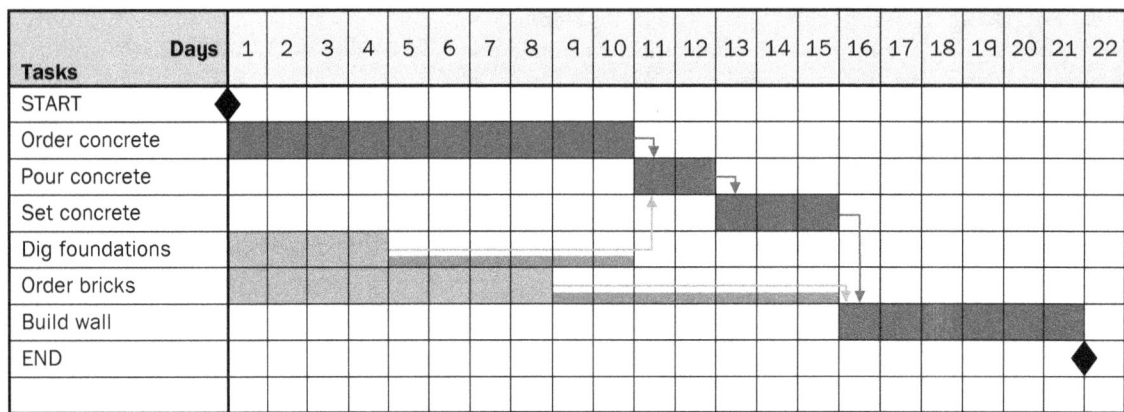

Gantt chart: slack time

'Dig foundations' could slide anywhere up or down that line and the project would still hit its deadlines. You'll notice that this now joins up to the task 'Pour concrete'. This makes sense as 'Dig foundations' needs to be completed before 'Pour concrete' can begin. Being aware of this slack allows you flexibility in terms of deciding exactly *when* you're going to complete these non-critical activities.

> **Activity: Gantt chart Steps 3 and 4**
> 1 Add non-critical tasks to your Gantt chart using the order determined in your network diagram.
> 2 Your software should show where you have slack (permissible delays) in your plan.

Step 5: Add and level resources

Finally, you need to add your resources. Identify all of the:

- Human resources, including:
  - You
  - Your supervisors – meetings, feedback, review
  - Technician – equipment set-up, support
- Physical resources, including:
  - Equipment – lab kit, recording devices, computers, samplers
  - Facilities – interview rooms, test beds, clean rooms
  - Materials – chemicals, alloys, cells, samples
  - Supplies – printer paper, lab book, journal
  - Software – statistics, modelling, algorithms, reference management, coding, email
- Data resources, including:
  - Participants – trials, interviews, focus groups, questionnaires
  - Archives – gatekeepers, permissions
  - Secondary sources – journals, papers, books.

Add these resources to the appropriate tasks. Remember that you can have *more than one resource allocated to each task.*

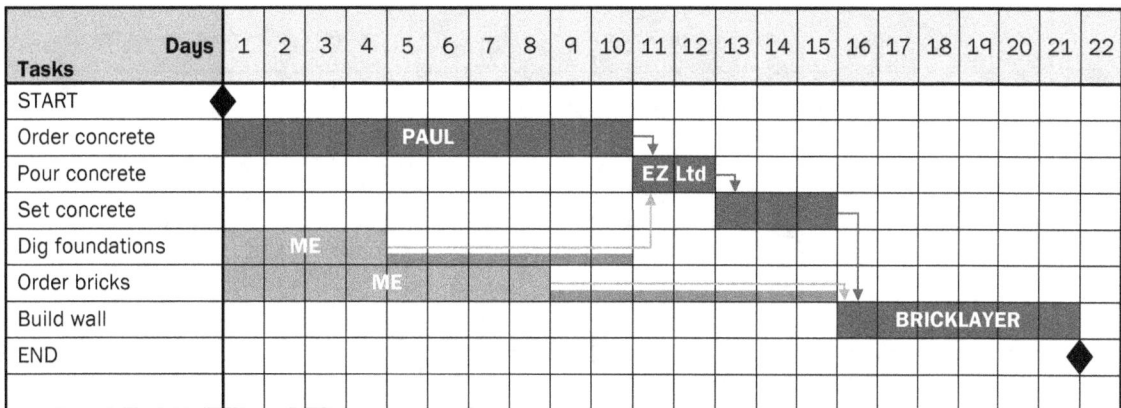

Gantt chart with resources

> **Resource breakdown**
>
> A resource does not need to be a single person or item. It could be a research group, industry collaborator or another team. That resource may break down their task into greater detail, but you don't need to, as long as you have sufficient information to create a helpful plan. For example:
>
> - In a clinical trial, your research partner is responsible for participant recruitment. In your WBS have a task 'recruit participants' and assign it to the partner. Your partner might break this down into smaller actions, but you don't need to in your own plan.
> - Perhaps you need the lab technician to set up a piece of kit. There are several tasks that they need to perform (break down existing set-up, reconfigure equipment, test and so on), but it's unnecessary for you to go to this level of detail in your plan. All you need to know is that it'll be ready in five days.

Your Gantt chart allows you see your busy times and quieter times. It also allows you to identify when you will need to schedule help from other people or schedule access to physical resources, such as equipment, both of which may be in demand elsewhere.

> **Activity: Gantt chart Step 5**
> - Add your required resources to your Gantt chart.
> - Consider all of the human, physical and data resources that you will need.

As part of this step, you can create a resource profile, shown as the last line of the Gantt chart. It summarises the total use of different resources at different points in your plan. Again, this is very straightforward: for each day of the project, add up how much work a resource is expected to be doing on that day. This will show who (and what) will be busy when and highlights any potential resourcing conflicts: where the same resource is working on multiple tasks.

Tasks \ Days	1	2	3	4	5	6	7	8	9	10	11	12	13	14	15	16	17	18	19	20	21	22
START	◆																					
Order concrete				PAUL																		
Pour concrete											EZ Ltd											
Set concrete																						
Dig foundations		ME																				
Order bricks			ME																			
Build wall																BRICKLAYER						
END																						◆
ME	2	2	2	2	1	1	1	1	–	–	–	–	–	–	–	–	–	–	–	–	–	–
PAUL	1	1	1	1	1	1	1	1	1	1	–	–	–	–	–	–	–	–	–	–	–	–
EZ Ltd (Supplier)	–	–	–	–	–	–	–	–	–	–	1	1	–	–	–	–	–	–	–	–	–	–
BRICKLAYER (External)	–	–	–	–	–	–	–	–	–	–	–	–	–	–	–	1	1	1	1	1	1	–

Gantt chart: resource profile

This is where project management software can be really helpful, as it automatically creates the resource profile for each resource. In our example, during days 1 to 4, 'Me' has two things ('Dig foundations' and 'Order bricks') scheduled at the same time, which is a potential resourcing conflict. There are three different ways to address a resourcing conflict:

1 **Ignore the conflict.** If you can manage these two tasks during the same time period, ignore the conflict.
2 **Ask for help.** If someone can help you out, it would resolve your resourcing problems. Unfortunately, you are often the only resource for your PhD! However, by asking another PhD student or your supervisor, you will find ways to do the task more quickly.
3 **Use slack.** When the project plan shows peaks and troughs of resourcing requirement (for example where you are really busy on days 1 to 4 but quiet on days 9 to 21), you can use slack to move around tasks and 'level' (even out) resource use. For example, 'Order bricks' needs to be completed before 'Build wall', but can happen anywhere up and down its slack line. To avoid a conflict, you could plan to do it on days 7 to 14. By smoothing out these peaks and troughs you have levelled your workload.

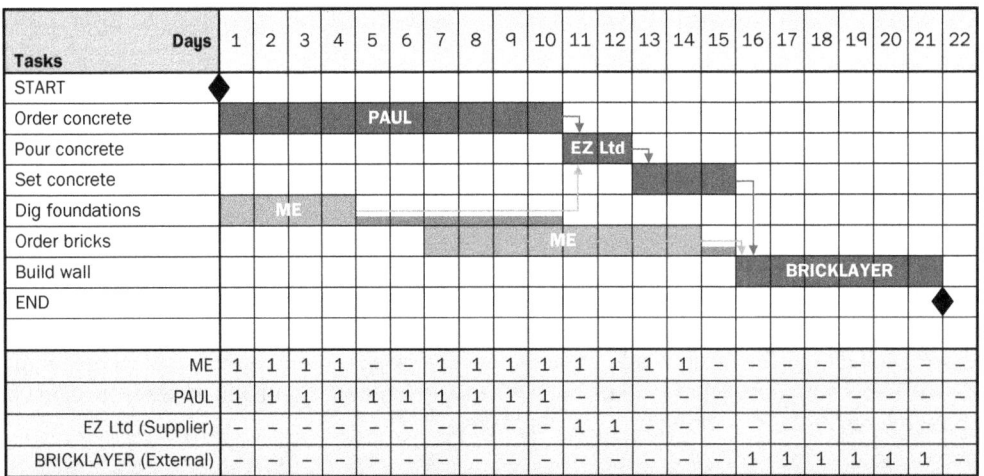

Gantt chart: using slack time to level resources

Being able to manipulate your schedule in this manner – and making your workload more manageable – is one of the key reasons for putting detail into the work breakdown structure, including both passive and active tasks.

For most non-critical tasks, slack is helpful because, if something is delayed, it gives you time to recover (for example, if you encounter a problem while digging foundations, you have time to fix it). Sometimes, however, having slack after a task can be unhelpful. For example, if you are using perishable materials (such as chemicals), you don't want them to arrive until just before you need them. Although there might be slack available in the timing of the task as it relates to the junction, the specifics of the task mean that you would need to schedule it 'as late as possible'. This means shifting the task to the end of the slack line (as in the example on page 132.).

If you find yourself in a situation where you cannot *level* to solve your resource issues, return to the project triangle. Remember, the project triangle always gives you three choices:

> **What if …?**
>
> A major advantage of using software to create Gantt charts is 'what if' scenarios. For example, you might look at a plan and think, 'It doesn't look as though I'll complete this task on time, *what if* it takes twice as long?' It is very quick and easy on the computer to make that adjustment, and the software will propagate that change through the plan, showing the knock-on effects on other tasks and deadlines. And, because you have made the change with a click of a button, you can undo it and revert to the original plan (always remembering to save the original as a back-up).

1 If you have a deadline (fixed time) and a set amount of work to complete (fixed scope), you are simply going to have to *work more hours per day* to get it all done (increased cost).
2 If you can only work a certain number of hours per day (fixed cost) and have a deadline to hit (fixed time), you have to *compromise on the amount of work* you complete (decreased scope). (This is a classic example of when to use must-haves, nice-to-haves and bells-and-whistles prioritisation.)
3 If you must complete everything on your to-do list (fixed scope) and can't increase the hours you work per day (fixed cost), *your deadline must move* (increased time).

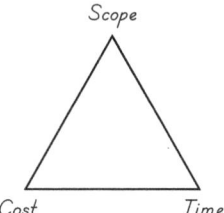

Examples of PhD Gantt charts

In the following example, notice how slack has been used to delay the order and delivery of perishable supplies like chemicals and bacteria until they are needed, to prevent degradation. The timeline is in days rather than weeks, because the task requires this level of specific timing.

134   Part 2 – How to Get Going

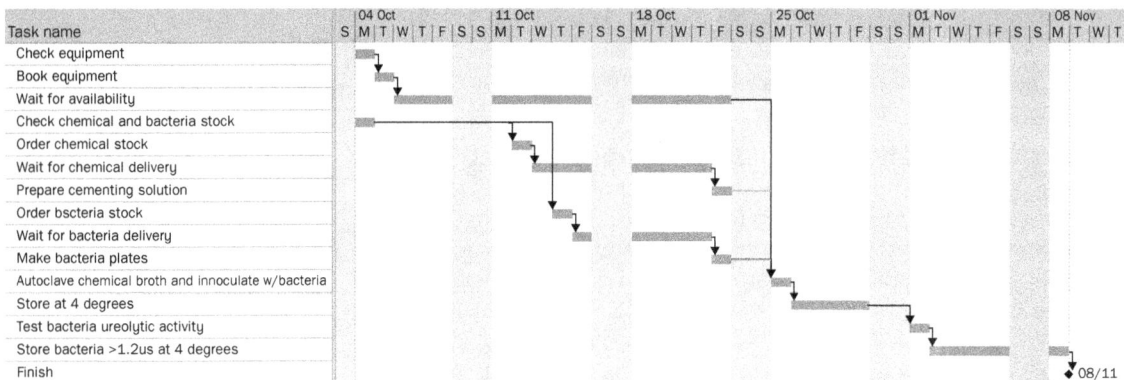

Five-week experiment

Notice that the timeline of the plan below is in weeks rather than days. These tasks don't demand day-by-day scheduling in advance. There are also regular milestones through the three-month study that allow for easier tracking and demonstrable signs of progress.

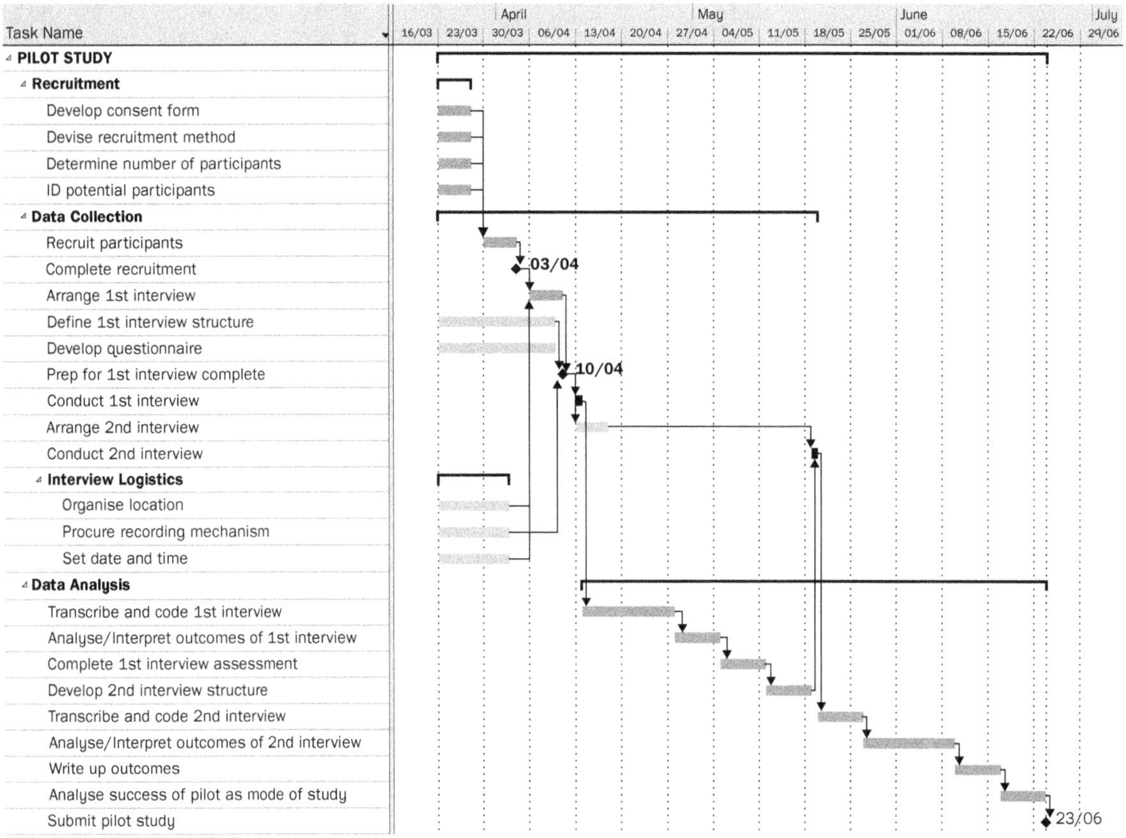

Three-month pilot study

> **✎ Activity: Gantt chart – levelling**
>
> 1. Add all of your required resources to your Gantt chart (you, supervisors, other people, equipment, facilities and so on).
> 2. Notice if you have any resourcing conflicts and try to either:
>   - Use slack to level them out
>   - Adjust your schedule using the triangle to assess the impact.

Summary

You need to be able to juggle the many different interrelated tasks of your PhD if you are to avoid inefficiencies and delays. The network diagram allows you to map out the dependencies between tasks and identify the most efficient route for your work. This mapping method pinpoints the critical, time-sensitive tasks that you must prioritise if you are to avoid delays. It also reveals the 'wriggle room' (slack) available for other tasks that you can use to accommodate insignificant delays and manage your workload to avoid stressful peaks and wasteful troughs. It then becomes a simple matter to transfer the tasks into a practical schedule via the Gantt chart. This also provides an assessment of the resources you need to achieve your tasks and, where necessary, allows you to take advantage of your wriggle room to avoid being overstretched.

> **Key points**
>
> - Understand your task dependencies: the order in which you need to do related tasks to maximise efficiency and avoid delays.
> - Prioritise your critical path: the tasks that will dictate the overall duration of the work.
> - Use any 'wriggle room' (slack) to balance your workload and resource usage.
> - Plotting tasks in a Gantt chart will allow you to manage your workload, accommodate delays and consider alternative scheduling options.

Further resources

Badiru, A., Rusnock, C.F and Valencia, V.V. (2021) *Project Management for Research: A Guide for Graduate Students.* Boca Raton, Fl: CRC Press.

Buttrick, R. (2019) *The Ultimate Guide to Directing and Managing Business-Led Projects,* 5th edn. Abingdon: Routledge.

Heagney, J. (2022) *Fundamentals of Project Management,* 6th edn. London: Harper Collins.

Wysocki, R.K. (2019) *Effective Project Management: Traditional, Agile, Extreme, Hybrid.* Indianapolis: Wiley.

11 Bulletproof Your Plan

How to ... Plan for things not going as planned

Stuff happens – Plan for the unexpected – Identify and assess risks – People, external and reputational risks – Risk checklists – Risk assessment team – Risk probability and impact – Mitigation considerations – Risk register

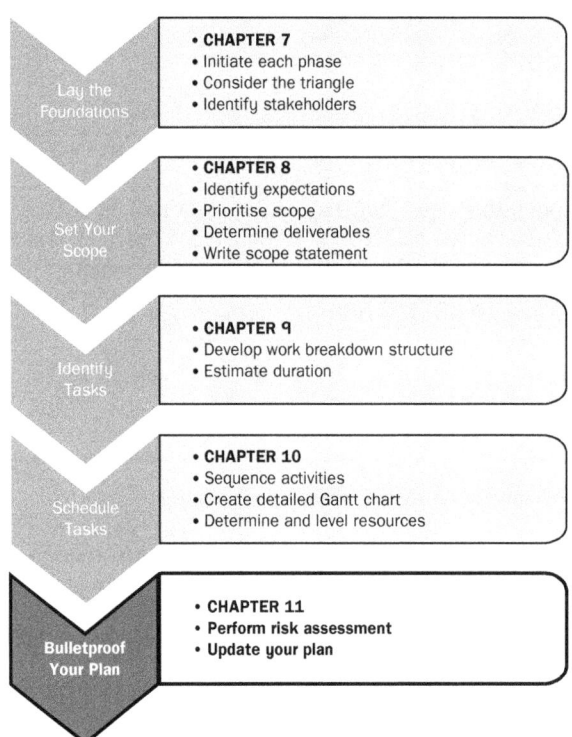

The planning process

It is in the nature of a PhD for unexpected things to happen. We often hear stories from PhD students about how their research was going really well until something happened that supposedly could never have been anticipated: the supervisor left, the equipment broke, the ethics committee rejected the proposal. However, many (not all, but the majority) of these 'unforeseen' events could have been anticipated or mitigated for with a little bit of forethought at the beginning of your PhD. The aim of risk management is to try to identify and deal with as many events that *could* happen before they *do* happen.

Anticipating risks is difficult for a PhD student because you don't know what could go wrong. Discussing potential problems might be interpreted as a sign of a negative attitude ('You're creating obstacles', 'You just need to get on and do it'). You might be accused of being pessimistic or paranoid if you highlight these issues. Alternatively, you might not want to think about problems because they are worrying or out of your control. You might prefer just to hope for the best.

Ignoring risks, however, or being unaware that they exist, doesn't make the problem disappear. Problems usually get progressively harder to resolve the longer you leave them (as shown in the following Cost of Change curve). In reality, spending some time thinking ahead to potential problems will make them easier to solve. You are unlikely to anticipate every risk in your project, but by spending time considering them at the start, you will identify more and be able to deal with them earlier, and your research will run more smoothly as a result.

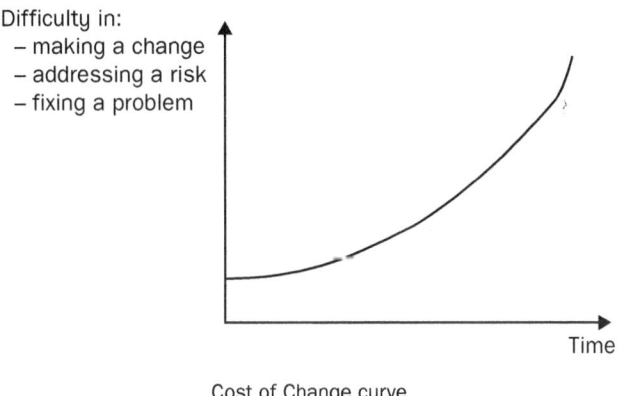

Cost of Change curve

The International Organization for Standardization (ISO, 2009) defines risk as the 'effect of uncertainty on objectives'. Uncertainty exists in everything you do, particularly in research, so you would be naïve not to consider it. ISO further states that a risk is 'a deviation from the expected – positive or negative'. So, risks don't always need to be threats. They can also be *opportunities*: things that are uncertain but which could potentially have a positive effect on your PhD. Where you might try to avoid or reduce a threat, you may try to actively exploit or enhance an opportunity. You can now see why it's so important to be aware of risks in your project from the start, as well as throughout, your doctoral journey!

Although you have been identifying potential problems or issues at every step of the planning process, this chapter will address how to deal with these risks and update your plan accordingly. Dealing with risks has three fundamental steps, which we will take you through in this chapter:

1 **Identify** – recognise that a risk exists.
2 **Assess** – estimate the likelihood of it happening and the effect on your work if it does.
3 **Respond** – decide what are you going to do to mitigate its impact or create a back-up plan.

These steps will allow you to create a risk register, which is a list of the risks and how you will deal them. A risk register template is on page 146. This chapter will walk you through the steps in completing one later.

Identify risks

There is one fundamental rule when performing risk identification:

If you think of something, write it down.

You may choose to ignore it later, but, making the *conscious decision* to ignore something is not the same as being unaware that it ever existed.

Identifying risks is the most important stage of the three-step process. You can't do anything about a problem if you don't know it exists. The different planning techniques in the previous chapters were all ways of proactively identifying risks, even if we didn't make that explicit at the time:

- **Scope statement, deliverables** – expectation risks
- **Work breakdown structure** – task-level risks
- **Network diagram** – dependency risks
- **Gantt chart** – schedule and resourcing risks.

 **Transferable skills**
Wherever you go in the world, any institution or organisation's risk policy will roughly follow the three fundamental steps given here. Almost all organisations now have risk-management policies, so skills in this area are highly transferable ones to develop in your PhD with application throughout the rest of your career.

When you applied these planning techniques during Chapters 7 to 10, you considered issues as they became apparent, and they informed your plan. For example, an important stakeholder has a particular expectation. Their involvement is crucial to the project, so there is a risk that, if their expectation isn't met, they could withdraw their support. You respond to the risk by making sure it is a 'must-have' and 'in scope'. There are, however, additional types of risks that the planning techniques don't always highlight.

People risks

The key use of the stakeholder analysis you began in Chapter 7 is to help identify people risks. Your stakeholder diagram is an excellent starting point for highlighting where potential opportunities or threats may lie in your PhD. For example:

- **Key academics.** Ensure you engage these stakeholders in meaningful discussion. People are more likely to want to contribute to your PhD success if they feel valued and included. Neglecting or ignoring them creates the risk of reduced involvement when you need them most.
- **Participants.** Are there risks around involvement (will they turn up) and input (will you get the data you need), as well as ethics, GDPR and data management?
- **Technicians.** Can you get the support and assistance you need when you need it?

You included time off and significant personal events in your timeline in Chapter 4, so have already taken steps to prevent this having an adverse impact on your PhD – you have been managing risk from the very start!

- **Family and friends.** They don't pose threats to your PhD, but the time you spend with them is time you're not spending on your research.
- **You.** Do you have all of the key skills to complete the work? Do you have personal or work commitments that could take you away from your research?

External risks

Sometimes, external risks – factors beyond your control – cause problems in your PhD; elements that don't seem to be connected to your project in any way, but still create issues, such as:

- **Strike action.** You turn up on campus for a meeting with your supervisor, have to pass through a picket line and then discover your supervisor isn't there.
- **Holidays.** You try to arrange meetings when you're available but find the people you want to meet with are on annual leave.
- **A pandemic.** Lockdown means you can't meet your supervisors or conduct interviews face to face.

> Assessing 'people risks' can uncover other important stakeholders. For example, one post-doc explained that they included 'weather' in their risk register, because it could have impacted on their ability to do their fieldwork. Identifying weather as a risk also highlighted other stakeholders who might be important to their work: meteorologists, protective-clothing providers, health-and-safety advisors. They were then able to go back and update their stakeholder diagram. *Your plans should always be always iterative and always under review.*

These are all true examples that happened to PhD students.

Reputational risk

Reputational risk is the danger of damage to your reputation and the reputation of your supervisors, your department and even your institution. This is *so* important, as reputation is the currency of research – if you lose your reputation, you will never be funded again! These types of risks are particularly important now that the world is so intimately connected through social media and (dis)information can be passed around quickly without you even knowing.

Reputational risks may be bigger than you. They could impact beyond your PhD and begin to affect your research group or even your university as a whole. But, don't worry: it is not your responsibility to deal with these risks. There are people higher up the hierarchy who are employed to worry about these things! It *is* your responsibility, however, to let others know if you think you have identified an issue that could cause a problem. All you need to do is send an email to your supervisor informing them of what might be a problem and why. The risk has then been 'escalated' (passed up the chain of command), and that is a perfectly acceptable professional response. Don't try to cope with everything on your own. In fact, if you are working in a research area where there are external groups who have particularly strong feelings about your work (for example animal welfare or human rights), your university will provide guidance on how to deal with these types of risks.

> ✏ **Activity: Revisit planning outputs and identify risks**
>
> 1 Look back at your stakeholder diagram.
>   For each stakeholder, consider any potential problems they could cause and write these in the 'risk' column of your risk register template (page 146), for example 'My supervisor is off sick when I need assistance.'

- Are there any opportunities that your stakeholders present? Note them down, for example 'Going to conference with my supervisor might mean I can be introduced to their network (great for career).'
2 Revisit your other planning outputs (as on page Xx) and use them to identify additional risks.
3 Add them to your risk register.

Risk checklists

Risk checklists can be very useful for identifying and proactively dealing with risks simply because they remind you of things you might otherwise forget. For each piece of work, go through the checklist and ask, 'Could any of these risks affect my project?' One of the notable features of checklists is that so many of them already exist. We've noted on several occasions that, although the output of your PhD is unique, most of the processes you go through are not. People have done very similar things before and, as a result, you can use the experience of others to guide your work. You may well be using risk assessment checklists already. Maybe you use toxic lab chemicals, or conduct fieldwork data collection, or use one for ethics reviews for research involving human participants. These are not always called 'risk checklists' but that is what they are. One advantage of using existing checklists is learning from people who have learned the lessons for you. They will tell you the risks to be aware of and also suggest potential preventative measures. There is no need to reinvent the wheel! You can adapt existing risk checklists to your own situation.

Activity: Search online for checklists

1 Search for 'research risk checklist ...' with some keywords from your particular topic. From the many hits, select those that are helpful and relevant.
2 Go through every task in your WBS, and use the checklist to determine if any of the risks exist in your PhD.
3 Add the risks to your risk register.

Risk assessment teams

One of the major problems with identifying risks within your own project is that you tend to be emotionally attached to your research, which can affect your judgement. This can hamper your ability to see potential problems and assess how serious they could be. To combat this, many large projects don't allow the project team to perform the final risk assessment. They bring in a risk assessment team (a RAT) – a group of people who are remote from the work and are able to more objectively assess risks, as well as strengths and weaknesses, of the plan, approach, ideas and methods.

You already have a RAT in your PhD: your supervisory team. They challenge your assumptions, pose difficult questions and can guide you away from your emotional attachment to the project. There are others too. The ethics committee, for example, is effectively a RAT. It assesses your research proposal for weaknesses and potential problems and, although this can sometimes seem time-consuming and even frustrating, when your proposal comes out of the other side, it is stronger, more rigorous and more robust as a result. Peer-review is another example of unattached people assessing your work. Probably the most intense RAT you'll encounter is in the Viva. Your work is put under scrutiny and interrogated by experts who don't carry the emotional attachment that you (or indeed your supervisors) have for the work.

It can also be very useful to establish your own informal risk assessment team for your PhD. When we run risk management courses for PhD students, we organise attendees in groups of mixed experience and mixed disciplines in which everyone asks questions about each other's research. It is amazing how often the researchers will say that they hadn't considered something or looked at their work in a particular way until these non-experts pointed it out.

> **➡ Action: Create your own informal risk assessment team.**
>
> It could be a group of colleagues from the same research group or department, or a group of PhD students you have met on a training course, networking event or writing retreat. Invite them to ask you questions about your research, highlight potential problems and challenge assumptions you've made – and you can return the favour to them. You will almost certainly discover aspects of your work that you hadn't previously considered.

Friends and family who are not linked to your PhD in any way often can make good risk assessors because they are not afraid to ask the seemingly 'silly' question – because they don't know the question might be 'daft'. Often, you find that this stupid question isn't actually stupid at all. It is very pertinent, but it was so obvious that you overlooked it.

> **✎ Activity: Risk assessment team**
>
> 1 Write down who you are going to ask to be on your risk assessment team:
>
>
>
> 2 Arrange dates to meet (bribe them with coffee if you need to!) and add those dates to your plan.
> 3 After you meet, update your risk register with risks that you hadn't previously identified.

Assess risks

Clearly, not all risks are equal. Some have the potential to be significant and you need to address them up front; others are of little consequence and, if they were to happen, you could easily cope with them. As such, you need to assess the *riskiness* of each risk and, based on that, determine an appropriate course of action. You should assess risks in two dimensions:

- **Probability** – the chance or likelihood of the risk occurring
- **Impact** – the effect it could have on your PhD should it happen.

It is possible sometimes to put numeric values on these assessments (for example, there is a 42 per cent chance of rain, or there will be a 16-week delay if this occurs). However, when undertaking a PhD, this is often not possible. This is probably the first major research project you've done, so you don't have the data to make such calculations. It is more appropriate to assess qualitatively, using a five-point scale:

> **Ask your RATs!**
>
> Risk assessment teams (supervisors, colleagues, post-docs and so on) can be really helpful when assessing risks. You might not have done these things before, but the chances are that they have, and you can use that experience to help.

- Very low
- Low
- Medium
- High
- Very high

Because the assessment of these values is subjective, you need to define what you mean by them, as in the following examples.

Probability assessment scale

Probability	Definition	Examples
Very low	Only happens very rarely	• Building burns down • Department closes • Global pandemic
Low	Happens occasionally – not often	• Lose all your data • Personal issues require significant time off • Irreconcilable disagreement with supervisor
Medium	Not unusual	• Supervisor leaves • Laptop gives up • Interviewees drop out
High	Quite common	• Struggle with a concept • A few days' illness
Very high	Happens in almost every PhD	• Loss of motivation • Writer's block

You should define in the same way for impact:

Impact assessment scale

Impact	Definition	Examples
Very low	Inconsequential, can cope easily	• Come into work late
Low	Inconvenient but can survive	• Supervisory meeting is cancelled • Equipment breaks so have to wait for resolution
Medium	Imposition, involves a bit of additional work	• Supervisor leaves and new one comes on board • Can't recruit enough participants so have to change approach
High	Significant, needs a lot of work to recover	• Completely redo data collection • Ethics proposal rejected
Very high	Means you might not get a PhD	• Mock Viva raises serious questions about quality of your work • You don't take supervisors' advice on board

Once you have assessed each risk, it's easy to categorise as red, amber or green, using the following table. (We've used grayscale approximations, but *everyone* uses colours in real life!) For example:

Risk: Small data set means examiners query the reliability of your findings.
Probability = Low. Impact = Very high.
Overall risk = Red.

Risk: Tide times mean you can't collect water samples when you'd like to.
Probability = Medium. Impact = Low.
Overall risk = Green.

Risk assessment categories

		Impact				
		V low	Low	Medium	High	Very high
Probability	Very low	Green	Green	Green	Green	Amber
	Low	Green	Green	Green	Red	Red
	Medium	Green	Green	Amber	Red	Red
	High	Green	Green	Red	Red	Red
	Very high	Green	Amber	Red	Red	Red

> ✏️ **Activity: Risk assessment**
>
> 1 Using the template on page 146, estimate the probability and impact of your risks.
> 2 If possible, ask other people with more experience for input.
> 3 Determine whether they are red, amber or green risks.

Respond to risks

Now that you've assessed the risks, you're in a position to work out how to deal with them. You should decide how you will respond to each risk individually, but the following general rules of thumb can help you.

Red risks

These are major, serious risks (with significant impact and/or probability). They are risks you should try to deal with now. Take the example of a risk that the cells you're growing become contaminated. You're not prepared to let that happen, so you'll completely sanitise your working area in advance. It will cost you some time, but it's worth it. Put a new 'Sanitise workplace' task in your WBS, network diagram and, therefore, Gantt chart – you have updated your plan to accommodate uncertainty.

Green risks

These are less significant risks and you probably can't really justify spending time up front dealing with them proactively (basically, wait and see if they happen). However, don't ignore them completely. Formulate a contingency plan to put into action if they occur: a set of mitigating measures you can use if and when the risk happens. For example, there is a risk that your fieldwork is delayed by bad weather, but your travel back to university is not until Monday, so you could use the weekend to catch up. You'll wait and see what happens: if the weather is great, then you'll finish Friday and relax ... but, if not, you have Saturday and Sunday in reserve.

Amber risks

These risks are neither big and scary (red) nor less significant (green), but somewhere in between. You have a choice: do you treat it as a red risk and do something immediately, or do you treat it as green and let it go for now, with a plan to review it? Ultimately, everything will become either red or green when you make a *conscious decision* how to deal with this risk. The only thing you can't do is ignore it!

Risk response and reward

Responding to any risk is going to cost you something. For a PhD, that will normally be time. Typically, however, the time spent addressing problems before they happen is justified by the much greater time saved further on. It's also possible that some risks, if not anticipated, can cause irreversible problems.

> **Are you feeling lucky?**
>
> Dealing with risks is always a gamble: they may never actually happen. But, if you could spend an hour now to prevent something from happening that could cost you a week later, is it worth doing? We think it probably is, and, for a PhD, it's usually much more difficult to fix a problem the further your research progresses.

You can respond to *any* risk, even if your response is, 'This is too risky – we'll do something different instead.' Most responses are not that severe, however, as in the following examples.

Risk	Response
My supervisor is always busy – it's difficult to get a meeting	Set meeting dates for six months at a time
The equipment I need is always in demand	Ensure to foster good relations with the technical staff as part of my support network
My data-management skills aren't great	Go on a training course
I'm a really slow typer; transcription will take for ever	Use a transcription company or app to do it for me
I find it hard to get motivated to write	Sign up to a 'Shut up and write' session or go to a writing retreat
I won't get the data I need	Spend more time on detailed research design and create a back-up plan just in case
I don't know what potential risk I'll face as I've never done this before	Communicate! Speak to everyone … supervisors, peers, post-docs. Read books. Go on courses.

It is rare to be able to get rid of a risk completely. An element of it usually remains after your response, but, hopefully, that response will reduce the probability and/or impact to an acceptable level. Essentially, you're trying to move all of your 'red' risks to 'green' so that all you have to do is monitor them.

Secondary risks

Finally, when you respond to a risk, you should be aware that responses can introduce new risks of their own. These secondary risks should be included in your risk register and assessed and responded to in the same way as any other risk. Take this true story as an illustration:

A PhD student was conducting research that involved interviewing people serving life sentences in prison. They identified a significant risk during their data collection phase: 'There is a risk that, due to the nature of the sensitive questions I need to ask, the participant could become violent. This could result in physical and mental personal injury.'

They assessed this as a red, unacceptable risk and determined that one risk response would be to have a prison officer in the room while they conducted the interviews. This would reduce both the probability and potential impact of the risk. However, it also introduced a 'secondary' risk. In this case: 'There is a risk that, due to the attendance of a prison officer, the participant does not answer the questions in the interview as fully (or at all). This could result in lower-quality (or a lack of) data.'

They now had to balance the impact of this new risk against the danger of the first one.

Identifying these potential problems in advance allowed the student to discuss and resolve them with the supervisory team, ethics committee and other key stakeholders.

> **Activity: Risk response**
>
> Using the template on page 146, write down potential risk responses.
>
> - For *red* risks: decide what you will do now and update your project plan (WBS, network diagram and Gantt chart) with these new actions.
> - For *green* risks: decide on your 'Plan B' should the risk manifest and write it in your risk register.
> - Identify and write down any secondary risks you have introduced.
>
> If possible, ask other people with more experience for input.

Template: Risk register

Risk	Probability VH, H, M, L, VL	Impact VH, H, M, L, VL	Exposure Red, Amber, Green	Response

Summary

One thing you can rely on during your PhD is that unexpected things will happen. Protect your PhD from the negative impact of unexpected events by undertaking a risk assessment at the start of every planning phase. This will also give you the chance to identify opportunities throughout your research project and to actively pursue them. Despite your lack of knowledge of the realities of PhD research, you can identify the range of risks you might meet. Review the risks identified through your planning activities and consider different categories of risk, such as people, external and reputational. Recruit additional help by establishing a risk assessment team and by looking at existing risk checklists. Assess the probability of the risks occurring and the impact they would have on your PhD. Having assessed these, decide what steps to take, if any, to reduce the likelihood of risks derailing your PhD.

Key points
- Expect the unexpected – stuff happens!
- Minimise the unexpected by thinking ahead and assessing possible risks.
- Don't do this alone – other people will see risks that you don't.
- Assess the likelihood of a risk occurring and its impact before deciding what, if anything, to do about it.
- If necessary, and possible, put measures in place to avoid or mitigate the impact of risks.

Further resources

Buttrick, R. (2019) *The Ultimate Guide to Directing and Managing Business-Led Projects*, 5th edn. Abingdon: Routledge.

Heagney, J. (2022) *Fundamentals of Project Management*, 6th edn. London: Harper Collins.

Wysocki, R.K. (2019) *Effective Project Management: Traditional, Agile, Extreme, Hybrid*. Indianapolis: Wiley.

Reference

ISO (2009) Guide 73:2009 (en) *Risk Management - Vocabulary*. Available at: iso.org/obp/ui/#iso:std:iso:guide:73:ed-1:v1:en [accessed 23 January 2023].

12 Take Charge of Your Time

How to ... Get the most out of every day

> Put plans into action – Time-blocking – Manage workload – Work-life balance – Circadian rhythms – Maximise productivity and brain power – Timer techniques

By using the planning techniques described in the preceding chapters you have created a plan to help you achieve sustained progress throughout your PhD. However, even the best-formulated plans rely on the ability to show up and do the work as planned. This means using your time effectively week by week and day by day.

A PhD can be a challenge to your time management, even if you have been quite good at it in the past. The scale and duration of the project, degree of uncertainty, steep learning curve and lack of short-term, externally-imposed deadlines can make it difficult to make the most of your time. This chapter provides a range of simple techniques to make the most of every week and every day. They will help you to take charge of your time and work productively. This will also help to reduce the stress of your PhD and build your confidence that you can stay on top of the work.

Take charge of your week

Having completed the previous chapters, you have a good idea of the tasks you need to work on in any given week. So, you shouldn't face your week wondering what you're supposed to be doing! However, your Gantt chart won't necessarily provide a detailed schedule on a day-by-day, hour-by-hour basis. It includes tasks that can't be completed in a few days but instead span a number of weeks. This means you need to be able to translate the scheduled tasks of the Gantt chart into an actionable plan for your week.

Additionally, new tasks will present themselves in the short term, which aren't included in your original Gantt chart, such as a request from your supervisors to provide information for a funding bid, a last-minute opportunity to submit a proposal for a conference poster, or a problem with equipment that demands immediate attention.

Take charge of your calendar: the time-blocking method

The best method for managing the day-to-day scheduling of your work in your calendar, is time-blocking. When we ask PhD students what they generally enter into their calendars, we get the following list:

- Meetings
- Classes or seminars

- Conferences
- Deadlines and reminders
- Personal appointments and social events.

In other words, events at a specific time. Time-blocking expands the practice of marking events and appointments in your calendar to tasks that don't already have a specific time attached to them. Instead, you schedule an *appointment with yourself*, to do the tasks. Time-blocking is particularly helpful for:

- Reducing confusion about what to do on a daily basis and helping to reduce the likelihood of procrastination
- Realistically assessing your workload – time allocated to key tasks is mapped in your calendar, allowing you to make better choices about what you can and can't take on
- Visually demonstrating your workload to others and providing evidence for the choices you make, such as taking on new demands or moving deadlines
- Creating flexible plans – it is easy to change the time-blocks in response to new demands and new opportunities
- Managing work-life balance – you time-block all aspects of your life and have an overview in one place
- Creating a sense of urgency that pushes you into work in advance of deadlines (particularly useful if you tend to procrastinate until deadlines are imminent).

Step 1: Enter fixed appointments

Identify all your appointments that have an allocated date, time and location – meetings, courses, events and so on. Put these into your calendar as and when they are agreed. Also enter key deadlines in your calendar, such as submission dates.

Note your personal and social events in your calendar as well as PhD-related appointments. Your work and personal lives affect each other. For example, you may have childcare commitments or a doctor's appointment that take up time that you might otherwise assume to be available for your PhD. Conversely, a major deadline for your PhD might mean it's not wise to schedule a weekend away with friends.

> **Digital vs analogue**
>
> A digital calendar will allow you to make the most of the time-blocking method, as its flexibility allows you to change your schedule easily in response to changes in circumstances. Colour-coding is also useful when time-blocking. If you are committed to an analogue version, you could, in principle, use a wall planner with dry-wipe pens or sticky notes, but it will be less efficient to update than a digital calendar.

If you are combining part-time work with part-time PhD study, it will be even more important to be able to view all your commitments at once, so you can assess how they might affect each other. If you don't want to put everything in one calendar, create different calendars that you can view at the same time. Colour-coding can help you to make sense of the different classes of demands.

Time-blocking: fixed appointments
© RDT&C

Step 2: Add preparatory work

Next, block out time for any work related to the fixed appointments and deadlines that are already in your calendar. For example, if there are seminars that require preparation, or a deadline for a grant submission that will require time to write and complete. Many of these tasks will already have been identified in your work breakdown structure, but time-blocking is another safety check to ensure all work is accounted for.

For simplicity, we're showing these time-blocks in the same week as the appointments or deadlines that require the work. In your own calendar, however, you can choose when to schedule the work, and it may span several weeks, depending on your workload. As long as the work is done before the deadline, it doesn't matter. For tasks that feature in your Gantt chart, you will already have listed an outline schedule for the work, taking account of deadlines and dependencies. You can now transfer these tasks into your calendar, choosing precisely the day and time to do them.

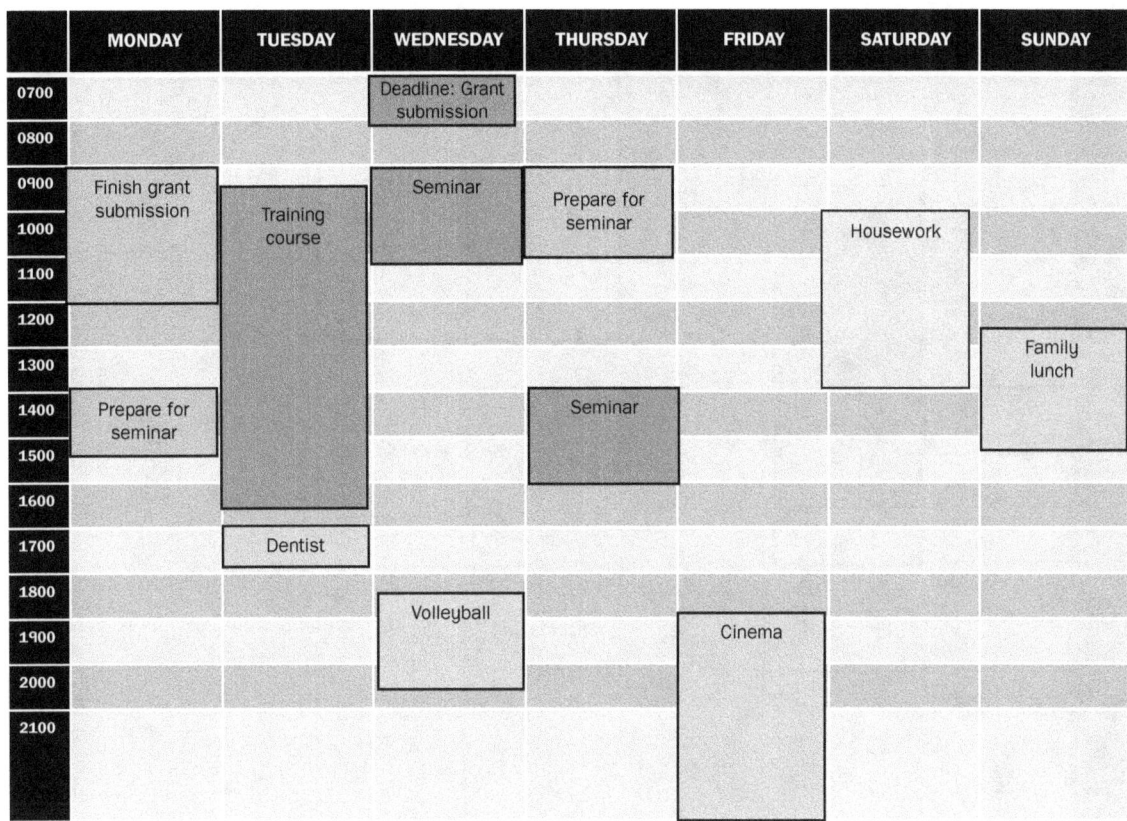

Time-blocking: appointment-related work
© RDT&C

Step 3: Create time-blocks for discretionary tasks

The final step is to create time-blocks: 'appointments' for which you have discretion over timing, such as tasks with timescales over multiple weeks. Most of these should be identified in your Gantt chart. However, rather than simply knowing that you will, for example, write your draft literature review between 1 and 30 November, you will create 'appointments' on specific days and at specific times between these dates to do the actual work.

Using the methods in Chapter 9, you have estimated the overall time you need to allocate to a task. Time-blocking is the process of blocking out the time needed for a task at a specific time in your calendar, providing clear structure for your work every day.

152 Part 2 – How to Get Going

	MONDAY	TUESDAY	WEDNESDAY	THURSDAY	FRIDAY	SATURDAY	SUNDAY
0700			Deadline: Grant submission				
0800							
0900	Finish grant submission	Training course	Seminar	Prepare for seminar	Read lit review papers	Housework	
1000							
1100				Read lit review papers			
1200							
1300							Family lunch
1400	Prepare for seminar			Seminar			
1500					Plan lit review structure		
1600	Prepare for supervision meeting			Update bibliography			
1700		Dentist					
1800			Volleyball				
1900	Gym	Plan holiday		Supermarket	Cinema		
2000							
2100							

Time-blocking: discretionary work
© RDT&C

Time-blocking tips

➔ Action

Avoid blocking out too much time.

Life (and PhDs) rarely happen the way you plan, so leave enough 'unblocked' time to accommodate inevitable problems and delays.

- Although your three-point estimations will account for this in your WBS tasks, having extra wriggle room allows you to incorporate new opportunities, extra meetings or additional routine work items as and when they crop up.

- It's impossible to create a hard-and-fast rule about how much time to leave unallocated, but we recommend committing *no more than 75 per cent* of your time to appointments and time-blocking. Where possible, leave at least an hour each day free. Don't see this as wasting time, as it always gives you the chance to begin your next task early. There's nothing better for your mood than feeling like you're ahead of the game.

➔ Action

Only block out 'working' time for work.

Don't make a habit of blocking out time in the evenings or weekends for your PhD work. The long duration of a PhD means that you must create a sustainable pace for your work, which means taking work-life balance seriously. If nothing else, your unallocated weekends may end up as contingency for the times when you do have to put in some extra work.

➔ Action

Hit the right level.

Don't attempt to time-block every task on your to-do list or you'll spend more time updating your calendar than doing any work. The aim of time-blocking is to allocate time to *key pieces of work* rather than every little task. The unallocated time is there to let you complete the shorter or less-important tasks. For example, block out time to read your methodology literature, but don't bother blocking time out to send an email or to print out a couple of documents.

➔ Action

Be flexible.

Be ready to move your time-blocks about, as necessary. Your calendar is not supposed to be set in stone. Time-blocks can be swapped around, as and when your demands change throughout the week. By resisting the urge to block out every hour of every day, you're building in flexibility.

➔ Action

Develop routines.

Put in regular time-blocks for routine tasks that might otherwise get overlooked, such as administration, record-keeping or reviewing your plans.

➔ Action

Pace yourself.

Don't try to time-block too far in advance. This granular level of day-by-day planning can be unwieldy to change. The further ahead you plan, the more changes you are likely to have to make, so find a balance that works for you. Put the deadlines and milestones from your Gantt chart for the next few weeks into your calendar and work backwards, blocking out the necessary working time. If you have a regular supervisory meeting, perhaps you can block out, say, 2p.m. on Wednesday for the next six months.

➡ Action

Colour-code.

Use colour-coding to distinguish different kinds of commitment in your calendars and get a quick visual representation of the shape of your week. You might want to differentiate between different areas of your life: PhD, personal, other work. More importantly, differentiate between fixed appointments, such as meetings and deadlines, and appointments that you have the discretion to move. For example, colour code the following categories of calendar entry:

- PhD events (such as meetings and training courses)
- PhD deadlines and reminders (submission deadlines, administrative dates)
- PhD time-blocked tasks (lab time, interviews, thesis writing)
- Social events (time with colleagues, friends and family, holidays)
- Personal/household appointments (medical appointments, tradespeople visits)
- Personal/home due dates and reminders (insurance, rent)
- Household time-blocked tasks (chores, maintenance).

✎ Activity: Choose your colour-coding

Identify the different categories of entry you will put into your calendar and assign a colour to that category

Category of calendar entry	Colour

You can see at a glance the entries in your calendar that are fixed – events and appointments – and those that you have more control over – time-blocked appointments. This gives you a very quick assessment of how flexible you can be and reduces the stress of handling the unexpected.

> **✎ Activity: Time-blocking**
>
> Using the time-blocking method and actions given here, time-block the key tasks for the next four weeks in your calendar.

> **Time-boxing**
>
> Time-boxing is a variation on time-blocking that can increase the speed and efficiency of your work. It is particularly useful if you're working under time pressure or if you tend to spend too long on your work, either because you get lost in the work or struggle to move on because of perfectionism (a common challenge for PhD students).
>
> Time-boxing is simply treating your time-blocked appointments as fixed. *You don't allow yourself to work beyond the allotted time.* This requires commitment and self-discipline, as no one is going to force you to adhere to this, but it can be a useful way of creating better boundaries around your work and increasing your focus.

Get the most out of every day

The time-blocking method, combined with the planning techniques from the previous chapters, means that you will be able to embark on every week confident that you know what to do and when. However, how can you get the best out of yourself every day?

Much PhD work is cognitively demanding. It requires reserves of mental energy and the ability to concentrate for long periods. By using the simple techniques that follow to maximise your mental energy, you will be able to work longer and better, and get the most out of every day. Once you have learned these techniques, you could incorporate these principles into your time-blocking methods.

> **➡ Action**
>
> Align your work with your body clock.

In Chapter 5, we explained that humans have biological patterns of alertness and sleepiness that affect us all every day. You can use these natural circadian rhythms to schedule different tasks at the ideal time of day. In simple terms, people are generally more alert in the mornings than in the afternoons, but there are subtle variations in alertness and cognitive state during the day that can help you choose the best tasks to do when.

> **Larks and owls**
>
> The concept of 'morning' people and 'evening' people is borne out by research. However, human 'owls' aren't nocturnal. They trail the 'larks' by only a couple of hours.

> For example, while Fraser is raring to go at 7.00, Rosie isn't really functioning well until about 9.30. However, she is happy to stay at her desk until 18.00 and, in fact, finds this later shift is often a productive time, while Fraser is ready to call it a day by 16.00.

Circadian rhythms		
Approximate times		**Mental and physical state**
'Larks'	'Owls'	
0800–1100	1000–1300	Working memory, alertness and concentration gradually increase.
1000–1100	1200–1300	Peak of concentration and focus.
1100–1200	1300–1500	Concentration and focus begin to decrease. Alertness remains high.
1200	1400	Verbal reasoning hits high point.
1200–1400	1400–1600	Cheerfulness peaks.
1400–1500	1600–1700	Metabolism slows. Sleepiness increases.
1500	1700	Long-term memory peaks.
1600–1800	1800–2000	Alertness increases.
1500–1900	1700–2100	Peak physical state: hand-eye coordination, muscle strength, blood circulation at their best.
2100–2200	2300–0000	Creativity peaks.

Because they are triggered by light, there are seasonal differences in circadian rhythms. It is easier to wake earlier in the summer because it gets light earlier, while dark winter mornings can make it harder to get out of bed. Although artificial light affects our circadian rhythms, there is evidence that we are still governed to a great extent by these inbuilt biological patterns.

The guidelines here are just that: guidelines. The exact timing of your circadian rhythms will be specific to you. Observe your own patterns of alertness to be more accurate when planning your day. Once you understand when your best times of day fall – after a bit of self-observation and honesty – you can schedule the right tasks for the right time of day. For example:

➜ Action

Schedule cognitive tasks that demand concentration in the morning.

Don't try to do tasks such as writing or data analysis when you are nodding off after lunch.

> **➡ Action**
>
> Schedule meetings in the early part of the afternoon.

Or at least meetings at which you can expect to be talking, and not just listening!

> **➡ Action**
>
> Get physical!

Counteract the sleepy time of day by doing things that require you to move about and generally be more physically active. This will help you to stay more awake. You can even use the science of circadian rhythms to choose when to go to the gym or when to pursue your creative hobby.

Example circadian rhythms plan	
Time	Best time of day for me to ...
0900–1000	Routine administrative tasks
1000–1230	Writing, data analysis, reading
1230–1430	Emails, note-taking, data entry
1430–1600	Meetings, interviews, interactive seminars, coffee/lunch dates, physical tasks
1600–1800	Reading notes, data entry, planning

The more flexibility you have in your schedule, the more you will be able to take advantage of your circadian rhythms to create an ideal plan for your day. It's unlikely that you will be able to follow this strictly all the time, but you can use this formula when possible to schedule appointments and events and time-block tasks. For example, if you're a 'lark', you might go into the office extra early to make the most of your best time for concentration. If you're more of an 'owl', you might shift your daily schedule slightly later, knowing you will produce better work.

> **Overriding your clock**
>
> You can override your circadian rhythms to some extent, if necessary, at least for the short term. For example, our training courses with European clients start at 7a.m. UK time. To make sure we're alert by the start of the course, we set our alarms early to allow plenty of time to wake up gradually (and, admittedly, drink plenty of strong coffee!). However, a job where we had to do this full-time might prove exhausting.

> ✏️ **Activity: Circadian rhythms plan**
>
> Organise a schedule of the best times to do certain types of tasks so that they align with your circadian rhythms. (The preceding example suggests some ideas.)
>
> | Time | My best time of day for ... |
> |------|------------------------------|
> | | |
> | | |
> | | |
> | | |
> | | |
> | | |
> | | |
> | | |
> | | |
> | | |

Maximise your mental energy

Much PhD work is mentally taxing and you will need high levels of concentration to undertake many complex cognitive tasks. Working in line with your circadian rhythms will help you to get the best from your brain. By carefully managing your brain energy throughout the day, you can increase your focus and boost your productivity.

When you're using your brain for the difficult 'thinking' work of your PhD – making sense of complex ideas, forward planning, decision-making, data analysis, writing and so on – you are largely relying on a particular part of the brain: the prefrontal cortex (PFC). The PFC is at the front of your head, behind your temples. It is often dubbed the CEO (chief executive officer) of the brain to reflect its importance. The PFC is very energy hungry and it also tires easily. If you take steps to preserve the energy of your PFC, you can extend the amount of time you can use it and as a result, increase your productivity.

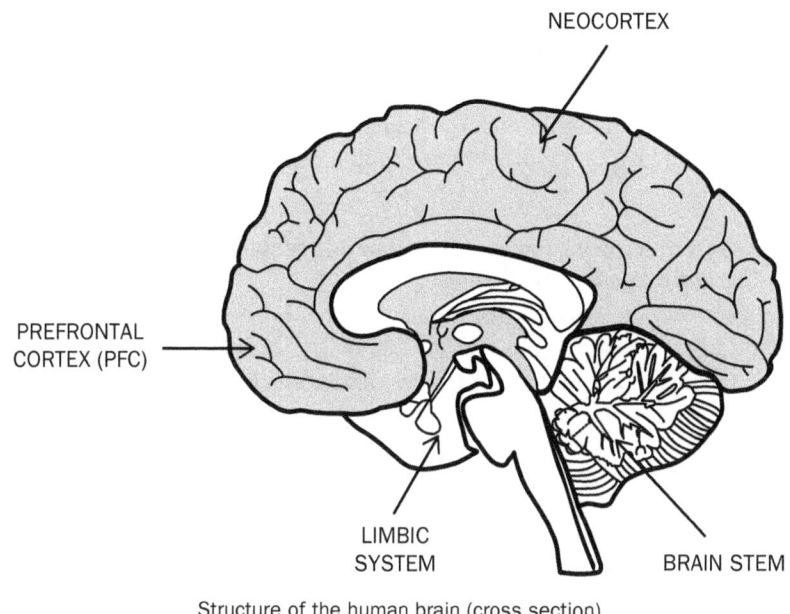
Structure of the human brain (cross section)
© RDT&C

There are two simple techniques you can use daily to preserve your PFC function:

- Limit concentration time
- Add variety.

Limit concentration time

We don't suggest you reduce the overall length of time you devote to work during the day – that would reduce your productivity rather than increasing it. Short bursts of concentration, however, with short breaks in between, will increase your concentration levels without sacrificing the overall amount of time you put into work.

How long can you actually sustain your concentration levels without a break? Imagine you block out three hours for reading journal articles in your calendar. If you then spend three hours at your desk, 'reading', the reality is that your attention will come and go. It's impossible to fully concentrate for the whole three hours. Research suggests that you can maintain your concentration fully for no more than 30 to 40 minutes at a time. Look to actively manage your concentration levels, by respecting the natural ebb and flow of your attention.

➡ **Action**

Use a timer to set short periods of concentrated work, interspersed by short breaks.

This kind of timer technique, is the principle behind the popular Pomodoro technique, devised by Francesco Cirillo (2018), which is based on:

- Working periods of 25 minutes, each followed by a 5-minute break
- After every fourth 'pomodoro' (25-minute working period), taking a longer break of 20 minutes.

Although you might think the frequent 'interruptions' for breaks would reduce your concentration levels, most people find the reverse is true. You'll find that your concentration improves during these short periods, and that you tire less overall.

You don't need to stick rigidly to the Pomodoro technique. Experiment to determine what time periods work best for you. You may also find that you use slightly different time periods depending on the work you are doing. For example:

- If you want to get a lot of work done in a short period of time, such as when revising a chapter or reading new literature, use the 25/5 regime.
- If you are doing work that is creative or requires deeper contemplation, such as research design or writing a first draft, try switching to a 40/10 regime.
- If you are doing a task that you hate or find exceptionally boring, you could even drop down to a 15/5 regime.

How you use the timer technique is up to you, as long as you stick to two important rules:

- **Don't use a timed work period of more than 40 minutes.** If you go beyond 40 minutes, you will lose concentration before the end of the work period, thereby undermining the value of the technique.
- **Always use a timer for your work periods**. It might be tempting just to look at the clock to keep track of the work periods. However, the point of this technique is to have short periods of very focused concentration. If you're stopping to check the clock every five minutes, you will lose your focus, so use a timer with an audio alarm.

Activity: The timer technique

1. Experiment with different versions of the timer technique – different work periods and different rest periods.
2. Observe the impact on your productivity.
3. Decide which version works best for you in each circumstance.

Version 1

Work period:	Rest period:	Type of work:
Impact on productivity:		

Version 2

Work period:	Rest period:	Type of work:
Impact on productivity:		

Version 3		
Work period:	Rest period:	Type of work:
Impact on productivity:		

Add variety

Adding variety into your working day is another way to preserve your brain energy and improve your concentration levels. Novelty has been shown to be refreshing to the PFC. Rather than slogging away on a single activity all morning, intersperse it with a different kind of task. For example:

- Alternate more passive thinking tasks, such as reading, with more active tasks that require typing or talking, such as writing an email or meeting a colleague.
- Alternate difficult cognitive tasks, such as data analysis or writing, with more routine tasks, such as data entry or filing.
- Alternate primarily cerebral tasks, such as reading or writing, with physically active tasks, such as walking across campus to collect some books or tidying your desk.

> ➡ **Action: Use the timer technique in conjunction with adding variety.**
>
> Rather than using your timer to cycle between periods of work and breaks, use the timer to alternate between different kinds of task. For example:
>
> - A 40-minute period of reading
> - Followed by 15 minutes on a routine task, such as data entry
> - Followed by a 5-minute break.

> ✏ **Activity: Build variety into your day**
>
> Schedule variety into your next working day.
>
> 1. Use time-blocking to schedule a variety of different tasks into your day (or rearrange your existing time-blocks if necessary).
> 2. Follow this schedule and observe the impact on your productivity and concentration levels.

Summary

To use your time most effectively, translate the schedule of your Gantt chart into a calendar-based daily schedule, using the time-blocking method. This allows you to make progress on your PhD, and accommodate new opportunities and additional tasks, without compromising on your research goals. It also allows you to manage your work-life balance, contributing to your well-being. On a daily basis, get the best out of yourself by scheduling different tasks in line with your natural circadian rhythms, to ensure you work *with* the natural patterns of alertness. Maximise your brain energy by looking after your pre-frontal cortex with timed periods of focused work interspersed with breaks and the conscious inclusion of a variety of tasks throughout the day.

> **Key points**
> - Translate your plans into action using your calendar.
> - Allocate time to make sustained progress on large tasks and create momentum in your week.
> - Maintain your work-life balance – schedule work time and your social and leisure activities.
> - Work effectively by scheduling tasks for the best time of day.
> - Take a brain-based approach to maximising your focus and concentration.

Further resources

Brann, A. (2013) *Make Your Brain Work*. London: Kogan Page.
Foster, R. (2022) *Life Time: The New Science of the Body Clock, and How It Can Revolutionize Your Sleep and Health*. London: Penguin Life.
Hills, J. (2016) *Brain-Savvy Business*. London: Head, Heart & Brain.
Newport, C. (2016) *Deep Work: Rules for Focused Success in a Distracted World*. London: Piatkus.

Reference

Cirillo, F. (2018) *The Pomodoro Technique: The Life-Changing Time-Management System*. London: Virgin.

13 Communicate Persuasively

How to ... Get what you need from other people

> Leverage your power – Bases of power – Best influencing strategies – Persuade through empathy – What's in it for me?

Throughout the planning process, you considered the role that stakeholders will have in the success of your PhD. You identified supervisors, funders, research subjects, family and so on, and additional people who will be your resources, such as technicians, librarians and participants. In order to deliver your plan, you need to be able to communicate with all these stakeholders so that you can get what you need from them. For example:

- Persuading research subjects to participate and provide access to data
- Proposing a course of action to your supervisors
- Gaining access to technical or scientific equipment or secondary data sources
- Drawing on research funds or expenses.

This chapter provides techniques to help you to be a more persuasive communicator – in other words, more easily getting what you want from other people. We begin by encouraging you to consider the power you hold in situations in which you want to exert influence. Then we offer a range of strategies that you can use to increase your influence.

> **Transferable skills**
>
> These communication skills are important to your PhD and they are transferable – vital for all collaboration and teamworking and always towards the top of the person specification for any job. You should view these techniques as part of your toolbox of professional skills.

Leverage your personal power

Your 'power' is the range of resources you draw on to exert influence on a situation. By power, we don't mean 'power over', the power to dominate other people. This is a narrow understanding and, as a PhD student, it's unlikely that you have that kind of power over the people around you. Think of power as *'power to'*: the power to *do* something.

As a PhD student, the different degrees and types of power at your disposal will depend on the situation and the people involved. For example, you may have a different level of power dealing with your supervisors than with a potential funder or with fellow PhD students. You should assess each situation individually to make informed decisions about how best to exert your influence.

The seven bases of power

This framework (Lipkin, 2013) identifies seven different types of power – power bases – to assess your power in any situation:

- **Legitimate** – drawn from formal status
- **Reward** – to provide a benefit in exchange for compliance
- **Coercive** – to impose sanctions in punishment for non-compliance
- **Expert** – drawn from expert knowledge and skill
- **Connection** – drawn from valuable relationships
- **Information** – drawn from access to useful information
- **Referent** – drawn from appealing personal qualities.

 Transferable skills

We explain each power base in detail because they can help you to be more influential during your PhD and they will be a useful tool in your wider career.

Power bases can function as a valuable professional development framework. You can increase your effectiveness and impact by consciously taking steps to increase your most important power bases.

These power bases are described in detail in the following pages, but, as you familiarise yourself with them, try not to get distracted by thoughts of whether or not you would *use* them. That will come later. The first step is to assess what power resources you have at your disposal.

Seven power bases	
Legitimate power Power drawn from formal status	The authority inherent in your formal status. For example: • A line manager has the right to ask (and expect) subordinates to comply with managerial requests. • Your supervisors have the power to request behaviour from you, simply by virtue of being your supervisors. • As a PhD student, you have little 'legitimate' power associated with your status, although you do have the right to certain kinds of support and resources, such as office space, supervision or financial resources.
Reward power Power to provide a benefit in exchange for compliance	The ability to provide benefits to people in exchange for compliance. Reward power can be a result of legitimate power, because the latter may bring with it access to rewards. For example: • The principal investigator might be able to reward you with access to travel expenses or the use of equipment. Rewards can also be symbolic, based on goodwill or patronage, rather than resource based. For example: • Being offered the chance to accompany your supervisor on a conference trip might be a reward that boosts your prestige in your research community. Don't assume that you have little reward power because of your PhD status. You may not control a large budget or be able to offer a promotion, but your labour and time are a valuable resource. For example: • You could help a PhD colleague with data entry or lab work, or assist your supervisor with proofreading. You may also have reward power drawn from other types of power, such as expert or connection.

Coercive power Power to impose sanctions in punishment for non-compliance	This is the power to be able to impose penalties – it is the flip side of reward power. Coercive power can be used as a threat to impose demands and is often associated with legitimate power. For example: • Your primary supervisor could refuse to put your research proposal to the progression board or reject your request for funding to attend a conference. Like reward power, coercive power doesn't have to be resource based. It can be expressed through the removal of favours or by excluding people. For example: • As a PhD student, you could exclude a fellow PhD student from a study group or a social event, or you might no longer offer your time to advise them or help them out.
Expert power Power drawn from expert knowledge and skill	The power drawn from the possession of valued expertise or skill is particularly potent in the academic world. In fact, expert power is one of the main currencies of academic success and is reflected in professional titles such as Professor or Fellow, as much as the formal line management titles (such as Director) that convey status in other types of organisations. Expert power confers credibility, meaning that your requests, opinions or suggestions carry weight. For example: • If you have already successfully submitted your research proposal to the ethics committee, your advice or opinions about ethics in research carry more weight because they are founded on the evidence of your expertise. Access to the knowledge that underpins expert power can also be used as a form of reward power. For example: • Because you have already successfully submitted to the ethics committee, you could offer to help a fellow PhD student with their ethics proposal, in return for their help with a grant submission. At the start of your PhD, you may feel you have little expert power. That may be true, but remember that you might have expert power drawn from your experience outside your PhD. If you have experience in industry, in a policy area or from your Masters dissertation, you might have expert power that can be useful in the academic context, despite your limited research experience. That said, it is important to realise that expert power is often context specific. Expertise is only a power when it is valued or deemed to be relevant. For example: • Before your PhD, you ran a department of 30 people and managed a budget of several million pounds. However, in the context of your PhD, this counts for very little. • Alternatively, in some professional settings, high-level academic qualifications such as a doctorate may be less valued than years of on-the-job experience.
Connection power Power drawn from valuable relationships	Connection power is the power of your networks. It comes from the way in which your perceived status is enhanced through your connections with important people and your profile. For example: • Other PhDs value connection with you because your supervisor is world-renowned in their field. Connection power is a very important form of power in the academic research world because of the focus on cross-disciplinary and cross-institutional collaborations. It can also be used as a reward power. For example: • You gain influence by offering access to useful people or networks.

	As a PhD student, you may have limited connection power, especially to begin with. However, in the same way that your professional experience before your PhD might offer expert power, it might also provide connection power. For example: • You may have industry contacts that are valuable in applied research or knowledge transfer partnerships • Or you may have previously studied at a different university, and have connection power through your contacts there.
Information power Power drawn from access to useful information	Information power is based on the possession and potential provision of useful information. It functions both as: • A status enhancer – people's perception of your power (and influence) will be increased if you are known to be someone with access to valuable information • A form of reward power – providing access to the information. Information power could take the form of: access to data, understanding of procedures such as grant applications, awareness of opportunities such as job vacancies or funding streams. There may also be information power drawn from 'insider knowledge'. For example: • Knowing what international travel grants are available for study trips *and* knowing what type of study trips are more likely to attract funding. As a PhD student, your greatest source of information power is likely to be your data. Don't undervalue it! Data is the raw material of the publications that fuel successful academic careers, but is time consuming and sometimes expensive to acquire. Providing access to your data (to your supervisors and other research collaborators) can be a very powerful asset when it comes to exerting your influence and building a future academic career. For example: • 'The main reason why my very critical examiner was persuaded by my research was the value of the qualitative data acquired through my interviews. Without that information power, it is unlikely I would have passed with "minor amendments" which was explicitly stated during my Viva.'
Referent power Power drawn from appealing personal qualities	Referent power is based on your personal qualities, such as friendliness, trustworthiness and charisma. Referent power means that people are well-disposed to you, or it may also be based on a desire to be associated with you and gain 'reflected glory'. The quality of your relationships will be the source of your referent power. Referent power is based on the way you conduct yourself with other people and how you treat them. As a PhD student, referent power is something you have direct control over. Your relationships will be built through your actions and behaviours – it is your choice whether to invest in them. For example: • Are you friendly and respectful when you deal with administrative or technical staff in your department? • Do you give your time to help other PhD students? • Do you deliver what you promise to your supervisors? • Or do you gossip about members of your research team?

When you are facing a situation in which you want to have influence, make an assessment of the level of each power base you have available, based on your status in the situation and the other people involved. To illustrate, here is a typical situation from a PhD student.

Ellen is a second-year PhD student at a UK university. She has kept in touch with her Master's dissertation supervisor, who has invited Ellen to attend a prestigious conference in the USA, where she now works. The former supervisor is part of the organising committee for the conference and has invited Ellen to attend the conference as her guest. Ellen hasn't submitted a conference paper or poster.

The conference will showcase some important research that is highly relevant to Ellen's PhD and her research group. Additionally, her relationship with her former supervisor means that Ellen hopes to be introduced to many of the researchers presenting at the conference.

Ellen needs to ask permission from her PhD supervisors to travel to the conference and to use some of her PhD research budget to pay for the travel expenses. Generally, there is no funding for conference visits, unless the PhD student is presenting a poster or a paper.

What level of each power base does Ellen have in this situation?

Example power base assessment	
Legitimate power	Ellen has little or no legitimate power in relation to her supervisors. Her status *does* allow her to ask for certain kinds of support, but she doesn't have *the right* to draw down her research funding when she isn't presenting at the conference.
Reward power	Ellen has *some* reward power in this situation, based on the connection and information power she might acquire through her conference attendance.
Coercive power	Ellen has no obvious coercive power in this situation.
Expert power	Although Ellen will be developing expert power related to her research topic, it is probably only weak as this stage of her PhD. It is unlikely to be relevant when trying to influence her supervisors, who currently have more expert power than she does.
Connection power	This is Ellen's greatest power in this situation. Her relationship with her ex-supervisor offers access to contacts who would be valuable to her current supervisors, the department and the university.
Information power	It is possible that Ellen will acquire information power through her conference attendance, such as information about research activity in the field, who is doing what, who is funding what and so on.
Referent power	The referent power Ellen possesses depends on the status of her relationship with her supervisors and to what degree has she accrued their goodwill through her conduct and actions during her time as a PhD student. This might influence their willingness to give her what she wants.

Having made this assessment, Ellen will be better equipped to decide how to persuade her supervisors to let her attend the conference and use her research funding to finance her expenses. Now she *understands* her power base resources, she can decide how to *use* them through the influencing strategies described next.

> ✏ **Activity: Perform a power-base assessment**
>
> Using the template on page 168, make your own power base assessment when you find yourself in a situation where you want to be persuasive.

Template: Power base assessment

Describe a situation in which you want to be persuasive	
1 Make a note of the circumstances: who is involved, what is the issue, etc.	
2 What outcome are you hoping for?	
Consider the level of each power you have in this situation.	
Legitimate power	
Reward power	
Coercive power	
Expert power	
Connection power	
Information power	
Referent power	

© RDT&C

Influencing tactics

By assessing your personal power bases, you have identified the resources you can draw on in order to be persuasive. You also need to decide how to leverage your power for the best chance of getting what you want. Research has shown the following influencing tactics to be successful (Kipnis et al, 1980). Some, although not all, depend on the availability of your power bases.

To decide on the best influencing strategy (or combination of strategies), consider the following questions:

- Do you have the resources available to use this tactic, for example a power base, time?
- To what extent do you want to convince the other person that you are right, or are you content simply with compliance?
- What impact might this strategy have on your future relationship with the other person?

Influencing tactics	
Bargaining Offering incentives in exchange for compliance or support	Bargaining is offering enough of an incentive to comply with your request or suggestion, whether or not the other person agrees with you. Bargaining is based on an *explicit transactional exchange* – a quid pro quo. You need reward power to bargain successfully because you need something to offer in return for compliance and, for bargaining to work, the reward you offer has to be something the other person values. For example: • Ellen might offer to teach extra seminars in her supervisors' modules if they let her go to the conference.
Coalition Adding weight to your argument by recruiting others to support your cause	Coalition is finding people who agree with you and using their agreement to put pressure on those you want to influence. It can be powerful and positive if the coalition or consensus provides evidence that your proposal is a good one. However, it can also be seen as a 'ganging up' and can alienate the people you are trying to influence. Coalition-building takes time as it requires you to work out how to influence the potential members of your coalition. It can also be high risk. If you can't convince the members of your coalition to support you, your influencing strategy will fall at the first hurdle. For example: • Ellen might say that all the other research group members think it would be a good idea if she's allowed go to the conference.
Direct instruction Using positional authority to request or demand compliance	Direct instruction is a straightforward use of existing legitimate power. In theory, this is a simple, effective influencing strategy, assuming you are working within the parameters of your authority. However, there can be challenges: first, the people you are requiring compliance from have to respect your legitimate power; second, it demands clear, confident communication skills and comfort in wielding this kind of power. This approach may only create compliance, and not necessarily conviction, so it may have only limited value, depending on your aims. For example: • Ellen could explain that, as a PhD student, she is entitled to use her research funding to make conference visits (but her supervisors still have the legitimate power to say no).

Friendliness Creating agreement and support through the development of goodwill	Friendliness uses existing goodwill developed through positive relationships by drawing on referent power. The advantage of friendliness is that people are complying for positive reasons and, presumably, happily. The disadvantage is that it is a very soft power. It isn't an approach designed to overcome strong objections. For example: • Ellen might hope for agreement from her supervisors because she has been an exemplary PhD student and has cultivated good relationships with them.
Reasoning Presenting rational grounds for support or compliance	Reasoning is based on using rational evidence to support your position. It can be powerful because you are making an objectively sound case. However, it has limitations: first, you may not be able to find enough evidence to support your position; second, people may disagree with you despite your sound reasoning. Other issues may affect their decision, such as politics or personal interests. For example: • Ellen might provide clear evidence of all the benefits likely to accrue to her research group from her conference visit. However, her supervisors may still refuse her request if they decide it is unwise to let her go and set a precedent to other PhD students.
Sanction Removing (or threatening to remove) symbolic or material privileges	Sanction relies on coercive power to enforce your position, whether or not the other person agrees with you. Sanction should only ever be used as a last resort, in a situation in which you have decided it is imperative that get what you want, irrespective of the lasting damage it will cause. It relies on enforcement, rather than persuasion and is likely to create resentment and bad feeling. For example: • It is unlikely that Ellen has much coercive power. She might be able to threaten to withdraw an earlier reward, for example her offer to cover teaching, but it would be extremely unwise to use coercive power and risk alienating her supervisors as a result.
Upward referral Invoking the power of others to support your cause	Upward referral is a way of co-opting the power of other people to add weight to your position, for example explaining that a senior colleague agrees with your request. The downside is that it reinforces your lack of power because you are relying on other people's power resources. It can also be viewed as sneaky or bullying and can create resentment. For example: • Ellen could tell her supervisors that the research director for the school thinks that it will be valuable for her to represent the department at the conference.

> **Activity: Perform an influencing tactics assessment**
>
> Using the template on page 171, make an assessment of the best influencing tactic/s for your own situation.

Template: Influencing tactics assessment

Consider each of the influencing tactics in relation to the situation in which you want to have influence.			
Description of the situation:			
Influencing tactic	Necessary resources, e.g. power, time	Potential benefits of this tactic	Potential risks of this tactic
Bargaining			
Coalition			
Direct instruction			
Friendliness			
Reasoning			
Sanction			
Upward referral			

Action plan

Which influencing tactic/s will I use in this situation?

How will I use the influencing tactic/s?

Swap your shoes: influencing through empathy

There's one further important approach that will help you to be more persuasive.

Put yourself in the shoes of the person you want to persuade.

In other words, to get what *you* want, first understand what the *other person* might want. For rewards or reasoning, or even sanctions, to work, they must align with the needs and preferences of the other person. For example:

- You offer to do some teaching for a fellow PhD student in return for them proofreading your thesis. However, they love their teaching and hate proofreading (bargaining).
- You provide evidence for the cost-effectiveness of your field trip to your supervisors (reasoning). However, they're not concerned by cost – they just don't have the time to complete the necessary risk assessments.
- You threaten to remove your colleague's agenda item from the next staff/student committee meeting unless they support your proposal (sanction). However, their agenda item isn't all that important to them. What's more important is that they fundamentally disagree with your proposal and they have no desire to be associated with it.

All these influencing tactics will fail because you haven't understood what's important to the people you wanted to persuade. It's understandable why people overlook this information: when we are trying to get something we want, it's easy to focus on our needs, our circumstances, our position. However, you can be a far more effective influencer by identifying what the other person wants and trying, as far as possible, to align your influencing strategies to fulfill their needs. This is the concept of:

WIIFM: What's in it for me?

The question to ask yourself is: If you were in their shoes and listening to you, do you know 'What's in it for me'? In marketing, WIIFM is used to highlight the features of a product or service that the potential customer cares about most. When you're trying to influence someone to help you achieve your PhD goals, you're essentially doing the same – you're 'selling' your idea. Let's examine how considering her supervisors' WIIFMs might help Ellen to be more persuasive.

Ellen's conference visit is obviously in her *own* interests. She wants:

- A nice trip to the USA and a chance to be a tourist
- To meet lots of interesting academics and listen to stimulating papers
- To see her former supervisor again
- To make contacts who will help her pursue an academic career.

What's in it for her supervisors, though? How might it benefit them? We're not suggesting that the only reason you will ever get support for your requests is if people can see a direct benefit to them – Ellen's supervisors might be happy to agree to her request out of good will. Your request will be more persuasive, however, if you can demonstrate its benefits. In Ellen's case, she might point out to her supervisors that her conference visit would potentially:

- Create an international profile for the research group's work (an international reputation can be very valuable for academics)
- Make contact with potential collaborators in the same research field (cross-institutional, international collaborations can be very important when it comes to securing research funding)
- Be cost-effective, with minimal impact on research budgets (budgets are always tight).

This draws upon Ellen's reward and connection powers, but makes it explicit how the reward will *deliver benefits* to the person she is trying to persuade. This approach could be enhanced by combining it with a reasoning tactic. For example, Ellen could provide evidence of:

- The potential contacts she could make, listing the key academics also attending
- Detailed costs of her travel expenses and the saving made by not having to pay for her conference pass.

> **Activity: WIIFM**
>
> Think about a situation in which you want to exert influence. Rather than thinking about what *you* want, put yourself in the shoes of the person you want to persuade, and consider:
>
> 1 What is important to them in the current situation?
>
>
>
> 2 How could my request deliver benefits that they value (their WIIFMs)?
>
>

We return to the concept of WIIFM later as it is one of those tools that can help you with more than your influencing skills. You can use it to:

- Help you to communicate with and engage your stakeholders (Chapter 7)
- Inform convergence and scoping (Chapter 8)
- Help you connect with your own motivation whenever you are feeling discouraged (Chapter 15) – you still need to remind yourself of your own WIIFM sometimes!
- Become a better negotiator and have an easier time resolving conflicts (Chapter 19)

Summary

The execution of your PhD plan rests, to a great extent, upon your ability to persuade your stakeholders to provide you with what you need to conduct your research effectively. Communication skills are also a key transferable skill that will serve you well in your future career. Your ability to persuade others is influenced by the power you can draw on in a particular situation. Assess your power resources by understanding and identifying the different types of power that are available to you, before deciding how to leverage them. Assess the circumstances of the situation, your power, the status of the relationships, what you want to achieve and what you are willing to risk before deciding on your best 'influencing tactic'. Choose and communicate your influencing tactics more effectively by first putting yourself in the shoes of the people you are aiming to persuade and understanding their needs and priorities.

> **Key points**
> - Understand where your power lies – you have different kinds of power to draw on in different situations.
> - Use the best influencing tactic depending on the circumstances and your available power.
> - The key to persuading people is to look at the issue from their point of view.
> - Whatever it is you want, make sure you point out its benefits to others.

Further resources

Carnegie, D. (2006) *How to Win Friends and Influence People*. London: Vermillion.
Cuddy, A. (2015) *Presence: Bringing your Boldest Self to your Biggest Challenges*. New York: Back Bay Books.
Lipkin, N. (2013) *What Keeps Leaders Up at Night: Recognizing and Resolving Your Most Troubling Management Issues*. New York. Amacom.
Neffinger, J. and Kohut, M. (2013) *Compelling People*. London: Piatkus.

References

Kipnis, D., Schmidt, S.M. and Wilkinson, I. (1980) Intraorganizational influence Tactics: Explorations in Getting One's Way, *Journal of Applied Psychology*, **65**: 440–452.
Lipkin, N. (2013) *What Keeps Leaders Up at Night: Recognizing and Resolving Your Most Troubling Management Issues*. New York: Amacom.

Part 3

How to Keep Going

Thanks to Parts 1 and 2, you have put everything in place to ensure that your PhD research can operate smoothly, efficiently and with the minimum of stress: well-founded and viable plans, constructive supervision partnerships, productive working habits and all the support networks you need. You are well equipped to take care of your work and yourself and already look ahead to your future. What can go wrong?

Well, unfortunately, something always goes wrong! Part 3 provides you with the means to deal with problems effectively and with the minimum of delay and disruption to your PhD. We address the problems that many PhD students face during their research project, such as how to:

- Find the stamina to keep going over the long haul
- Deal with unexpected changes and setbacks
- Cope when work doesn't go according to plan
- Address conflicts with stakeholders.

This section provides a range of tools and techniques to enable you to deal with the psychological and practical dimensions of the problems you may face, and help you to stay on track.

- In Chapter 14, you learn how to develop the resilience to meet the substantial demands of a PhD head on, reduce your stress and sustain your efforts over the long term.
- Chapter 15 considers how to overcome the procrastination that plagues all PhD students at some point. It helps you to identify the specific reasons behind your procrastination so that you can choose the best techniques to get moving again.

- In Chapter 16, you draw on the planning methods from Part 2 to quickly assess your progress against your plans. You then learn new techniques to decide what, if anything, you should change in the light of your progress and incorporate the lessons into your ongoing plans.
- Chapter 17 ensures that you don't neglect the career-building opportunities of your PhD and instead position yourself as well as possible to make a smooth and successful transition into your career beyond your PhD.
- Being able to bounce back quickly and positively from setbacks has a substantial impact on motivation and momentum, and Chapter 18 introduces tools to move quickly to action and reduce the likelihood that you will be derailed by a setback.
- Chapter 19 provides conflict-resolution skills to deal promptly and confidently with conflicts that might otherwise compromise your interests. Powerful communication techniques equip you to expertly navigate the negotiations of conflict resolution and, if necessary, stand your ground.

As we said in Chapter 11, the only thing guaranteed to happen during your PhD is that something will change, and we can't prevent problems occurring. However, in Part 3, we provide the knowledge to help you minimise the negative impact of the problems that will inevitably crop up. As well as providing you with tools to deal with problems as they arise, knowing you have these tools at your disposal will boost your confidence that you can handle whatever your PhD throws at you.

14 Boost Your Resilience

How to ... Be ready for the demands of a PhD

> Stress is subjective – Reframe your perception of challenges – The ABC method – A happiness prescription – Sleep hygiene – Exercise – Mindfulness

In the UK, a PhD takes a minimum of three years. In other countries, it can be even longer. It's a long time to sustain effort and commitment to one project, especially such a challenging one. To see this through successfully, you will need resilience. Resilience is the degree to which you can handle stress and draw on your psychological, emotional and physiological resources to push through stressful demands and bounce back from setbacks and failures. In Chapter 18, we focus on bouncing back after setbacks, but first, in this chapter, we focus on what you can do to boost your resilience and build stamina. Our purpose here isn't to advise you how to avoid the challenges of your PhD, but to ensure you have the resilience to withstand pressure and make the most of your experience.

This chapter provides three practical techniques to boost your resilience:

- Learn to manage your thoughts in such a way that you minimise stress
- Increase the happiness-boosting activities in your life
- Use well-being measures to support your resilience.

Stress, the brain and the body

Before we explore resilience-building techniques, it is helpful to understand some of the ways in which stress plays out in your brain and body, and how this stress affects your resilience.

Stress per se isn't bad. Biologically speaking, stress is simply a mental or physical demand that requires effort. Stress can be a positive force. For example, in sport and exercise, we need to put our bodies under stress to develop stronger muscles and better cardiovascular performance. Without this 'stress', we would never improve. In the workplace, research has shown that, while too much stress can reduce performance and cause burnout, too little stress results in lethargy and poor performance.

To paraphrase Goldilocks, stress levels need to be 'just right' in order to stimulate performance and development. Unfortunately, there's no algorithm to calculate the level of stress that's 'just right' for you. It's highly individual. Your resilience will dictate the degree to which you can handle stress.

Our stress responses were established hundreds of thousands of years ago as our species evolved. The biological mechanics of stress responses have not changed, although the kinds of stress we experience have. Stress responses developed to ensure survival in physically dangerous situations, for example when under attack by predators.

When you experience stress, a cascade of hormonal activity is kicked off by the brain that in turn creates the biological readiness for fight or flight: your heart rate increases; additional blood sugar is made available; your breathing rate increases; your immune system is suppressed. Once the immediate threat has passed, these hormones dissipate, and you return to normal. Psychological threats, such as the fear of failure, humiliation or social rejection, trigger exactly the same hormonal responses, even though they present no physical danger.

Individual acute stressful events don't cause long-term problems. However, chronic low-grade stress or repeated acutely stressful events *do* affect our mental health and general well-being. Stress hormones put pressure on our body. There is evidence that chronic stress compromises immune-system functioning and, perhaps more significantly for a PhD student, has been associated with reduced cognitive function, such as the capacity to deal with complex problems and make decisions.

When facing a PhD, with its not inconsiderable demands, how can you reduce your stress levels? Well, you could avoid 'demands' – which probably means not signing up for a PhD in the first place – or avoiding as many challenging demands as possible. But that would mean avoiding the opportunities offered by a PhD and, ultimately, undermining the whole reason for undertaking a PhD. What you can do is take steps to increase your resilience so that demanding events cause you less stress. This approach will protect your performance and well-being during your PhD – and in your life in general.

> **✎ Activity: What causes you stress?**
>
> Write down some tasks or aspects of your PhD that cause you particular stress. (You will soon have ways to deal with these!)

Manage your thoughts to reduce stress

Most of the stresses experienced during your PhD aren't physical, but psychological. It's unlikely (although not impossible) that you will be in physical danger. What types of experiences you find psychologically stressful, and to what degree, depends on your individual perception of the experience. All of us, faced with a physical threat, would probably experience it as a stress that required a vigorous response – fight or flight – but we all have very different perceptions of what constitutes a stressful psychological demand. The thought of presenting at a conference might create huge stress for you and only moderate stress in others. You might sail through unexpected changes to your research that would cause great stress for other PhD students. The prospect of confronting your supervisor about a difference of opinion might cause you sleepless nights, but not everyone.

Here's the good news: Because your individual *perception* of an experience dictates how stressful it is for you, by *adjusting your perception* of the experience, you can reduce the stress it causes. This might sound too good to be true, but extensive research done in the field of cognitive behavioural therapy (CBT) demonstrates that, by consciously adjusting our *thoughts* about an experience, we can change the way it affects us. Don't worry – we won't insist you have 'therapy'. CBT has developed many simple techniques, that people use on a daily basis, to help you adjust your perception of events and change their impact, for example reducing anxiety, minimising phobias and reducing stress.

Central to this approach is the principle of reframing. This is the process of consciously substituting a more helpful thought about an experience in order to reduce the negative impact of the experience. Reframing can be done equally for:

- *Prospective* **experiences** – something you are facing in the future
- *Past* **experiences** – something that has already happened.

The ABC method

One widely used reframing technique is the ABC method (Ellis, 1991), which provides a simple, memorable framework to structure your perception of a potentially stressful experience in order to reframe it and reduce the stress it triggers.

A: the Activating event – the experience that is causing you stress
B: the Beliefs – the thoughts you have about the experience
C: the Consequence – the impact of the 'beliefs' on your feelings and actions.

Use the ABC method to identify your perception of the experience, and the impact of this perception, so that you can use the reframing technique to:

Change the beliefs

Which will in turn ...

Change the consequence.

You might be thinking, 'That's ridiculous! My beliefs about this stressful experience are based on fact and I can't just change the facts.' No, but we can change the *impact* of the facts. There will be unchangeable factual elements linked to an experience. For example, when presenting at a conference, you *will* have to stand up in front of an audience of academics and make your case. Those are facts. However, how you personally perceive those facts will be what makes the prospect of the presentation stressful or not. Do you:

- See it as an opportunity to impress people with your research?
- Assume the questions from the audience will be hostile?
- Expect that you will be too nervous to do yourself justice?

It is these *thoughts* (the beliefs) that dictate how stressful you find the experience (the activating event), rather than the simple facts. The beliefs, in turn, trigger different consequences. These consequences will be feelings: anxiety, fear, enthusiasm and so on. The consequences will also be behaviours and actions that have a material impact on you and your PhD, such as procrastination or avoidance of criticism.

Let's look at a range of different beliefs that different PhD students might have about an Activating event and consider what the impact might be in terms of consequences.

A **Activating event**	Example: Submission of research proposal to the ethics committee			
B **Beliefs**	What a waste of time this whole process is. Ethics aren't even relevant to my research.	If they reject this proposal, I am going to have to redesign my data collection and I'll fall way behind.	This is one of those formalities I just have to go through for my research. It's not that important.	This is a chance to put my research to a wider audience and make sure it's academically robust. It's a great opportunity.
C **Consequences**	Feelings of resentment or frustration; reluctance to get on with the work.	Feelings of anxiety and stress; struggling to get on with work, or overcompensating and spending too much time on the work.	Relaxed; little stress about the work, and perhaps too little effort.	Motivation and determination; putting effort into the submission for the best response; seeking advice to ensure good work.

Impact of beliefs on consequences

You can see how your beliefs will impact on your reaction to an activating event. There may be a range of reasons for your beliefs. They may be based on your personality – are you an optimist or pessimist, confident or suffer from imposter syndrome? They may be based on prior experiences – did you have a rough ride at a previous conference, or do you enjoy presenting to an audience? Don't judge the rationality of your beliefs, or try to work out where they come from. The point is to become *aware* of the thoughts you have so that you can *substitute more helpful thoughts*. You don't even need to *believe* these new thoughts! You are simply sending yourself different messages, and our brains are supremely sensitive to these messages. They will have a direct impact on your psychological and emotional state and, as a result, your stress levels. And reduced stress means greater resilience.

The ABC method can have even greater power if you use it repeatedly. We all know people who are a bit pessimistic and those who are more 'glass half full'. Many people tend to have either pessimistic or optimistic thinking habits, but we can develop new thinking habits in the same way that we can develop new behavioural habits. Remember, from Chapter 5, that habit formation requires commitment to repeating a process over time, until it becomes automatic. By repeating the ABC exercise, you start to default to the more constructive beliefs and become 'unconsciously competent' at influencing the degree of stress you experience during your PhD. Practise until positive thinking becomes automatic!

> **Activity: The ABC method**
>
> If you're facing a particularly stressful challenge, use the ABC method to help uncover and then reframe some of the stress-inducing beliefs associated with the challenge.
>
> 1. Using the template on page 181, complete sections A, B and C to clarify your default view of the situation and your reaction to it.
> 2. Then reframe your beliefs to create alternative, more constructive ones.
> 3. Note the consequences of the reframed beliefs in terms of how you feel and what you are ready do next.

Template: The ABC method

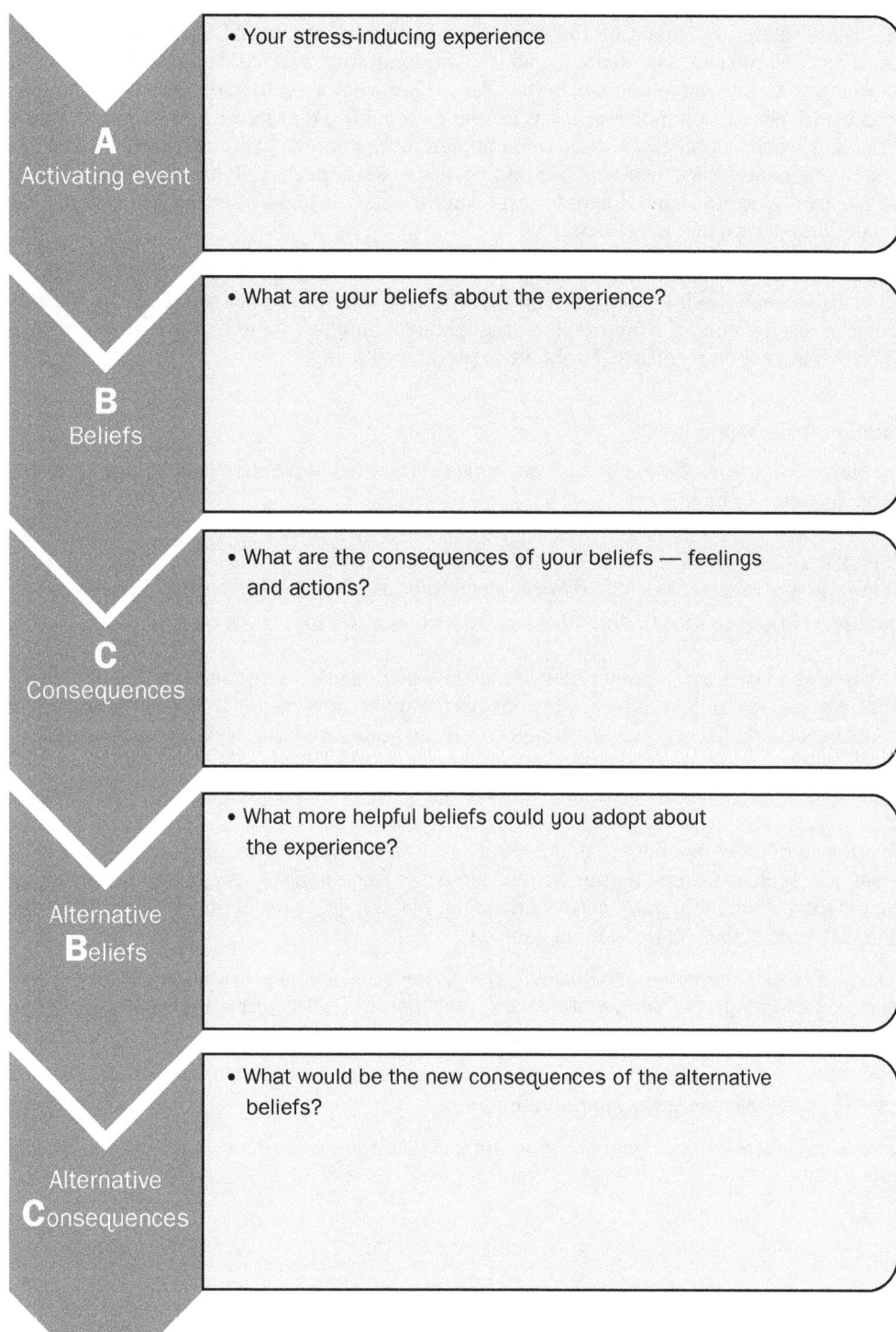

The power of happiness

The ABC method uses your thoughts to create a more positive emotional state, thereby reducing the experience of stress. You can also create a positive emotional state and build your resilience by engaging regularly in activities that make you feel better. Remember what we said about habits in Chapter 5? This is your chance to develop a happiness habit! Do things regularly that make you happy. In this context, we aren't taking a philosophical perspective on human fulfilment; we just mean doing things that make you feel good. Happiness has a measurable, relaxing, hormonal impact. Activities that you find rewarding, stimulate the 'feel good' hormone dopamine and can produce the class of hormones called endorphins, which are our body's own anti-depressants.

How can you decide what happiness boosting activities to build into your PhD? The things that we find pleasurable are probably self-evident, but pleasure is only part of the answer. Luckily, there has now been extensive research into the factors that create human happiness and that have been demonstrated to have positive impact on resilience, health and mental well-being.

A prescription for a happy life

Professor Martin Seligman (2004) and his colleagues in the field of positive psychology identified three different components of happiness:

- **Pleasure** – activities that make us feel good while doing them
- **Meaning** – the awareness that we are contributing to something bigger than ourselves
- **Engagement** – activities that involve us so deeply that we lose track of time.

Seligman's model doesn't try to prescribe what specifically brings every individual happiness – we are all very different. Instead, it provides a framework so you can consider how to create each of those components in ways that suit you, allowing you to write your own happiness 'prescription'.

Pleasure

Pleasure is the simplest component to understand as we all recognise what gives us pleasure. This could be quite passive, such as watching your favourite box set, listening to music or savouring a good meal, or it might involve something quite active – dancing, playing sport or having a laugh with friends. It's something that makes you feel good in the moment.

Some activities associated with your PhD will also (hopefully!) be pleasurable, for example reading an interesting paper, writing a perfectly crafted paragraph, getting the experimental results you were hoping for or discussing your data with fellow students.

> **Activity: Consider what brings you pleasure.**
>
> Write it down regardless of whether or not you currently do this regularly. (You will plan to make it happen shortly.)

Meaning

Meaning is the sense that we, and our activities, connect with something bigger and more important than ourselves individually. It might come from involvement with family, politics or religion. Meaning is linked to the experience of doing something that benefits the greater good and provides a sense of purpose. Meaning is often associated with the sense of being part of a community.

As a PhD student, it is likely that aspects of your research will be a powerful source of meaning in your life. During your research, step back now and then and consider the 'meaning' of the work: whether that's the feeling of belonging in a research group, or the benefit your research might provide to others.

> **✏ Activity: Consider what brings you meaning.**
>
> Write it here.

Engagement

Engagement refers to the state you reach when you're engrossed in an activity that requires concentration, effort and some degree of skill. When you're engaged, you forget yourself and lose track of time, but you aren't 'zoning out'. You might lose track of time watching a box set, or chatting with friends, but that's not 'engagement' because you aren't exercising an active skill. Engagement is often achieved through skilled sporting activity or some kind of skilled leisure activity such as a craft.

It's highly likely that you will find periods of engagement in your research work, for example becoming enthralled by the results from an experiment or delving deeply into an archive.

> **✏ Activity: Consider what brings you engagement.**
>
> Write it here.

While all three components of happiness will make a positive difference to you, meaning and engagement have been demonstrated to have the most impact on happiness levels. Pleasure alone doesn't shift the needle very much, but it can function as the 'icing on the cake' when the other two components are present.

Having a happy life isn't something that just happens. To build and maintain your resilience during your PhD, you need to make a conscious effort to build in activities that will keep you happy. This is particularly important for you as a PhD student because the demands of a PhD may cause you to neglect the things that make you happy. Ensure that you continue to invest time into happiness-creating activities, remembering that this is an investment in your well-being that will help you get through your PhD successfully. Happiness isn't a luxury during your PhD!

Don't forget that social connection is another way to create positive psychological states and reduce stress (see Chapter 6).

✏ Activity: The happiness planner

Complete the happiness planner template on page 185. Use the happiness-boosting activities you have already identified in this chapter as a starting point.

For each of the three components of happiness (pleasure, meaning, engagement):

1. Identify the happiness-boosting activities you already have in your life
2. Identify any additional activities you could do to fill the gaps in your happiness prescription
3. Schedule one happiness-boosting activity for every day of the next week.

Template: Happiness planner

Pleasure	Meaning	Engagement
1 What happiness boosting activities do I currently incorporate into my life?		
(e.g. play video games; go out with friends)	(e.g. volunteer at a charity; post about my research on social media)	(e.g. go running; bake cakes)

2 What else I can do to fill any gaps?
   - Remember to prioritise meaning and engagement over pleasure.
   - It might help to think about things you enjoy but have neglected during your PhD.

3 Choose happiness activities for the next week and schedule them into your calendar.

Happiness activity	Date/time

© RDT&C

Support your well-being

Finally, consider how you can boost your resilience by supporting your physical and mental well-being. The demands of your PhD mean that, if you can ensure you're in good shape, the greater your mental and physical stamina. The following suggestions have been shown through extensive research to contribute to increased well-being and resilience. They are also aspects that can easily be neglected as you prioritise the work of your PhD. Each of these dimensions could fill a chapter, and detailed recommendations are beyond the scope of this book, but we raise them as areas that, especially if you are neglecting them, are worth paying attention to during your PhD.

Good sleep

There is ample research demonstrating the importance of good sleep to optimal functioning. Studies have shown that quite modest sleep deficits can impair mental functioning, immune-system functioning and stress hardiness. A resilient, highly functioning brain (and body) is, in part, supported by good sleep patterns, which means getting a decent amount of sleep (seven to nine hours per night on average for adults) and good-quality sleep.

The UK Sleep Charity (2020) has a range of sleep hygiene recommendations: measures that help you improve the duration and the quality of your sleep, including:

- Go to bed and get up at similar times every day, to programme your body for sleep
- Ensure your bedroom is cool, quiet and dark; use earplugs or an eye mask if needed
- Take moderate exercise during the day to relieve stress and to tire you physically
- Cut down on stimulants such as caffeine in tea or coffee in the late afternoon and evening
- Avoid overindulging in food or alcohol close to bedtime
- Switch off screens an hour before bedtime
- If worry is preventing you falling asleep, consider making a list of the things you are concerned about before you go to bed, so you can put it aside and forget about it until the next day.

Activity: Improve your sleep

Use this checklist to list the measures you will use to improve your sleep. Try them for one week and observe the impact on your sleep.

Good-sleep measures	Mon	Tues	Wed	Thur	Fri	Sat	Sun
	☐	☐	☐	☐	☐	☐	☐
	☐	☐	☐	☐	☐	☐	☐
	☐	☐	☐	☐	☐	☐	☐
	☐	☐	☐	☐	☐	☐	☐
	☐	☐	☐	☐	☐	☐	☐

Impact on the quality of sleep

Exercise

It's very easy to neglect exercise when most of your working life might be spent sitting in front of a screen for long periods of time. Like sleep, the benefits of exercise are well evidenced in research, linked to positive outcomes such as general health, reduction of depression, and longevity, as well as resilience. The well-being benefits of exercise do not demand athletic prowess or marathon-levels of endurance. Some studies suggest that even 20 minutes of moderate exercise, three times a week, can have a positive impact in numerous ways, for example:

- The long-term health benefit of a stronger body, with improved muscle mass and increased cardio-vascular capacity
- The biochemical results of moderate to vigorous exercise on the brain, through the production of endorphins – the body's own anti-depressants
- The release of tensions and pent-up energy
- Outdoor exercise in sunlight, which increases vitamin D production (particularly important for those of us in northern climes) – important for stress hardiness and immune-system functioning.

Even if you're not a natural 'gym bunny', create simple, sustainable exercise habits, such as taking a short, brisk walk every lunchtime, that you can sustain throughout your PhD. This is especially important when pressures of work may lead you to neglect other important well-being activities. You can even try multitasking ways to combine exercise *with* work as an efficient way of integrating exercise into your day:

- Use a standing desk rather than sitting down.
- If you need to travel between university locations, walk, bike (or run) rather than using the car.
- Fraser used to have 'walking meetings' around campus with his supervisors and found that vigorous pacing released his thoughts, as well as providing much-needed exercise.
- Rosie used to walk briskly around her nearby park during writing up her PhD, whenever she felt stuck.

✎ Activity: Increase your exercise

Add some exercise measures to the checklist that you can integrate into your working week. Try them for one week and review the impact on your well-being.

Exercise	Mon	Tues	Wed	Thur	Fri	Sat	Sun
	☐	☐	☐	☐	☐	☐	☐
	☐	☐	☐	☐	☐	☐	☐
	☐	☐	☐	☐	☐	☐	☐
	☐	☐	☐	☐	☐	☐	☐
	☐	☐	☐	☐	☐	☐	☐

Impact of exercise on well-being

Mindfulness and meditation

Regular meditation (sometimes called mindfulness) has been demonstrated through many studies to reduce stress and increase resilience. Whether you go for full-blown transcendental meditation or opt for a ten-minute daily mindfulness exercise, it's a powerful way of reducing your stress levels. Research indicates that meditation produces changes in the areas of the brain associated with reduced anxiety and a lowered stress reaction. Studies have even shown that regular meditation can enhance cognitive function, increasing your ability to pay attention and focus – something that might just be useful for a PhD student!

Although mindfulness and meditation aren't a magic bullet, for a relatively small investment of time, they can have a very positive impact. The more regularly you do it, the greater the accumulated benefits. There are plenty of free resources available online or via apps to help you develop a mindfulness practice. We recommend that you try a few in order to see which suit you best. The key thing here is to do this *regularly* – ideally daily.

> 'I was quite cynical about mindfulness. It all sounded a bit ... well, not really my sort of thing. But after my mental health suffered – in part due to the stress of doing a PhD – I started using a popular app to do a short meditation exercise each day. Wow – it changed my life! I still encounter stressful situations and suffer from anxiety, but the intensity of the sensation is reduced massively simply by applying some very straightforward guidance.'

Activity: Mindfulness

You can use this simple ten-minute mindfulness exercise to get you started.

1. Find a quiet, private place to sit comfortably, where you won't be interrupted.
2. Close your eyes and breathe slowly and deeply in and out five times.
3. Continue breathing deeply and, in your mind, count down from ten to one.
4. Allow your breathing to find its natural rhythm.

   Your breathing should be quite relaxed and slow by now. It can help to focus on the out-breath, and let the in-breath happen naturally.

5. Stay in that relaxed state for approximately five to ten minutes.

   You won't be able to monitor the time because it would interrupt the process. You could set a timer, but make sure the buzzer is gentle, so it doesn't shock you out of your relaxed state. You could instead use a relaxing track of music that plays for the appropriate length of time.

6. During this time, simply notice any thoughts that enter your mind.

   Don't get involved in the thoughts or try to stop them. Instead, observe them in a detached fashion as they pass through your mind. Think of them as clouds passing across the sky of your mind.

7. When you are ready to end the exercise, count back up from one to ten, then open your eyes.

You can also use this technique as an emergency measure if you suffer an acute attack of anxiety.

✏ Activity: Commit to daily mindfulness

Choose a mindfulness activity to do daily for one week, then observe the impact on your well-being.

Mindfulness activity	Mon	Tues	Wed	Thur	Fri	Sat	Sun
	☐	☐	☐	☐	☐	☐	☐
What was the impact?							

Important: The suggestions in this chapter are designed to help you reduce stress and increase your resilience. However, if you are suffering from serious mental health problems, for whatever reason, they are not a substitute for proper professional help.

Please contact your university's support services if you think you might benefit from professional intervention. A PhD can be hard, and you don't have to face it alone if you are struggling to cope.

Summary

Your resilience levels provide you with the stamina to see your PhD through to the end, whatever the challenges you face. Taking steps to boost your resilience makes it easier to deal with the stress of your PhD and take advantage of the opportunities it provides. The degree of stress you experience is affected by the way you perceive the challenges you meet. By changing your perception, using the cognitive behavioural technique of 'reframing', you can reduce the stress you experience.

Your happiness will contribute to your resilience, as positive emotions stimulate stress-reduction hormones. Invest in your happiness during your PhD as a resilience measure. Incorporate regular activities that bring you pleasure, meaning and engagement in your life. Physical and psychological well-being boosts resilience. Measures such as good sleep, regular exercise and mindfulness activities will contribute to your well-being and give you the personal resources to meet the demands of a PhD. See all of these measures as valuable investment in your success.

Key points

- Resilience is vital to meet the demands of a PhD – and you can increase your resilience.
- Stress itself is not necessarily a bad thing – it stimulates us to grow and develop.
- Increase your resilience by changing the way you think about stressful demands.
- Happiness boosts your resilience – do things that give you pleasure, meaning and engagement.
- Simple measures to protect your physical and mental well-being will maintain your resilience during your PhD.

Further resources

Gillihan, S.J. (2020) *Cognitive Behavioural Therapy Made Simple: 10 Strategies for Managing Anxiety, Depression, Anger, Panic and Worry*. London: Sheldon Press.

Hills, J. (2016) *Brain-Savvy Business*. London: Head, Heart & Brain.

Miller, C.A. and Frisch, M.B. (2021) *Creating Your Best Life*. New York: Sterling.

Reivich, K. and Shatte, A. (2003) *The Resilience Factor: 7 Keys to Finding Your Inner Strength and Overcoming Life's Hurdles*. New York: Broadway Books.

Seligman, M. (2017) *Authentic Happiness: Using the New Positive Psychology to Realise Your Potential for Lasting Fulfilment*. London: Nicholas Brealey.

Williams, M. and Penman, M. (2011) *Mindfulness: Finding Peace in a Frantic World*. London: Piatkus.

References

Ellis, A. (1991) The revised ABCs of rational-emotive therapy (RET), *Journal of Rational-Emotive & Cognitive-Behavior Therapy*, **9**(3): 139–172.

Seligman, M. (2004) *The New Era of Positive Psychology*. Available at: ed.ted.com/lessons/martin-seligman-on-positive-psychology [accessed 23 January 2023].

The Sleep Charity (2020) *Sleep Hygiene*. Available at: thesleepcharity.org.uk/information-support/adults/sleep-hygiene/ [accessed 23 January 2023].

15 Overcome Procrastination

How to ... Get going again if you get stuck

> Six drivers of procrastination – What if vs What is – Disputation – Affirmation – Get organised – Do something! – Iterative process – Reward yourself – WIIFM revisited – Breaking bad habits

However diligently you plan and conscientiously you time-block, procrastination can still create an obstacle to getting on with your work. You might know exactly what you're supposed to be doing on any given day and still find yourself avoiding it. Many PhD students struggle with problems of procrastination. It's not surprising: the scale, duration and difficulty of a PhD can trigger procrastination in the most committed people. This chapter helps you to identify the drivers behind your procrastination and provides practical techniques to address those specific causes.

Procrastination is literally the Latin for putting a task off until tomorrow:

pro = towards
crastinus = tomorrow

We generally procrastinate about something to avoid (or at least delay) the *discomfort* of engaging with the task. Unfortunately, the longer you avoid the task and the worse things get, the more discomfort you will face, which can create a vicious circle of procrastination. Frequent procrastination can also be toxic for your self-esteem by undermining your confidence in your ability to stay on top of work. The truth is that procrastination will make it harder to excel regardless of your abilities.

The only cure for procrastination is to do the task.

That's easier said than done, however. To help avoid procrastination, or at least overcome it once it starts, consider what is driving it. This will be different for everybody and can also change for the same person in different situations. Once you understand what's driving your procrastination, it's easier to find appropriate solutions, rather than wasting time using the wrong techniques.

In this chapter, we describe six common drivers of procrastination and provide techniques to address each one, so that you can identify your drivers and choose the techniques best suited to solving your particular problems.

- Fear and anxiety
- Disorganisation
- Overwhelm
- Perfectionism
- Lack of motivation
- Habit.

192 Part 3 – How to Keep Going

To make best use of the information in this chapter:

1 Consider a task you are procrastinating about right now.
2 Identify the key drivers that are behind your procrastination.
3 Try out some of the suggested techniques to overcome the drivers of your procrastination.

Although you may feel that you are dealing with all six drivers at once, you will find it more useful if you can identify the most significant drivers and target them in your response.

✏ Activity

Note a task you are currently procrastinating about.

Fear and anxiety

Important: Please be aware that the advice in this chapter is not designed to address severe, anxiety-related, mental-health problems such as panic attacks. If you suspect you may be suffering from an anxiety disorder, while some of the tips here may help you handle your anxiety, please consult a suitably qualified mental-health professional. Your university is able to help and will have dedicated expert resources for student health and well-being.

What you may notice

- **Psychological signs:** Dwelling on negative thoughts: how badly things might turn out; imagining hostile or critical reactions; catastrophising – imagining disastrous and highly unlikely events; going over things that have gone badly in the past.
- **Emotional signs:** Feeling fearful, weepy or helpless; generally low in mood.
- **Physical signs:** Feeling jittery, tense; in severe situations, trembling or breathlessness and difficulty sleeping.

What's going on?

Fear and anxiety can be the primary drivers of your procrastination. They can also be the *result* of procrastination driven by other factors. The more you delay or avoid a task, the more anxious you are likely to feel about it. If your anxiety is a symptom of other causes of procrastination, you will be better served addressing the original drivers. Your anxiety will lessen once you make progress on the task.

For many people, however, the fear or anxiety itself can drive the procrastination. You are avoiding a specific task because you are anxious about it. By avoiding the task, you are trying to avoid experiencing the anxiety.

What to do about it

If your anxiety has increased to the extent that you are feeling physical effects, such as jitteriness, racing heartbeat, accelerated breathing, the first thing to do is to calm yourself. These are the signs of the fight-or-flight state, caused by a belief that you are under threat. Your nervous system has gone on high alert.

Address the physical symptoms

> ➡ **Action: Breathe**
>
> Deep, slow breathing is the quickest way to calm your nervous system. It slows the heart rate.

Breathing through your nose is also understood to be particularly calming as it stimulates the release of nitric oxide, which relaxes the blood vessels and allows oxygenated blood to circulate freely (which will also help with your brain function, as we will explore further in Chapter 18).

> ➡ **Action: Move**
>
> Take a brisk walk to calm your anxiety.

Moderate physical activity will help the stress hormones to dissipate and discharge some of the restless energy you might be feeling as a result of your anxiety. Movement also fulfills the 'flight' demand that your brain is signalling and calms the anxiety response that way.

Address the psychological causes

If your anxiety is manifesting itself through negative thoughts rather than physical symptoms, you need to deal with the thoughts. Remember the concepts of CBT introduced in Chapter 14: your thoughts (beliefs) about the task (the activating event) may be driving the procrastination (consequence). Try to become fully conscious of these thoughts – you're probably not even aware of them most of the time. Reflect for a moment and identify the thoughts circulating in your head when you turn towards the task. Don't try to edit or reject the thoughts, and don't worry if they seem unrealistic or even irrational! Whether you're thinking, 'The last time my supervisor read my work, they were heavily critical,' or, 'My supervisor hates me!', simply notice these thoughts. These are what is driving your anxiety. Once you're aware of the thoughts, you can take steps to counter them.

> Try using the mindfulness activity from Chapter 14, page 188.

If your anxiety is based on fear that you don't have the skills to complete the task successfully, you can take practical steps to deal with the lack of skill.

> ➡ **Action: Objectively reflect where you are.**
>
> First, remember your conscious competence cycle (Chapter 1, page 8). You're probably in the 'conscious incompetence' phase. It's quite normal to feel anxiety. In fact, it's a good sign. It shows that you are learning new skills.

194   Part 3 – How to Keep Going

> ➡ **Action: Take action if you can.**
>
> Second, if you can, do something to *gain the competence* that you fear you lack. Ask for advice, attend a course, practise and so on. Taking action is itself an antidote to anxiety.

> ➡ **Action: 'Reframe' the anxiety-inducing thoughts.**
>
> Use the ABC method from Chapter 14 (page 179). You can also use CBT techniques (Chapter 14) to address the anxiety-inducing thoughts directly.

The following are some other quick and simple CBT techniques you can use to reduce anxiety. All of these are based on the principle that, by changing your thoughts, you can change your psychological and emotional state.

The 'What is' technique

Anxiety-inducing thoughts often focus on 'What ifs?', such as:

- What if my work isn't good enough?
- What if I'm not intelligent enough to do a PhD?
- What if my supervisor thinks my work is lousy?
- What if all my experiments go wrong?
- What if I run out of time to do my work?

This can add up to a continual narrative of potential failures. To counter the 'What if' thoughts, focus instead on 'What is' by bringing your attention back to the *facts* of your present situation rather than imagining all the possible future negative outcomes. For example:

What if my supervisor thinks my work is lousy?

What is: I am working on my draft literature review.

What if all my experiments go wrong?

What is: I am taking care in the design of my experiments.

What if I run out of time to do my work?

What is: I am making progress on my work.

> ✏️ **Activity: What if vs What is**
>
> Write down some of the 'What if' thoughts that are driving your fear and anxiety and substitute some 'What is' thoughts.
>
> | What if ...? | What is ... |
> |---|---|
> | | |

What if ...?	What is ...

The disputation technique

To use the disputation technique, remind yourself of *evidence* that counteracts the fearful thoughts. For example:

- I have been accepted on a PhD programme, which means I have the potential to complete my PhD.
- My supervisor was critical of my work before and I used the criticism to improve my work to a higher standard.

✏ Activity: Disputation	
Note the evidence that disputes your fearful thoughts.	
Fearful thought	
Disputation	

The affirmation technique

The affirmation technique might sound peculiar, but it is surprisingly powerful, with research evidence for its efficacy. In this technique, you identify affirmations – affirmative statements – as alternatives to negative thoughts. These affirmations are expressed in the present tense and in the positive (the state you want, not the state you wish to avoid). For example:

Negative thought: My supervisor will hate my work and be really critical.

Affirmation: *My supervisor provides me with useful feedback that I use to improve my work.*

Negative thought: I will never be able to make sense of my data.

Affirmation: *I find clear conclusions when I interrogate my data.*

Negative thought: No one will agree to participate in my research.

Affirmation: *People are keen to participate in my research.*

Here, you don't need to seek factual evidence to counteract your anxiety-inducing thoughts, as you do in the disputation technique. You are simply making a statement that describes a positive state of affairs. You then *repeat* the statement – whether saying it out loud (although probably not in front of anyone!) or writing it out a few times. Repeat them whenever you feel your anxiety increasing.

Activity: Affirmation

Note down some of the negative thoughts that are causing fear and anxiety. Then write affirmations to counteract them.

Negative thought	Affirmation

Activity: Identify your preferred techniques

If fear and anxiety are driving your procrastination, consider which technique/s to use to overcome that. Note them here and check them off when you have used them successfully.

Techniques I will use to overcome my fear and anxiety	
	☐
	☐
	☐
	☐
	☐
	☐

Disorganisation

What you may notice

- You are unsure of what you should be doing next.
- You are ready to get on with a task but you give up after (or at the thought of) a lengthy search for the materials, equipment or information needed to begin.

What's going on?

Disorganisation can take two forms:

- **Temporal** – a problem of knowing what to do when or next
- **Material** – a problem in organising the 'stuff' you need to do your work, whether equipment, digital or paper documents, information and so on.

What to do about it

There's no 'quick fix' for this problem. Disorganisation demands a programme of organisation. It is another example of 'sharpening your saw'. If you have identified 'temporal' disorganisation as one of your drivers of procrastination, this is a planning problem, and everything you need to know to solve it is contained in this book!

If you're struggling with 'material' disorganisation, you need to implement organisational structure, whether that's information-management systems, digital folders and filing systems, or an old-fashioned filing cabinet.

The degree of organising that each individual needs is quite personal. We know that, for some people, piles of papers on a desk, or an unsorted email inbox might be a problem, while others have a clear sense of where everything is, despite it looking like chaos. The test of your self-organisation is whether you waste time and ultimately lose momentum because you can't find things. If that's the case, you need to organise yourself.

The systems you need are specific to you, and probably also particular to your discipline or methodology. There is no 'one size fits all' answer, and our main recommendation is to seek help!

> ➡ **Action: Enrol on a training course.**
>
> Your university is likely to have a range of courses available to help you with information management during your PhD.

> ➡ **Action: Speak to others.**
>
> Find out how other PhD students organise themselves and their research. If you have a friend or colleague who is particularly organised, see if they can help you set up some simple systems (for example, a partner, who understands nothing of your PhD, may be able to help you get organised because they are someone who finds it easy to be systematic).

> ➡ **Action: Read.**
>
> There is a myriad of academic and non-academic books and resources on 'getting organised'. (Some of our favourites are listed at the end of this chapter.)

✎ Activity: Get organised

If disorganisation is driving your procrastination, decide what steps to take to overcome it. Note them here and check them off when you have used them successfully.

Action I will take to overcome my disorganisation	
	☐
	☐
	☐
	☐
	☐
	☐

Overwhelm

What you may notice

- Not knowing where to start
- Not being able to see the wood for the trees
- Feeling helpless or defeated by the task ahead
- Feeling that your PhD is such a big task that it's pointless even starting.

What's behind it

Feelings of being overwhelmed are quite common when undertaking a PhD. It is a big thing, after all! This drives procrastination because the thought of all the work you need to do can be paralysing. Some of the planning tools explained in Part 2 can be really helpful in preventing overwhelm, especially the work breakdown structure (Chapter 9), because it divides the enormous whole into specific tasks.

What to do about it

As well as implementing all your planning techniques, there really is only one short-term solution to procrastination that is driven by overwhelm:

> ➔ **Action: Do *something*!**
>
> Choose one thing and do it. It doesn't have to be the 'right' thing. Just do something, and ideally, something small to start with – the aim here is to get you moving.

Often just doing *something* breaks the impasse and you will be off and running, or you may find you do one small thing and then you have to grit your teeth and do another small thing. In either case, you feel better for having made some progress. It's like the famous proverb, attributed to the philosopher Lao Tzu:

> A journey of a thousand miles begins with a single step.

> ✎ **Activity: Take steps**
>
> If overwhelm is driving your procrastination, consider what small things to do and which planning techniques to use to overcome it. Note them here and check them off when you have used them successfully.
>
> | Small things I will do to overcome overwhelm | |
> |---|---|
> | | ☐ |
> | | ☐ |
> | | ☐ |
> | | ☐ |
> | **Planning techniques I will use to reduce overwhelm** | |
> | | ☐ |
> | | ☐ |
> | | ☐ |
> | | ☐ |

Perfectionism

What you may notice
- Making a negative assessment of the gap between your aspiration and the reality of your skill or work
- Repeatedly judging your work negatively
- Feelings of hopelessness, resulting from the above.

What's going on?
If you already have a tendency towards perfectionism – which might manifest itself in never being satisfied with your work or being highly self-critical – a PhD is likely to reinforce this character trait. As we explored in Chapter 1, coming up against the limits of your competence is a necessary part of the learning process of a PhD and you should recognise it as a positive step in your development as a researcher.

What to do about it
First, don't waste time telling yourself not to be perfectionist! The aim is to circumvent perfectionism as a cause of procrastination, not to embark on a major personality transformation. It is far better to harness your perfectionism in the service of a more constructive version of excellence.

> ➡ **Action: Remind yourself that a PhD is an 'iterative process'.**
>
> *Everything* you do in your PhD is subject to a cycle of review, criticism and improvement. Think about it:

You submit your work to your supervisors

They tell you all the things that are wrong with it so you can go away and do it better

You submit a paper to a journal

The editors tell you all the ways it could be improved, even if they accept it

At the very end of the PhD process, you submit your thesis – 100,000 words you've sweated over

You then have a Viva exam, in which experienced academics tell you all the ways they think your thesis should be improved

In other words, no one is expected to complete everything perfectly first time around. The sooner you can understand and accept this, the lesser chance that your perfectionism will sabotage your progress

> **➡ Action: Acquaint yourself with the expected standards at each stage of your PhD.**
>
> It can be hard to quantify these standards, so don't expect any absolutes, but inform yourself by asking your supervisors about your progress against their expectations.

> **➡ Action: Use time-based boundaries to force you to move forward.**
>
> Decide how long you will spend on a task, and don't allow yourself to go over the allocated period, however much you want to add a few more finishing touches.

Review the time-boxing technique in Chapter 12, page 155.

> 💬 'One of the most useful illustrations of the iterative process that I had during my PhD was at a PhD conference workshop. We were shown an article that had been submitted to a prestigious journal. We were asked whether we thought it was of publishable quality. Everyone said, "No, definitely not!"
>
> It was then explained that the paper had indeed been published, but not in the form of the initial submission – which we had read. It was only after numerous reviews and rewrites, i.e. an *iterative* process, that it had reached publication standard.'

> **✏ Activity: Let go of perfect**
>
> If perfectionism is driving your procrastination, decide how you will overcome it. List your actions here and check them off when you have used them successfully.
>
> | Measures I will take to counteract my perfectionism | |
> |---|---|
> | | ☐ |
> | | ☐ |
> | | ☐ |
> | | ☐ |
> | | ☐ |
> | | ☐ |

Lack of motivation

What you may notice

- Lethargy and lack of momentum
- Boredom
- Feelings of pointlessness
- Resistance or resentment.

What's going on?

Every PhD student will suffer from a lack of motivation at some point; for most students, numerous times. It's inevitable that a project that is long and difficult will be characterised by ups and downs. So don't be surprised, and don't panic, if you struggle with motivation at times.

It's helpful to differentiate between a lack of motivation that is simply down to boredom and more deep-rooted problems of motivation that might result from losing track of the purpose of your PhD.

What to do about it

If your procrastination is because a task is just plain *boring or unpleasant*:

> ➡ **Action: Add some variety.**
>
> This is a version of the advice from Chapter 12.

If something is dull or routine, break it down into short, timed periods, and cycle between the boring task and more interesting ones. For example, consider mixing up 'thinking' tasks with 'admin' tasks.

> ➡ **Action: Reward yourself.**
>
> Give yourself a reward in return for doing the dull task.

This can be the reward of different, more interesting work, or something non-work related that you will enjoy – coffee with a friend, time on social media, a bar of chocolate – whatever makes you feel good. Do remember though that the reward should be commensurate with the effort. Five minutes updating your bibliography probably shouldn't be rewarded by taking the rest of the day off and heading to the shops!

> ➡ **Action: Get real!**
>
> A PhD, just like any work, will include dull, routine tasks that nevertheless are vital to the success of the overall project. Sadly, boredom isn't a reason to not get on with your work. Give yourself a mental push and suck it up!

If your procrastination is a result of a *deeper lack of motivation*:

> ➡ **Action: Rediscover your purpose.**
>
> Go back to your 'personal goals' (Chapter 2).

Remind yourself what you are aiming to achieve from your PhD work. If necessary, review and update these aims, to reflect what's important to you at this stage.

> ➡ **Action: Identify your 'WIIFM's.**
>
> We covered 'What's in it for me?' in Chapter 13, when considering how best to persuade other people.

Here, look at *your* WIIFMs. How will *you* benefit from getting on with your work and stopping procrastinating? Look for *benefits that you genuinely value*, not what you think you are *supposed* to want. Wanting to complete your PhD so you can finally show your dad you're 'cleverer' than your older sister is ok if it's really true for you. One PhD student admitted that a reason they wanted a PhD was so they could use the prefix Dr – not for intellectual kudos, but because they had heard it would get them flight upgrades! Of course, there will be more worthy, professional goals as well. Sometimes the WIIFM is short term: 'If I get this done today, I can really enjoy my weekend away', or 'I can take a half day tomorrow.' Sometimes it will be about changing your future: 'It's my first step towards a Nobel Prize!' Towards the end of your PhD, your most powerful WIIFM is likely to be that it will be finished!

✎ Activity: What are your WIIFMs?

Think of some WIIFMs that will motivate you to persevere with your work.

✎ Activity: Find your motivation

If lack of motivation is driving your procrastination, choose techniques to use to overcome that. Note them here and check them off when you have used them successfully.

Techniques I will use to overcome my lack of motivation	
	☐
	☐
	☐
	☐
	☐
	☐

Habit

What you may notice
- Not consciously choosing to avoid a task, but instead 'finding yourself' doing other things
- Procrastinating about tasks you feel all right about.

What's going on?
If you're a chronic procrastinator – whatever the initial reasons for your procrastination – you may have established it as a habit over many years. This means that your default, inbuilt response to facing tasks is to do something else. Often, people need the pressure of a deadline or an insistent demand from

someone else to break through the procrastination habit. Over time, this sets up another habit, of relying on the pressure of a deadline or external demand before you can get on with things, which reinforces procrastination.

What to do about it

The good news is that, if habit is driving your procrastination, you don't need to do anything other than create new, better habits. We've already discussed habit formation (Chapter 5): repeated, sustained effort is the key, until the new habit becomes automatic and effortless. There are some extra steps to take when overcoming bad habits rather than just establishing new, good habits:

1. *Identify the cues* that create the habitual response, in this case work avoidance and procrastination. If you tend to procrastinate about specific types of task, such as writing or making phone calls, you may notice that this is the trigger for the procrastination.
2. Once you're aware of the cue, you need to consciously *choose a different response* to the cue. This will be hard work at first because you are resisting an automatic response and it will take some will-power and conscious effort, but don't give up – it will get easier.
3. Don't focus on resisting the bad habit. Instead, consciously *substitute a new (positive) habit* for the bad habit of procrastination.
4. *Repeat the new habit* whenever you experience the 'cue' until it is associated with the original cue and becomes automatic.

New habits (especially new habits that break old habits) take time and effort to establish at first and you will inevitably relapse along the way – as anyone who has given up smoking, drinking or chocolate knows all too well! The key is persistence.

✎ Activity: Commit to breaking the procrastination habit

If habit is driving your procrastination, consider which cue(s) trigger your procrastination and what new 'habit' you can link to these cues. Write them here and check them off when the new habits have been established.

Cue(s) that trigger your procrastination:	What new 'habit' you will link to the cue:	
		☐
		☐
		☐
		☐
		☐
		☐

Having reflected on each of the six drivers of procrastination, identified which ones are causing your procrastination and determined actions you can take to mitigate them, you're in a great position to continue your PhD with confidence. Even if you get 'bitten' by procrastination again, you can always come back to this chapter at any point during your research and use the tools to get back on track.

> **Eat your frog!**
>
> If you don't want to spend time considering what lies behind your procrastination and simply want to bust through it, this is a brilliant technique devised by time-management specialist Brian Tracy (2013).
>
> Your 'frog' is the task on your to-do list that you like the least. As such, it is the task you are most likely to procrastinate about. Instead, *start your day* by eating your frog – doing that task first.
>
> Not only does this mean that your frog has been eaten, but the rest of your day will be more pleasant and productive as a result of not having the dreaded task hanging over you. You'll also feel pretty pleased with yourself for having faced your frog.
>
> Your 'frog' should be manageable in a relatively short period of time. The idea is to face it, get it done and have the rest of the day free to get on with other work. If your frog is large, for example writing a chapter, or reviewing all your data, identify a manageable chunk of it, such as writing 500 words or working on it for 15 minutes. That's your frog for the day.

> **✎ Activity: Eat your frog**
>
> Try eating your frog every day for a week. Every morning, note that day's frog. Tick 'done' once you have eaten your frog that day.

Frog		Done
Mon		☐
Tues		☐
Wed		☐
Thurs		☐
Fri		☐

Summary

Procrastination can befall all PhD students regardless of whether or not they already have a tendency towards procrastination. It is a way of avoiding discomfort, and the challenge and uncertainties of a PhD can mean there is plenty of discomfort to avoid. Procrastination can reinforce itself because anxiety is only increased by the knowledge that you are putting off a task and falling behind. Procrastination can also become a habit, so it is important to nip it in the bud before it becomes established, or address it as soon as you notice it. Taking the time to reflect and identify what underpins your procrastination, and choosing techniques to directly address the relevant drivers, means that you will be more successful in overcoming your procrastination. Don't beat yourself up about procrastination. Accept it as an inevitable part of a PhD, but take steps to overcome it as soon as possible.

> **Key points**
>
> - Procrastination is a common experience for every PhD student because research is challenging and often uncertain.
> - Procrastination can have different causes. Identify your causes before you try to solve it.
> - Understand the power of your mind and changing your thoughts when it comes to overcoming procrastination.
> - Planning and organisation can counter many causes of procrastination.
> - Finding reward and purpose in your work can rekindle motivation.
> - Use the power of habit to address chronic procrastination.
> - When all else fails, just do it!

Further resources

Allen, D. (2015) *Getting Things Done: The Art of Stress-free Productivity*. London: Piatkus.
Forster, M. (2006) *Do It Tomorrow and Other Secrets of Time Management*. London: Hodder and Stoughton.
Gillihan, S.J. (2020) *Cognitive Behavioural Therapy Made Simple: 10 Strategies for Managing Anxiety, Depression, Anger, Panic and Worry*. London: Sheldon Press.
Morgenstern, J. (2005) *Never Check E-mail in the Morning: And Other Unexpected Strategies for Making Your Work Life Work*. New York: Fireside.
Pychyl, T.A. (2013) *Solving the Procrastination Puzzle: A Concise Guide to Strategies for Change*. New York: Jeremy P. Tarcher / Penguin.
Tracy, B. (2013) *Eat That Frog!* London: Hodder.

Reference

Tracy, B. (2013) *Eat That Frog!* London: Hodder.

16 Track Your Progress

How to ... Know what and when to change

> Plan-check-do – Little and often – Ask yourself three questions – Project triangle revisited – Review your goals – Beware the WIBNIs – Assess the impact of change – Learn your lessons

Keeping going doesn't mean never stopping to think. A crucial part of 'keeping going' is knowing where you're 'at' with your work. To do this, you need to stop and consider your progress to date and decide whether you need to make adjustments. Regardless of your discipline, you will roughly follow this method of inquiry in your research:

1. Form research questions, objectives, hypotheses and so on based on the extant literature.
2. Collect your data.
3. Analyse the data and draw conclusions.

You follow a similar iterative process when you're managing your PhD, except that we would use the terms: plan, do and check. You *plan* your project using all the techniques in the previous chapters. You then *do* the work you've planned. At various points in the 'doing', you should *check* whether things are going as anticipated. This chapter explains how to assess the progress of your PhD and how to make any necessary adjustments to your plan.

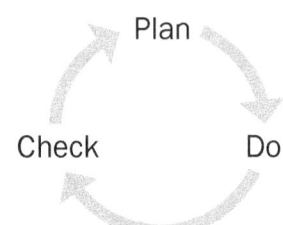

Running, tracking and controlling your PhD is a lot like driving a car. You don't drive down the motorway at 150mph, veering wildly through the traffic. As you drive, you monitor the controls and your environment, and make minor adjustments. You make small alterations as you're steering, you accelerate and brake as the traffic around you changes, you change gear, you check your mirrors, you keep an eye on your speed, you might look at your fuel gauge. You make minor modifications as and when your journey requires it. It is much the same in terms of driving your project. You have all the controls you need, for example your supervision ground rules, working habits, support networks, stakeholder diagram, scope statement, goals, SMART deliverables, WBS, network diagram, Gantt chart and so on.

In the same way that you don't U-turn on a motorway, you're unlikely to completely rip up your plan and start again from scratch. Instead, as your PhD progresses, you periodically refer back to your controls to see if anything has changed or if you need to make adjustments. This is why you spend time planning before you start the next phase of work. It gives you a series of benchmarks against which to monitor your progress and make minor adjustments as necessary.

The ongoing management of any project demands you repeatedly ask three simple questions:

1. Where am I?
2. Where did I expect to be?
3. Do I need to change anything?

Your advance planning equips you to answer these questions, track your progress and make any necessary adjustments.

> ➡ **Action: Assess your situation.**
>
> Reflect on your current situation, by asking the three questions given here.

Tracking progress

Tracking is the assessment of how well you are executing your plan: comparing where you are with where you planned to be. In a PhD, tracking progress can be difficult. In some projects, it's very easy to say that you are 75 per cent of the way through something, such as building a house, but research is often less tangible and, therefore, harder to assess. Even if you can put a percentage against your progress, it's not always appropriate. For example, you may have written 20,000 words of your 80,000-word thesis but this doesn't necessarily mean that 25 per cent of the work has been completed. Similarly, having spent five days on a task that you estimated would take ten to finish doesn't mean you're halfway through. So, in terms of assessing task progress, it is often more appropriate to ask two questions:

1. How much work have you done?
2. How much more do you need to do?

For example, you have worked five of the original ten days allocated (How much have you done?) but, after reflecting on your rate of progress, you re-estimate that you'll need probably another seven days to complete everything (How much more do you need?). This is usually a much easier and, more importantly, accurate method of understanding progress and getting a clear view of the health of your PhD progress.

> ➡ **Action: Track your progress.**
>
> Get into the habit of regularly assessing your progress by asking these two questions. Schedule regular quick tracking reviews in your calendar.

Knowing whether or not you are on track then allows you to decide whether or not you need to make adjustments: to your plan, your scope or your work method. The project triangle is the best way of making these decisions.

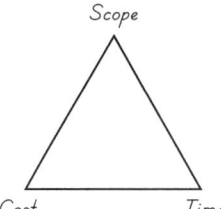

For example:

- Tasks are taking longer than expected. You can:
  - Work more hours per day to hit to original deadline (increase cost)
  - Extend the deadline (increase time)
  - Adopt a different approach or cut some work – take out some nice-to-haves or bells-and-whistles (reduce scope).
- You're completing the work more quickly than expected. You can:
  - Work fewer hours per day on this and invest those hours elsewhere (reduce cost)
  - Finish and deliver everything more quickly (reduce time)
  - Reintroduce some of the nice-to-haves or even bells-and-whistles you had earlier decided to omit (increase scope).

Ultimately, the options you have all come back to the project triangle: scope, cost and time. The project triangle now really comes in to its own as it always provides you with three different options to move forward!

Updating your plan

One of the reasons that we recommend you create your Gantt chart digitally is that when things change (as they inevitably will), the software can very quickly show the impact of that change on the rest of your PhD. For instance, if you find that one task is likely to take double your estimate, by updating that single task in the computer, the change will be propagated through the rest of your plan, immediately updating your timeline. For example, the following plan has 'Conduct Experiment 1' as five days, which means that the whole phase of work is due to finish on 16 August.

Task Name	Duration	Start Date	End Date
⊿ EXPERIMENT 1	23 days	Mon 17 July	Mon 16 August
START	0 days	Mon 17 July	Mon 17 July
Design Experiment 1	4 days	Mon 17 July	Thu 20 July
Setup Experiment 1	2 days	Fri 21 July	Mon 24 July
Conduct Experiment 1	5 days	Tue 25 July	Mon 31 July
Analyse results	10 days	Tue 1 August	Mon 14 August
Write Up	2 days	Tue 15 August	Wed 16 August
END	0 days	Wed 16 August	Wed 16 August

Tracking Gantt chart: original plan

As you are conducting the experiment, you discover that it will actually take longer than planned (now eight days). In the software, you simply update that single duration (change '5' to '8') and the rest of your project is amended accordingly.

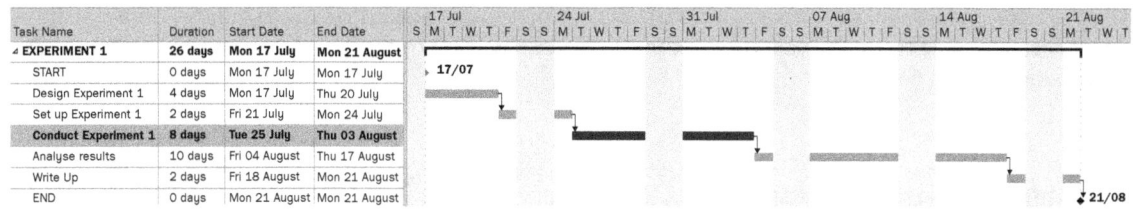

Tracking Gantt chart: after update

This immediately shows the new predicted finish of 21 August. You can now decide whether this new deadline is acceptable. If not, revisit the triangle: you need to work more hours per day (increase cost) or cut back on the work you're doing (adjust scope) – anything else is impossible!

As we've said before, don't worry if things don't go exactly to plan. Things very rarely do go *exactly* to plan. If you find during tracking that your estimates weren't very good, don't fret. This is actually quite positive because it gives you feedback and tells you that, for the next bit of work you're planning, you need to increase your durations. You are learning as you are going.

> **Activity: Tracking**
>
> 1 Looking at your plan over the past two weeks, assess:
>   - How much have you done?
>   - How much is still to go?
> 2 Update your Gantt chart accordingly.
> 3 Have a quick look (ten minutes) at your stakeholder diagram, deliverables, WBS and estimates. Based on the last two weeks, is there anything that needs updating?
>
> Repeat this *every* fortnight.

Revisit your goals

As you proceed through your PhD, both your maturity as a researcher and the maturity of your research idea will develop. One of the major benefits of planning in detail only for each small phase of your PhD is that, as you and your project develop, your work plan can develop in tandem.

As you initiate each new 'bite of the elephant', you have the opportunity to create a detailed day-to-day plan and can reanalyse your project as a whole. At the start of each phase, ask yourself:

- What were your original goals when starting a PhD and are they still going to be met?
- Is your research still moving towards your goal, or does that need to be re-examined?
- Are you taking advantage of the additional opportunities you identified as part of your personal goals?
- Is your work-life balance as you had hoped?

The iterative 'plan-do-check' nature of a PhD allows you to pause and reflect regularly on all of these critical issues so as to ensure that your experience is delivering everything you require academically, professionally and personally.

> **✎ Activity: Revisit your goals**
>
> 1. Go back to the most recent version of your goals (from the template on page 22) and review them. Are they still important to you? Have you changed them?
> 2. Assess to what extent your PhD is contributing to the achievement of your goals so far.
> 3. Identify any changes you need to make to your plans or goals.
>
> *Repeat this at least every six months.*

Dealing with unexpected issues

Having performed your risk assessment in Chapter 11, you will have reduced the number of 'unexpected' events likely to occur during your PhD by proactively mitigating potential problems. This is the real world, though, so things will happen that you didn't anticipate or plan for. This means that, during the research project itself, you'll have to change what you're doing, how you're doing it or when you're doing it. In fact, change is the only thing that is guaranteed to happen during your PhD!

So far in this chapter, you've updated your plan to address changes that are identified when you're tracking, so, changes primarily linked to your schedule. Whether you're hitting your deadlines or not, are tasks taking longer than expected and so on? You will also encounter issues beyond your control that necessitate changes in your PhD, for example:

- A supervisor leaving
- The ethics committee not approving your plan
- A lack of participants for your study
- Peer-review suggesting major alterations to a paper
- Equipment that isn't working or is unavailable.

You might also choose to make changes around issues that you've encountered yourself, for example:

- Adjustment of focus based on results
- Tweaking your approach based on experience
- Amending your objectives as you read more literature
- Adopting a different method because the current one is too complicated.

As such, your plan needs to be flexible enough to accommodate these inevitable changes too.

Wouldn't it be nice if ...

When you do encounter unexpected issues, don't be overly concerned about the ones that require major changes. Don't worry if you accidentally burn down the building. Actually, let's rephrase that: *do* worry if you burn down the building, but, you'll notice this happening and you'll respond accordingly! By contrast, the changes that can cause you the most significant problems are often an accumulation of the small, seemingly trivial things.

We call these small changes WIBNIs (Wouldn't it be nice if…). You might be reflecting on some work you've just completed or, often, you're in a supervisory meeting reviewing progress and someone suggests, 'This is looking really good; wouldn't it be nice if you did this as well?' To which you respond, 'Great idea! It'll only take a couple of days. I'll do it.' If this isn't familiar yet, it will be before the end of your PhD! Two days doesn't seem a lot and seems realistically achievable. However, if you have ten of these two-day WIBNIs, you're adding 20 days of work to your plan – the equivalent of four 5-day weeks: a whole month! It is frequently these multiple, unmanaged little changes that cause your timeline to become pressured.

The purpose of having a plan is not to prevent these changes, but instead, as with changes to your planned timeline, to provide an easy way of understanding the impact an issue will have and then choosing an appropriate course of action. Each change should be assessed by asking three simple questions:

1. What are the benefits of making this change?
2. What is the impact of this change on everything else you're doing?
3. Therefore, is it worthwhile to go ahead and make the change?

> ➡ **Action: Determine the impact of change.**
>
> Every time you want to make a change in your project, ask those three questions. You can then make an *informed decision* whether to go ahead and do it. Having used all the techniques from Part 2 to create a robust plan, this should only take a few minutes.

These questions should be assessed in the context of the information gathered through the preparatory planning activities in Chapters 7 to 11. In addition, every potential change should be reflected against the project triangle:

- **Scope**
  - Can you still do everything you want to do?
  - Is the change a must-have, nice-to-have or a bells-and-whistle?
  - What are the benefits of making this change?
  - What are the risks of not doing it?
  - Does the change take you closer to your goal?
  - Will your key stakeholders' expectations still be met?
  - Do you need to add tasks to your WBS – if so, what is the impact on the network diagram and Gantt chart?
- **Time**
  - How long will it take to make this change?
  - Can that be absorbed into your timeline or will everything take longer?
  - Are there any new dependencies linked to this change?
  - Do you have the time for this new activity/exercise/item?
- **Cost**
  - How many hours will this change take?
  - Will that mean you have to work more hours per day or over a weekend?
  - Do you have the resources for it?
  - Are the resources available when you need them?

The purpose of asking these questions is not to prevent you from making changes to your plan, but to allow you to make informed, conscious decisions about the relative merits of a change for your PhD. The project triangle also arms you with objective evidence to use in discussions with your supervisor about the difficulty of incorporating additional work or performing extra activities in light of your current workload. Instead of, 'No', you might be saying, 'Yes, but ...' in conscious acknowledgement of the impact that change can have. This will help you to assert boundaries around your work and reduce the risk of overload. For example:

Supervisor: These findings are really interesting. What would be great is if you extended the analysis to compare them with XYZ.

Student: Great idea. Thanks for the suggestion. It does mean that ABC won't be finished on time though. Is that ok with you?

Jump on the small ones ...

Get into the habit of doing this for every change in your project – especially the small ones (it takes just a couple of minutes). If you start letting the small changes go, the bigger ones will also start to slip and your plan will soon become so out of step with real life that it becomes unusable.

✏ Activity: Assess a potential change

When you encounter an unexpected issue of any size in your PhD, complete the following steps using the template on page 213 to help you.

1. Identify the change that is needed (and/or desired) to address the issue. Write it in the template.
2. Using the planning artefacts you developed previously, consider the impact that making this change will have on your PhD plan. Add it to the template.
3. Ask the questions in the checklist on page 211 and consider the change against the project triangle. Update the template.
4. Decide: Do you still want to do this?
   - If yes, update your plan accordingly by revisiting the techniques in Chapters 7 to 11 as appropriate.
   - If no, you have the evidence to back up your decision.

The more you do this, the quicker and easier it will become. You're establishing another new habit!

📄 Template: Change assessment

Details of the proposed change:

What impact will the change have on your project plan?

How will the change affect the corners of the project triangle?	
Scope	
Time	
Cost	

Do you want to make this change?	Yes ☐ No ☐
If yes, update your project plans to reflect the change.	Done ☐

How often should you review your plan?

Tracking and assessing progress are important psychologically as well as practically. They will provide regular, demonstrable signs of progress that will help to maintain your motivation for, engagement in and commitment to the work. You will need these boosts throughout your PhD, and so will your supervisors. Tracking progress regularly isn't just about giving yourself a pat on the back for work completed, it can also show where your progress is slow. Surprisingly perhaps, this is really positive. The earlier you know things aren't going quite to plan, the earlier you can do something about it. Hiding problems or being unaware of them won't make your PhD any easier in the long run, so, be positive and confident about good *and* bad news. Acknowledging both will help you to finish more quickly and easily.

There is no rule for how often you should assess the progress of your PhD. There will be some major milestones that you must align with, such as first-year reviews, but tracking should also be done regularly for your own benefit. For the high-level plan that you created in Chapter 4, checking-in once every couple of months is fine. For the more detailed plan you created in Part 2, perhaps tracking once a fortnight would be more appropriate. Tracking is not intended to be an onerous task – just five minutes asking those initial three questions: Where are you? Where did you expect to be? What do you need to change?

As you get closer to significant milestones or deadlines, you might want to check-in more often. If you're doing a particularly complex bit of work, you may want to keep a really tight rein and check where you are every couple of days. This is not an exact science, so we can't give you a definitive instruction. A good general rule of thumb is to track your work often enough that if something bad happens you are aware of it early enough to address it. For example:

> A collaborative partner is recruiting participants for your study and has estimated the recruitment will take five months. It would be prudent to check in every month on how things are going because if you know after one month that you have only one person lined up, you can make some adjustments to your plan. It's a much better situation than only discovering that you have one person after five months of waiting.

Tracking regularly not only gives you a clearer picture of how your work is progressing but also makes it much easier to report on your progress when required. You will find that you don't need to spend a lot of time preparing for a supervisory progress meeting because all the relevant information is at your fingertips. When you submit formal reports and reviews to your university, funder, doctoral college, CDT and so on, it shouldn't take you very long because you are already on top of your work progress.

Plan, do, check … plan

Finally, at the end of each phase you need to consider what's coming next. This takes you back to the start of a new loop of the plan-do-check cycle. For the next 'bite of the elephant', return to Chapter 7 and go through the whole process again, but it won't take as long this time. As well as getting better at research, you're getting better at planning your PhD; and you now have a basis to work from. You won't need to spend much time identifying stakeholders and their expectations, for example, because you've done it already. This time you will focus on:

- The detailed scope for the next phase (Chapter 8)
- Determining the associated deliverables (Chapter 8)
- Creating a work breakdown structure (Chapter 9)
- Time estimation (Chapter 9), sequencing (Chapter 10) and scheduling (Chapter 10) in exactly the same way as you did before.

> **✏ Activity: Plan the next stage**
>
> 1. Create a schedule for your tracking activities and put it in your calendar.
> 2. Make a note of each time you go round the plan-do-check loop and rate how easy you found the planning process.
>
> | 1. Date ___ ☺☻☹ | 6. Date ___ ☺☻☹ |
> | 2. Date ___ ☺☻☹ | 7. Date ___ ☺☻☹ |
> | 3. Date ___ ☺☻☹ | 8. Date ___ ☺☻☹ |
> | 4. Date ___ ☺☻☹ | 9. Date ___ ☺☻☹ |
> | 5. Date ___ ☺☻☹ | 10. Date ___ ☺☻☹ |
>
> We don't promise that the research will get any easier, but we hope that, by keeping this record, you'll notice that your planning ability and your transferable skills are developing during your PhD.

Learn your lessons

It's worthwhile at the end of every phase to run a final 'check' or 'evaluation' of how the work went. Again, spend just 10 or 15 minutes (which you can easily afford in a three-year-plus project). Reflect, of course, on the outputs themselves, what you learned and so on from a research perspective, but also consider how effectively you performed the work.

The formal term for this is 'lessons learned' and the main reason for doing it is to inform future planning: identify what didn't go as expected, work out the reasons for these deviations and try to avoid them in the future. We can't emphasise how important this reflection is – plan, do, *check*. Your PhD will become a little easier if you can learn as you go and incorporate that learning into managing yourself and your workload. When undertaking a lessons learned assessment, ask the following questions.

How accurate were your estimates? Was anything significantly longer (or shorter) than expected?	This informs your **comparative estimates**. You might be doing completely different tasks in the next phase, but if you consistently underestimated last time, and most things took 50 per cent longer than expected, then maybe you should add 50 per cent to every estimate this time.
What issues did you encounter that you didn't anticipate?	These become risks you address during your **risk assessment** next time.
Was there anything that went particularly well that you want to make sure you repeat?	Improve the planning now you have **comparative data**.
Did anything go badly that you want to try to avoid in the future, and what were the reasons?	Use your **comparative data** to inform the planning and **risk assessment**.
Have any new stakeholders emerged that you need to consider?	Update your **stakeholder diagram**.
Are all the expectations aligned and managed and key stakeholders remain satisfied?	Revisit **convergence** and the **scoping** tools.
Are your goals still relevant, viable, achievable and en route to where you want to go?	Revisit your personal **goals** and check that your **deliverables** still align.

> ✏ **Activity: Lessons learned review**
>
> At the end of your next planning phase, take some time to answer the questions in the template on page 217. Identify the changes you need to make when you plan the next phase of your work.

📄 Template: Lessons learned review

At the end of your next planning phase (or bite) answer the questions below and identify the changes when you plan the next phase of work.	
How accurate were my estimates? Was anything significantly longer (or shorter) than expected?	
What issues did I encounter that I hadn't anticipated?	
What went particularly well that I want to repeat?	
What went badly, and why?	
Have any new stakeholders emerged?	
Are all the stakeholder expectations aligned and managed and do key stakeholders remain satisfied?	
Are my goals still relevant, viable, achievable and en route to where I want to go?	
In summary, what changes will I make for the next phase of work?	

Summary

Good planning follows a cycle of: plan, do, check – and plan again. The planning tools you have used so far mean that you have everything you need to monitor and assess your progress and make any changes necessary to keep on track. The plan you have already drawn up includes the benchmarks against which you can check your progress quickly and spot problems as soon as they arise. Little and often is the best approach for tracking. If you identify problems, assess the likely value and the potential impact of any changes before deciding whether to make them. Beware the WIBNIs – those small changes that can add up and accumulatively create delays. Once you have reviewed your progress and identified any necessary changes, always incorporate them into a new iteration of your plans. Finally, always learn the lessons of your review and incorporate this knowledge into your future planning.

Key points

- Track the progress of your PhD using the plan-do-check cycle.
- Checking 'little and often' is the secret to good tracking.
- Review and, if required, adjust your short- and long-term plans based on your progress to date.
- Frequent checking will improve your estimations and provide lessons learned.
- Changes in your PhD are inevitable. Always update your plans to accommodate their impact.
- Resist the temptation of the small changes – they can add up to make big problems!

Further resources

Buttrick, R. (2019) *The Ultimate Guide to Directing and Managing Business-Led Projects,* 5th edn. Abingdon: Routledge.
Heagney, J. (2022) *Fundamentals of Project Management,* 6th edn. London: Harper Collins.
Portnoy, J.L. and Portnoy, S.L. (2022) *Project Management for Dummies,* 6th edn. Hoboken NJ: Wiley & Sons.
Wysocki, R.K. (2019) *Effective Project Management: Traditional, Agile, Extreme, Hybrid.* Indianapolis: Wiley.

17 Look Ahead

How to ... Get a head start on your future career

> Your future happens sooner than you think – Invest in employability as well as research – CV development planning – Skills audit – Use your existing networks – Build new connections – Strengthen your networks – Keep in touch

The middle stages of a PhD, especially in full-time study, can be all-consuming. This is one of the joys of a full-time PhD, of course: a chance to immerse yourself in your topic and your research. This immersion can, however, cause tunnel vision that obscures other important issues, one of which is your future career. If you focus solely on the substantive research to the detriment of all else, you run the risk of leaving career development at the bottom of the pile and ignored until the thesis is submitted. This may leave you scrambling to find your next step at the end of your PhD and mean that you miss valuable opportunities during the PhD to make progress on your future career. Invest time and effort in your employability *during* your PhD – the skills and experience that employers value – as well as on your research.

You may feel as if your supervisors want you to focus only on your PhD during your funding period, which is understandable from their perspective. However, in order to make the most of *all* the opportunities a doctoral degree offers, we recommend that you don't leave thinking about 'life after the PhD' to the end or, even worse, to chance.

If you are in part-time study and combining your PhD with work in industry, you will remain more connected to the workplace. However, the challenging balancing act of undertaking research alongside another professional role can squeeze out all but immediate demands at the cost of investing in your future.

You may have embarked on your PhD with a clear sense of what you want to do next, but many PhD students are unsure where they want their PhD to lead them. Whether you have clear ambitions or not, making time to explore where you (might) want to be professionally *after* your PhD, can ensure that you use the opportunities *during* your PhD to build progress towards this professional future. For example, attending conferences – whether academic or industry based – might help to clarify your preferred professional 'tribe'. Taking on teaching duties during your PhD would be a great way of finding out whether the demands of a traditional lecturer position would suit you.

> **Transferable skills**
>
> Even if you really don't have a clue what you're going to do after your PhD, engaging in professional development opportunities is never going to be a waste of time because you will be building *transferable* skills that will be useful irrespective of what you end up doing.

Whatever your career aims, *you* need to take charge of your career development. If you are aiming to stay in academia, your

PhD means you are well placed to do this. Your PhD experience is, as we have already said, an apprenticeship in academic research. However, this doesn't mean you can sit back and wait for it to happen. Academia is a notoriously competitive professional field. You will have to make the most of the opportunities provided and be proactive in creating your professional edge.

If you know you are seeking a career outside academia, you'll probably have to make more effort to seek out relevant opportunities that will support you in your career aims. The more you can stay connected to your personal goals (see Chapter 2), even as they change and develop, the easier it will be to ensure that your PhD provides a stepping stone to your future career. Whatever your ultimate professional aims, the sooner you start positioning yourself for future success, the better.

This chapter helps you to make a start on two important career development activities. In the first part of the chapter, you consider a programme of 'CV building' through the strategic acquisition of relevant skills and experience. In the second part, you take steps to develop your professional networks. Building on the professional support networks examined first in Chapter 4, we introduce a more strategic element to networking, with a view to establishing contacts who can provide access to future career opportunities.

Build your CV

One valuable thing to do during your PhD to increase your chances of securing your next career step, is to create your own CV development plan. This guides you to use the opportunities available during your PhD to acquire the skills and experience necessary to secure your desired job post PhD. It also means that, by the time you're ready to secure your next professional role, you have built a CV that puts you in a good position to compete in your chosen job market.

The template on page 226 provides a step-by-step approach to building a CV development plan. You can complete it section by section as the chapter takes you through it.

Step 1: Identify your career goals

To be able to develop your CV effectively, you need to find out what skills and experience are required for your next career step. This is easier if you know what you want to do next. You began envisioning your future in Chapter 2 by creating some personal goals. If you're still not sure exactly what you want to do next, you can create some broad parameters for your preferred next step. For example:

- **Broad sector** – something in education, something in conservation, something in marketing
- **Type of role** – management, R&D, training and development, consultant
- **Level of role** – senior management, post-doc, frontline technical support, self-employed.

However clear or vague your career ambitions, you can still usefully focus on acquiring the transferable skills and experience that will serve you well in *any* professional role. For example, all employers are likely to value:

- Communication skills
- Teamworking skills
- Leadership or managerial skills
- Problem-solving and decision-making skills.

> **✏️ Activity: CV development plan – Step 1**
>
> In the template on page 226, note the type of role you aim to secure on completing your PhD. If you're not exactly sure, note down some broad parameters, such as:
>
> - A post-doc at a UK university, in the field of conservation biology
> - An advisor role in a national educational policy unit
> - A self-employed documentary film director.
>
> It's fine to be ambitious! Write down your true aspirations.

Step 2: Identify required skills and experience

The next step is to find out the kind of skills and experience you will require in order to secure the role (or type of role) you are aiming for. You can do this by:

- Looking at relevant job descriptions to find out the desired and required skills and experience
- Using your network to contact people who work in a similar field or position that you are aiming for and ask about the skills and experience valued by potential employers that will give you a competitive edge
- Developing a mentoring relationship with someone occupying a more senior position and get advice about the key skills and experience that you would benefit from developing (your supervisors are the obvious people to fulfill this role if you're aiming to stay in academia)
- Taking a summer placement with an organisation you'd like to work with.

> 💬 'I undertook a full-time internship with the Scottish Government. It meant taking three months off the PhD, but the opportunities for my future career were fantastic. It was really good experience of research in an environment outside academia and also improved my focus coming back to the PhD.'

> **✏️ Activity: Identify required skills and experience**
>
> Decide how you will find out more about the skills and experience needed to achieve your career goals. Make some notes here.

> ### ✏ Activity: CV development plan – Step 2
>
> In the template on page 226, note the *skills and experience you think you will need* to secure your desired career role: For example:
>
> - A post-doc at a UK university, in the field of conservation biology
>   - *Project management*
>   - *Journal publications*
>   - *Teaching experience*
> - An advisor role in a national educational policy unit
>   - *Teamworking*
>   - *Knowledge of UK education policy*
>   - *Journal publications*
> - A self-employed documentary film director
>   - *Pitching film treatments*
>   - *Knowledge of funding sources*
>   - *Project management.*

Step 3: Assess your existing skills and experience

Next, run a skills audit. That means, first, comparing the skills and experience you need to achieve your career goals with your current skills and experience. It also helps to note how you have acquired and used these skills. This will be important when you come to apply for jobs, as it will be a way of *demonstrating* to potential employers that you have the skills and experience.

> ### ✏ Activity: CV development plan – Step 3
>
> In the template on page 226, note *the skills and experience you already have*. For example:
>
> - A post-doc at a UK university, in the field of conservation biology
>   - Project management
>   - Journal publications: *Two submitted publications and one accepted, in review*
>   - Teaching experience: *Taught on two UG modules*
> - An advisor role in a national educational policy unit
>   - Teamworking skills
>   - Knowledge of UK education policy: *PhD topic/literature review*
>   - Journal publications
> - A self-employed documentary film director
>   - Pitching film treatments: *Attended 'pitching' training course run by the BFI*
>   - Knowledge of funding sources
>   - Project management.

Step 4: Identify your development priorities

Next, assess your development priorities by identifying the required skills and experience that you *don't* currently have. This will help you to set your priorities for CV development during your PhD and help you to make good choices about how to spend your (scarce) time, pursuing the most relevant opportunities. For example:

> Chapter 23 suggests tips on translating your PhD skills into the skills desired by future employers.

- If you hope for a post-doc after your PhD, put time into academic conference submissions and submitting research papers for publication.
- If you aim to secure a job outside academia, you may reject some of the opportunities to participate in academic activities and instead seek out activities more relevant to the industry and position you are aiming for, such as opportunities to project-manage an event or society, whether at university or elsewhere, to demonstrate your managerial and leadership skills. You might focus the dissemination of your research findings in industry or trade publications rather than academic journals.

Another way in which the skills audit helps you to prioritise your CV-building activities, is by encouraging you to go beyond the comfort zone of your current strengths and focus on developing the skills and experience you *lack* (your conscious incompetence). For example:

- You want to find work in an R&D function in the construction industry. Your PhD research may furnish you with the technical skills and material knowledge you need to excel in the substantive work of this function. Moreover, perhaps this is the kind of work you love, spending time in the lab, testing the functional properties of new forms of environmentally friendly concrete. However, when you investigate the skills required to compete in this sector, you discover that, as well as sound technical abilities and knowledge, you need excellent presentation and project management skills. This knowledge gives you the chance to acquire these additional skills by taking up opportunities to hone your presentation skills through seminar or conference presentations or by signing up for project management training provided by your university.
- Perhaps you want to stay in academia as a lecturer. You've discovered that you love the teaching part of academic work and you've taken up every teaching opportunity offered during your PhD. However, you discover that your pathway to an academic job will be via a post-doc position and, as such, you need to be able to demonstrate research outputs. Knowing this might mean that you decline some teaching duties in favour of putting work into submitting papers for publication.

Activity: CV development plan – Step 4

In the template on page 226, highlight *the skills and experience you want to develop*. For example:

- A post-doc at a UK university, in the field of conservation biology
    - *Project management*
    - Journal publications: Two submitted publications and one accepted, in review
    - Teaching experience: Taught on two UG modules
- An advisor role in a national educational policy unit
    - *Teamworking skills*
    - Knowledge of UK education policy: PhD topic/literature review
    - *Journal publications*
- A self-employed documentary film director
    - Pitching film treatments: Attended 'pitching' training course run by the BFI
    - *Knowledge of funding sources*
    - *Project management.*

Step 5: Plan how to acquire necessary skills and experience

Once you've identified your priorities for further CV development, the next step is to *acquire* the necessary skills and experience. Clearly, the pressure of a PhD means that you will have limited time available. Your first priority *must* be successful completion of your PhD. However, there are plenty of ways you can incorporate CV-building activities into your PhD without causing too much distraction. Indeed, your research work itself will offer opportunities to develop relevant substantive and transferable skills. The following are some suggestions for how to develop your skills and experience during your PhD:

> **➜ Action: Volunteer**
>
> Volunteer for activities associated with your PhD that offer you the chance to develop different skills.

Such as:

- For event management skills, organise a seminar programme or a social event for fellow PhD students
- For communication skills, take on the dissemination of important research or policy information to the rest of your PhD cohort
- For presentation skills, offer to present your research findings at university seminars.

> **➜ Action: Take advantage of training opportunities**
>
> As well as research-skills training, most universities offer programmes of short courses in more general transferable skills.

For example, these are some of the courses that we offer at universities for PhD students:

- Project management
- Risk management
- Leadership and teambuilding
- Professional communication skills
- Time management.

> **➜ Action: Learn from your peers and mentors**
>
> We've emphasised throughout the book the value of your supervisors and other colleagues as sources of advice and guidance. For CV-building purposes, consider who, in your communities of practice, might possess the skills you want to develop.

Proactively find ways of learning from them, whether that's informally through observation or by asking for advice and guidance. For example:

- Your supervisors are a valuable source of research knowledge, but perhaps one of your supervisors is particularly good at time management or is a fantastic communicator. Observe how they do this.
- Consider the previous work experience of your fellow PhD students. Have they had positions that demand the skills and knowledge you would like to develop? Ask their advice.
- Don't forget your wider stakeholders: funders, research participants, end users and so on, who may all be valuable sources of knowledge, expertise and advice.

✏ Activity: CV development plan – Step 5

In the template on page 226, plan *how* you will develop the skills and experience you lack. For example:

- A post-doc at a UK university, in the field of conservation biology
    - Project management: *Attend university project management course*
    - Journal publications: *Two submitted publications and one accepted, in review*
    - Teaching experience: *Taught on two UG modules*
- An advisor role in a national educational policy unit
    - Teamworking skills: *Volunteer for the working group organising this year's PhD conference*
    - Knowledge of UK education policy: *PhD topic/literature review*
    - Journal publications: *Speak to Supervisor about publication options*
- A self-employed documentary film director
    - Pitching film treatments: *Attended 'pitching' training course run by the BFI*
    - Knowledge of funding sources: *Ask research development staff for information on current funding sources for my field*
    - Project management: *Attend university PM course.*

Template: CV development plan

Target job/role			
Key skills/experience	Current skills/experience	Development priorities	Action to acquire skills/experience

Networking: it's not (just) what you know; it's who you know

We explored the importance of support networks for emotional, psychological and professional support in Chapter 6. We've also described the value of your networks as a form of personal power – connection power – in Chapter 13. In this chapter, we suggest how you can develop professional networks that will help you achieve future career success. Much of this will occur naturally as an outcome of your research work, so it won't distract from completing the substantive PhD work. However, there are real benefits to being strategic, and even instrumental, in choosing how to build your networks and developing your profile in line with your career ambitions, not least because it will be more efficient and less time-consuming to be more focused about networking.

There's no doubt that professional networks are important to your career success. Good networks can provide a range of professional development benefits, such as:

- **Information and advice** – for example on how to secure post-doc funding
- **Opportunities** – for example in jobs, conferences, research funding
- **Links with potential collaborators** – researchers, business partners, research subjects and so on
- **Building your profile and reputation** – perhaps disseminating your research, publicising achievements and awards.

Despite the demonstrable value of professional networks, we have found when running networking courses for research staff and students that there can be resistance to, and even distaste for, the concept of networking. This seems to reflect a belief that networking as a professional activity is somehow exploitative and manipulative; that it involves the creation of inauthentic relationships for the selfish purpose of personal gain. This misrepresents the purpose and the value of good professional networks and the way they operate. Networking is simply the creation and maintenance of social relationships, which is what humans do (and need) anyway. The concept of *professional* networking merely refers to something that you should be doing already – finding your community of practice, learning from peers and mentors, developing social relationships with colleagues – and suggests that by doing it more consciously, you can do it better.

The best social relationships are built on some degree of reciprocity, which means mutual benefit. This doesn't have to be as blatantly transactional as, 'You scratch my back and I'll scratch yours.' Instead, the benefit emerges from the relationship, whether through goodwill, shared interests and goals or the exchange of information. For example:

- Your supervisors have a relationship with you, meaning they know you and value your research and your attitude to work (your referent power, see page 166). As a result, they may help you to find a post-doc position so they can continue to work with you.
- You are active in and contribute to a social networking group linked to your field of research in midwifery. This means that you find out about new developments and opportunities, through informal communication, that might otherwise have been unknown.
- You have developed good relationships with some of the stakeholders involved in your research on discrimination in education because you are all committed to reducing inequality. As a result, if funding becomes available in that field, that information will be shared among the network, with a view to trying to use it to improve educational outcomes.

Networking can be time consuming and hard work. We're also very aware that, for some people, it can be a daunting prospect. The following practical actions can help you to approach the task of networking with purpose and confidence and to build professional networks that contribute to your career success.

Set your networking objectives

When it comes to networking, it's definitely a question of quality rather than simply quantity. There is some value in just getting 'out there' as much as possible as, clearly, the more people you come into contact with, the greater your chance of making valuable connections. Online tools and social media provide easy access to a far wider pool of people than having to go and meet people face to face, but it can also mean that you end up with a proliferation of networks to maintain, with lots of contacts, few of whom can provide you with what you require, so, a balance is needed.

To stay focused, we would recommend that, first, you identify some networking objectives linked to your current and future career needs. Some of these may link directly to the skills and experience you want to develop that you identified in your CV development plan (page 226). For example, you might want to:

- Contact people in a particular industry sector in order to understand the key skills required for your desired role
- Make links with researchers working at the most active research universities in your field to find out about post-doc opportunities
- Develop connections with staff in educational policy units, to raise the profile of your research in the hope of developing potential collaborations
- Connect with people who've received funding for documentary film projects, so you can find out how it's done.

Once you've identified your current networking objectives, you can focus your networking activities more efficiently.

Activity: Set your current networking objectives

Identify your key networking objectives, by reviewing your CV development needs and considering any other current requirements for your PhD.

Networking objectives	
	☐
	☐
	☐
	☐
	☐
	☐

Review and use your current networks

Before you put effort into making new contacts, stop and consider whether your existing networks can help you achieve your networking goals. It's easy to overlook and take for granted the people we're already familiar with.

- Look at your stakeholder diagram developed in Chapter 7. This will be an excellent summary of the people you are connected to with through your research.

- Create a network map of your contacts, including key stakeholders. Add categories to include people you know through, for example:
  - Previous and current employment
  - Previous studies
  - Leisure activities, clubs, societies and so on
  - Community or voluntary activities
  - Friends and relations.

Similar to stakeholder identification in Chapter 7, when you review your existing networks, drill down to specific individuals rather than just categories. Networking is done between individuals. So, for example, rather than stating 'previous employment', name the people with whom you have kept in touch or with whom it would be easy to make contact again. Just mark them on your network map using their initials to keep it simple.

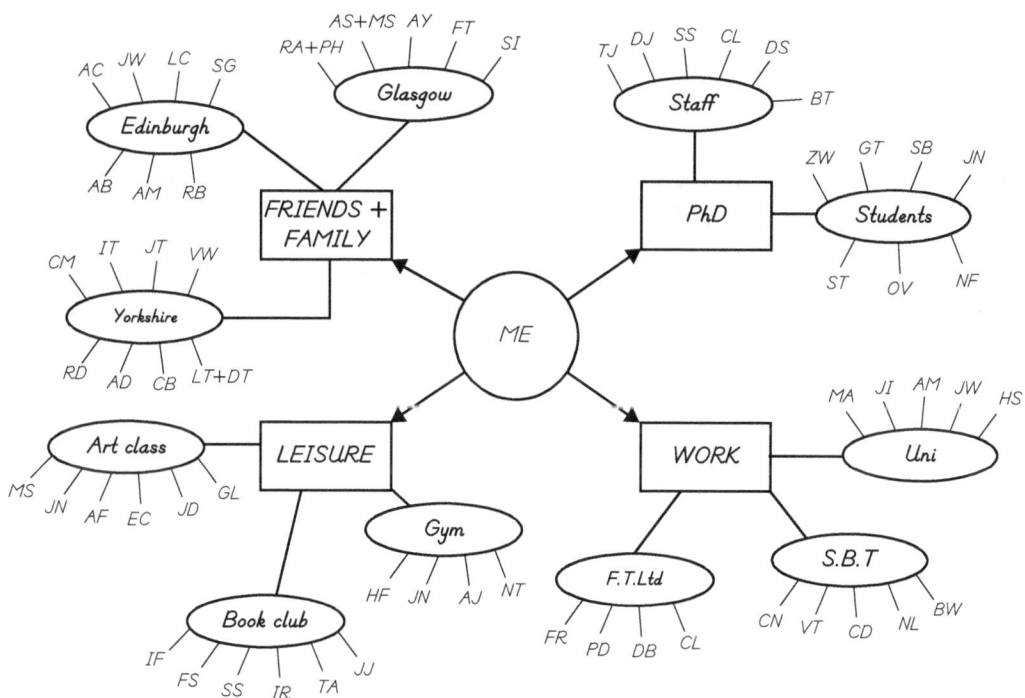

Network map of contacts

Once you have reviewed your network map, pick out any people who could help you achieve your goals and decide how you can get the help you need from them. For example:

- 'Dr Smith, my ex-supervisor, is now working at a DTI-funded management research institute. I can contact them and ask if there are likely to be any post-docs advertised in my field in the next year.'
- 'My friend's partner works in the Scottish Government Policy Unit. I can ask them to give me some advice about recruitment into this department.'
- 'My ex-boss was always really brilliant at making presentations. I can contact them and ask for their advice so I can improve my presentation skills.'

Second-level contacts

Don't forget your 'second level' contacts, i.e. your contacts' contacts.

'I found a work opportunity ideally suited to my skill set in conservation development in Central America through one of my partner's contacts.'

✎ Activity: Review and use your current networks

1. Review your current networks by creating a network mind map.
2. Identify people in your current network who can help you achieve your networking goals.
3. Decide how they can do this, perhaps provide advice, information, additional contacts.

Make new connections

The next step in your networking strategy is to develop your networks by increasing the number and range of contacts you have. Use your networking objectives to guide your priorities when it comes to making new connections. Remember: quality not quantity. You don't have time during a PhD to service a vast network of contacts. Consider what kind of contacts you need more of – for example, industry professionals, academic mentors, potential customers, potential job providers – in order to achieve your networking objectives. You can even identify specific people you want to make contact with. We are not recommending 'stalking' anyone, but it is perfectly reasonable to try to make contact with individuals in professional spheres. Social media has been a great boon in this respect: democratising access to fellow professionals. While you might not try to get a meeting with a highly respected professor to discuss your career plans, you could reply to one of their posts and make yourself known to them that way.

To develop the new connections you want, seek out opportunities through which to make contact. Consider identifying:

- Virtual or face-to-face events at which you will meet people you wish to include in your networks
- Social media opportunities to make contacts, whether discussion groups, social media hashtags and so on
- Other people's status in networks (in other words, *their* connection power) and 'piggy-back' on this, whether face to face or online – for example, if you're attending a conference with your supervisors, ask them to introduce you to people you want to make contact with.

✎ Activity: Network development

Identify individuals or the type of contacts you want to include in your network. Decide how you will make contact with these people. List them here and check them off when you have contacted them.

Contacts to include in my network	How I will contact these people	
		☐
		☐
		☐

		☐
		☐
		☐
		☐
		☐
		☐

Keep in touch

Building a network isn't done through one meeting. When we talk about networks, we are talking about *relationships*, and these take time to develop. Making an initial contact is the starting point; then you need to invest time in maintaining and developing your networks. This means keeping in touch and maintaining your presence. The following are some ideas for staying in touch.

How to strengthen your connections

Be interested, not just interesting	Showing genuine interest in the other person is a great way to build relationships. Focus on finding out about the people you meet rather than feeling pressure to fascinate or impress them.
Be a connector	Look for opportunities to bring people on your network in contact with each other if you think that would be useful for them. Your status and profile in a network are enhanced by your role as a 'connector' (your connection power).
Pay it forward	Do favours without the expectation of getting something back immediately in return. Remember, good networking is not simply transactional. You are building referent power through your networking activity.
Use it or lose it	Make regular use of your network as a means of keeping in contact. Ask for advice and information. Crowd-source solutions for your problems on social media. You will find out something and strengthen your network.

Every time you communicate with your networks, for whatever reason, you are *strengthening* your networks.

✎ Activity: Plan regular contact

Plan (and schedule) what you will do on a weekly basis to keep in touch with your networks. Tick the box when you've added it to your calendar.

What I will do to keep in touch with my networks:	
	☐
	☐
	☐
	☐
	☐
	☐

Summary

It's never too soon to position yourself for your future career. Running career development activities alongside your research will mean that you can make a seamless transition into the next phase of your life. It also means that you won't squander the career development opportunities provided by your PhD. If you're not sure exactly what you want to do next, you can still develop your employability by building the transferable skills that most employers want. Undertake a skills audit to assess your existing skills and your skills gaps. Then you can strategically identify what skills to develop and how.

Continue to build your professional networks, with a view to developing the contacts who can help you to achieve your next career goal. Networking should be an ongoing activity that you balance alongside your substantive research work. Using your networks by being visible, being a connector and keeping in touch will strengthen the power of your networks. Together, CV building and networking during your PhD will put you in the best position to take your next step.

Key points

- It is never too early in your PhD to think about your future career.
- Consider what skills and experience you will need in order to get where you want to go in your career, and take action now to acquire them during your PhD.
- Build the right professional networks to support your future career.
- Use it or lose it – maintain strong networks through frequent contact.
- Don't underestimate the value of your contacts' contacts.

Further resources

Blake, J. (2017) *Pivot: The Only Move That Matters is Your Next One*. New York: Portfolio/Penguin.
Bolles, R.N. (2022) *What Color is Your Parachute? Your Guide to a Lifetime of Meaningful Work and Career Success*. New York: Ten Speed Press.
Burkus, D. (2018) *Friend of a Friend: Understanding the Hidden Networks that Can Transform Your Life and Your Career*. Boston and New York: Houghton Mifflin Harcourt.
D'Souza, S. (2011) *Brilliant Networking*, 2nd edn. Harlow: Pearson.
Ferrazzi, K. and Raz, T. (2014) *Never Eat Alone: And Other Secrets to Success, One Relationship at a Time*. London: Penguin.
Newport, C. (2016) *So Good They Can't Ignore You*. London: Piatkus.

18 Deal with Setbacks

How to ... Bounce back when things go wrong

> Survival threats – Amygdala hijack – Reframing revisited – Growth and fixed mindsets – Action cures fear – Circle of control – Effort-impact matrix – Quick wins and essential challenges

We've said many times already that it's very unlikely that your PhD will go completely smoothly. So, every PhD student must prepare themselves for the experience of disappointment and failure, whether simply critical feedback on their work, experiments that don't turn out as expected, right up to global pandemics! Additionally, unforeseen personal problems, such as illness, family crises or financial problems can also threaten to derail your PhD. This isn't to suggest that these setbacks aren't serious or difficult to handle but rather to reassure you that most, if not all, successful PhD candidates have to deal with setbacks along the way. It's just life – and also a significant part of the uncertainty and emergent nature of research.

After using the techniques from Chapter 14 to build your resilience, you will already be better equipped to withstand setbacks. In Chapter 16, we provided techniques to handle the impact of changes on the management of your research project. In this chapter, we offer tools to help you bounce back from the psychological impact of these setbacks.

We revisit the impact of stress on the brain and the 'reframing' technique explored in Chapter 14 to consider how you can use this to reduce the negative fallout of setbacks and failures. In addition, we introduce some new techniques to help you move forward from a setback and take practical steps to minimise the negative impact.

Stress and the brain, revisited

Let's briefly revisit the impact of stress so that you can understand the impact of a setback on your brain and what it means for your ability to respond constructively. In Chapter 14, we explained how demands that challenge our abilities can trigger a stress response. A setback is a particularly stressful type of challenge. Unconsciously, a setback is experienced as a threat to our survival. In evolutionary terms, it's the difference between gearing up to chase down fleeing prey and being the potential prey. Often, a setback is also combined with a sense of shock: it's something bad that happens for which we aren't prepared.

This means that a setback can trigger our fight-or-flight response – our unconscious reaction to a threat. You don't choose this; it just happens. This is also called an amygdala hijack because the trigger of stress hormones involves parts of the brain called the amygdala. The stress reaction 'hijacks' your brain in the service of your fight-or-flight response and sidelines rational, conscious thinking processes for the duration of the stress reaction. Remember your prefrontal cortex (PFC) from Chapter 12? This part of your brain is particularly important in high-level cognitive tasks, such as rational thinking and decision making. Your amygdala and PFC function like two ends of see-saw. When your amygdala are fired up, the functioning of your PFC is suppressed. This is why, when you face a shock, you sometimes can't think straight.

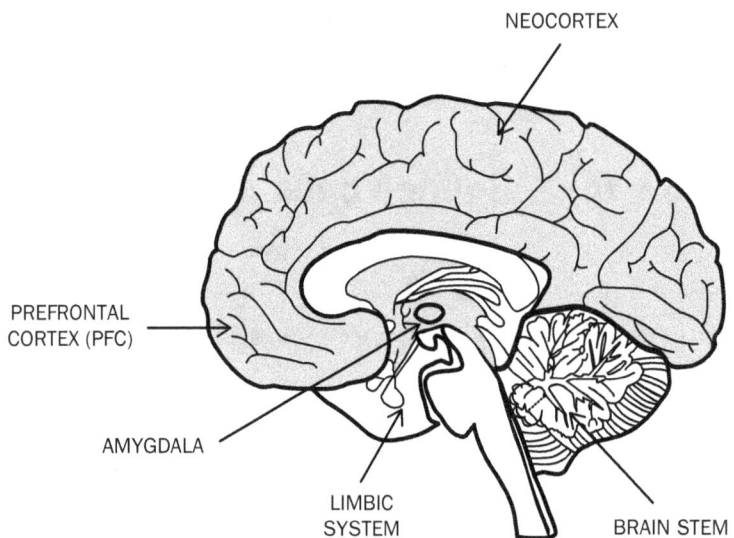

The human brain: prefrontal cortex and amygdala

This type of stress reaction evolved to handle survival threats. Speed of reaction is key to survival. In your PhD, your survival isn't under threat. The best reaction isn't fight or flight, but rather to engage the PFC and make considered decisions. If your supervisor suddenly pulls apart your carefully drafted chapter, the best response isn't to hit them (fight) or to run from their office (flight) – however much you might want to! If your important conference proposal is rejected, rather than throwing your laptop across the room (fight) or vowing you'll never submit a conference proposal again (flight), you'd be better to engaging your PFC and deciding how you can do better next time. Easy to say, but not easy to do when you're experiencing that flood of fight-or-flight hormones.

Understanding what's going on in your brain when you experience the shock of a setback can help you to deal with it and recover your equilibrium more quickly. Don't make important decisions when you are in that state; wait until you've calmed down, the stress hormones have had time to disperse and your PFC is back in charge. This might seem obvious, but, sometimes, if you're caught off guard by a problem, you can feel under pressure to respond immediately. There are things you can do to help you regain control:

➡ **Action: Breathe.**

Slowing down your breathing counteracts the shock.

➡ **Action: Speak.**

Language re-engages your sidelined PFC. Speaking rationally about what's happening will help you to regain control over the strong emotions of the situation.

➡ **Action: Take time out.**

Take some time to allow the hormonal impact of stress to fade and to collect yourself, rather than rushing to make decisions in the heat of the moment.

Once the biological response to the immediate stress of a setback has passed, you are left with the ongoing fallout. Psychological impact of the experience may leave you feeling anxious, angry, discouraged or helpless. There will also be a practical impact – what do you need to do to recover the situation? To help you recover from the psychological impact of the setback, we are going to return to the technique of managing your thoughts that we explored first in Chapter 14.

Manage your thoughts

In Chapter 14, we explained the technique of reframing your 'beliefs' about 'activating events' to generate resilient responses to them (consequences). You can take the same approach to help you respond more effectively to setbacks. We will use the concept of mindset pioneered by Stanford psychologist Professor Carol Dweck (2017). It provides a kind of template to guide your reframing of your beliefs about setbacks and to reduce the likelihood that they will derail your PhD.

In her research into success, Dweck observed that one of the factors that determined whether school children coped well with failure and sought out new challenges was their *attitude to their own abilities*. She dubbed this perspective their 'mindset' and identified two different mindsets: 'growth' and 'fixed'. These had a significant impact on the children's performance. The research was subsequently widened to demonstrate the validity of the concept in parenting, business and sport, as well as education. The attributes of the two mindsets are as follows:

- **Growth mindset** is a belief that innate talent, intelligence and ability are merely the starting point when it comes to performance and that *they can be increased by effort, training and experience*. People with a growth mindset have been shown to be more likely to respond better to setbacks, to experience greater success, and sustain their improvements in performance.
- **Fixed mindset** is a belief that all talent, intelligence and ability is *inborn and static*. Education and training provide the opportunity to *demonstrate* inborn ability, rather than increase it. As a result, failure is experienced as being due to a lack of ability. People with a fixed mindset have been shown to be more likely to give up in the face of challenges or setbacks.

There are some nuances to the model that are important in understanding the mindsets and deciding how you can use the framework to help you deal with setbacks you face in your PhD:

- Your mindset is formed during your early experiences as children, in the family and at school, and may even be somewhat influenced by genetics. It's not something you have consciously chosen. Don't waste time beating yourself up if you have a fixed mindset.
- You might have a fixed mindset about some things in your life (and your PhD) and a growth mindset about others.
- It is possible to change from a fixed to a growth mindset over time, through consciously adopting growth-mindset attitudes and reframing your thinking.
- The mindsets are *not* linked to ability. It is perfectly possible to have a fixed mindset and be a high achiever because of an innate talent or academic prowess. The problem is that, with a fixed mindset, if you reach the limits of this innate ability, for example, by experiencing a failure, you are less likely to overcome it and bounce back compared with someone who has a growth mindset.
- A growth mindset is *not* the same as positive thinking. It isn't an invitation to ignore setbacks or pretend failures haven't happened or aren't important. A growth mindset manifests in the way that these failures are then interpreted and addressed.

How could this help you to cope with setbacks in your PhD? A fixed mindset has been shown repeatedly in research to result in a tendency to be discouraged by failure and to give up rather than bounce back. A growth mindset will help you to see the setback as something to be dealt with and overcome. The mindset framework is a useful reframing template to help you respond to setbacks. Essentially, this is another version of the ABC method (page 179) with the addition of the mindset concept with which to construct a more helpful 'belief'.

Reframing your mindset

> **1 ➡ Action: Revisit your 'beliefs' in the context of mindset.**
>
> Use the framework to reflect upon your 'beliefs' about a setback and identify whether they are representative of a fixed or growth mindset.
>
> **2 ➡ Action: Reframe a fixed mindset.**
>
> If you discover that you have been using a fixed mindset, use the reframing techniques to switch to a growth mindset, thereby shifting your reaction to a more constructive mode.
>
> **3 ➡ Action: Reflect, reframe, repeat.**
>
> Over time, repeated reframing will retrain your thinking patterns so that you increasingly default to a growth mindset.

If you discover that you already have a growth mindset in relation to your PhD, then you're already psychologically well-equipped to respond constructively to setbacks. Congratulations! However, be alert for new situations in which you might have a fixed mindset. For example, you might be able to handle academic criticism of your research work with a growth mindset, but, when competing with others for professional jobs, or developing non-academic skills such as presenting or networking, you might find that these trigger a fixed mindset.

Although you react with a different mindset to different kinds of setbacks, it's not the inherent properties of the setback that dictate the mindset. It is your *perception* of the challenges and then the mindset response (the belief) that shapes the impact of the setback. For example, imagine that your conference paper is rejected. The mindset of your belief about this setback will have a knock-on effect in terms of the impact of the setback:

Activating event: My conference paper submission is rejected	
Fixed mindset belief My research isn't original enough to warrant a conference presentation	**Growth mindset belief** One this occasion, I didn't clearly represent the value of my research to the conference selection committee
Consequence Discouragement; self-doubt; lack of confidence for future submissions	**Consequence** Disappointment; determination; another attempt

Fixed vs growth mindsets: beliefs and consequences

How can you spot that your response to a setback is fixed or growth? There are some linguistic clues you can watch out for:

- Fixed mindset responses are often couched in absolute terms, for example never, always, everyone, every time.
- Growth mindset responses usually have a sense of impermanence, such as not yet, on this occasion, next time.

Just shifting the language that you use to *think* about your experiences, from fixed to growth, can have a powerful effect. Fixed-mindset thoughts can lead to a sense of helplessness, defeat and powerlessness. In contrast, a growth mindset leads to a sense of agency, determination and hope for the future.

Fixed-mindset language	Growth-mindset language
I'll *never* be able to write well.	My academic writing isn't good enough *yet*.
I *always* end up finishing my work at the last minute.	*This time*, I ended up finishing my work at the last minute.
My experiments fail *every* time	I now know this doesn't work. *Next time*, I'll try something different.

Fixed vs growth mindset language

Don't underestimate the power of these thoughts. They are the messages you give to your own mind and they have a significant impact on how you see yourself, your experiences and your world. The more you repeat them, the more you create the 'thinking habits' that shape your experiences and dictate their consequences. Choose these messages wisely.

✎ Activity: Mindset reframing

Whenever you encounter a setback, use this table to reframe your beliefs if necessary.

Activating event Note the details of the setback you are facing.	
Beliefs Consider the thoughts you have about the setback.	
Identify your **mindset**	Growth ✗ ✓ Fixed ✗ ✓
Reframe If your beliefs are from a fixed mindset, give yourself some alternative growth beliefs about the setback.	

238 Part 3 – How to Keep Going

Take action to overcome setbacks

By attending to your mindset, you will minimise the negative psychological impact of setbacks and be able to focus on what you can do practically to bounce back. There is a valuable saying (from Schwartz, 2007) for dealing with challenges and setbacks:

Action cures fear.

This reminds you that, however stressful the situation, the best strategy is *always* to take action and get moving again.

How do you know what action you should take? The actions available to you will be entirely down to the specifics of the situation you find yourself in. However, there are two tools you can use to assess your options and decide on your best course of action. These tools are useful in all sorts of PhD circumstances – from helping you make good decisions to spending your time wisely. They are particularly useful in the aftermath of a setback because they will get you moving again. The key to making good choices about your next steps is to assess:

- **Control** – what actions are available to you
- **Impact** – what difference your actions will make.

The Circle of Control

Let's look first at how you can assess the control you have by using the circle of control tool. This is based on a concept introduced by Stephen Covey (2020). He recommends that, in any situation requiring action from you, you must first assess what aspects are under your control and then distinguish the degree of control available according to three different 'circles'.

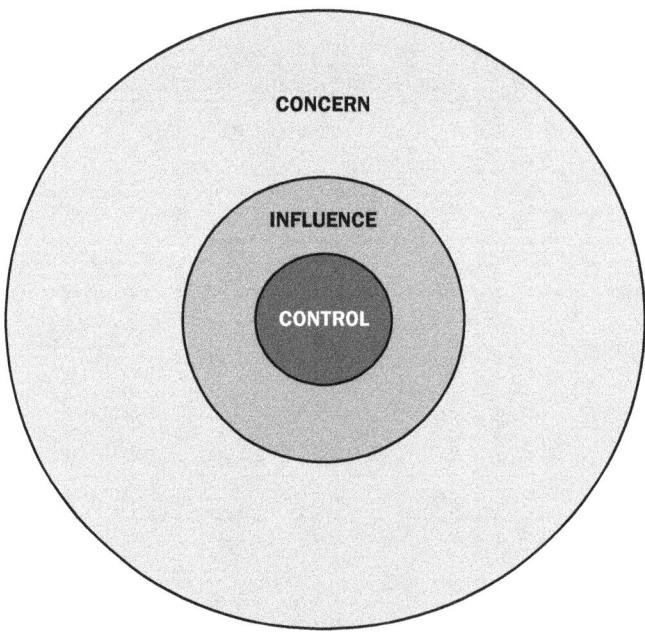

Circle of control

- **Your circle of *control*** – Actions you can take that have direct control over the outcome.
- **Your circle of *influence*** – Actions you can take that may affect the outcome.
- **Your circle of *concern*** – Issues that you have no control or influence over.

By assessing which possible responses to a setback fall into which circle, you can see where best to put your efforts to salvage the situation:

- Do/act on (some of) the things that fall into your circles of control and circles of influence.
- Let go of the things that fall into your circle of concern. Don't waste your time.

> **Transferable skills**
>
> Control is a very important factor in human functioning. Repeated studies on the causes of stress in the workplace show that one of the key factors in the degree of stress experienced in a situation is the amount of control we feel we have. A lack of control is highly stressful. By using this tool to take control of what you can you will feel better about your problems and reduce your stress, now and in your future career.

Imagine a setback where you have had your conference submission rejected. What issues fall into each circle?

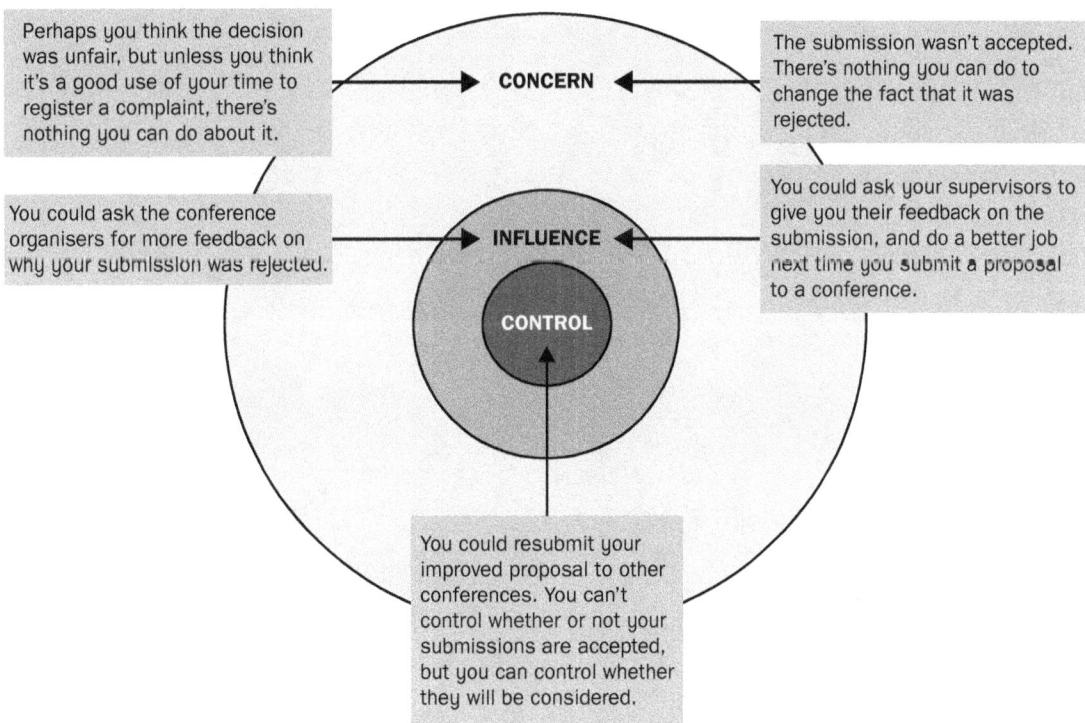

Circle of control: conference submission rejection

Using this tool helps you to focus on where you can make a difference rather than wasting your time bemoaning or regretting things in your circle of concern. This is empowering and improves your sense of self-efficacy, which will, in turn, build your confidence and resilience. It also makes you appear more effective to those around you. We all know people who spend their time complaining about things they can't do anything about rather than doing something constructive and, conversely, those people who are pragmatic and do what they can.

> **✎ Activity: Circle of control assessment**
>
> Use the template on page 241 to assess your options in the wake of a setback. Make this assessment whenever you want to bounce back from a setback.

📄 Template: Circle of control assessment

Complete this assessment whenever you are dealing with a setback.	
Note the details of a current setback you are facing:	

Circle of control: List the actions that you could take that would definitely have a positive impact on your recovery from the setback:

Circle of influence: List the actions you could take that would have a positive influence on your recovery from the setback:

Circle of concern: List the issues that fall outside your circles of control or influence, that you can let go of:

© RDT&C

Take action that makes a difference

If you have a range of actions that fall into your circles of control and influence, we recommend a simple tool to help you assess the best course of action: the effort-impact matrix:

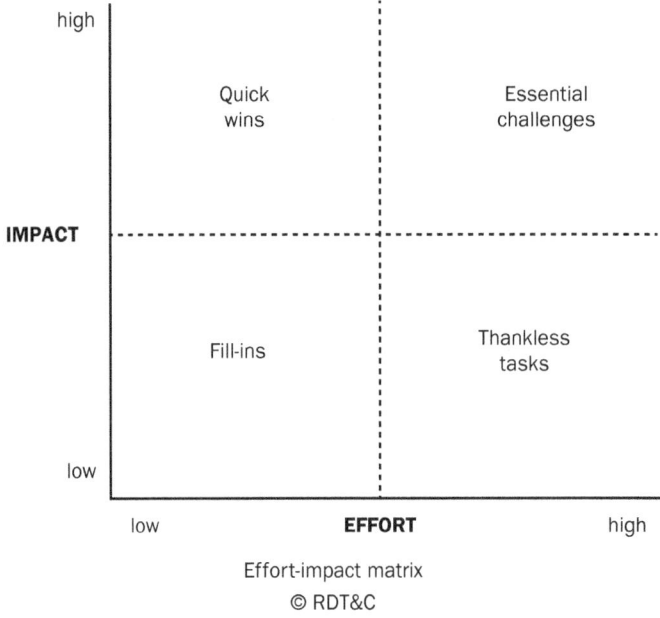

Effort-impact matrix
© RDT&C

To use this tool:

- Assess the *effort* required to undertake the action – this might be hours you'll need to spend, equipment you have to use, and so on.
- Assess the likely positive *impact* of the action – what difference it will make.

Combining the degree of effort and impact produces four categories of actions which help you to identify where best to focus your time and energy.

Categories of action from the effort-impact matrix

Quick wins	Actions that are low-to-medium effort and medium-to-high impact. It's a no-brainer – do these!
Essential challenges	Actions that are medium-to-high effort and medium-to-high impact. These may take more effort, but their impact means they are worth the investment. The higher the impact, the more value in making the investment.
Fill-ins	Actions that are low-to-medium effort and low-to-medium impact. They are not worth it. Don't bother.
Thankless tasks	Actions that are medium-to-high effort but low-to-medium impact. There's really no reason for doing these things! They take up a lot of time and they won't have any positive impact. A complete waste of your time.

Let's see how we could apply the effort-impact matrix to our example of the rejected conference submission. These are the potential actions identified from the circle of control on page 239:

1. Complain to the conference organisers that your proposal was rejected unfairly.
2. Ask your supervisors to give you their feedback on the submission.
3. Ask the conference organisers for more feedback on your submission.
4. Read examples of successful submissions, to see how they are better than yours.
5. Resubmit proposals to other conferences.

By using the matrix to plot the effort and impact attached to each of these options, you can:

- Decide which to do and which to avoid
- Prioritise and schedule your actions, to take advantage of your 'quick wins' and make time for your 'essential challenges'.

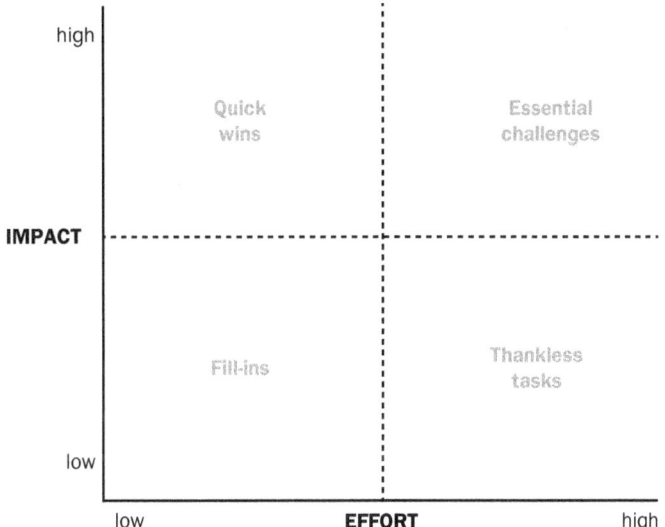

Effort-impact matrix: conference submission rejection
© RDT&C

In this example, it's clear that:

- The best quick win is:
    - To ask the conference organisers for more feedback on your submission.
- The essential challenges are:
    - To read examples of successful submissions, to see how they are better than yours
    - To submit proposals to other conferences.

Perhaps even more importantly, it makes it clear that the thankless task, which can be dropped, is:

- To complain to the conference organisers that your proposal was rejected unfairly.

Activity: Effort-impact assessment

Using the template on page 245:

1. Note the setback.
2. List the actions you *could* take.
3. Plot them in the effort-impact matrix, according to the effort required and the likely impact and classify them according to the segment they fall into.
4. Decide which actions you will take.

Deal with Setbacks **245**

Template: Effort-impact assessment

The situation/setback:	
Potential mitigating actions	**Which matrix segment?**

```
           high │
                │      Quick           Essential
                │      wins            challenges
                │                │
       IMPACT   │────────────────┼────────────────
                │                │
                │      Fill-ins       Thankless
                │                     tasks
            low │                │
                └────────────────┴────────────────
                 low          EFFORT           high
```

Action plan: Which actions I will take

© RDT&C

Summary

It's inevitable that you will experience setbacks during your PhD. The key is to be able to bounce back from them as quickly and constructively as possible. A setback is experienced as a threat. It can trigger your body's fight-or-flight mechanism, which makes a rational, practical response very hard.

By taking practical steps to re-engage your rational brain, you can quickly restore your equilibrium. You can minimise the psychological fallout of a setback by using the concept of a growth mindset to reframe your reaction. Cultivating a growth mindset over time will insulate you against setbacks and help you to bounce back more quickly. Taking action will help you feel more in control and less helpless in the face of setbacks, as well as repairing any damage to your research project. By assessing what you can do and what concerns to let go of, you can focus your efforts on the most beneficial course of action. Choosing what actions to take according to their impact and effort will ensure that you don't waste your time on pointless tasks.

Key points

- The key to a successful PhD isn't to avoid setbacks but to learn how to bounce back from them.
- Give yourself time before making important decisions – your rational brain needs to recover from the shock of setbacks.
- Cultivate a positive mindset in order to take setbacks in your stride.
- Take action to rebuild your feelings of control and reduce your stress.
- Don't waste your time on pointless reactions – choose responses to setbacks that will deliver most benefit, ideally for least effort.

Further resources

Covey, S. (2020) *The Seven Habits of Highly Effective People*. London: Simon and Schuster.
Dweck, C. (2017) *Mindset: Changing the Way You Think to Fulfil Your Potential*, 6th edn. London: Robinson.
Gillihan, S.J. (2020) *Cognitive Behavioural Therapy Made Simple: 10 Strategies for Managing Anxiety, Depression, Anger, Panic and Worry*. London: Sheldon Press.
Hills, J. (2016) *Brain-Savvy Business*. London: Head, Heart & Brain.
Miller, C.A. and Frisch, M.B. (2021) *Creating Your Best Life*. New York: Sterling.
Reivich, K. and Shatte, A. (2003) *The Resilience Factor: 7 Keys to Finding Your Inner Strength and Overcoming Life's Hurdles*. New York: Broadway Books.

References

Covey, S. (2020) *The Seven Habits of Highly Effective People*. London: Simon and Schuster.
Dweck, C. (2017) *Mindset: Changing the Way You Think Tto Fulfil Your Potential*. London: Robinson.
Schwartz, D.J. (2007) *The Magic of Thinking Big*. Gleneden Beach, OR: Fireside Press, p51.

19 Handle Conflict and Confrontation

How to ... Have those difficult conversations

> Conflicts of interest – Conflict-management modes – Communication skills – Non-verbal language – Active listening – Open questions – I-statements – The broken-record technique

At some point during your PhD, you are likely to find yourself in conflict, whether a stand-off with your supervisors about the direction of your research or tensions with fellow PhD students. A conflict is more than disagreement. A conflict is a situation in which people feel that their *interests are threatened* by the opinions or actions of other people. Robust disagreement is part of academic discourse and learning how to handle it will be an important part of your professional development during your PhD, but you may also face true *conflicts* in which your interests are potentially compromised. For example, you might have concerns about shortcomings in the conduct of your supervision; there may be changes to the focus of your PhD, meaning that it no longer aligns with your personal goals; or you might face difficult behaviour from colleagues that prevents you working effectively. These issues aren't just a difference of opinion. They are problems that might affect the successful completion of your PhD. Knowing how to confront such issues promptly and constructively before they escalate will minimise the disruption to your PhD.

Conflict isn't necessarily problematic. It can be a valuable process, leading to greater mutual understanding and creative solutions to problems. For example, addressing supervision shortcomings rather than ignoring them might result in improvements or a change of supervisor; or raising your misgivings about the focus of your research might mean that you can shift it in line with your needs. Some conflict is inevitable when people are working together. Having the skills to deal with conflict constructively and confidently will ensure that you can gain the benefits of well-resolved conflicts.

 Transferable skills

Conflict is an inevitable part of teamworking and collaboration. Conflict-management skills are therefore highly valued by employers, especially if you're aiming to occupy leadership and management positions.

You might well be asked in an interview to provide an example of a conflict situation in the workplace and how you resolved it. So, keep a note of any conflicts you resolve during your PhD.

This chapter provides a conflict-resolution tool to help you decide on your best strategy for handling a conflict. It also includes communication techniques to help you handle the difficult conversations that might be needed in order to resolve conflicts.

The persuasive communication techniques in Chapter 13 will also help you to handle confrontation and conflict effectively.

Conflict management strategies

The specific details of any conflict will demand different conflict-resolution approaches, for example: How important is the issue? What else is at stake? How likely are you to achieve your aims? The Thomas-Kilmann (1974) 'conflict management modes' framework is a well-established conflict-resolution approach that can help you to decide how (and whether) to deal with conflict. This framework is based on two dimensions:

- **Assertiveness** – the degree to which you assert your own needs and get what *you* want
- **Cooperativeness** – the degree to which you work to ensure other people get what *they* want.

The combination of assertiveness and cooperativeness produces a set of five conflict-management modes to choose from.

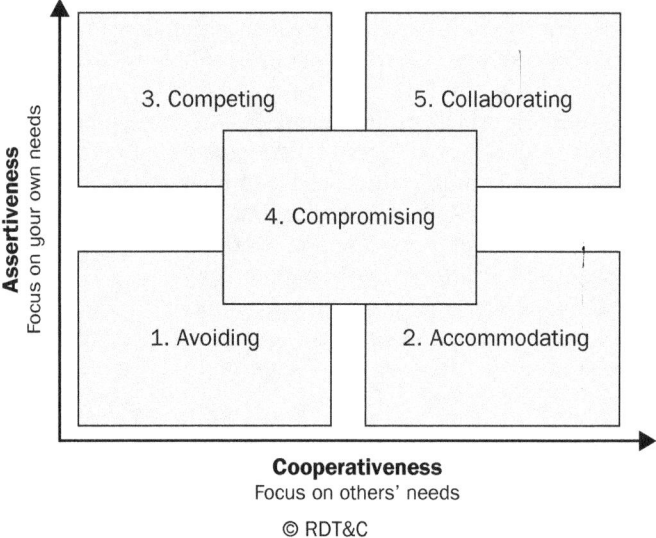

The following examples from PhD students illustrate how you might use each conflict management mode.

1. Avoiding

- Assertiveness: low
- Cooperativeness: low.

You neither attempt to fulfill your own needs, nor do you try to facilitate the fulfilment of the needs of the other people. You just ignore the conflict. For example:

> You share an office with a PhD student who regularly has loud phone conversations. You find this interrupts your concentration, but you decide to live with it rather than ask them to take their calls out of the office.

Use *avoiding* when:

- The issue isn't all that important and won't affect your PhD work
- Addressing the issue will cause more disruption than it's worth
- You are unlikely to find a resolution to this conflict.

Be careful:

- Don't use the avoiding mode purely because you fear conflict.
- Always consider the possible longer-term impact of the avoiding mode, as issues that are not addressed may become more problematic later.

2. Accommodating

- Assertiveness: low
- Cooperativeness: high.

You take steps to ensure that other people get what they want, but don't make an effort to have your own needs fulfilled. You give way to the other person. For example:

> Your supervisor asks you to work at the weekend as the whole research group will be there. You agree even though you'd already made plans to visit friends.

Use *accommodating* when:

- The issue is more important to them than to you
- It won't cost you much to accommodate their needs
- It will create goodwill or a sense of obligation that you might be able to draw on later
- The disruption of refusing to give in will be more damaging than giving way.

Be careful:

- Too much accommodating might make you seem (or feel!) weak, and other people may take advantage of you.
- Be wary of defaulting to accommodating because you dislike conflict.
- Don't be accommodating on the *assumption* that you will get a quid pro quo.
- Using the accommodating mode with someone who is generally dominating or takes advantage of you will only reinforce that dynamic.

3. Competing

- Assertiveness: high
- Cooperativeness: low.

You focus your efforts on getting what you want and pay no attention to the needs of the other people. For example:

> You refuse your supervisor's request to work at the weekend, and stick to your original plans.

Use *competing* when:

- It is vital to you to get your own way
- You are dealing with people who will otherwise take advantage and you want to assert yourself and show strength
- When the other party uses the competing mode and you need to fight back.

Be careful:

- You must have confidence and determination to use the competing mode.
- You may need power or status to back this up.
- This won't make you any friends.
- If other people feel they were poorly treated, it may build up resentments.

4. Compromising

- Assertiveness: moderate
- Cooperativeness: moderate.

You work to create a solution that meets *some* of the needs of everyone involved. For example:

> Rather than working the whole weekend, you offer to come in on Sunday, which means you can spend Saturday with your friends.

Use *compromising* when:

- Conflicting demands cannot be completely resolved
- You need a temporary solution that will allow you to move forward, with the intention of revisiting the problem later
- It's the best you can hope for.

Be careful:

- Although a compromise can be a practical option, don't assume it's the best you can do. Taking the extra time needed to use the collaborating mode might create innovative solutions that can fulfill all needs.

5. Collaborating

- Assertiveness: high
- Cooperativeness: high.

You work together to find new, innovative or creative solutions that meet everyone's needs. For example:

> You discuss with your supervisor the work they want done at the weekend and discover that you could instead come in the following weekend, when you don't have plans, and still complete the necessary work.

Use *collaborating* when:

- Both sets of concerns are too important to be compromised
- You can create a much better solution by working together and taking different perspectives
- You want to ensure that everyone is satisfied and committed to the agreed solution.

Be careful:

- Collaborating takes time – don't use it if there are significant time pressures.
- Successful collaborating relies on everyone genuinely committing to the process.
- There may not be a collaborating solution. Be ready to go back to compromising as a best option.

> **Activity: Apply conflict management modes to a conflict**
>
> Use the template on page 253 to apply the conflict-management modes to a conflict you are facing. (The following example demonstrates how to do this.)

Conflict management mode assessment: example

Use the conflict-management modes to resolve a conflict or raise a difficult issue.
1 Think of a conflict you are involved in and note some of the details.
My primary supervisor wants me focus on any link between vaping and laryngeal cancer. I want to focus on the links between traditional tobacco use and cancer. Another of their PhD students has been told to look at traditional tobacco usage and cancer. My supervisor has already published in the emerging field of the health impact of vaping.
2 What do you want?
I want to focus my research primarily on the impact of traditional tobacco usage on cancer prevalence because tobacco usage is still rising in developing nations where it is causing health problems and where there is often poor healthcare provision.
3 What do the other people want? (Or what do you think they want?)
I think my supervisor wants to continue building their reputation by publishing research on vaping, which is a newer area than traditional tobacco use. The four PhDs recruited to the research group applied to conduct cancer research. None, other than me, is particularly favouring one topic.
4 Assess the conflict management modes.

Mode	Potential benefits	Potential risks
Avoiding	I don't have to confront my supervisor.	It's central to my personal goal for taking a PhD. I could suffer motivation issues and fail to satisfy my main reason for going into research – to help people in developing nations.
Accommodating	My supervisor will be very helpful to my research because of their knowledge. I may be able to capitalise on their reputation and get published more easily.	Tobacco usage is what interests me most. It will affect my commitment to the whole project.
Competing	I would be able to do the research topic that interests me most.	I'm not sure I have the nerve to go up against my supervisor. I would risk alienating them and losing their support.
Compromising	If I could find a way of partly doing what they want – perhaps a comparison. I could keep them on board and still do the research my way.	The scope of my PhD would end up too wide and I won't be able to complete all of the work.
Collaborating	If I explained my reasons, my supervisor might be able to suggest another way of incorporating my areas of interest into the workstream I've been assigned to.	Can't see any!

5 Which conflict management mode/s will you use and how?

Collaborating:
  – I will double-check whether any of the other PhDs would like to focus on vaping instead of me, so I can propose it as a solution.
  – I will raise my concerns with my supervisor and explain why I would like to focus on traditional tobacco usage, and ask their advice.

Template: Conflict management mode assessment

Use the Conflict management modes to resolve a conflict or raise a difficult issue.		
1 Think of a conflict you are involved in and note some of the details.		
2 What do you want?		
3 What do the other people want? (Or what do you think they want?)		
4 Assess the conflict-management modes.		
Mode	**Potential benefits**	**Potential risks**
Avoiding		
Accommodating		
Competing		
Compromising		
Collaborating		
5 Which conflict management mode/s will you use and how?		

Communication skills for conflict management

You will rely on your communication skills to successfully *use* the conflict-management modes. The following four sets of communication techniques will help you to resolve conflict.

Non-verbal language

Non-verbal language is what you say without words:

- **Body language** – eye contact, facial expression, posture, hand gestures
- **Vocal tone** – the pitch, pace and melody of your voice.

Research by Albert Mehrabian (1971) suggested that non-verbal elements of language are responsible for 93 per cent of the messages we convey to others in face-to-face communication! This is particularly the case when the non-verbal elements are at odds with the verbal elements. If your words are saying one thing, for example, 'I am keen to find a compromise,' but your non-verbal language says, 'I am not interested in what you are saying,' the message of the non-verbal elements will supersede the words.

Becoming aware of and managing your non-verbal communication is a hugely powerful tool in improving the impression you make on other people in all kinds of situations. When you are confronting potentially difficult issues, present yourself confidently by:

> **Transferable skills**
>
> Although these communication skills are featured in this chapter on conflict, they are all highly transferable and can be used to improve your communication in any situation.

- Maintaining direct eye contact
- Sitting or standing firm and upright
- Avoiding 'closed' body language, such as slumped shoulders or folded arms, which can convey defensiveness
- Not fidgeting, which can convey uncertainty or a lack of concentration
- Ensuring your facial expression accurately mirrors the impression you want to convey, for example friendly, enthusiastic, serious
- Using a clear, strong voice – many people undermine their verbal message because their voice is soft or hesitant
- Using a measured pace when speaking to give weight to your words.

It can be difficult to know what your non-verbal language conveys as it is mostly unconscious. If you want to identify aspects to improve, you could:

- Watch a video of yourself, for example giving presentations, or film yourself
- Ask for feedback on your non-verbal language from a friend or colleague
- Pick a non-verbal component that you suspect needs improving, perhaps eye contact, and consciously practise it.

Activity: Improve your non-verbal communication

Decide what areas of non-verbal communication to focus on and how you will address them. Note them here.
Consciously practise using them in discussions (not just conflict resolution) and observe what impact they have.
Check them off when you notice an improvement.

What I will do to improve my non-verbal communication:	
	☐
	☐
	☐
	☐
	☐
	☐

Active listening

Listening is an underrated but extremely powerful communication technique, especially in conflict resolution. This can come as a surprise as people often think that conflict resolution is all about telling the other people what you want. Listening to the other person's position, rather than simply putting your own case forward, will help you to:

- Show respect
- Better understand other people's perspectives and positions
- Access better information about the situation
- Find points to use in negotiating a resolution.

Listening as a communication skill is a particular type of listening, called active listening. Active listening is not just listening, but also *demonstrating* that you are listening. In order to use active listening effectively:

➡ **Action: Truly listen!**

Genuinely pay attention to what the other person is saying.

➡ **Action: Listen without judgement of their position (at least at first).**

Focus on trying to understand their position. This conveys respect and will help you to appreciate their perspective.

➡ **Action: Avoid interrupting.**

Keep quiet and let the other person have their say.

➜ Action: Use body language to show that you are listening.

Maintain eye contact, nod and display an open posture.

➜ Action: Don't rush in to have your say or make suggestions.

First, summarise what you have understood from the other person. This shows that you have been listening and is also a chance to double-check your understanding.

✎ Activity: Improve your active listening

Decide which area of active listening to improve and when you will do it. Make notes here.
Decide when you will practise using them, in conversations or meetings, and observe what impact they have.
Check them off when you notice an improvement.

Aspects of active listening I will practise:	
	☐
	☐
	☐
	☐
	☐

Open questioning

Using open questions rather than closed questions can be another key communication tool in conflict resolution. A closed question invites just a yes/no response or some other simple information as an answer. For example:

- 'Can I use the optical emission spectrometer next Tuesday?'
- 'What time have you booked the small meeting room in the grad school?'
- 'How many words should my literature review chapter be?'

An open question encourages and allows greater freedom in the response, and is often prefixed by 'How', 'What', 'In what ways', 'Why.' For example:

- '*How* would it affect you if I used the optical emission spectrometer next Tuesday?'
- '*What* work do you plan to do in the grad school's small meeting room?'
- '*What* is the best way to structure my literature review?'

Open questions are particularly useful when using the compromising or collaborating conflict-management modes because they:

- Help you to find out more about the other person's perspectives and needs and allow you to suggest appropriate solutions

- Stimulate thinking and reflection in the person you are questioning, and may generate new ideas
- Pave the way for truly collaborative problem-solving
- Reduce the adversarial nature of conflict by showing curiosity and respect for the other person's perspective.

For example, if you ask a fellow PhD student, 'Can I use the optical emission spectrometer next Tuesday?' they will either say yes (great!) or no. If you ask, 'How would it affect you if I used the optical emission spectrometer next Tuesday?' they will explain how it would affect them, potentially giving you scope to find a way of using the kit that suits your needs but doesn't inconvenience them. It sets you up to use the compromising or collaboration modes.

Activity: Improve your open questioning

Choose a situation in which you could practise open questioning, such as a supervision meeting or research group meeting. Note some examples of open questions you could use.
Reflect on whether it makes any difference to the outcome of the conversation.

The situation

What I want to know	Open questions
e.g. Is my data analysis chapter of a high-enough standard?	• What else do I need to do to improve my work? • What are your expectations for my data analysis chapter?

Asserting techniques

As we explained, dealing with conflict isn't all about cooperativeness. It also requires assertiveness. Whether you want to use the competing mode and insist on your needs, or to provide clarity as the precursor to compromising or collaborating, you need to be able to assert your position unambiguously. The following techniques are useful when you want to make your needs clear and, if necessary, stand your ground.

Part 3 – How to Keep Going

The I-statement technique

The I-statement is a short statement that sums up your key need, opinion or request, without explanation, justification or qualification. It starts, 'I think …' or 'I want …' or 'I need ….' If this seems obvious, you probably have no problems expressing your needs, opinions or demands clearly! Many people, however, for personality or cultural reasons, feel uncomfortable with such direct communication, although there is nothing inherently aggressive or disrespectful about an I-statement. It is simply a clear expression of your position.

The shift to an I-statement can be small, but powerful in its impact.

I-statement examples

Statement	I-statement
I am interested in attending the conference.	I *want* to attend the conference.
I'm not sure that my second supervisor is well-equipped to be part of my supervision team.	I *want* an alternative second supervisor.
I'm unhappy about using a survey-based research design to obtain my data.	I *want* to use qualitative interviews to obtain my data.
I am a bit worried about the deadline to submit my draft ethics submission.	I *want* to postpone the deadline for my draft ethics submission.

The I-statement helps you when you are resolving a conflict because:

- The process of constructing it gives you *clarity about your own needs* – you will be in a stronger position to assert yourself and to negotiate
- Articulating your I-statement makes it *easier for other people to understand* what you want and think – using an I-statement isn't trying to bully them into agreeing or giving in to you; they can always say no
- An I-statement may make the process of conflict resolution quicker as you are clear up front about what you want
- I-statements reduce the chance of misunderstandings and false 'resolutions'
- An I-statement can sometimes resolve perceived conflict which may be based on misunderstandings about what everyone wants or needs.

Be careful:

- Don't *only* communicate in 'I-statements'. Save the technique for when you need to be firm and clear.
- The I-statement doesn't include any explanations or qualifications of your point, so it can also be valuable to be explain, justify and support your requests (see Chapter 13).
- You need to use confident non-verbal language to back up your I-statement.

> **Activity: Create and use your I-statement**
> 1. Think of a situation in which you want to assert yourself. Note the details her.
> 2. Consider what you want to assert (your opinion, need or request)
> 3. Create an I-statement to convey that key message.
> 4. Decide when you are going to use your I-statement.
> 5. Once you have tried it, note the impact.

Details of the situation	
What you want to assert	
Your I-statement	
When you plan to use it	
What was the impact?	

The broken record technique

Another useful technique when you want to stand your ground, particularly in the face of indifference or resistance, is the broken record technique. This builds on the I-statement and is well-suited to the competing conflict management mode.

To use the broken record technique, start with your I-statement and then repeat it to ensure that it is not ignored. Always include an 'acknowledge' step to demonstrate that you are also listening to the other person to avoid annoying or alienating them. The formula is:

1 Acknowledge (what the other person has said).
2 Repeat your I-statement.

The following two versions of the same conversation demonstrate how the technique works in practice. The first uses an I-statement (italic). The second adds the broken record technique.

Conversation 1: I-statement

PhD Student: There's a lot of noise in my data. *I want to re-run my experiment.*
Technician: There's no more lab time available for you to re-run the experiment.
PhD Student: I don't think it will take a lot of time. How much time can I have in the lab?
Technician: There's no time. I'm already running behind the project schedule.
PhD Student: How far behind is the project? What if I re-run it over the weekend?
Technician: There's no budget for overtime to keep the lab open over the weekend. Can't you account for the noise during your analysis?
PhD Student: But that means adjusting the statistical basis for the analysis, which I don't have time for.
Technician: That's something you can make time for later.

There's nothing particularly wrong with this discussion. The student has been clear about what they want by using an I-statement, but the technician clearly doesn't want to agree to the request. The student is trying to counter all the objections with constructive proposals, but the technician isn't interested, so the student doesn't get what they want.

Now look at the same conversation again. This time however, the PhD student uses the broken record technique to push their point.

Conversation 2: Broken record

PhD Student:	There's a lot of noise in my data. *I want to re-run my experiment.*
Technician:	There's no more lab time available for you to re-run the experiment.
PhD Student:	I realise it will mean finding some extra lab time [acknowledge], but *I want to re-run the experiment.*
Technician:	There's no budget for tech staff overtime in the lab.
PhD Student:	I will avoid overtime [acknowledge] so *I can re-run the experiment.*
Technician:	The rest of the research team can't give up their lab time for you.
PhD Student:	I will ensure I don't take their time [acknowledge], but *I want to re-run the experiment.*
Technician:	Ok. If you can find time that doesn't mean disrupting the other lab work, you can re-run it.

The broken record technique is designed to overcome stubborn or unthinking refusals. If you suspect someone just isn't listening to you or giving your request any serious consideration, you can bring out the broken record technique.

There are different situations in which you might want to use the broken record technique:

- You want to insist on (or refuse) something and you will stand your ground come what may (however unpopular this might be)
- Someone is being obstructive and refusing to accept your point
- You are happy to negotiate the practicalities of implementing your request or proposal, but you want it to be accepted in principle before you negotiate
- You are dealing with someone who tends to ignore or not listen to you.

Be careful! Be wary of how you use this technique in discussions with people who have higher status than you, including your supervisors. It can seem disrespectful if you don't have the authority to make demands or insist on yours. In some cultures and organisations, the broken record technique might not be appropriate, for example in a very hierarchical culture. That said, using it with a light touch – repeating your I-statement occasionally during a discussion, along with acknowledgements of the other position – can be a useful and perfectly collaborative way of keeping the focus on your priorities and ensuring that other people have clearly heard and understood your needs, whatever the power dynamics.

✏ Activity: Use the broken record technique

1 Think of a current situation in which you need to stand your ground and which is appropriate for the broken record technique.
2 Create an I-statement to convey your key message.
3 Decide when you will use the technique.
4 Note the impact once you have tried it.

Details of the situation	
Your I-statement	
When you will use the broken record technique	
The impact of the technique	

Summary

A conflict is more than a simple disagreement – it's a situation in which you think that your interests are threatened. Conflict-resolution skills will help you to protect your interests during your PhD and in your career. Assessing the context and desired outcome of a conflict situation will allow you to decide whether to address a conflict at all and which conflict management mode is most likely to get the outcome you want.

A strategic approach to conflict resolution needs good communication skills to back it up. Communication techniques such as managing your non-verbal language, active listening and open questioning will be key when creating rapport and the mutual respect needed for successful conflict resolution and mutually satisfying outcomes. Asserting techniques, such as the I-statement and the broken record, when used appropriately, can enable you to stand your ground in situations when you face resistance or when you want to insist on your needs being met. Understanding and practising the conflict management modes and these communication techniques will build your confidence and help you to face conflicts more effectively.

Key points
- Conflicts will be an inevitable part of your PhD and can be a useful opportunity to solve problems and improve understanding.
- Be strategic about how (and whether) you address conflicts, depending on who is involved and the outcome you desire.
- Aim to find mutually satisfying solutions to conflict.
- Develop good communication skills so that you can navigate difficult conversations successfully – body language is as important as good verbal ability.

Further resources

Back, K. and Back, K. (2005) *Assertiveness at Work*. Maidenhead: McGraw Hill.
Bungay-Stanier, M. (2016) *The Coaching Habit*. Toronto: Box of Crayons Press.
Fisher, R., Ury, W. and Patton, B. (2011) *Getting to Yes: Negotiating Without Giving In*. London: Penguin.
Goulston, M. (2018) *Just Listen: Discover the Secret to Getting Through to Absolutely Anyone*. New York: Amacom.
Navarro, J. (2011) *Louder Than Words*. New York: Harper Collins.
Schein, E.H. (2021) *Humble Inquiry: The Gentle Art of Asking Instead of Telling*, 2nd edn. San Francisco: Berrett-Koehler Publishers.

References

Mehrabian, A. (1971) *Silent Messages*, 1st edn. Belmont, CA: Wadsworth.
Thomas, K.W., & Kilmann, R.H. (1974). *Thomas-Kilmann Conflict Mode Instrument*. Mountain View, CA: Xicom.

Part 4

How to Get It Finished

Part 1: How to Make a Good Start → Part 2: How to Get Going → Part 3: How to Keep Going → **Part 4: How to Get It Finished**

In this final part of the book, we focus on the 'home straight' of your research, approximately the last six months, during which your primary focus will be writing up and submitting your thesis. We also look beyond submission, to your Viva and embarking on the next phase of your career. We address the main issues PhD students face during the last months of their PhD, such as how to:

- Submit a high-quality thesis on time
- Reduce stress and panic in the run up to submission
- Keep going in the face of the pressure of the last few months
- Deal with the task of writing up
- Feel good about your Viva
- Get the job you want after your PhD.

You will discover that, thanks to the earlier parts of this book, you already have many of the skills and techniques to make the most of the final phase of your PhD. There's no need to spend precious time in these last months learning lots of new skills. Your saw is already sharp!

The following chapters guide you through how best to adapt the techniques from earlier chapters to the demands of writing up, submission, Viva preparation and securing your next job. The aim of Part 4 is to ensure that you stay on track with as little effort as possible and maximise your time to focus on completing your thesis, before shifting focus to the Viva and beyond. Our aim is not only to help you finish but to equip you to finish well: produce a superb thesis, have an excellent Viva and get the job you want.

- In Chapter 20, you revisit planning techniques once more and use them to ensure that the final stage of your PhD runs as smoothly and with as little stress as possible.

- Chapter 21 considers how to maintain your momentum throughout this demanding final phase by using the productivity and anxiety-reduction tools that you've already learned and by tapping into your motivation. You also learn new techniques to help you handle writing up.
- In Chapter 22, you focus on preparing yourself for the Viva so that you can do your research justice. Once again, planning is key, along with using techniques to build your confidence and perform well in spite of nerves.
- Chapter 23 looks beyond your PhD and examines how to capitalise on the transferable skills you have developed during your PhD when applying for future positions. You can find your competitive edge in the employment market by demonstrating your value to a potential employer, whether in academia or beyond.

We can't make the final months of your PhD easy. They may be some of the hardest of your whole doctoral experience. However, if you use the advice in these chapters, they will be as easy as they can be and, perhaps more importantly, as successful as they can be, ensuring that you end your degree with pride and confidence about what comes next.

20 Get It All Done

How to ... Plan the final stage

> Painting by numbers – Writing up is not just writing – Planning tools revisited – Fixed time vs flexible cost – Focus on the must-haves – Scope with your supervisors – WBS your thesis – Schedule feedback

As you enter the final months of your PhD, the planning focus shifts. In earlier chapters of this book, the emphasis was on detailed planning for the short term that rolled forward as you progressed through your PhD. This allowed you to incorporate your learning as you went and to accommodate the inevitable uncertainties and changes that characterise PhD research. As you approach the end of your PhD, with its final deadline, you can – and must – be more definitive about identifying and scheduling the tasks that will get you over the finish line.

In this chapter, we revisit some of the planning techniques from Part 2 and apply them to the specific demands of the final six months of the PhD. In doing so, the last few months of completion and write-up become a simple 'painting by numbers' exercise. All the work required has already been determined and it just becomes a matter of getting it done. This clears your way to focus on the academic endeavour of producing a high-quality thesis rather than the management of the work, confident that everything has been identified and considered.

Students often think of the final stages of the PhD in terms of one task: sitting alone, spending hours writing up, but there are many other tasks that are necessary to complete on time. Writing up itself isn't just one task; that of sitting at your laptop and typing away. You need to plan for input from other key stakeholders, such as the time for supervisors to review drafts and provide feedback. In Chapter 21, we provide techniques to make the work of writing easier but, for now, we want to help you *plan* your writing. We also ensure that you incorporate all the necessary 'external inputs' into your final plan, including all the practical, 'nuts and bolts' activities that are required for your PhD, such as setting aside time for printing and binding, completion of university submission forms and Viva preparation. All of these are easy to overlook when you are, understandably, focused on finishing the thesis.

To create a comprehensive plan for your final months, follow the process laid out in Part 2, with some subtle variations for this stage, which we highlight in the following sections.

Scoping

Scoping (see Chapter 8) gives you a clear picture of the work you need to do in order to complete your thesis. As you approach the final months of your PhD, this becomes critical because you have a hard deadline by which you must be confident you have done everything required for submission.

To explain, let's revisit the project triangle. The project triangle links the three manipulable elements of project delivery: scope (what you will do), time (when it will be done by) and cost (how many hours' work it will take). The corners of the triangle must always be linked. If one corner changes, it must impact the other two.

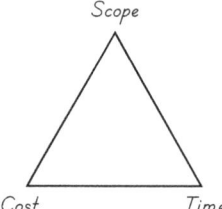

At this stage in your PhD, time is fixed. You may not have an exact date for submission, but you will have an approximate idea. You will certainly know when your funding or contract expires. This means that you can manipulate only cost or scope in order to manage delivery of your thesis on time.

If you are unsure about your submission deadline, it's a good idea to *agree an end date* with your supervisors. Without one, it is very difficult to plan for these last few months. If they are reluctant to pin things down, at least get them to agree an approximate date with you. Explain that, for your own peace of mind and so that you can begin to plan the remaining work, you need an indicative deadline to work towards.

> **Activity: Set yourself a deadline**
>
> I will submit my thesis on or before:

With a deadline in place (however approximate it may be) you can plan your final 'bite of the elephant'! You know the time: your deadline. So, the next step in planning is to join the corners of the triangle by establishing the other two elements, scope and cost. Cost is relatively straightforward as there are a finite number of hours before your deadline. However, identifying how many hours each task within this 'bite' will take is particularly difficult because it is difficult to estimate writing time. Instead, it is more useful to set yourself *milestones* for the completion of the necessary sections or chapters and accept that you simply have to work the hours (cost) to meet each milestone. Remember: your final deadline (time) is essentially fixed, so you can't push that back.

At this stage, it is vital that you also define your scope. You need to know exactly what you must complete before your deadline. To do this, go back to the categorisation technique introduced in Chapter 8 and identify your must-haves.

- **Must-haves** – essential – you will not be awarded a PhD without it (many of these will be pre-defined in university regulations)
- **Nice-to-haves** – very valuable but not essential – might be something of real interest to you or your supervisor, but you can pass without it
- **Bells-and-whistles** – little add-ons, a bit of fun – of personal interest or aesthetic, but not contributing greatly to the work.

There is always so much that you could include in your final thesis. Most PhD students collect far more data than they can use. When you add in all the non-writing tasks you need to complete it's often clear that you don't have enough time to do everything you would like. Trust us on this! Categorisation will help you to stay focused. Examine all the work you have to do and categorise by asking one simple question:

What is required for me to get my PhD?

Focus on the must-haves first

Everything else can wait. Almost regardless of how much you or your supervisor want to complete a nice-to-have, doing so to the detriment of an essential element risks compromising your whole PhD. This can be very difficult because you might have a strong emotional attachment to work that isn't a must-have, but, at this stage, you need to be pragmatic and complete the elements that will get you over the line. If you find you have time for a nice-to-have once all the must-haves are done, by all means, revisit it, but do the key parts first. If you're struggling to categorise your priorities, use the work breakdown structure (page 107) for more detail, and ask your supervisor or someone who has already submitted their own thesis for advice.

> **Remember your goals**
>
> If you truly feel that neglecting one of your nice-to-haves completely undermines your personal reason for undertaking the PhD, then include it in your plan but recognise that to do it will probably mean working more hours per day or, potentially, requesting an extension.

Create a scope statement

As you approach your final deadline, it is important to engage with the expectations of your supervisors. Create a Scope Statement, as described in Chapter 8, which explicitly describes what you intend to include in your thesis and what you will exclude. This allows you to plan and is a way of ensuring that you are confident in your understanding of what will be required to complete your PhD. By involving your supervisors in creating your scope statement, and asking them to agree to it, you are double-checking that you have identified all the must-haves.

Your 'out of scope' list will also help you to write about the limitations of your study and explain why you did not pursue certain aspects of the research. This list will be useful when preparing for the Viva, as an examiner might ask whether you considered an idea that was outside your scope and you have a justifying explanation ready-made.

✏ Activity: Scoping

1 Using the template on page 268, determine the must-haves, nice-to-haves and bells-and-whistles for your final plan.
2 Based on this, determine what will be in and out of scope.
3 Mark when you have completed each item. Make sure you complete your must-haves first!

Template: Prioritisation for final six months

Task/deliverable	Must-haves	Nice-to-haves	Bells-and-whistles	Completed
	☐	☐	☐	☐
	☐	☐	☐	☐
	☐	☐	☐	☐
	☐	☐	☐	☐
	☐	☐	☐	☐
	☐	☐	☐	☐
	☐	☐	☐	☐
	☐	☐	☐	☐
	☐	☐	☐	☐
	☐	☐	☐	☐
	☐	☐	☐	☐
	☐	☐	☐	☐
	☐	☐	☐	☐
	☐	☐	☐	☐
	☐	☐	☐	☐

Beware of late changes

At this stage, even more than at any other time during your PhD, be very wary of changes. There will inevitably be some changes that are necessary to complete your thesis to a high standard, but it can be very tempting to try to include extra elements just because you can. Remember the WIBNIs ('Wouldn't it be nice if' changes) in Chapter 16? It's often the accumulation of these small additional elements that throw you off track. Towards the end of your PhD, you can't afford to deviate too far from your plan. Be very strict and only include late changes that add considerably to the quality of your thesis.

To help you with this, revisit the WIBNI questions on page 211. Every time you (or your supervisors) have a bright new idea, consider the impact on the project triangle:

- Can you still complete everything else to the required level (scope)?
- Can you do it all by your deadline (time)?
- Do you have to work more hours per day to include it (cost)?

You can also apply the prioritisation of must-haves, nice-to-haves and bells-and-whistles to each change. Ask yourself:

- What difference will this really make?
- Can I complete and submit without it?

We're not saying that you must not make changes but, before you do, consider how important they are to your PhD. Will it make a big difference to the final thesis or is it really just additional, unnecessary stress?

Work breakdown structure

So far, you have used the WBS to identify the detailed tasks needed to complete a phase of your PhD project (Chapter 9). Adopt the same method for the final stage of your PhD by identifying:

- The additional administrative tasks associated with submission, such as thesis printing and university form-filling
- The final responsibilities you must fulfill, for example teaching
- The opportunities you still want to take advantage of before you compete your PhD, such as training or conferences.

However, the centrepiece of your WBS for the last phase of your PhD will be the writing of the thesis itself.

By now, you should have an idea of the structure and content of your thesis. The number and form of chapters will be similar to other PhD theses, especially those sharing your methodology. There are standard chapters for almost all PhD theses: introduction, literature review, methodology, data collection, discussion/findings and conclusions. Within each of these generic areas, you will have headings and sub-headings that are specific to your own PhD. This means you have a structure upon which to build a WBS of your thesis. For each chapter, drill down to identify the sections and content that belong in that chapter. For example.

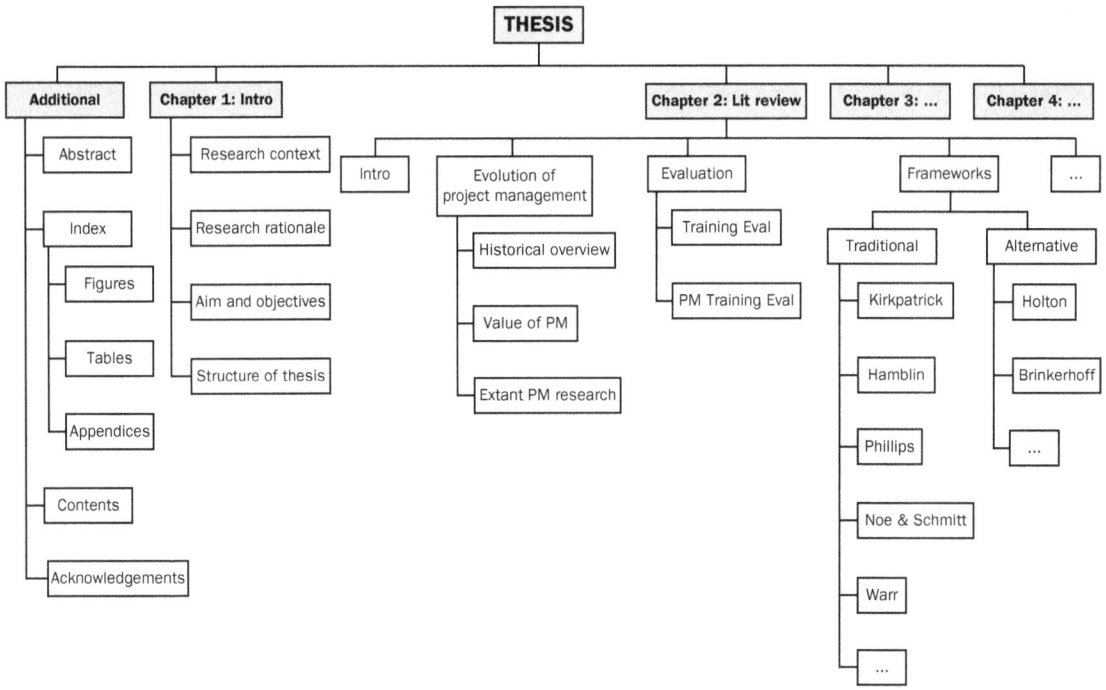

Work breakdown structure: thesis completion

Structuring a WBS to represent the content of your thesis has the dual benefit of making the tasks needed to complete the thesis (your ultimate project deliverable) clearly identifiable and making the task of writing almost like 'painting by numbers'. You know exactly what must go in each section and it's just a matter of writing it. Some people even put word counts against tasks or sections. Clearly, this is underplaying the challenge of the actual writing itself but, from a process point of view, it's as simple as filling in the boxes.

As well as the thesis content, it is crucial to include the *passive* (or 'not you') tasks. The most important of which is feedback from supervisors. Along with the writing, feedback will be the key part of the process of producing the thesis. Although these tasks don't demand you as a 'resource', you must build in the time it will take for you to *receive* the feedback. Your writing progress will be dependent on this supervisory guidance. It is imperative that these passive tasks are included in your WBS so that they can then be incorporated into your network diagram and finally, scheduled in your Gantt chart. At the beginning of the in-depth writing stage, speak with your supervisors about the best way for this feedback loop to work.

Determine the feedback process

In order to determine exactly how the feedback process will work, ask your supervisors the following questions.

- What works best for you both – little and often, or longer sections and less frequent?
- Can they review your work in small chunks, or does it require longer sections to make contextual sense?

- How long does it take to have feedback returned – a week, a fortnight? (This isn't to pressure your supervisors, but to better manage *your* expectations.)
- How will feedback be delivered – face to face, printed out and annotated, electronic annotation or comments?

To represent this process in your WBS, break down your chapter sections into several different discrete tasks to allow you to optimise your schedule. For example:

- Draft chapter and submit for review
- Wait for supervisory feedback
- Incorporate feedback and redraft
- Finalise section
- Finalise chapter
- Wait for supervisory feedback
- Incorporate feedback and finish.

Despite increasing the level of complexity of the WBS, this level of detail actually helps you to estimate more accurately and get a firmer grasp of all the small component activities that need to come together. Now, more than ever, what might seem like a lengthy planning process when you're feeling the pressure of your fast-approaching deadline, is a worthwhile investment. It will mean that you know exactly what you need to do to complete your thesis, and can therefore plan accurately, and having this step-by-step plan to follow will dramatically reduce the stress of writing up.

Once you have completed a WBS for the writing of your thesis, incorporate all the other tasks you need to perform to complete submission, any outstanding responsibilities you must fulfill and any final opportunities of the PhD you want to take advantage of. You might have conferences you want to attend; papers to produce; new publications to keep on top of; teaching and marking to complete. You have administrative tasks associated with your PhD, such as printing and binding your thesis, and completing university submission forms. There might be non-PhD activities that you want to complete too, such as taking advantage of training courses while they're still free to access. You may be involved in job-seeking activities, such as applications and interview preparation. Ensure that these are also included in your WBS as they will take up precious time and need to be accounted for. It's also good to get away from the writing occasionally – as the saying goes, a change is as good as a rest.

> **✎ Activity: Work breakdown structure**
>
> - Similar to the process in Chapter 9, use a blank sheet of paper to create a WBS; this time formatted around the structure of your thesis.
> - Make sure that you include any final substantive research tasks you still need to complete and any other PhD admin activities you need to perform.
> - Add any other tasks (training courses, holidays and so on) as appropriate.

Network diagram

Once you have your WBS, you can use the network diagram (from Chapter 10) to identify the dependencies that exist between the tasks. For your writing-up, do this for *each chapter* (or even section of chapter)

272   Part 4 – How to Get It Finished

individually. Attempting to create a single network diagram for your entire thesis will almost certainly be too complicated, as in the following diagram.

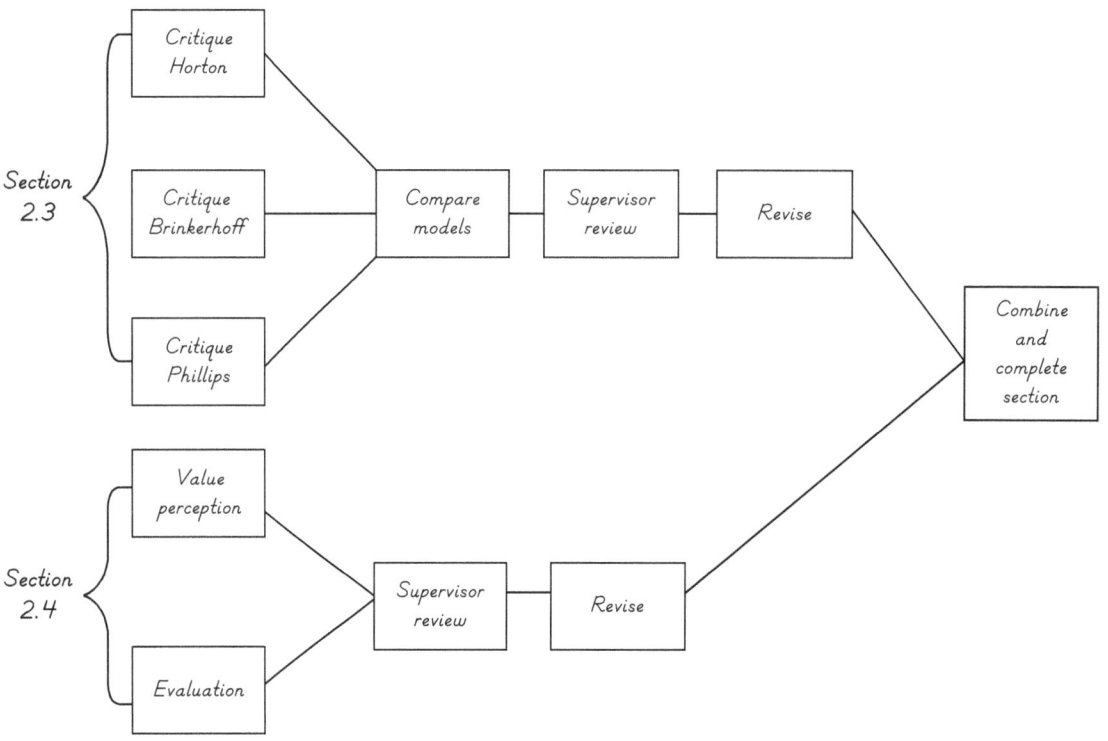

Network diagram: section completion

> 'This was so useful, as it allowed me to progress other bits of work while I was waiting for feedback from my supervisors. It made me feel in control of the write-up process.'

✏ Activity: Network diagram

Write your WBS tasks on sticky notes and, as described in Chapter 10, create a network diagram. Remember to consider *only* task dependency at this stage.

Gantt chart

Once the network diagram is complete, you arrive, once again, at the Gantt chart. For this final timeline, craft it in the same manner as you have throughout your PhD (see Chapter 10). Hopefully, by now, this will be a quick and simple exercise as you will have created many charts over the lifetime of your research. The only real difference at this stage is that, rather than estimating how long the writing will take using the techniques from Chapter 9, you will find it easier to work to *fixed milestones* – dates by which tasks, chapters or chapter sections must be finished. Writing time is hard to estimate because of the recurring write-edit-review loop. You don't know how much rewriting the feedback will require you to do. Instead, consider when you would like each chapter to be completed. Be warned: setting these milestones is an acknowledgement that you are prepared to work however many hours it takes to hit that deadline, so do not be over ambitious.

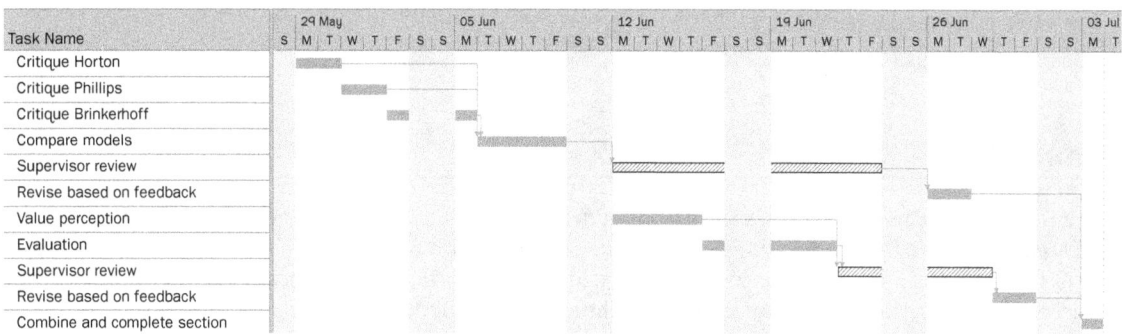

Gantt chart: section completion

In this example, a couple of days each has been allowed to write the critique of Horton, Phillips and Brinkerhoff, followed by a few days to compare their models. The most important date here, though, is the commitment to give your supervisor a copy for review on Monday of the third week. As long as the draft is ready for review by that Monday, how many hours you spend getting to that point isn't important. It must be done.

Setting these milestones also helps in negotiating the involvement of your supervisors. However busy they are, by committing to a deadline (and keeping to it), you are allowing them to incorporate time into their busy schedule to review your work and provide feedback. It's therefore crucial that the milestones are realistic to avoid frustrating your supervisors with late delivery.

Including the 'supervisor review' passive tasks in the timeline also allows you to schedule other non-dependent work in that time. It means that, while you are waiting for feedback on one part of the thesis, you can make the most of the time you have available to work on other things. 'Waiting' tasks should never be 'dead' time for you. Optimise your workload.

Finally, make sure you include the non-writing tasks in the Gantt. The PhD tasks could include final completion of the substantive research or others more closely related to admin. Add any important personal commitments, training courses, job interviews, holidays and so on, too, just as you did when you created the high-level timeline in Chapter 4.

Once you have completed your Gantt chart, go back to the time management techniques in Chapter 12 to ensure that you make the most of your time and as much progress as possible on your planned work on a day-to-day basis.

> **Working hours only**
>
> Notice in the example that you commit to delivering your draft to your supervisor on a Monday. When you are considering the *effort* you will put in, only ever plan for your typical working hours (perhaps 9 to 5, Monday to Friday). *Do not create a plan – particularly at this late stage – that includes regular evening or weekend work.*
>
> You *will* have to work some evenings and weekends, but that time is reserved for dealing with unexpected events and when you need to play catch-up. If you already have work planned for the weekends, there's no space to incorporate 'extras' and means that either you won't get everything finished or you'll miss your deadline. Weekends and evenings are the contingency time you need!

> **✏️ Activity: Gantt chart**
>
> Using your software of choice, create a Gantt chart based on the order defined in your network diagram.
> - Make sure you include any final substantive research tasks you still need to complete and any other PhD admin activities you need to perform.
> - Add any other tasks (training courses, holidays and so on) as appropriate.
> - Ensure that you make the best use of the time available by scheduling other tasks while you're waiting for feedback.

Summary

In the final six months of your PhD, the planning methods you have learned and used throughout can be used again to ensure that you complete a high-quality thesis with the minimum stress. Plan for your final 'bite of the elephant' with the same tools you have already used. The only difference now is that you have a hard end point – your agreed submission deadline – which will demand even more ruthless prioritising and even stricter scheduling. Keep in mind that, despite the time pressures of the final phase of your PhD, effort spent planning will save you time, reduce confusion and free you up to concentrate on the quality of your work. Include your key stakeholders in your planning, especially your supervisors. This ensures that your plans are stress-tested, that you can be confident in the accuracy of your scoping, and that your supervisors' availability won't delay your work.

Scheduling tasks only on working days and during working hours leaves you with a little bit of contingency for unexpected problems or overruns. Comprehensive planning for the final months of your PhD will mean that you can juggle the different tasks of this phase alongside completing your thesis on time.

> **Key points**
> - Revisit all your planning techniques – with the view of meeting that final submission deadline.
> - Ruthlessly prioritise your must-haves.
> - Crush unnecessary changes – they can easily accumulate and throw you off track.
> - Create a comprehensive plan to get your PhD finished – one that includes tasks such as administration and printing, as well as the writing-up.
> - Allow for the 'passive' tasks, such as waiting for feedback.
> - Use your planning techniques to plan the writing of your thesis in detail.

Further resources

Badiru, A., Rusnock, C.F. and Valencia, V.V. (2021) *Project Management for Research: A Guide for Graduate Students*. Boca Raton, Fl: CRC Press.
Heagney, J. (2022) *Fundamentals of Project Management*, 6th edn. London: Harper Collins.
Portnoy, J.L. and Portnoy, S.L. (2022) *Project Management for Dummies*, 6th edn. Hoboken NJ: Wiley & Sons.
Wysocki, R.K. (2019) *Effective Project Management: Traditional, Agile, Extreme, Hybrid*. Indianapolis: Wiley.

21 Hang in There

How to ... Keep moving and stay motivated

> Hitting the wall – Well-being measures – Work-life balance – Mood management – Productivity techniques – Reward yourself – Micro-goals – Writing is hard – Creating and revising – Stop on the downhill slope

You're nearly there. After years of hard work, the end is in sight. At this stage, you might experience a new burst of energy and motivation, or you might find yourself in panic mode, struggling to maintain your motivation in the face of that last climb towards the summit. We've often observed that, during the final months, many PhD students entertain thoughts of giving up. It is the equivalent of 'hitting the wall' in the last stage of running a marathon. The chances are that you'll experience all these different moods and more during the final months of your PhD.

The techniques in the previous chapter help you to maintain your momentum by creating a clear, step-by-step plan to follow. Even if you know exactly what you should be doing, however, you still have to find the energy and focus to do it! In this chapter, we want to help you maintain your motivation and sustain your productivity during this final stage. We remind you of earlier techniques that are even more valuable now and we provide some new tips and tools that are particularly useful in this phase of your PhD. We also offer techniques to support your progress on the big task of this phase: the writing-up.

How to handle the stress

As you head into the final months of your PhD, there's no doubt that you will suffer from some additional stress as the submission deadline approaches. It's important to continue investing in your mental and physical well-being despite the pressure of the increased workload. Try the following suggestions.

> **➡ Action: Reduce stress.**
>
> Revisit the resilience-boosting techniques in Chapters 14 and the solutions to anxiety-induced procrastination in Chapter 15.

> **➡ Action: Take care of yourself.**
>
> We discussed the importance of well-being measures such as good sleep, exercise and mindfulness in seeing you through your PhD (Chapter 14).

As you head into the final stages, it's a good time to take stock of your well-being needs and recommit to some regular habits. You may have to discipline yourself to spend time looking after your well-being because deadline pressures can make it easy to neglect activities that aren't 'work'. However, investment of regular time in well-being activities will make your work easier and more productive.

- Sleep hygiene measures, page 186
- Exercise, page 187
- Mindfulness, page 188

✎ Activity: Take care of your well-being

Choose some simple daily and weekly well-being measures to optimise your physical and mental resilience during the final phase of your PhD.

Every day, I will:

-
-
-
-

Every week, I will:

-
-
-
-

➡ Action: Maintain a work-life balance.

It can be tempting to focus entirely on work to the exclusion of all else during the final months of your PhD, in the belief that you need to give all your time to your thesis. However, pleasure, social connection and rest are key to maintaining optimal cognitive functioning.

Your social support networks (Chapter 6) and happiness-boosting activities (Chapter 14) become even more important when facing the pressure of the submission deadline.

Revisit some of the techniques from earlier chapters to make it easy to manage your work-life balance. For example:

- Use the time-blocking method to set boundaries for working time and to schedule social contact, rest and happiness-boosting activities
- Look after your 'social biome' by drip-feeding different kinds of daily social contact rather than chaining yourself to your desk all day
- Use the 'happiness prescription' to devise a programme of activities that will keep your happiness levels topped up as work gets more intense.

- Time-blocking, page 148
- Social biome factors, page 61
- Prescription for a happy life, page 182

✏️ Activity: Put the 'life' in your work-life balance

Note some of the social and happiness-boosting activities you will include in your daily and weekly schedule during the final months of your PhD.

Social activities
Happiness-boosting activities
Pleasure:
Meaning:
Engagement:

➡ Action: Manage your mind and your mood.

Maintaining a positive attitude during this demanding time will help you to sustain your momentum.

It can be easy to find yourself plagued by anxiety and self-doubt in the face of the pressures of the final months of your PhD. However, as explained in Chapters 14 and 18, your 'beliefs' about stressful demands will play a significant part in the impact of these experiences.

- The ABC method, page 179
- 'What if' vs 'What is', page 194
- Affirmations, page 195
- Growth mindset, page 235

Revisit the CBT tools from Chapter 14 to help you create a positive state of mind. The following techniques will be particularly useful to help you perform at your best in the final phase of your PhD.

The ABC method

Use the ABC method to identify negative 'beliefs' about your work and substitute alternative thoughts that will produce a 'consequence' of confidence and productivity.

'What if' vs 'What is'

The approaching submission deadline can easily stimulate fear of the future – and you may find you dwell on anxiety-inducing 'What if' thoughts. Substitute simple, factual 'What is' thoughts to keep you focused on what needs to be done in the present.

For example, rather than:

- 'What if my examiners ask me a question that I can't answer?'
- 'What if I don't finish in time to hit my deadline?'

Think:

- 'I will prepare for the Viva in due course,'
- 'I am using my planning and time management techniques in order to be confident of meeting my deadline.'

The affirmation technique

Try devising a few affirmations to use daily that will put you in the right frame of mind for your work. These will be very personal to you, but some examples are:

- I am working hard and effectively
- My research contribution is well-founded
- I am enjoying writing up.

Remember that these don't have to be true right now! You are sending these messages to your brain to put you in a positive mood about your work.

Rosie returned to the affirmation technique when writing the first draft of this book. She started the working day by writing four affirmations that expressed positive statements about her writing. For example:

- I write easily and clearly
- I have lots of valuable information to share with my readers
- I enjoy putting words on paper
- I am making good progress on this book.

She wrote each one out five times and then read them out loud to herself. The improvement in her attitude to her work and the boost to her productivity was immediate.

✏ Activity: Manage your mind

Choose some of the mind-management techniques from the book to introduce into your daily routine to optimise your mental attitude to your work.

Mind-management techniques	When/how often

✏ Activity: Well-being planner

Using the template on page 280, create an overall well-being plan for the activities you have identified during this chapter. Update this planner every month.

📄 Template: Well-being planner

Well-being activities	Schedule (Daily, 1x a week, 2x a month etc.)	✓
e.g. Meditate for 10 minutes	e.g. Every morning before breakfast	
Week beginning:		
Week beginning:		
Week beginning:		
Week beginning:		

How to sustain your productivity

The writing-up period can cause a blip in momentum and productivity. Many students, expecting to relish the freedom of weeks and months of 'just' writing, feel a bit lost. Good planning techniques (as in the previous chapter) help you to create structure and momentum, and revisiting Chapter 12 will help you to take charge of your time. The following techniques are also particularly helpful during this phase of your PhD to sustain your productivity.

Visit **https://www.mheducation.co.uk/professionals/open-university-press/olc/doyle-robertson-the-phd-handbook** for a printable version of this template for your weekly checklists.

> ➡ **Action: Revisit the timer techniques.**
>
> Use timer techniques to improve your focus and conserve mental energy during the day.

By breaking work down into fixed time periods interspersed with short breaks (as in, for example, the 25/5 regime of the Pomodoro technique), you will be able to work better and more productively.

Timer techniques, pages 159–161

Remember: even when you're tempted to just keep working, you shouldn't extend your work period beyond 40 minutes before taking a short break if you want to capitalise on the brain's natural powers of concentration.

We recommend the timer technique during the writing-up phase because:

- Writing requires deep concentration – the timer technique increases your ability to focus
- Writing is mentally hard work and tiring – using the timer technique preserves your brain energy, helping you to sustain effort for longer
- Writing doesn't really correspond to very small tasks that you can tick off on your to do list – by focusing on the measurement of time, you can break down the writing work into manageable chunks.

> ➡ **Action: Choose the best time to write.**
>
> To get the best out of your writing, do it when you are at your best according to your circadian rhythms.

Normally, this is in the morning, but, by this stage, you should know yourself and your work preferences well enough to choose to write precisely when you are at your best, even if this means adjusting your schedule to allow for this:

> If you know that you are at your brightest from 7 to 11 in the morning, write during that time, and leave other tasks for other times in the day. Alternatively, if you are better from 10a.m. to 1p.m., write then. If you're most productive early in the evening, then write then.

> ✏ **Activity: Schedule your day using your circadian rhythms**
>
> Decide the best times of day for you to write and to attend to other kinds of tasks needed to complete your PhD.
>
> Note anything you need to do differently to spend your time most effectively, for example reorganise your schedule, set your alarm an hour earlier.

If you don't have control of your schedule because of work or family commitments, do the best you can. For the last months or weeks of your PhD, you may want to adjust your schedule or get additional help to allow you to work when you are at your best and most productive.

Circadian rhythms, pages 155–158

> **➔ Action: Reduce distractions.**
>
> Writing is hard and intensive; the last thing you need are unnecessary distractions.

Give yourself the benefit of focus by trying the following:

- **Switch off electronic notifications**.
  Emails, messages, social apps … switch off your notifications, at least for part of your day. You can't maintain your concentration if it's constantly being interrupted by pop-ups and pings.
- **Find a quiet space**.
  Or, if you can't find a quiet space, consider using earplugs, noise-cancelling headphones or even earbuds playing white noise – there are plenty of free apps.
- **Get help**.
  If you're juggling other demands, such as work or family responsibilities, consider using holidays or finding support to let you have a full day now and then so you can connect deeply with the writing work.

💬 'I used to decamp to a café now and then when writing up my thesis, especially if I was a bit stuck. The change of location was energising (as well as the nice cup of coffee!) and I found that the background chat functioned as a kind of 'white noise' and I could concentrate better there than in the silence of my office.'

'I was finishing my PhD while juggling a young family. I'm lucky to have access to a weekend cottage by the sea. Being able to go to the cottage alone sometimes meant I could focus completely on my writing and get a lot of work done.'

✏️ **Activity: Reduce distractions**

Decide what you will do to reduce distractions while you are writing up.

I will reduce distractions by:

How to stay motivated

For many PhD students, there's something about facing this last mountain to climb that is so daunting that motivation can falter. Unfortunately, you can't afford to lose much time to dips in motivation. Instead, work proactively to maintain your momentum through the following measures.

> ➡ **Action: Reward yourself.**
>
> Use small, regular rewards – pleasures and treats that make you feel good – to give yourself an incentive for getting on with your work.

For example:

- Short breaks and rest periods throughout the day (this boosts brain energy as well as providing a reward)
- A treat or a particularly pleasurable leisure activity at the end of the day
- A bigger treat at the end of the week – or simply allowing yourself a weekend off if you've worked hard during the week.

Schedule some greater rewards for after submission to provide further motivation to get through to the end. For example:

- Book a holiday, city break or overnight trip
- Buy tickets for a concert or festival
- Arrange to visit friends you've had to put on hold during your writing-up period
- Pick up a leisure activity that you haven't had time for.

Only you know what makes a meaningful reward for you, so choose what feels good. It might seem weird or self-indulgent to itemise rewards, but it's a very efficient productivity strategy.

Rewards function as incentives to keep going, but they're also good brain management. Remember the feel-good hormone, dopamine? (See page 182.) Rewards, and just the contemplation of them, have been shown to boost dopamine. There is evidence that, as well as making you feel good, dopamine improves cognitive functioning. You may find your rewards boost your ability as well as your motivation.

✏ Activity: Plan a schedule of rewards

Complete the table with different personal rewards.

	My planned rewards
During the day	
At the end of the day	
Weekly	
After I've finished my PhD	

➜ Action: Set micro-goals.

There is evidence that achieving your goals also gives you a valuable dopamine boost.

This works for small, short-term goals as well as major life goals. For dopamine boosts every day, break down your work into short tasks of no more than 15 to 30 minutes (ideally, the shorter the better) that function as micro-goals for the day. As you work through them, you will get a repeated boost from the sense of achievement. For the job of writing, you might aim to complete so many words that day, or so many 'pomodoro' periods, for example:

- I will write 600 words of the chapter today
- I will write 300 words in the morning and 300 words in the afternoon
- I will compete eight 'pomodoro' periods of writing.

✎ Activity: Set your micro-goals

- Complete the table for your next working day.
- Copy it (or just make a list on blank paper) to use every day to help your motivation.

Date:	
My micro-goals for completion are:	
	☐
	☐
	☐
	☐
	☐
	☐
	☐
	☐
	☐
	☐
	☐
	☐

➜ Action: Reconnect with your WIIFMs.

Reminding yourself of your WIIFMs (What's in it for me) for your PhD (see pages 201–202), or discovering new ones, is a great way of tapping into powerful motivation to keep going.

Your WIFFMs are the personal benefits you will get from completing your PhD. Some of these will be linked to your personal goals for your future (see Chapters 2 and 17), such as securing your next job, acquiring the credibility of the title 'Dr'. Some of them, at this stage, will be linked to the benefits of *finishing* your PhD: having more time for family; feeling less stressed.

✏ Activity: Three WIIFMs to keep you going as you finish your PhD	
	When my PhD is finished I will ...
WIIFM 1	
WIIFM 2	
WIIFM 3	

How to generate momentum in your writing

We've heard so many PhD students describe how much they hate writing and how much they procrastinate about it. We find writing hard as well – both when we wrote our own PhD theses and writing the book that you're now reading. There's a good reason for this: writing *is* hard! We say this not to discourage you – quite the reverse. We want to reassure you that it's normal to find writing difficult. But the fact that it's hard isn't a reason to give up!

As recommended in Chapter 5, the more you've practised writing during your PhD, the easier the final stages of writing up will be, practically and psychologically. Nevertheless, the demands of the writing-up phase are a challenge to pretty much every PhD student. The following tips and techniques will help you to keep up your writing momentum.

Separate creating from revising

Approach the work of writing by separating the process into two different modes of activity.

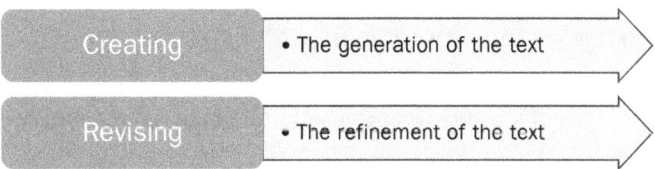

These two modes require a completely different way of thinking:

- **Creating** is expansive and open, for example expressing new ideas, identifying questions, making connections, following insights.
- **Revising** is precise and critical, for example testing assumptions, clarifying meanings, assessing quality, editing out surplus.

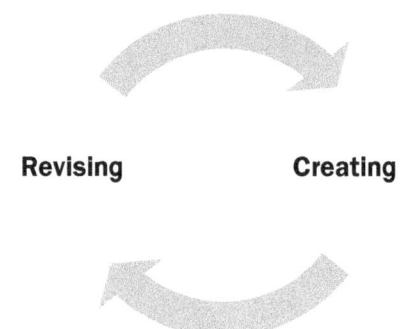

The two modes build on each other and are *equally important* if you are to produce a well-written thesis.

You will revisit each mode numerous times in the process of producing a good piece of writing. Trying to do both at the same time causes tension and is likely to keep you stuck. If you *separate* the act of creating text and the act of revising your text, your writing will go more smoothly and it will be of better quality.

- You can cycle in and out of the two modes for long periods of time. For example, you might stay in creating mode for a few days, while producing the first draft of a chapter, before switching to revising mode for however long you need to edit and review.
- Alternatively, you can cycle in and out for short periods, for example creating for half an hour to generate a new short section and then revising for 15 minutes to tighten up the text.

The following recommendations will help you to make the most of each of the modes.

The creating mode

The aim of the creating mode is to generate text – but not just random text. When writing your thesis, you will have some kind of focus and, using a WBS (page 270), you will have identified a series of short sections. When you are in the creating mode, you aren't just 'writing up' existing material; you are writing *about* it. This means *describing, interrogating and thinking* about your research through the act of writing. The following are some tricks you can use to make your creating mode as productive as possible.

> ➡ **Action: Don't judge the quality of your writing.**
>
> It is fine during the creating mode to write rubbish! Your aim is not to produce excellent writing – that comes later. Your aim is to produce the raw material of text and stimulate your ideas.

> **Action: Write as if you're having a conversation with yourself.**
>
> You can even write yourself questions and then write your responses to your own questions.

> **Action: Write as if you're having a conversation with someone else.**
>
> For example, your supervisor, a stakeholder, or a research user. Thinking about your writing from their perspective will stimulate new ideas – put yourself in their shoes.

> **Action: Ignore spelling, grammar, sentence structure and overall structure.**
>
> That's the work of the revising mode.

> **Action: Don't waste time trying to find the 'right' word.**
>
> Use a good-enough word for now. You will find the right word when you are in revising mode.

> **Action: Don't worry about repetition.**
>
> In fact, you might express the same idea a few times in slightly different ways as you explore it.

> **Action: Don't interrupt the flow of creating.**
>
> If something comes to mind during the creating mode that you need to check later, make notes in the text, identified by brackets or different colours so that you can easily deal with them later.

> **Action: Use short bursts of timed 'freewriting'.**
>
> Freewriting is writing without stopping for a short, set amount of time – between ten and twenty minutes.

The key principle here is to *keep writing* for the time period, come what may. If you don't know what to write, write 'I don't know what else to write …' and then just keep going.

- Freewriting is a good way of busting through procrastination.
- A short loop of freewriting can help to energise you during the creating mode. If you are stuck or are starting to slip into revising mode, set your timer and write without stopping for 10 minutes.

> 💬 **Don't forget to read**
>
> 'I didn't realise quite how much reading there was when writing! Not just revising my own thesis, but keeping up to date with all the new publications in my field.'

288 Part 4 – How to Get It Finished

> ✎ **Activity: Choose 'creating mode' techniques**
> 1 Commit to the techniques you will use to optimise your creating mode.
> 2 Check them off as you try them out.
>
> | I will: | |
> |---|---|
> | | ☐ |
> | | ☐ |
> | | ☐ |
> | | ☐ |
> | | ☐ |
> | | ☐ |

The revising mode

Most PhD students (and we include ourselves in this) drastically underestimate the amount of time needed to properly revise a written thesis. When it comes to planning the final months of your PhD, bear this in mind and schedule *more time* than you probably assume is necessary for the revising stages. Revising isn't just the final polishing stage of proofreading, it is still part of the process of writing. The aim of the revising mode is to:

- Organise and reorganise content to focus and hone your arguments
- Tighten and improve your language to make clear, powerful points
- Strengthen the evidence you use
- Cut out unnecessary text.

The following tips will help to make your revising mode as effective as possible:

> ➡ **Action: Differentiate the modes.**
>
> Consider making the change from creating to revising explicit by moving to a different place or using different materials, for example from the desk to the armchair, from typing to handwriting. These cues signal to your mind that you are in a different mode.

> ➡ **Action: Get some distance.**
>
> Take a break from whatever it is you have been creating before you go back to revise it.

Your perspective on the writing will be much clearer, and it will be easier to revise as a result. If you're under pressure to finish a piece of writing on the same day, at least take half an hour between the creating and revising modes.

> ➡ **Action: Get some feedback.**
>
> Invite feedback on your writing from your supervisors or a 'PhD buddy' and use their comments during your revision.

➡ **Action: Keep every draft.**

Some of this is good document management – so that you don't mistakenly press the delete button and lose everything! You may also find that, as you revise (which will include a lot of cutting), you might want to go back to reincorporate some of the original writing you had edited out.

➡ **Action: Sharpen your saw!**

Revising is a skill that takes specialist knowledge. Read a good book on academic writing (some suggestions are offered at the end of the chapter) or sign up for a thesis-writing course that will also include tips on helpful software to use.

➡ **Action: Set up templates.**

Early in the writing process, set up a formatting template for your thesis to standardise layout, font size and style, headings and so on.

Use this from the outset when you write your chapters. It will save you time in the final preparation of the manuscript. In addition, you will be able to make changes easily and apply them to the whole manuscript rather than going through, manually updating every heading or paragraph. Learn how to use your software's styles, outline, navigation and template functions to do this simply.

➡ **Action: Learn to let go.**

Every word should count in a good thesis.

Revising means a lot of cutting. This can be really hard. It can mean letting go of writing you are proud of or information that you think is interesting. If it helps, keep everything you cut from earlier drafts, 'just in case'. You never know. You might get the chance to use it in a later paper or report. You can use the 'must-haves, nice-to-haves and bells-and-whistles' technique to focus.

> 💬 'The best thing I ever did was to go on an MS Word training course before I started writing up. I thought I knew how to use Word but the handling of a 100k-word single document is a challenge.
>
> The one-hour course was a great investment, helping me manage the formatting and organisation of the thesis easily and efficiently. That one hour literally saved me days!'

> **✏ Activity: Choose 'revising mode' techniques**
>
> 1 Commit to the techniques you will use to optimise your revising mode.
> 2 Check them off as you try them out.

I will:	
	☐
	☐
	☐
	☐
	☐
	☐

Keep on writing

Cycling through the two modes of writing helps you to maintain your writing momentum. The switching of modes provides energising variety. It can still be very difficult, however, to face the page day-in day-out, as you must do to complete your thesis. The following tips can help you to keep on writing.

> **➡ Action: Write first.**
>
> This comes back to using your best time of day for writing. Give your writing focused attention, *before* other distractions, demands and worries come in. This means, write first – before you check your emails, review your to do list or chat with your office colleagues.

> **➡ Action: Give it enough time.**
>
> Time-block sessions that are long enough to let you find your way into the writing, whether in creating or revising mode.
>
> Writing well demands deep concentration if you are to make real progress, and not just fiddle about making some superficial tweaks. Try to schedule sessions of at least two to three hours (although always remember to divide this time into work periods of no more than 40 minutes to maintain brain power and concentration – see page 159).

> **➡ Action: Pace yourself.**
>
> Be realistic about how much you can do in a day and set a pace you can sustain.
>
> When you're in a good place, it might be tempting to go hard and write for ten hours. You might do great work on that day, but you'll probably find you're too tired to get much done the following one. Better to put in four good hours every day, at a pace you can sustain, and then spend the rest of the day doing everything else associated with your PhD.

> **➡ Action: Stop on the downhill slope.**
>
> Always finish your writing session at a point where it will be easy to pick it up again.

For example:

- Don't stop in the middle of a difficult section – add that extra bit to finish it before you set it aside
- Spend five minutes at the end of your writing session deciding where you will start next time
- Write the first few sentences of the section you are going to work on next, so you can pick it up easily
- Note some quick bullet points of your next paragraph, so you have a basic structure to get started on
- Print out the chapter you will be revising.

> ➡ **Action: If it's not working, stop.**
>
> If you're really stuck or just having a bad day, put your writing aside.

As long as this isn't a frequent occurrence (which would suggest that your writing schedule *isn't* sustainable), it is probably better to accept when it isn't working and take a break from it.

> ✎ **Activity: Choose 'writing momentum' techniques**
>
> 1 Commit to the techniques you will use to maintain your writing momentum.
> 2 Check them off as you try them out.
>
> | I will: | |
> |---|---|
> | | ☐ |
> | | ☐ |
> | | ☐ |
> | | ☐ |
> | | ☐ |
> | | ☐ |

Summary

The pressure of the final phase of your PhD can create new momentum and, just as easily, produce dips in your motivation. These final months are a time of increased stress and intensive demands on your energy and stamina. Prepare for this by reviewing and recommitting to the well-being and productivity techniques provided in this book. Invest time in your well-being, your mood and your motivation to ensure that you can keep working at your best right through to submission. The challenge of writing up your thesis can be a daunting prospect. Understanding and taking charge of the writing process, by separating the creating mode from the revising mode, will allow you to write more easily and increase the quality of your writing. Using techniques to maintain momentum will help you to sustain your writing output throughout the final months of your PhD.

> **Key points**
> - Motivation can falter in the final stages of your PhD.
> - Recommit to your physical and mental well-being measures so that you can cope well with the increased pressure.
> - Use your productivity and time-management techniques to maintain a steady work output.
> - Preserve your work-life balance.
> - Actively manage the writing process to keep your momentum.

Further resources

Bolker, J. (1998) *Writing Your Dissertation in 15 Minutes a Day*. New York: Holt Paperbacks.

Dunleavy, P. (2003) *How to Plan, Draft, Write and Finish a Doctoral Thesis or Dissertation*, 3rd edn. London: Red Globe Press.

Elbow, P. (2003) *Writing with Power: Techniques for Mastering the Writing Process*, 2nd edn. Oxford: Oxford University Press.

Gillihan, S.J. (2020) *Cognitive Behavioural Therapy Made Simple: 10 Strategies for Managing Anxiety, Depression, Anger, Panic and Worry*. London: Sheldon Press.

Hills, J. (2016) *Brain-Savvy Business*. London: Head, Heart & Brain.

Miller, C.A. (2017) *Getting Grit: The Evidence-Based Approach to Cultivating Passion, Perseverance, and Purpose*. Louisville, CO: Sounds True.

Newport, C. (2016) *Deep Work: Rules for Focused Success in a Distracted World*. London: Piatkus.

Reivich, K. and Shatte, A. (2003) *The Resilience Factor: 7 Keys to Finding Your Inner Strength and Overcoming Life's Hurdles*. New York: Broadway Books.

22 Get Ready for the Viva

How to ... Prepare yourself to perform confidently

> Preparation is key –Thesis summary spreadsheet – Literature map – Play devil's advocate – Practise, practise, practise – Visualise success – Power poses

Congratulations! Thesis submitted. Just the Viva stands between you and the coveted title of Doctor. It can be a daunting prospect. After writing a beautiful thesis, it can seem like an unreasonable extra hurdle to have to *discuss* it as well. Remember though: the PhD is an apprenticeship not an undergraduate assignment. Yes, the thesis is the representation of your research, but the Viva is the point at which you demonstrate that you can engage with a debate about your research, that your apprenticeship is over and you have *become* an academic researcher. This skill is just as much a part of your expertise as all the other research skills you have evidenced in your thesis.

Many guides exist on good academic preparation for the Viva. You should also receive advice from your supervisory team on preparation for this crucial test. So, our focus is on some of the aspects of preparing for the Viva that are acknowledged but not always explored in depth – in particular, addressing how to plan your preparation so that you feel confident and can manage the anxieties that you will face both in the lead up to and the actual Viva itself.

This chapter reminds you how best to plan your Viva preparation and provides tools to create the aides-memoires that will carry you through the Viva itself. We suggest techniques to reduce your anxieties about the Viva so that you can 'get out of your own way' when preparing for it. We revisit the concept of 'reframing' and provide techniques to create confidence-building thinking habits that you can adopt to minimise your anxiety. We emphasise the role of 'rehearsal' and why it is so important in optimising your Viva performance.

Your chance to shine

What UK universities call the Viva (short for *viva voce*) is called a thesis 'defence' in some countries. We think that's a shame as it sets you up to enter the Viva with the expectation that your examiners' aim is to attack. There's no doubt that your examiners will be testing your thesis (and the research that underpins it). We believe, however, that approaching the Viva as an opportunity to *show off your research* with experienced academics who understand your topic puts you in a better frame of mind. Your examiners want to see if you know what you're talking about; if you can justify your choices; if you understand the limitations of your work; that you have a well-rounded knowledge of the field and the research that backs up the thesis. They want to see if you are ready to be their peer.

Before our Vivas, we both, independently, had a similar experience. Some fellow students who had already completed their Vivas told us how much they had *enjoyed* the experience because it was a chance to discuss their research with other academics in an in-depth and knowledgeable way. Both of us thought this was highly unlikely and even a bit arrogant! But it turns out they were right. Despite the challenges of the Viva, we did enjoy the opportunity to spend a few hours with senior academics in our respective fields, whose literature we'd referenced, being treated like an equal and having a serious discussion about our research. You might not get to the point where you are looking forward to your Viva, but you should realise at least that this will be an opportunity as much as a test.

Things to think about:

- *Very few people fail a Viva.* According to a study (on DiscoverPhDs.com) of over 26,000 UK PhD students between 2006 and 2017, only 3.3 per cent! Unless you have ignored the advice and support of your supervision team, or somehow managed to circumvent all the checks and balances put in place by your institution, you will not fail.
- *Very few people pass a Viva with no corrections* (the same study gives the figure as 4.1 per cent). It's just not the 'academic way'. Remember, the iterative process? This is one more stage of iteration. Corrections don't mean failure – simply improvement.
- *The Viva isn't a box-ticking exercise.* What you say during the Viva will make a difference to the final decision. Whatever the examiners' assessment of your thesis going in, they will make their final assessment based on your performance in the Viva. Rosie went into the Viva anticipating major corrections (according to her primary supervisor). The discussion with the examiners resulted in minor corrections only. Fraser had the opposite experience!

 Call me doctor

'Remember the old joke about what one calls the person who graduates last in his medical school class: "Doctor". The same holds true for those who just squeak by their thesis defenses ... And no one will ever ask you about your performance at the event at which it was accepted' (Bolker, 1998).

Whether your thesis is accepted without corrections, or after minor or major corrections, the outcome will be the same. *You will be able to add 'Dr' to your name.* How you get there is irrelevant.

Preparing yourself for the Viva

For a successful Viva, preparation is key. Good preparation will also increase your confidence and reduce your anxieties. To prepare effectively, reach again for the planning methods we have described during the book.

1. Use the prioritisation technique (page 94) to define the scope of your preparation.
2. Create a WBS for the preparation for your Viva, in the same way that we recommended for writing up (page 270), making sure to include all the 'admin' and passive tasks.
3. Draw network diagrams (page 120) to identify the interdependencies between the different preparation tasks.
4. Create a Gantt chart (page 127) to schedule all the work.
5. Use the time-blocking method (page 148) to ensure that you fit all the preparation time into your schedule. This is particularly important because you are likely to have other work to do alongside your Viva preparation, whether a new job or applying for jobs, or submitting publications. It can be easy to neglect the Viva preparation in the face of other demands.

What to include in your Viva preparation

> ➡ **Action: Get advice.**
>
> As well as reading academic guides, seek advice from the people around you who have been through it.

Your supervisors will be able to advise you on what your examiners will be looking for, which will help you to prepare. Perhaps more importantly, ask fellow PhD students who have recently completed their Viva for some tips. Ask them what worked for them *and* what they wish they'd done differently.

> ✏ **Activity: Get advice on preparing for your Viva**
> Note down who you are going to seek out and what you want to know from them.
>
> | Who to ask | What to ask |
> |---|---|
> | | |

> ➡ **Action: Remind yourself of what you wrote and why.**
>
> Ensure that you are as familiar as possible with your thesis, and the research underpinning it.

Your Viva might happen months after you completed your thesis and you may be surprised just how much you've forgotten in the intervening period. You will be asked very detailed questions about the content of your thesis and will have to discuss the research that lies behind what you've written.

> ➡ **Action: Create a thesis summary.**
>
> You can't memorise a 100,000-word thesis. Instead, make a summary of your thesis content.

The act of creating this thesis summary spreadsheet will remind you of its contents. The artefact you create will also become one of your key study aids in memorising the detailed content and flow of your thesis. You can also take it in with you into the Viva as a reference. This example is an extract from Fraser's preparation spreadsheet. It made sense to him at the time!

Page #	Sec.	Summary
80	3.5/3.6	Purposive sampling follows BKHs method - more can be learnt from great triumphs and abject failures than averages. Getting positive participants is not a serious concern as this research is not about evaluating the specific training course itself (ie only *what* people value), it is attempting to investigate also *how* and *why* people value, with the aim of creating a better evaluation method for PMT.
81	3.6/3.6.1	Used IMPACT to link back to data - this could be criticised by saying you'll simply reproduce findings in the lit. Review by coding like this, however the *conv ints* also allowed unexpected benefits to augment the findings as well as supporting (or not) scholarly arguments. **Transcription:** I imagine time is an issue in a lot of professional doctorates - it certainly was with me - so I outsourced the transcription but it was read and reread while listening back to the interviews to ensure close familiarity with nuances etc.
82	3.6.1/3.6.2	No need for verbatim transcription - not keeping recordings like many OH projects. Also dangerous to read too much into nuances and personal opinions of the participants as described in 3.8 Strengths & limitations **Coding:** initially checking for "trustworthiness" by reading and rereading. But major omissions or inconsistancies can also be helpful - but you only get these if you're also have memory as a focus.
83	3.6.2/3.7	Coding generally using IMPACT categories... some lower level codes developed but were latterly subsumed by higher levels (ie materials, handouts, exercises etc all went in to 'content')
84	3.7	True OH is about giving a voice (∴ anonymity is not encouraged). This is still giving a voice to participants but without identifying them. We felt it would be safer.
85	3.8	Mitigating personal research agenda by discussing axiology (s3.2.3), research rationale (s1.2), insider/outsider debate (s3.4.1) and reflection throughout thesis.

Thesis summary spreadsheet example extract

> **✎ Activity: Create a thesis summary spreadsheet**
>
> 1 Similar to the example above, compile a very simple, three-column table in a spreadsheet package that summarises the content of your thesis. Alternatively download the template from OLC available at: https://www.mheducation.co.uk/professionals/open-university-press/olc/doyle-robertson-the-phd-handbook.
> 2 For <u>every page</u> of the thesis, include:
>   - Page number
>   - Section of thesis
>   - <u>Very</u> brief summary of the main argument/contention/discussion on that page.

➡ Action: Have the summary to hand.

In advance of your Viva, print out the spreadsheet to take into the exam room with you, or have it available electronically, if permitted.

You will be asked questions such as, 'What, in the extant research, supports your assertion on page 172?' and, if you're anything like us, you'll be thinking, 'What on earth happens on page 172?' Rather than having to open your thesis, read page 172, then glance at pages 171 and 173, by referring to your spreadsheet, you can quickly orientate yourself to the question. You will, of course, refer to your full manuscript as well, but this allows you to answer quickly and confidently. It should also reduce your anxiety about having to rely on your memory to answer questions in the pressured environment of the exam room. The stress of the Viva can trigger your fight-or-flight response with its negative impact on your prefrontal cortex, reducing your ability to think quickly. Anything you can do to avoid that will help you to stay calm and collected.

> **Action: Map your literature.**
>
> As well as the content of your thesis, it can be useful to summarise the key literature within which your research is situated.

To do this, use a mind map to display the key themes, sub-topics, seminal works and authors, as in the following example.

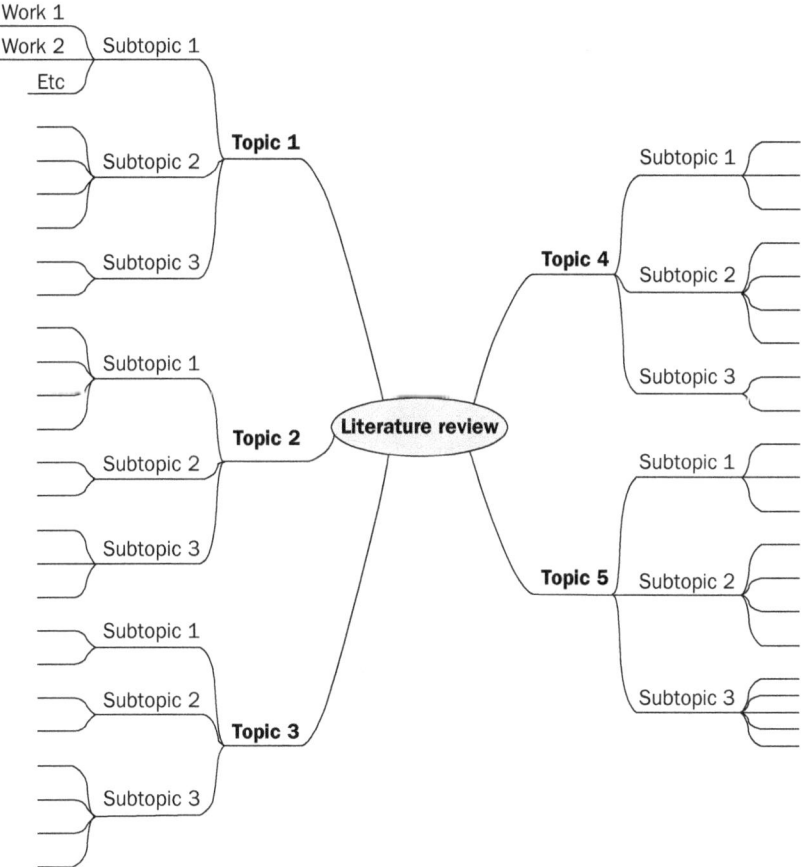

Literature map outline

Similar to the spreadsheet summary earlier, your literature map has a dual purpose: to help to prepare for the Viva and to be of use in the exam itself. Rather than having to remember all the references, the key ones are presented in a graphic that is easy to read and navigate. This does not have to be an exhaustive list. As in the following example, it should be an aide-memoire to assist you in the pressurised exam situation.

298 Part 4 – How to Get It Finished

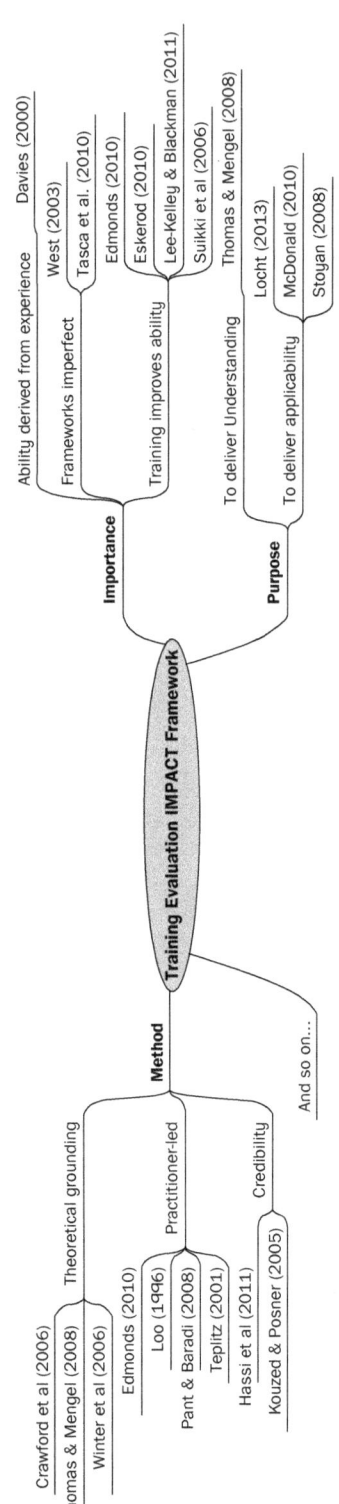

Literature map example

> **Work breakdown structure**
>
> If you prefer, you could adapt the WBS to perform a similar task if that layout appeals to you more.

> ✏️ **Activity: Create a literature map**
>
> 1. On a blank sheet of paper or in software, draw a mind map that reflects the findings of your literature review.
> 2. Include categories/topics of literature.
> 3. Note the *key* texts that underpin your thesis.
>
> Feel free to annotate and colour the map in any way that will help you to navigate it easily.

> ➡ **Action: Ask yourself questions.**
>
> The Viva isn't a memory test. You have to be able to discuss, interrogate and defend your research in response to your examiners' questions. To prepare yourself for this aspect, practise answers for potential questions.

You won't know exactly what you will be asked, but typical questions that are asked in a Viva include:

- Who are the top academics in your field at the moment, and what influence has their research had on your work?
- Why did you decide to take this specific approach to your study and not this other approach?
- What is the biggest contribution you feel this work has made?

Many academic guides have lists of likely Viva questions. Ask other PhD students who have completed their Viva what questions they were asked. They won't be exactly the same questions you will be asked, as every piece of research is different, but it will give you some ideas of the sorts of questions you might face.

Once you have a list of potential questions, write out answers and memorise them. Even if you aren't given the same questions, you will find that the memorised answers will make it easy to bring to mind relevant information in response to the questions you *are* asked.

> ✏️ **Activity: Prepare yourself for questions**
>
> 1. Make a list of potential questions that you might face in your Viva.
> 2. Write example answers for each question.
>
> We also advise you to practise saying these answers out loud. More on this shortly ...

> ➡ **Action: Find your weaknesses.**
>
> This can be a painful process, but facing up to shortcomings of your research, and knowing about them going into your Viva, will make you a stronger, more confident candidate. Demonstrating that you have thought about and have been able to identify potential weaknesses demonstrates that you are a mature researcher, ready to be a peer.

You will have done this already to some extent in the limitations section of your thesis. In preparation for your Viva, take another look at these limitations and consider what else you could have done or would do in future research. Don't just identify weaknesses, but identify the reasons for the weaknesses and changes you would make – and ensure they are justifiable reasons, not just, 'I messed up'! More important is the next stage of the thinking – how could such weaknesses be avoided in future research?

The devil's advocate technique

The devil's advocate technique is a great tool for revealing the shortcomings of any project, not just your research. A devil's advocate is someone who criticises something for the purposes of testing an idea, not necessarily because they believe the criticism is valid. Playing devil's advocate for your own research relieves you of any defensiveness you might otherwise feel in the face of criticism. The criticisms are not necessarily real; they are *potential* criticisms. Once you have collected a number of potential criticisms, you can decide on the validity of them and come up with defences or solutions. It's easier to do this by asking other people to be devil's advocate for you – in the same way that you used a RAT to identify risks (page 140). It overcomes the emotional attachment you would have to your research. However, if that isn't possible, you can be your own devil's advocate.

1. Ask each devil's advocate to give you as many potential criticisms of your research as possible. They don't have to explain or justify the criticisms.
2. List the criticisms. *Don't* engage with or otherwise argue against the criticisms at this point. Just record them.
3. Once you have listed the criticisms, go back and assess the validity of each one. You have two possible responses:
   - Refute the potential criticism, and provide evidence for the refutation
   - Accept the criticism as valid and then provide an explanation for the necessary limitations of your research, and/or explain what could be done differently in future research to avoid the criticism.

For example:

Criticism	**Refutation**	**Mitigating action**
The number of participants in the study is too low to draw any real conclusions from the data.	The purpose of the research was not generalisability or statistical significance, but a deep investigation into subjective assessment, therefore a small data set doesn't prevent this.	
The research would have been greatly enhanced by also considering an additional data modelling technique during the analysis.		It was considered, but, due to feasibility within a PhD study, it was decided to focus on these other models first. Use of the additional modelling technique would provide an excellent follow-on project.

Devil's advocate: refutation and mitigating action

> **✎ Activity: Devil's advocate technique**
>
> 1 Find other people to be your devil's advocates (or be your own).
> 2 On the template on page 302, note all these potential criticisms of your research.
> 3 Rebut or accept each criticism and provide mitigating action depending on its validity.

Template: Devil's advocate technique

Criticism	Refutation	Mitigating action

> ➡ **Action: Practise, practise, practise.**
>
> The Viva is an *oral* exam, not a written one. It's full title, the Viva Voce, is Latin for 'with living voice'. Part of good preparation for your Viva, therefore, will be to ensure that you are ready to *speak* about your research. This means *rehearsal*: speaking out loud and live!

Rehearsal will improve and increase:

Fluency	Talking about your PhD out loud is a very different proposition from reading or writing about it. Aim for natural fluency. Try to avoid scripted responses: just speak cogently.
	Have (and practise) key points about your research. This is a bit like politicians staying 'on message' – although, unlike politicians, don't avoid answering questions! Having some key points ready helps you to navigate the discussion.
Authority	Present yourself *confidently* while talking about your research to increase the authority of your answers. This is not just down to what you say, but how you say it. As explained in Chapter 19, a lot of communication is conveyed by the non-verbal aspects of conversation, not just the words. Even if you are generally quite a confident and articulate speaker, the challenge of the Viva will test you – so practise looking and sounding confident.
	There is evidence that your body language can create a positive feedback loop with your mind. Confident body language will make you feel more confident as well as seem more confident to other people.
Readiness for questions	Practise answering questions. Obviously, this is the whole point of the Viva! Practise fielding unexpected questions, without losing confidence or becoming defensive. Practise pausing and thinking – you don't have to respond immediately. It's fine (good, in fact) to take time to think about your response. This demonstrates that you are engaging fully in the debate.
Self-belief	The better you prepare, the better you will feel about the whole thing. And, the more confident you feel, the better you will perform on the day.

There are two aspects to rehearsal: practising *speaking* about your research out loud and practising *thinking on your feet*. If you can, find someone to play the role of your examiners so you can answer their questions live. Even if they don't know much about your research (perhaps are a family member, flatmate or friend) and therefore won't be able to enter into deep debate, they're a real person to respond to. Furnish them with a variety of questions to throw at you, and they can choose in which order to ask them so there's at least some element of surprise.

Alternatively, find a Viva prep buddy among your PhD colleagues and help each other prepare. Even if they don't know your topic in detail, they will know enough about research to engage with questioning. Make sure that you trust them to be positive partners. You want to practise the difficult questions you might get asked by your examiners, but you don't want your confidence destroyed by someone who is feeling competitive or defensive. Nor should you do that for them.

Your supervisor may be happy to hold a practice Viva with you. Many universities organise a formal 'mock' Viva before the real thing. All of this preparation should be in addition to that final dress rehearsal. If nothing else, practise on your own, speaking out loud.

304 Part 4 – How to Get It Finished

Activity: Draw up a rehearsal schedule
1 Note below who you will rehearse with.
2 Time-block preparation and rehearsal time into your calendar.
3 Check it off when you have had some practice.

Repeat the process as often as necessary.

I will rehearse with:	When?	Done
		☐
		☐
		☐
		☐
		☐
		☐

Activity: Write a viva preparation checklist
- Add to this list any further items that you want to include in your preparation.
- Check off the items as you use them to prepare for your Viva.

Viva preparation items/events	✓
Preparation schedule (Gantt chart)	☐
Advice from others	☐
Thesis summary spreadsheet	☐
Literature map	☐
List of potential questions	☐
Check what is permitted in the exam room (print-outs etc.)	☐
Practise answering questions	☐
Devil's advocate/identify weaknesses	☐
Rehearsal/mock Viva	☐
	☐
	☐
	☐
	☐

Handling nerves

You will be nervous in the run up to the Viva, and even more so on the day itself. It's inevitable. Remember that your examiners expect you to be nervous, so they make allowances. We offer some suggestions for reducing your nervousness here, but you should also accept it. It is a sign that you are gearing up for something. A little bit of adrenaline will keep you sharp and give you energy!

Although you should accept some degree of nerves, there are actions you can take to reduce your nervousness to a level where it won't get in the way of your performance in the Viva. Some of these techniques have already featured in the book, and you can adapt them to the demands of the Viva as follows.

> ➡ **Action: Reframe your nerves.**
>
> A tried-and-tested method is to call your nerves 'excitement', rather than anxiety. You have the same physical responses in both cases. One experiment (Robson, 2022) showed that students who had been told that their nerves would improve their performance in their exams performed better than students who had not been given that message. Embrace your nerves rather than resist them.

> ➡ **Action: Be prepared.**
>
> Knowing that you have prepared well will soothe your nerves and boost your confidence. Follow the steps in the first half of this chapter and you can approach your Viva knowing that you're in the best place you can be to perform well.

> ➡ **Action: Manage your mind (again).**
>
> Carefully attend to your 'beliefs' about the Viva.

Use all the techniques described in the book to create constructive thoughts (Chapters 14 and 18):

- Resist the temptation to catastrophise about the Viva. Don't feed your mind frightening 'What if' stories (see pages 194 and 278), such as, 'What if my mind goes blank and I can't remember anything? What if the examiners think my research is worthless? What if I make a fool of myself?'
- Rather, use affirmations to create positive attitudes about your abilities and about the nature of the Viva itself (pages 195 and 278). Repeat them daily, for example:
  - My Viva is a unique opportunity to discuss my research with a respected academic
  - My Viva is a chance to explain the value of my research
  - I am well prepared for my Viva.
- Avoid the scare stories! There are always stories circulating of terrible Viva experiences. Yes, some students have a bad time, but it's a small proportion. Your Viva will be difficult – there's no doubt about that – but it will be difficult in a way that you can prepare for and overcome.

> ➡ **Action: Visualise success.**
>
> In the weeks running up to the Viva, use the visualisation technique introduced in Chapter 2 to prepare your unconscious mind for success.

The use of visualisations to improve performance was pioneered in sport. It's the process of imagining a successful outcome, for example winning a race – or having a successful Viva! Repeating the visualisation activity regularly will really help to prepare you, so do it as often as you can or turn it into a habit (for example every night just before you go to sleep).

> ✎ **Activity: Visualisation**
>
> 1 Sit somewhere quiet and comfortable, where you won't be disturbed.
> 2 Breathe deeply and close your eyes.
> 3 Visualise yourself successfully going through your Viva:
>
> - Make the image as vivid as possible – sights, sounds, feelings.
> - Imagine being in the room (or in a room if you don't know the room where it will take place).
> - Visualise feeling and looking confident.
> - See yourself answering questions articulately and confidently.
> - See the impressed responses of the examiners.
> - Visualise exiting the Viva, knowing that you've done yourself proud.
>
> 4 Repeat this regularly – it's another example of training your brain and body through repeated effort.

Look after yourself

In the weeks before the Viva, recommit to all the self-care practices associated with resilience, for example:

- Get a good night's sleep (page 186). You might not sleep well the night before your Viva but, if you've looked after your sleep in the weeks before, one night's poor sleep won't derail you.
- Keep your mindfulness practice going (page 188). You can combine it with the visualisation technique. Mindfulness has been shown to have an accumulated positive impact on your brain; it makes you less reactive to stress and improves cognitive function.
- Don't overlook regular exercise. It's less about staying fit at this stage, and more about ensuring that you have a flow of the body's natural anti-depressants – endorphins – circulating regularly.
- Draw on your social support networks (Chapter 6). The Viva is a big challenge. Don't face it alone if you can avoid it.

> 💬 **On-the-day support**
>
> 'My partner very sweetly took a day off work to drive me to and from my Viva. It made a huge difference to my nerves to have them with me before it and to know that they would be waiting for me afterwards.'

> ✎ **Activity: Manage well-being**
>
> Write below what you commit to do to manage your well-being and reduce anxiety in the lead up to your Viva.
>
> **I will:**

Get ready: the day before your Viva

It will help to minimise your stress if you have everything you need laid out and ready the night before, for example:

- Clothing
- Documents (including your thesis, thesis summary and literature mind map) printed or available electronically
- Details about the location
- Water bottle, coffee cup, chocolate
- Money
- Fully charged phone and chargers
- Notepad and pens.

> **Transferable skills**
>
> All of these 'getting ready' tips for the day before the Viva are equally applicable when preparing for a job interview.

Activity: Draw up a Viva checklist

Write down everything you need to have ready for your Viva so you don't need to think about it.

Viva checklist	✓
Thesis	☐
Thesis summary	☐
Literature map	☐
	☐
	☐
	☐
	☐
	☐
	☐
	☐

Get ready: the day of your Viva

- Give yourself plenty of time to get to your Viva – so you don't end up rushed and stressed.
- Consider moderating your use of stimulants. One cup of coffee or tea might help you to feel alert, but don't overdo it. You don't want to add to any jitteriness.
- Try some deep-breathing and mindfulness exercises to reduce the physiological impact of stress.
- Do your visualisation one last time.
- Use power poses.

In Part 3, we mentioned that your body language can send signals to *your* mind as well as to the people observing you. Using confident body language can make you *feel* more confident. Psychologist Amy Cuddy

(2015) has popularised this notion through her concept of power poses – postures that use expansive, strong, open body language. Her research demonstrated that adopting a power pose for two minutes resulted in a measurable boost of the power hormone testosterone and reduced the stress hormone cortisol.

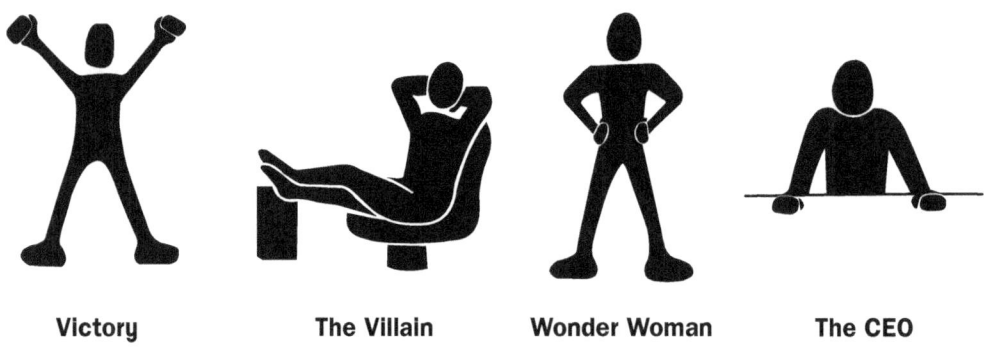

Victory   **The Villain**   **Wonder Woman**   **The CEO**

Image: Zoë Robertson

Power poses

Now go, give 'em hell!

> **✏ Activity: Boost your confidence**
>
> Immediately before your Viva, spend two minutes somewhere private in one of the power poses shown here (time yourself, as it tends to feel like a long time). You might feel a bit silly, but they can *really* work!

Summary

Your Viva is the final hurdle of your PhD, but it's also the culmination of your achievements. See it as an unrivalled opportunity to show off your research as much as a test. Remember that the Viva is not a formality. A good performance at the Viva can improve the assessment of your research.

Good preparation is key to a successful, and also less stressful, Viva, so don't skimp on it. Use your planning tools to ensure you allocate enough time to prepare thoroughly. Engage with the content of your thesis by preparing summary artefacts that can serve as aides-memoires, devising answers to potential questions and addressing the shortcomings of your research head on.

Although nerves are inevitable, keep them at a manageable level by using the anxiety-reduction techniques and well-being measures you have learned throughout this book, both in the run up to the Viva and on the day itself. Good preparation will ensure that you feel confident enough to make your Viva the crowning achievement of your PhD. Do yourself justice and feel proud!

> **Key points**
>
> - Your Viva is a unique chance to show off your research – make the most of it.
> - Good preparation is the single biggest factor in ensuring that you have a good Viva.
> - Plan your preparation schedule carefully to make sure you get everything done.
> - Reacquaint yourself with your thesis, in detail.
> - Rehearse your Viva.
> - Take steps to handle your inevitable nerves before and during your Viva.

Further resources

Brann, A. (2013) *Make Your Brain Work*. London: Kogan Page.
Cuddy, A. (2015) *Presence: Bringing your Boldest Self to your Biggest Challenges*. New York: Back Bay Books.
Iornem, K.S. (2021) *A Social Science Student's Guide to Surviving Your PhD*. London: Open University Press.
Murray, R. (2015) *How to Survive Your Viva: Defending a Thesis in an Oral Examination*, 3rd edn. Maidenhead: Open University Press.
Phillips, E.M. and Johnson, C.G. (2022) *How to Get a PhD*, 7th edn. Maidenhead: Open University Press.
Rugg, G. and Petre, M. (2020) *The Unwritten Rules of PhD Research*, 3rd edn. London: Open University Press.

References

Bolker, J. (1998) *Writing Your Dissertation in 15 Minutes a Day*. New York: Holt Paperbacks, p 134.
Cuddy, A. (2015) *Presence: Bringing Your Boldest Self to Your Biggest Challenges*. New York: Back Bay Books.
Discover PhDs.com (no date) PhD Failure Rate – A Study of 26,076 PhD Candidates, available at: discoverphds.com/advice/doing/phd-failure-rate#:~:text=Summary,and%20are%20awarded%20a%20doctorate [accessed 25 January 2023].
Robson, D. (2022) *The Expectation Effect*. Edinburgh: Canongate, p 143.

23 Take the Next Step

How to … Use your PhD as the launch pad for your future career

> Give yourself a pat on the back – A PhD isn't enough – Leverage your transferable skills – Identify, articulate, evidence – WIIFMs one more time – Features and benefits – STAR technique

Stop for a moment and congratulate yourself for getting this far. The successful completion of a PhD is a huge accomplishment, one which only a small percentage of the population achieves. Recent OECD (2021) data states that only 2 per cent of the UK population has a doctorate. As you've come to realise, completing a PhD is about so much more than the research. It's a long, challenging process requiring degrees of intellect, persistence, resilience and self-organisation that not everyone possesses. So, please do give yourself a big pat on the back and revel for a moment in your success.

But what now? As we said right back in Chapter 2, it will be different for every PhD student. However, by identifying your personal goals from the start, reviewing them frequently and taking steps to make progress towards them during your PhD, hopefully, you won't have landed at this stage with no clue about what comes next. We hope the vision of your future, your 'glimmer of light', has become clearer and brighter throughout your PhD and you are now ready to make it a reality.

In this chapter, we want to make sure that you can leverage the value of your PhD in the service of your career, so that you have a competitive edge with potential employers, funders or collaborators. When designing the structure of this book, it has sometimes been hard to know what to focus on when – particularly when we really want to say, 'You need to do all of this, all of time.' Clearly, that wouldn't be very helpful! Instead, we chose to use a chronological order for the content. As a result, this chapter falls at the end of the book, but we really hope that you started on the process it describes much earlier in your PhD (as recommended in Chapter 17).

We don't wish to burst your bubble, but, on its own, having a PhD will not get you a job. The award demonstrates that you have conducted a robust research project that has produced some new knowledge in, let's face it, a fairly niche field. That alone isn't going to have future employers beating a path to your door, unless you are one in the miniscule proportion of PhD students whose research has produced a world-changing, immediately profitable, patentable innovation. If that's you, then congratulations, good luck, and get a good lawyer! Everyone else has to be able to demonstrate why their PhD has equipped them with the skills and attributes that make them a valuable asset to a potential employer. This is equally true whether you are continuing in academia or going out into a different industry. The level you have now attained means that everyone competing for the jobs you aspire to is also likely to have a PhD – this isn't denigrating your achievement, it merely reflects how far you've come.

Don't feel discouraged. We aren't saying you must go straight out after submitting your thesis and get even more expertise. All you need to do is learn how to identify, describe and evidence all the expertise you have already acquired through your PhD to a potential employer. You've done all the hard work. You just need to know *how to talk about it* in a way that shows off your assets.

We've frequently described a PhD as an apprenticeship in academic research. However, your PhD is so much more than research skills. It's a complex project that required good self-organisation, time management, planning and monitoring. It's a long, difficult undertaking that required self-motivation, resilience and determination. It required collaboration and communication skills. It required excellent writing and information management skills. The broad range of skills you have used and developed along the way are going to be equally (and sometimes, more) valuable than the award itself.

This is important because all jobs, including those in academia, demand this broad range of skills, not only the research-specific skills associated with a PhD. This is particularly the case if you're aiming to work outside academia. The Higher Education Policy Institute (Hancock, 2020) claims that 70 per cent of PhD holders will not be working in academia three and a half years after graduation. Even if you're in the other 30 per cent, the other 'non-research' skills you've developed will be extremely important for future employment.

Don't assume the 'non-research' skills required to complete a PhD will be obvious to a potential employer. For one thing, not all PhD students will have developed these skills – especially those who haven't read this book! The PhD can also be something of a 'black box' for people outside academia. Potential employers may just think it means you're very clever (which is true!) and that you know a lot about some very specific topic (which is also true!). They may not realise just what the successful completion of a PhD entailed. Worse, in some fields, there may even be negative associations attached to a PhD. It may be assumed that you're an ivory-tower intellectual who has nothing practical to offer the real world. It is up to you to show that your 'ivory tower' skills are just as relevant and valuable in the 'real world' of the potential employer.

> 'I found out this week that I was successful in the interview [with commercial pharmaceutical research organisation]. I begin my role as project coordinator next month. Thanks again for the training and introducing me to a career I had never previously thought of!'

Even in academia, where a PhD is a required part of the standard career path, the range of skills you have developed during your PhD may not be understood. Expert subject knowledge alone is not enough to progress through to a permanent academic contract. You also need to be able to put bids together, run research groups and lead collaborations. You must be able to demonstrate that you have these skills.

Our aim in this book has been to provide you with knowledge, techniques and tools that equip you to complete your PhD successfully and to make the most of the opportunities that a research degree provides. More than that, we know these skills and attributes will be useful to you in your career and are the qualities that employers will seek in their employees. This whole book adds up to a comprehensive toolbox of professional expertise termed transferable skills. These are skills that you can equally utilise in academic research or industry R&D or space engineering or agriculture or public policy development or marketing or nursing or art-gallery management. In other words, they are useful in whatever direction you want your career to take you. Employers, be they in academia or industry, want employees who have the ability to be independent and do not need 24/7 supervision. They want employees who *bring value as quickly as possible*. The time it will take you to get up to speed in a professional workspace is going to be considerably reduced because you already have such a wide portfolio of skills.

Remember too: not all PhD students will have read this book. We hope that our book gives you a competitive edge in the highly competitive job market. Compare your position with that of another candidate who has a fantastic thesis but no transferable skills, or a candidate who doesn't *realise* that their PhD has provided them with transferable skills and therefore doesn't flag these up to a potential employer.

This chapter guides you through a process that prepares you to capitalise on the knowledge and skills you've fought so hard to develop during your PhD, using three steps:

1 **Identify your skills** – ensure that you are aware of your full portfolio of relevant skills.
2 **Articulate your skills** – describe the most relevant skills in such a way that a potential employer will see the value they offer.
3 **Evidence your skills** – demonstrate that you can apply these skills successfully in a work setting.

As an extra bonus, this process will also give your confidence a boost. It helps you become aware of – and truly value – the full range of skills you've developed during your PhD. This can do wonders for your self-belief and aspirations when embarking on the next stage of your career.

Identify your skills

Let's go back to Chapter 1 and remind you of the conscious competence model (page 8). Back then, we were preparing you to find yourself frequently in the 'conscious incompetence' phase during your PhD; discovering just how much you didn't know about doing research. At the end of your PhD, you are occupying the 'unconscious competence' stage for many of the skills developed over the intervening years. You may have forgotten just how many new skills you've acquired because you have become expert and now take them for granted. Not only does this mean that you overlook them and may forget to mention valuable skills in the job market, but you may also overlook the fact that *not everyone* you are competing with has these same skills. They may be the very things that give you your competitive edge.

Your PhD will have furnished you with specific technical and research skills and knowledge that may be required for your next step. Some of these will be the research skills associated with your PhD, for example:

- Conducting a literature review
- Data analysis
- Academic writing
- Teaching.

Some will be related to the specifics of your PhD topic, such as:

- Handling and transporting fragile archival material
- Coding a data dictionary in R statistical software
- Conducting an oral history interview
- Extracting blood samples from sea eagle nestlings.

These skills won't be enough on their own to guarantee you a job, however. Instead, you need to demonstrate your transferable skills: the skills required in any job at a senior level. The following is a summary of the generic skills most employers will be looking for in a potential employee:

- Communication
- Leadership and teamworking
- Planning and organising
- Research and information management
- Problem-solving and decision-making

- Presentation and public speaking
- Self-management.

In preparation for competing in the job market, take another look at your PhD and identify all the skills you have developed under each category. Then think of situations in which you have used (and thereby demonstrated) these skills.

The table that follows provides examples of how you could think about all your transferable skills and your competitive edge.

Skill identification examples		
Skill category	**Skill**	**Examples of use**
Communication	• Written communication • Oral communication	• 80k-plus-word thesis • Academic paper, peer-reviewed and published in journal • STEM ambassador performing outreach at local schools
Leadership and teamworking	• Goal-setting • Influencing skills	• Used SMART objectives method to specify key research goals for PhD • Represented PhD students at researcher-development meetings and successfully lobbied for additional resources for conference expenses
Planning and organising	• Project management • Risk management	• Used PM techniques (WBS, estimation and Gantt chart) to create a realistic plan that helped to complete PhD on time • Successfully achieved CAPM accreditation • Performed formal risk assessment sub-tidal fieldwork, mitigating serious risks and developing work around plans for small risks
Research and information management	• Data management	• Developed and abided by a data management plan that passed through ethics approval with no changes and aligned to GDPR regulations for oral history depositions of cancer patients
Problem-solving and decision-making	• Testing potential solutions • Data analysis	• Used project triangle tool to assess value of potential changes to PhD • Management recommendations for child protection social work in thesis conclusions based on analysis of qualitative data
Presentation and public speaking	• Presentation skills	• Presented at conference on research topics to audience of 250 academics • Teaching 300 students on undergraduate module • Entered university's Three-minute Thesis competition
Self-management	• Personal time management	• Hit all PhD deadlines through efficient personal time management • Implemented strategies to avoid procrastination, work more effectively and be productive for longer

The specific examples of use that you've included in this table could be applied to several different parts of the job-seeking process, for example covering letters, CVs, job applications. They will be especially useful during interviews as an answer to the very common 'Give me an example of a time when you ...' questions used by interviewing panels.

You can use the table as a general reminder of the skills you've developed and the experience gained over the course of your PhD, and in response to the specific requirements of particular jobs you're applying for. It helps you to identify and articulate your 'unique selling point' – what differentiates you from all the other candidates.

> **✎ Activity: List skills and examples**
>
> Using the template on page 315, list your skills and examples.
>
> If you are doing this at the point of applying for a specific job, use the job description and person specification to identify the skills you need to demonstrate. If that is the case, substitute the details from the job description into the left column of the template.

Template: Skill identification

Skill category	Skill	Examples of use
Communication		
Leadership and teamworking		
Planning and organising		
Research and information management		
Problem-solving and decision-making		
Presentation and public speaking		
Self-management		

Articulate your skills

One of the major issues for PhD graduates applying for positions is the difficulty they have in describing the transferable skills they've developed through their degree. It's also something we've encountered recruiting in industry: candidates find it difficult to articulate the skills developed other than in relation to the very research-specific tasks of the study. Given how increasingly competitive the job market is, being able to articulate everything that you can bring to a role is imperative. There are usually three aspects of this articulation you need to pay attention to:

- **Specification**: making your skills explicit and clear
- **Translation**: changing the research/discipline-specific language to vocabulary that will be understood by the potential employer
- **Value**: explaining how a research-related skill can be relevant and useful in the employment setting you are aiming to enter.

If you are staying in academia, this work of articulation (describing your skills in a job application or interview) requires less of a shift, as you will share the perspective of the employment destination. Don't assume, however, that even an academic interviewer will automatically be aware of your skills and their relevance. The steps of articulation are still important in making certain that your potential value to an employer is accurately understood.

Often, the most significant issues in explaining your transferable skill set to others are simply down to *terminology*. Particularly if you are moving out of academia, the language used isn't the same as the lexicon of research, so, being able to translate your experiences into the vocabulary of your audience is a crucial skill to develop. A fundamental rule of any type of communication is that it is *not* the audience's job to take a message on board, it is *your* job to put the message across in an accessible way.

Employers do not pay you solely for your expertise. *They pay you to bring value.* What employers really want to know is:

- How will your expertise (which is what your PhD demonstrates) be of benefit to this institution, department, research group, company or project?
- Can you work effectively and efficiently within their environment and how quickly will you get up to speed?
- Do you have the skills required to manage your workload and deliver to deadlines without needing to be micromanaged?
- Can you integrate, communicate and establish professional working relationships within the existing team structure?
- How well can you overcome challenging situations, setbacks and adversity (one of the most common interview questions)?
- How do you deal with the inevitable conflict that comes with work in a high-pressure environment?

When you articulate your skills, be explicit about how they will provide value for the employer. Go back to the WIIFM concept introduced in Chapter 13.

> ➡ **Action: Find the WIIFMs**
>
> Put yourself in the shoes of your potential employer and view your experience and skills from their perspective. This will make it easier to reframe and explain your skill set in a way that directly aligns to the job requirements. Ask yourself: Why should they care if I understand the thermal

behaviour of bisoprolol fumarate? What difference will it make to them if I won the Donachy Prize for best conference presentation? How will it benefit them if I can assess and mitigate risk?

The features and benefits technique

Once you have worked this out, make sure that you clarify these WIIFMs when you articulate your skills. A quick trick to help with this is the features and benefits technique. This is a way of describing something in terms of its *features* (the facts) and the way that the features provide *benefits* to the intended audience, in this instance, the potential employer. For example:

- **Feature**: I work as part of research group on a large collaborative project with many different partners
- **Benefit**: Which means that I am used to working as an effective team member, and communicating with and managing the expectations of key project stakeholders

Or:

- **Feature**: My supervisor was off sick for three months, so I had to make progress without regular oversight
- **Benefit:** Which means that I am able to work productively and independently without the need for micro-management.

Activity: Identify features and benefits

Identify the features of your key skills and the potential benefits they offer to an employer.

Features	Benefits to the employer

Evidence your skills

The job application process is often described in terms of being 'competency based'. This means that you have to demonstrate your ability to use a particular skill, not just that you have the knowledge or a qualification. To do this adequately, you need to provide evidence that you have already put that skill into practice successfully.

You have now started the process of thinking of situations when you have used your skills in the skills identification and articulation processes. These examples will be the raw material you can choose from for applications and job interviews. Select the examples that are *most relevant* to the employment setting and those that will *differentiate you* from other candidates. For example, you may have noted that you have used written communication skills in your thesis, in journal articles and in conference posters.

If you are applying for a post-doc, you will be best served using the evidence of your journal articles, especially if they have been accepted. Why not just your thesis? Because every single candidate for that post-doc has produced a thesis. It doesn't mark you out. However, not every PhD student has articles published.

What if you're applying for a job outside academia? Perhaps in an R&D role in industry? Do you tell them about your thesis in detail? Probably not. Having a staff member who can write a 100,000-word document isn't helpful in itself. However, the employer might be interested in someone with the ability to take complex information and streamline it into a 20-minute conference presentation with accompanying slides. That's a more relevant example of evidence for this job.

The STAR technique

Once you have strategically selected evidence for your skills, there's a technique you can use to make your evidence especially convincing in a job application or an interview setting. This is the STAR technique. STAR is an acronym for:

- **S**ituation
- **T**ask
- **A**ction
- **R**esult.

Use the STAR structure to build the description of the evidence of a skill to an employer, so that its *value* is emphasised and your *competence* in the skill is clear.

Situation

> ➡ **Action: Describe the situation in which you used the skill.**
>
> It can be especially impressive if you can identify a problem to solve, or an opportunity to take advantage of. For example, 'The research team wanted to stimulate industry engagement and potential funding partners. The government-backed Catapult Network conference was the chance for me to present my PhD research to a new set of industry representatives in the UK.'

Task

> ➡ **Action: Describe what you needed to achieve through the use of the skill.**
>
> For example, 'I had to create a presentation that would demonstrate the commercial value of the research to industry.'

Action

> ➡ **Action: Describe the action you took that demonstrates the use of the skill.**
>
> For example, 'I only had 20 minutes for my presentation, so I had to make sure I chose the most relevant information for my audience. I selected the research outputs from my PhD that would be most suitable for patent development and illustrated the relevance with similar examples that had already produced viable patents in the industries represented at the conference. I also highlighted the government funding our research project had received, to emphasise the credibility of our work.'

Result

➡ **Action: Describe the (positive) impact of the action you took.**

Only pick examples that have a positive result! For example, 'After my presentation, I received follow-up enquiries from four separate organisations that were interested in the work of our research team.'

✏ **Activity: STAR template**

1. Select the most relevant examples of evidence for key transferable skills or that are linked to a specific job application.
2. Write a STAR version of each example, using the template on page 320.

Template: STAR assessment

Skill	Evidence example	STAR version			
		Situation	Task	Action	Result

Summary

A successfully completed PhD isn't just the culmination of your PhD journey, it is the first step on the next phase of your career. The award itself is only one small part of the benefits that the PhD has provided and, perhaps, not even the most important for your future career, however great the achievement. In order to use your PhD as the launch pad for your future career, you need to leverage the portfolio of transferable skills you have acquired along the way, as well as the research skills.

Don't assume your skills are obvious to a potential employer, whether in academia or elsewhere. Instead, make sure to identify, articulate and evidence your skills, demonstrating the practical value they will offer in your employment setting of choice. Take particular care to demonstrate the skills you have developed that other PhD holders may not have, especially the toolbox of professional skills you have acquired by reading and using this book. This is your competitive edge.

> **Key points**
> - The skills you have used in successfully completing your PhD are highly transferable to a wide range of other work settings.
> - Non-research skills developed during your PhD will be just as important in differentiating you to potential employers as your research skills (if not more so).
> - Articulating and evidencing the relevant skills you have developed during your PhD will enhance your employability and give you a competitive edge in a crowded job market.
> - Explicitly linking your skill set to the needs of potential employers in a language they understand will clearly demonstrate your value as an employee.

Further resources

Cuddy, A. (2015) *Presence: Bringing your Boldest Self to your Biggest Challenges.* New York: Back Bay Books.
Kelsey, K. (2015) *The Professor is In: The Essential Guide to Turning Your PhD Into a Job* New York: Three Rivers Press.
Newport, C. (2016) *So Good They Can't Ignore You.* London: Piatkus.
Ryan, R. (2016) *60 Seconds and You're Hired!*, 3rd edn. New York: Penguin.
Vick, J.M., Furlong, J.S. and Lurie, R. (2016) *The Academic Job Search Handbook*, 5th edn. Philadelphia: University of Pennsylvania Press.
Your university careers service

References

Hancock, S (2020) *The employment of PhD graduates in the UK: what do we know?* Available at: hepi.ac.uk/2020/02/17/the-employment-of-phd-graduates-in-the-uk-what-do-we-know [accessed 4 September 2022].
OECD (2021) *Education at a Glance 2021: OECD Indicators*, Paris: OECD Publishing.

Afterword

Congratulations – you've finished the book. If finishing the book coincides with finishing your PhD, even bigger congratulations! But you haven't finished *with* the book.

We explained in the introduction that we would help you to 'sharpen your saw'; that investing time up front in learning how to use the techniques in the book would make your research experience easier, better and more enjoyable. However, every PhD and every PhD student are unique, with different challenges, priorities and goals, which is why we didn't write a book of 'golden rules'. Instead, we've provided you with a full toolbox (not just a saw!) that equips you with the means to handle whatever your PhD throws at you. We also hope you find reassurance in the book, knowing that you are not alone in your trials and tribulations. The points we address are common to many doctoral research students.

If you have reached the end of the book having only *read* it, we politely suggest that you go back and *use* it! This book is not intended to be a one-time read. It's designed as a workbook, full of activities and templates, so you can *try all of the techniques yourself*. You'll see the immediate effect of applying the techniques to your own PhD, but it's by revisiting them as your research progresses that you will truly learn how to use and benefit from these tools. Reading about them isn't enough. You need to use them to understand how they work, to decide whether they're relevant to you and, if necessary, to adapt them to your needs. It's another part of your apprenticeship. Try everything a few times and only then pick and choose the tools that suit you best: because of your situation, year of study or personal preference. You might find that something that didn't seem relevant to you when you first read about it will be exactly what you need on another occasion.

In a book like this – as it presents tools to handle the challenges of a PhD – there's always a danger of focusing too much on problems. Our intention, however, has been to help you get more out of your degree than you otherwise might; to make the most of the opportunities it provides; and to enable you to reach the end of your PhD celebrating your successes – not only the graduation, but to feel pride in each step you took to get this far.

And finally, although the primary focus of this book has been as a companion guide to get you successfully through your PhD, its value won't end there. Wherever you end up next in your career, you have a toolbox that is transferable to any environment, whether academia, industry, public sector or self-employment. It may even help in your personal life!

A PhD is hard, but it's worth it. It's a transformational experience. You will not be the same person at the end of your PhD as you were when you started. Your mind will have been opened, your intellect will have been honed; you may see the world differently. You will have developed new skills and abilities, increased your confidence and you will leave your PhD embarking on a new phase of your career. We hope that, in some small way, our book will be part of making your PhD a positive and powerful experience.

Good luck with your PhD and with whatever comes next!

Rosie and Fraser
January 2023

Glossary

ABC method   A CBT method of creating more constructive responses to challenges or setbacks and thereby reducing stress and anxiety.

Active listening   A communication technique to build rapport, convey respect and acquire information.

Activities   See **Tasks**.

Affirmation   A statement in the present of a positive state of affairs or mood.

Affirmation technique   A CBT method of reducing anxiety by creating positive statements in the present tense and repeating them.

Amygdala   Areas of the emotion-processing area of the brain central to our reaction to threats and the fight-or-flight response.

Amygdala hijack   An overwhelming reaction to a severe psychological or physical threat in which the fight-or-flight response sidelines conscious, deliberative thought.

Bells-and-whistles   Unimportant items of scope.

Broken-record technique   An assertiveness technique in which a person repeats their key message.

Circadian rhythm   The regular biological pattern of alertness and sleepiness over a 24-hour period; our 'body clock'.

Circle of control   A concept popularised by Stephen Covey, to identify where we can have the greatest impact in a situation.

Closed question   A question that invites a yes/no answer or other short answer.

Cognitive behavioural therapy (CBT)   A psychotherapeutic approach based on techniques to change a person's thoughts in order to produce more constructive emotional responses and behaviours.

Community of practice   A group of practitioners with common goals or professional interests who share expertise and learning by spending time together.

Comparative estimation   Estimation based on a comparison between the current task and the duration of a similar task done before.

Conflict management modes   A framework developed by K.W. Thomas and R.H. Kilman that proposes five different behaviours during conflict management.

Conscious competence framework   The process of acquiring new expertise through initial awareness of a skill deficit, the development of the ability and ultimately automatic use of the ability.

Contingency   A little extra time added into a plan to allow for unanticipated events.

Convergence method   The technique of identifying individual expectations before looking for convergent and divergent ideas.

Cost   The number of hours you must spend to complete your scope.

Critical path   The sequence of tasks in your plan with the longest duration.

Data analysis   The phase of a PhD during which the raw data collected is interrogated.

Data collection   The phase of a PhD when raw data is acquired through experimentation, sampling, fieldwork, modelling, interviews, meta-analysis, archival material etc.

Deadline   A completion date you have either been given or committed to (often linked to a **milestone**).

Deliverable   One of the outputs that you will produce to ensure that your PhD satisfies its purpose.

Dependency   The relationship between tasks in a project plan.

Devil's advocate technique   A method for checking the potential weaknesses of an argument.

Disputation technique   A CBT method of reducing anxiety about a challenge by finding evidence from the past that refutes the anxieties about outcome or performance.

Dopamine   A chemical messenger in the brain associated with reward, motivation and attention.

Duration   The length of time from the start to the end of an activity/event/project.

Effort-impact matrix   A framework for assessing the most productive course of action in a situation.

Employability   The degree to which a candidate has the transferable and job-specific skills and knowledge that employers seek in their employees.

Endorphins   Hormones released during vigorous or pleasurable activity which relieve pain and reduce stress.

Expectation   An opinion that a stakeholder has of the correct direction, approach or outputs (of your PhD).

External risks   Risks that are beyond your control but could impact your PhD.

Features and benefits   A technique to make explicit the ways in which a product, service or skill will provide value.

Fixed dates   Dates that are set in your calendar and are immovable (conferences, contract end, birthdays etc.).

Fixed mindset   The belief that our talent, intelligence and ability are inborn and static.

Freewriting   Writing without stopping for a short, fixed period of time in order to push through mental blocks and get moving on writing.

Gantt chart   See **Timeline**.

Goal   A desired achievement or state of affairs for the future resulting from personal effort.

Ground rules   Jointly agreed rules for the conduct of professional activities such as meetings and communication.

Grounded theory   A research methodology where ideas, concepts, hypotheses and theories emerge from the collected data instead of being the initiating framework for data collection.

Growth mindset   The belief that our talent, intelligence and ability can be increased through focused effort over time.

Habit   Automatic and routine behaviour in response to an environmental stimulus.

Hard dates   See **Fixed dates**.

Impact   The effect or benefit your research has on others.

Imposter syndrome   A feeling of inadequacy that persists despite success.

In scope   The work you are going to do during the next phase (of your PhD).

Initiation   The period spent planning before beginning any piece of work.

I-statement   A succinct expression by a person of their opinion, request or need.

Iterative process   The process of improving the quality of a piece of work by repeated cycles of feedback and amendment.

Junction   In a **network diagram**, where two or more paths converge.

Known knowns   Events that you know will occur or skills that you know you possess.

Known unknowns   Events that you know could occur but it is uncertain whether they will, or skills that you know you need but currently don't possess.

Lessons learned review   The process of reflecting on how well your work has progressed to date and any changes you can make to improve going forward.

Levelling   The act of trying to spread the workload evenly across the full project duration and avoid times of extreme busy or quiet.

Literature map   A mind map representing the content and findings of your literature review, for use in preparing for your Viva and during the Viva.

Literature review   The phase of a PhD where the research is positioned within the existing literature, noting key works, seminal authors and potential contribution to knowledge.

Managing expectations   Agreeing in advance with stakeholders on the direction, approach or outputs (of your PhD) to avoid disappointment.

Masters degree   A first-stage post-graduate degree (usually taught with a dissertation).

Micro-goals   Small, daily goals that will take no more than 15–30 minutes' work to achieve.

Milestone   A marker in your plan that denotes the completion of an important piece of work (such as first year report submitted).

Mindfulness   Focusing awareness on the present to allow calm acknowledgement and acceptance of thoughts and feelings.

Mind map   A diagram used to organise concepts or ideas graphically through grouping and hierarchies.

Mindset   The established set of attitudes and beliefs we hold about ourselves and the world.

Most-likely estimate   In three-point estimation, the normal time for a task to take.

Must-haves   Essential items of scope.

Network diagram   A visual representation of the theoretical order of tasks within your PhD plan; the stage before the Gantt chart.

Network map   A mind map used to graphically represent professional networks.

Networking   The creation and maintenance of positive and useful social relationships, usually in professional spheres.

Networks   The collection of an individual's professional relationships.

Nice-to-haves   Valuable, but non-essential, items of scope.

Non-verbal language   Communication without words through our body language and vocal characteristics.

Open question   A question that invites expansive answers.

Optimistic estimate   In three-point estimation, the quickest time a task could take.

Out of scope   Ideas you have considered but have decided not to pursue during the next phase (of your PhD).

Parametric estimation   Using simple maths to calculate a value.

Passive task   A task that doesn't require any human resource (a 'waiting' task).

Pessimistic estimate   In three-point estimation, the longest time a task could take.

Phase   A high-level piece or stage (of your PhD).

PhD   Doctor of Philosophy (you soon!).

Pomodoro technique   A method of increasing your productivity by interspersing 5-minute rest periods in between 25-minute periods of focused work.

Positive psychology   A school of psychology focused on research into enhancement of human well-being and optimal functioning.

Power bases   A range of different types of personal power, including expert, coercive and referent.

Power pose   A posture that uses expansive, strong, open body language to boost feelings of confidence.

Prefrontal cortex   The area of the brain associated with high-level cognitive functions, such as forward planning, problem-solving and goal-directed behaviour.

Project   An undertaking to create a unique output within a set time period (doing something you haven't done before by a deadline – much like a PhD!).

Project management   Organising and leading the efforts of a project.

Project plan   All the artefacts required to effectively run a project (timeline, risk register, stakeholder diagram, scoping document etc.).

Project triangle   A model linking the three major project constraints: scope, cost and time.

R&D   Research and development (often in a commercial setting).

Reframing   A CBT technique in which a more constructive or helpful interpretation of an event or experience is consciously substituted for the automatic interpretation.

Reputational risk   Risks that could damage your reputation or the reputation of your supervisors, department or even institution.

Research journal   An informal written record of your research work, reflections and ideas, with the purpose of noting and developing your research thinking.

Resilience   The capacity to deal with challenges and bounce back from setbacks.

Resource profile   An indication of what resources are required and when throughout a project; allows identification of potential issues due to conflicts or over-allocation.

Resources   The people, equipment, facilities, materials, supplies and data you need (to complete your PhD).

Risk   A potential event that, if it happens, could have a negative (or sometimes positive) impact (on your PhD).

Risk assessment team (RAT)   A group of people remote from your PhD who are able to objectively assess risks as well as strengths and weaknesses of the plan, approach, ideas and methods.

Risk checklist   A list of common risks (associated with your type of PhD).

Risk management   The process of trying to identify and respond to negative events that could happen before they do happen.

Risk register   A document used to keep track of risks and mitigation actions.

Risk response   The act of addressing a risk.

Schedule   See **Timeline**.

Scope   The work you need to complete and the outputs you need to produce.

Scope statement   The documented agreement of the scope for your next piece of work.

Secondary risk   A risk only introduced to your project as a direct result of an earlier risk response.

Skills audit   Assessing existing competencies and identifying gaps against the necessary or desired skills required for career success.

Slack   The amount of time a task can be delayed without impacting on your deadline.

SMART   An acronym for assessing deliverables: Specific, Measurable, Achievable, Realistic, Timebound.

Social biome   The ecosystem of relationships and social interactions that constitute your regular social connections.

Stakeholder   Any person who can impact on the success (or otherwise) of your PhD (or project).

Stakeholder diagram   A mind map used during stakeholder identification.

Stakeholder identification   The process of uncovering all of your PhD stakeholders.

STAR technique   A method of building evidence of a skill set for use in job applications and interviews: Situation, Task, Action, Result.

Stress   A physical or psychological demand that requires action or attention.

Stress hormones   Hormones, such as cortisol and adrenaline, secreted in response to a perceived physical or psychological threat, to prepare the body for the fight-or-flight response.

Supervisor   A person (normally academic but could be from industry) responsible for guiding, supervising and advising on your PhD.

Supervisory team   The team of supervisors overseeing your research.

Support network   A set of social relationships that provide emotional and/or professional support.

Tasks   The discrete actions you need to perform to complete PhD work.

Thesis summary spreadsheet   A detailed summary of your thesis content used to revise for your Viva and as an aide-memoire in the Viva.

Three-point estimation   Introducing allowance for uncertainty into an estimate by taking three data points.

Time   The duration of a task.

Time-blocking   The time-management technique of creating calendar appointments with yourself to designate times during which you will work on specific tasks.

Timeline   A table visually representing the tasks you need to complete plotted against a time axis.

Tracking   The act of assessing how well you are executing your plan.

Transferable skills   The core set of skills you have developed during your PhD that you can apply in a wide range of different jobs, sectors or industries.

Unknown unknown   An event that you couldn't anticipate, or skill that you don't yet know you need.

User   Any stakeholder who will use the output of your research.

Vision board   A visual representation of a future state, using a collection of symbols of success.

Visualisation technique   A process of purposeful imagining of the circumstances of a future desired state based on the achievement of personal goals.

Viva   Oral exam after thesis submission; short for *viva voce* ('with living voice').

Weighted average   Adding a weighting value to the calculation of an average (normally, the mean) to account for uneven data distribution.

WIBNI   'Wouldn't it be nice if …' – a term used for a small (often unnecessary) change in scope.

WIIFM   'What's in it for me?' – the benefits provided to a person by a product, service or situation.

Work breakdown structure (WBS)   A tool that subdivides pieces of work into low-level, manageable tasks.

Writing up   Normally, the final phase of a PhD, where the focus is on completing the writing of the thesis.

Index

ABC method
   definition of 179–81
   final stage of PhD 277
   mindset 236
   procrastination 193–4
   template: the ABC method 181
Active listening 255–6
Active task 108, 133
   see also Task
Activity
   see Task
Affectionate communication
   see Social biome
Affirmation technique
   definition of 195–6
   final stage of PhD 278
   procrastination 195–6
   Viva preparation 305
Alertness
   scheduling work 51
   see also Circadian rhythms
Amygdala hijack
   definition of 233–4
   recovery from 234
   see also Fight-or-flight
Annual leave
   see Holidays
Anxiety
   amygdala hijack 233–4
   fight-or-flight 178, 193, 233–4
   final stage of PhD 276
   getting started 3
   mindfulness 188
   procrastination 192–6
   Viva 305
   see also Procrastination; Stress; Cognitive behavioural therapy
Apprenticeship 26, 66, 294, 311
Asserting techniques
   broken record 259–61
   I-statement 258–9

Behavioural norms 29, 32
   see also Habit
Bells-and-whistles 94–5, 133, 266
   see also Prioritisation; Scope statement; Tracking
Body clock
   see Circadian rhythms

Body language 254, 256, 303
Broken record technique 259–61

Calendar 148–55
   see also Time-blocking
Cameron, Julia 50
Career
   community of practice 66–7, 69, 227
   curriculum vitae 219–26
   demonstrating value 316–7
   development priorities 222–3
   features and benefits technique 317
   goals 16, 19–20, 220
   planning 221–6
   skills audit 222
   STAR technique 318–9
   training 224
   see also Curriculum vitae; Employability; Industry; Networking, Support networks; Transferable skills
Catching up
   see Social biome
CBT
   see Cognitive behavioural therapy
Change
   managing 77–8, 207–8, 210–2, 269
   project triangle 77–8, 207–8
   template: change assessment 213
   tracking progress 207–9
   see also Wouldn't it be nice if
Checklists
   change 213
   estimation 112
   exercise 187
   getting started 4–5
   risk 140
   sleep 186
   Viva 307
   Viva preparation 304
Circadian rhythms 155–8, 281–2
   see also Larks and owls
Circle of control 238–40, 241, 243
   see also Setbacks
Code of practice, supervisors 25, 28–9
Cognitive behavioural therapy
   ABC method 179–80, 277
   affirmation technique 195–6, 278, 305
   anxiety 193–6

definition of 178–9
disputation technique 195
final stage of PhD 277–9
procrastination 193–6
reframing technique 179, 305
Viva 305
What is technique 194–5, 278, 305
see also Stress
Collaboration 32, 60, 257
see also Conflict management modes; Ground rules
Communication
  active listening 255–6
  assertiveness 258–61
  broken record technique 259–61
  career development 312–5, 316–9
  conflict management 254–61
  impact of change 78
  influencing tactics 169–71
  I-statement 258–9
  networking 231
  nonverbal language 254–5
  power bases 164–7
  open questioning 256–7
  social biome 61–2, 68, 276
  supervision 24, 28
  Viva 303
  work breakdown structure 109
Community of practice
  definition 66
  networking 227
  social biome 68
  social media 68
  support networks 66–9
  template: community of practice development planner 69
  unconscious competence 66
Comparative estimation 113
Concentration 156–8, 159–60, 254, 281–2
  see also Time management
Conferences
  career development 220, 223
  dealing with nerves 178
  networking 68, 227, 230
  PhD opportunities 16, 44
  planning for 44, 271, 148–9
  skills identification 313
  final stage of PhD 269, 271
Conflict
  active listening 255–6
  advantages 247
  body language 254, 256
  broken record technique 259–61
  conflict management modes 248–51
  definition of 247

difficult conversations 247
  I-statement technique 258–9
  nonverbal language 254–5
  open questioning 256–7
  resource allocation 132–3, 135
  vocal tone 254
  see also Conflict management modes
Conflict management modes
  accommodating 249
  avoiding 248–9
  collaborating 250, 256, 257
  competing 249–50, 257, 259
  compromising 250, 256, 257
  conflict management mode assessment example 252
  template: conflict management mode assessment 253
  Thomas-Kilmann conflict management modes 248
  see also Conflict
Confrontation
  see Conflict
Conscious competence
  community of practice 66, 67
  definition 10
  framework 7–13, 35
  habit forming 51, 57
  procrastination 193–4
  skills audit 223
  skills identification 312
  supervision 35–6
  template: conscious competence framework 13
  transferable skills 312
Conscious incompetence 8–11, 35, 38, 51, 193, 223, 312
  see also Conscious competence
Contingency 115, 116, 143, 153, 273
  see also Estimation; Risk
Contingency plan 143
Convergence method
  step-by-step method 90–3
  template: convergence table 93
  tracking 215
Cost
  changes to 78, 133, 208–9, 211, 213
  definition of 77
  final stage of PhD 266, 269
  see also Project triangle
Cost of change curve 137
Covey, Stephen 238
  see also Circle of control
Critical path
  critical path analysis 123–6
  definition of 124
  Gantt chart 127–9
  slack 124–5
Cuddy, Amy 307
  see also Power poses

Curriculum vitae
  conscious incompetence 223
  development 220–6
  development priorities 222–3
  goals 220–1
  networking 228
  skills audit 222
  stakeholders 224
  template: CV development plan 226
  training 224
  volunteering 224
  see also Career; Transferable skills
CV
  See Curriculum vitae

Data analysis 56, 67, 95, 156–7, 161, 312
Data collection 42, 113, 145, 269
Data management 56–7, 67, 91–4, 138, 313
  see also Information management
Data resources
  see Resource
Dates, Fixed
  see Fixed dates
Deadlines
  final stage of PhD 266
  high-level timeline 43–5
  planning for submission 265–74
  tracking 214–5
  see also Milestones; Time-blocking
Delays
  dealing with 124–5, 128–30, 153, 207–8
  impact of 124–5, 128–30, 133, 142, 207–8
  procrastination 191
  updating the plan 207–8
Deliverables
  control 99
  examples 100
  phrasing 98–9
  SMART 98–100
  template: deliverables 101
  work breakdown structure 107
  see also Expectations; Planning
Dependencies
  see Tasks
Devil's advocate technique
  Viva preparation 300–1
  template: devil's advocate technique 302
Disorganisation
  material 196
  procrastination 196–7
  temporal 196
Disputation technique 195
Doctoral degree guidelines 24, 88–9
Dopamine 182, 283, 284

Duration 42–3, 76, 77, 112–6, 123–5
  see also Time; Estimation; Planning
Dweck, Carol 235
  see also Mindset

Eat the elephant
  definition 40
  deliverables 98, 99
  final stage of PhD 266
  initiation 76
  scope 95, 103
  tracking 209
  work breakdown structure 107
  see also Planning; Phases
Eat your frog 204
Effort-impact matrix 242–5
  see also Setbacks
Eisenhower, Dwight D. 39
Empathy 172
  see also What's in it for me
Employability
  CV development 220–6
  features and benefits technique 317
  goal-setting 19–22
  skills articulation 316–7
  skills identification 312–4
  STAR technique 318–9
  training 224
  what's in it for me 316–7
  see also Career; Curriculum vitae; Transferable skills
Endorphins 182, 187, 306
Engagement 182, 183–4
  see also Happiness
Essential challenges 242–3
  see also Effort-impact matrix
Estimation
  accuracy 111
  comparative estimation 113
  considerations 112
  contingency 115, 116
  duration 41–3, 112–6, 123–5
  estimation methods 113–6
  high-level PhD timeline 43
  lessons learned 215–6
  parametric estimation 113–4
  ranges 111–2
  template: three-point estimation 117
  three-point estimation 114–6
  time-blocking 152
  tracking progress 207
  updating plan 208–9
  using ranges 190–1
  work breakdown structure 108
  writing-up 271, 273

Events
  induction 4, 44, 62
  online 63
  university 62–3
  see also Support networks
Exercise
  mindfulness 188
  physical 186, 187, 275, 306
  visualisation 18–9
Expectations
  convergence method 90–3, 215
  deliverables 98–100
  differences 92
  ground rules 32–3
  managing 3, 24–5, 32–3, 81, 88–9, 94
  prioritisation 94–5, 267
  research community 88
  scope 88–90
  stakeholder 81, 88–90
  supervisor 24–5, 88–9, 267
  university 88
Expert
  learning from 26, 66, 68
  power 164, 165, 167
  risk assessment team 40
  transferable skills 311

Features and benefits technique 317
  see also Career; Industry; Transferable skills
Feedback process 270–1
Fight-or-flight 178, 193, 233–4
  see also Amygdala hijack
Fill-in tasks 242–3
  see also Effort-impact matrix
Fixed dates 43–4, 149–50
  see also Planning; Time management
Fixed mindset
  see Mindset
Freewriting 287
  see also Writing

Gantt chart
  change 211
  creating 127–33
  critical path 128–9
  definition of 120
  examples 133–4, 208–9, 273
  final stage of PhD 270, 272–4, 294
  high-level 41–6
  network diagram 127–9
  non-research tasks 45–6
  resource levelling 130–3
  resources 130–2

risk management 138, 143
slack 129–30
software 128
task definition 107–10
thesis completion 270, 272–4
time-blocking 149, 150, 152, 294
tracking 206–10, 214
updating 208–9
viva preparation 294
see also Scheduling; Planning
Goals
  career goals 220–1
  clarifying goals 17
  future goals 16–7
  goal-setting 19–20
  importance for PhD 15–6
  lessons learned 215–7
  micro-goals 284
  motivation 201, 285
  networking objectives 228
  procrastination 201
  revisit and review 17, 209–10, 215–6
  revisiting 352–3
  stakeholder identification 83
  template: goal-setting planner 22
  tracking 209–10
  visualisation technique 18–9
  walking in fog 17–8
Ground rules 32–3, 34
Growth mindset
  see Mindset

Habit
  ABC method 181
  annotating literature 57
  cues 50, 53, 202
  definition of 50
  forming 50
  happiness 182
  information management 56–7, 197
  office hours 51
  procrastination 202–3
  repetition 50
  research journal 55
  showing up to the page 50
  social biome 61–2
  supervision 32, 33
  support networks 60, 61
  thinking 180, 237, 294
  time management 153
  uniform 53
  using this book 2
  visualisation for viva 305
  working day 51–2

workspace 52–4
writing 54–6
Happiness
　engagement 183
　final stage of PhD 276
　hormones 182
　meaning 183
　pleasure 182, 183
　power of 182–4
　prescription for 182, 276
　template: happiness planner 185
High-level timeline
　deadlines 43–5
　eating the elephant 40
　estimating durations 42–3
　fixed dates 43
　Gantt chart 41
　step-by-step process 41–6
　level of detail 39–40
　main phases of a PhD 40–1
　template: high-level PhD timeline 47
　time axis 42
　work-life balance 45–6
Holidays 32–4, 41, 46, 139, 54, 273
Hormones
　dopamine 182, 283, 284
　endorphins 182, 187, 306
　stress 60, 178, 193, 233–4
Human resources
　see Resource

Impact
　Effort-impact matrix 242–5
　of change 208, 211–2, 269
　research impact 89–90
　risk assessment 141–4
　stress 177–8, 233–4
　see also Expectations; Risk; Project triangle
Imposter syndrome 7, 11–2, 180
In scope
　see Scope statement
Induction 4, 5, 25, 44, 62, 68
Industry
　bringing value to 316–7
　career planning 16, 89, 219, 223, 230, 311
　community of practice 67
　creating links to 89, 228, 230, 233
　power bases 165, 166
　research expectations 92, 95
　stakeholders 89, 92, 95
　translating PhD skills 316–9
　see also Transferable skills
Influencing tactics
　bargaining 169

coalition 169
direct instruction 169
empathy 172–3
friendliness 170
reasoning 170
sanction 170
template: influencing tactics assessment 171
upward referral 170
what's in it for me 172–3, 316
see also Power bases
Information management
　habits 56–7, 197
　procrastination 197
　software 56
　supervisory guidance 29–30, 56
　transferable skills 311–3
Initiation 76
I-statement 258–9
Iterative process
　convergence method 91
　goals 84
　perfectionism 199, 200
　stakeholders 84
　using this book xix
　Viva 294
　writing 207

Job interview, preparation for 307, 314, 320
　see also Transferable skills
Joking around
　see Social biome

Known knowns 37
　see also Known unknowns; Risk; Unknown unknowns
Known unknowns 37
　see also Known knowns; Risk; Unknown unknowns

Larks and owls 155–6
　See also Circadian Rhythms
Lessons learned 215–7
Literature map 297–8
Literature review
　annotating 57
　planning 38–40, 42–3, 95, 99, 113, 152
　Viva preparation 304
　work breakdown structure 299

Meaning 182–3
　see also Happiness
Meaningful talk
　see Social biome
Meetings
　ground rules 32–3, 4

note taking 57, 103
scheduling 157
supervision 24, 32–3, 43, 148
time-blocking 148
Mehrabian, Albert 254
Mental health 189, 192
see also Anxiety; Stress; Well-being
Micro-goals 284
Milestones
deliverables 99
estimation 118
final stage of PhD 266, 273
Gantt chart 128, 134
PhD network diagram 121, 122, 126
planning 39
time-blocking 154
tracking progress 214
Mindfulness
final stage of PhD 276
technique 188–9
Viva preparation 306, 307
Mindmaps
literature 297–8
network 230
stakeholder 80–1, 83
Mindset
ABC method 236
definition 235
fixed 235
growth 235
language 236–7
reframing 236
see also Setbacks
Most likely estimate 114, 115
Motivation
creating 7, 49–50
final stage of PhD 283–5
goals 17, 201, 285
hitting the wall 275
lack of 201–2
maintaining 214, 283–5
procrastination 201–2
what's in it for me 201–2, 284–5
Moving away 4
see also Support networks
Must-haves 94–7, 267–8
see also Prioritisation

Needs analysis, supervision 29–31
Negotiation
see Influencing tactics; Power bases
Network diagram
calculating duration 123–5
creating 120–5

critical path analysis 124
examples 126, 272
final stage of PhD 271–2, 295
Gantt chart 127–30
junctions 123–4
milestones 121–2
passive tasks 108, 270
risk assessment 138
slack 124–5
thesis completion 271–2
tracking progress 206
Viva preparation 295
Network map 230
Networking
benefits 227
community of practice 67
connection power 227
network development 230–1
network map 229
objectives 228
referent power 227
risk assessment team 141
stakeholders 227
supervision 29
Nice-to-haves 94–6, 97
see also Prioritisation
Nonverbal language 254–5
Norms
see Behavioural norms

Open questioning 256–7
Optimistic estimate 114–5
Out of scope
see Scope statement
Outputs
see Deliverables
Overwhelm 198–9

Parametric estimation 113–4
Part-time 3, 78, 149, 219
Passive tasks 108, 270, 273, 294
see also Tasks
Peer review 140, 210
Peer support
see Support networks
Perfectionism 155, 199–200
Pessimistic estimate 114–5
PFC
see prefrontal cortex
Phases
common PhD xvi, 40–1
planning in 39–40, 42, 72, 109
structure of book xvi
see also Planning

Physical resources
  see Resources
Plan
  see Planning
Plan-do-check 207, 210
Planning
  contingency 115
  critical path analysis 123–6
  deadlines 43–5
  definition of a good plan 39–40
  deliverables 98–101
  estimating durations 41–3
  final stage of PhD 266–74
  fixed dates 43–4, 149–50
  Gantt chart 41–7, 127–35, 206, 208, 272–4, 294
  high-level PhD plan, step-by-step process 41–6
  level of detail 39–40
  main phases of a PhD 40–1
  network diagram 120–6, 271–2, 294
  passive tasks 108, 270, 273, 294
  phasing 39–40, 42, 72, 109
  planning process 39
  project triangle 77–8, 133, 266, 269
  purpose for a PhD 38–9
  resources 130–1
  sequencing 120–3
  starting to plan 76
  supervisory meetings 32
  timescales 42, 766
  tracking 205–6, 207–8
  Viva 294
  what if scenarios 133
  work breakdown structure 107–9, 269–71, 294, 299
  work-life balance 45–6, 149, 153
  writing-up 269–70
  see also Eat the elephant; Estimation; Gantt chart; Initiation; Network diagram; Project triangle; Tasks
Pleasure 182, 183, 283
Pomodoro technique 159–60, 281, 284
  see also Time management
Positive psychology 307
Positive thinking 180, 235
Power bases
  coercive 164, 165, 167, 170
  connection 164, 165, 167, 227, 230–1
  examples 167
  expert 164, 165, 167
  information 164, 166, 167
  legitimate 164, 165, 167
  referent 164, 166, 167, 170, 227, 231
  reward 164, 165, 166, 167, 169
  template: power base assessment 168

Power poses 308
Prefrontal cortex
  amygdala hijack 233–4
  brain structure 159
  description 158–9
  mental energy 158–9, 161
  setbacks 234–5
  stress 234–5, 297
  Viva preparation 297
Priorities
  career development 158–9
  for PhD 15–6
  supervision 26–9
  see also Convergence method; Prioritisation
Prioritisation
  categorisation 94–5
  change 211
  final stage of PhD 266–7
  numeric 94
  resource levelling 133
  scope 94–5
  template: prioritisation 97
  template: prioritisation for final six months 268
  tracking progress 208
  writing-up 289
Probability
  see Risk
Problems
  see Risk
Procrastination
  ABC method 193–4
  affirmation technique 195–6
  anxiety 192–6
  conscious incompetence 193
  definition of 191
  disorganisation 196–7
  disputation technique 195
  drivers 191, 192–204
  eat your frog 204
  freewriting 287
  goals 201
  habit 202–3
  iterative process 199
  lack of motivation 200–2
  overwhelm 198
  perfectionism 199–200
  reframing technique 194
  time-blocking 149
  time-boxing 155, 200
  what is technique 194–5
  what's in it for me 201–2
  work breakdown structure 198
  writing-up 287

Productivity 50, 53, 158–61, 277–8, 281–2
    see also Procrastination, Circadian rhythms, Time management
Professional support networks
    see Support networks
Project initiation
    see Initiation
Project management
    see Planning
Project triangle
    change, impact of 77–8, 133, 207–8, 211, 269
    cost 77
    definition of 77–8
    final stage of PhD 266–7, 269
    planning 133, 266, 269
    resource levelling 133
    scope 77
    time 77
    tracking 207–8
    see also Cost; Planning; Scope; Time

Quick wins 242–3
    see also Effort-impact Matrix

Referent power
    see Power bases
Reframing 179, 235–6, 237, 294
    see also Cognitive behavioural therapy
Rejection
    See Setbacks
Reputational risk 139
    see also Risk
Research impact
    see Impact
Resilience
    ABC method 179–81
    circle of control 238–40
    definition of 177
    exercise 187
    happiness 182
    mindfulness 188
    sleep 186
    support networks 59–60
    Viva 306
    well-being 186–9, 276
    see also Setbacks; Stress; Work-life balance
Resource profile 131
    see also Resources; Gantt chart
Resources
    allocation 130
    conflict 132–3
    data 130
    human 130

identification 108, 130
levelling 130–3, 135
physical 130
planning 108
prioritisation 133
project triangle 133
resource profile 131–2
Resumé
    see Curriculum vitae
Rewards 283
    see also Motivation
Risk
    assessment 141–3
    assessment team 140–1
    categories 143
    checklist 140
    cost-of-change curve 137
    definition of 137
    external risks 139
    Gantt chart 138, 143
    identification 138–40
    impact 141–3
    lessons learned 215
    people risks 138–9
    probability 141–3
    reputational risks 139
    response 143–5
    risk register 138, 146
    secondary risks 144–5
    stakeholders 138–9
    template: risk register 146
    transferable skills 138
Risk assessment team 140–1, 300
    see also Risk
Risk Impact
    see Risk
Risk register 138, 146
    see also Risk
Routine
    see Habit
Rumsfeld, Donald 37

Scheduling
    see Planning
Scope
    changes to 77–8, 133, 208, 211, 269
    convergence method 90–3
    definition of 77
    final stage of PhD 266–7, 269
    identification 90–2
    managing expectations 81, 90–2, 94
    prioritisation 94–6, 266–7
    research impact 89–90
    see also Project triangle; Scope statement

Scope Statement
   definition 102
   final stage of PhD 267
   in scope 102–3
   out of scope 102–3
   template: scope statement 104
   writing 102–4
Secondary risks 144–5
Seligman, Martin 182
Setbacks
   amygdala hijack 233–4
   assessing 238
   circle of control 238–40, 243
   dealing with 238–45
   effort-impact matrix 242–4
   mindset 235–7
   reframing 236–7
   regaining control 234
   taking action 238–45
   template: circle of control assessment 241
   template: effort-impact assessment 245
   see also Stress; Prefrontal cortex
Showing up to the page 50
Skills audit 222–3
Slack
   calculating 124–5
   Gantt chart 129–30
   levelling resources 130–5
   network diagram 124–5
   see also Critical path analysis
Sleep 186, 275, 306
SMART deliverables
   see Deliverables
Social biome 61–62, 68, 276
Social connection
   see Support networks
Social media
   community of practice 68
   distraction 53, 282
   networking 63, 68, 228, 230
   reputational risk 139
Social support
   see Support networks
Stakeholders
   advantageous 79
   adverse 79
   change 211–2
   communication 163
   convergence method 90–3
   definition of 79
   examples 79–80
   expectations 81, 84, 88–90
   final stage of PhD 266
   identification 79–84

   identification questions 81
   impact 84, 89–90
   level of detail 81
   mindmap 80
   networking 227, 228–9
   review 84
   risks 84, 138–9
   software 84
   support networks 60
   template: stakeholder identification 82
   see also Expectations; Stakeholder Diagram
Stakeholder diagram
   creation of 80–4
   examples 80, 83
   first level stakeholders 80
   level of detail 81
   mindmap 80
   networks 228–9
   review 84
   second level stakeholders 83, 230
   third-level stakeholders 83
   see also Stakeholders
STAR technique 318–20
   see also Career; Industry; Transferable skills
Stress
   ABC method 179–81, 194, 236, 277
   brain structure 234
   control 239
   cognitive behavioural therapy 178–9, 193–4, 277
   definition of 177–8
   fight-or-flight 178, 193, 233–4
   final stage of PhD 275–6
   hormones 60, 178, 193, 233–4
   increasing well-being 186–9, 276
   managing 178–9, 234, 275–80
   mindfulness 188–9, 276
   reframing 179, 235–6, 237, 294
   responses 177–8
   social connection 59–60
   time-blocking 149–55
   Viva 304–6
   see also Anxiety; Setbacks
Submission
   administration 266, 269, 271
   dealing with pressure 275–80
   feedback process 270–1
   Gantt chart 272–4
   identify tasks 269–70
   motivation 283–5
   network diagram 271–2
   planning for 265–71
   prioritisation 266–8
   setting a deadline 266
   work breakdown structure 269–70

Supervision
  apprenticeship 26
  characteristics of 25–7, 28, 29
  code of practice 28
  conscious competence 35
  convergence method 90–3
  feedback process, writing-up 270–1
  ground rules 32–4
  holidays 32
  meetings 32, 57, 149, 157
  needs analysis 29–31
  problems with 28
  professional support networks 67
  purpose 25
  risk assessment team 141
  stakeholder expectations 88–9
  stakeholder identification 79
  supervisor expectations 89
  template: supervision ground rules 34
  template: supervision needs analysis 31
  when it goes wrong 28
Supervision team
  see Supervision
Supervisor
  see Supervision
Support networks
  career development 59, 227–8
  community of practice 66–9
  establishing and maintaining 61–5, 66–8
  importance for PhD 59–60
  network map 230
  networking 227–32
  online 63, 68, 230
  peer support 60
  professional network 60, 66, 227–32
  social 60–5
  social biome 61–2, 68, 276
  social connection 60
  social media 63, 68, 228, 230
  stakeholders 60, 227
  stress hormones 60
  supervision 67
  template: social support network development planner 65
  unconscious competence 66
  well-being 60
  see Work-life balance

Tasks
  active 108, 133
  critical 123–6, 128
  dependencies 120–2
  estimation 111–7
  identification 107, 109–10, 265, 269–70
  non-critical 129, 133
  non-research 45–6, 265
  passive 108, 270, 273, 294
  sequencing 120–3
  using verbs 109
  work breakdown structure 107–9, 267–21, 294, 299
  see also Gantt chart; Network diagram; Planning
Thankless tasks 242, 243
  see also Effort-impact matrix
Thesis
  feedback process 270–1
  Gantt chart 272–4
  planning write-up 269–74
  thesis summary spreadsheet 295–6
  work breakdown structure 269–70, 299
Thomas-Kilman conflict management modes 248
  see also Conflict management modes
Three-point estimation 114–6
Time
  changes to 208, 211, 269
  contingency 115, 116, 153, 273
  duration 42–3, 76, 77, 112–6, 123–5
  project triangle 77, 266
  change 77–8
  lessons learned review 215–6
  see also Estimation; Planning; Time management
Time management
  calendar 5–6, 149–55, 159, 207, 304
  circadian rhythms 155–8, 281–2
  concentration 156–8, 159–60, 254, 281–2
  part-time study 78, 149
  pomodoro technique 159–60, 281, 284
  task variety 161
  Viva preparation 294
  work-life balance 149, 153, 276–7
  see also Timer techniques; Time-blocking; Time-boxing; Procrastination
Time-blocking 148–55, 161, 276, 294
Time-boxing 155, 200
Timeline
  see Gantt chart
Timer techniques
  Pomodoro technique 159–60, 281, 284
  task variety 161
  writing-up 281
Timescales
  see Time
Tracking
  change assessment 210–3
  frequency 214–5
  Gantt chart 208–9
  goals 209–10
  lessons learned 215–7
  plan-do-check 207, 210

progress 207–8
project triangle 207–8, 211
reviewing the plan 206–7, 214–5
template: lessons learned review 217
Wouldn't it be nice ifs 210–11
Training
career development 197, 223–4, 271
research skills 9–11, 16, 44, 62, 112, 271, 289
Transferable skills
articulation 316–7,
career development 219–20, 224, 232, 311–4
circle of control 239
communication 163, 254
conflict management 248, 254
CV development 220–6
definition of 15, 311
evidencing 317–20
features and benefits technique 317
goal-setting 15
ground rules 32
how to use this book xviii
identifying 312–5
information management 311
job interview 307, 317–20
job market 12, 220, 311– 4, 316
mindmaps 84
power bases 164
project management 73, 84, 107, 223
risk 138
skills identification example 313
stakeholder diagram 84
STAR technique 318–9
template: skill identification 315
template: STAR assessment 320
training 224
Viva preparation 307
what's in it for me 316–7
work breakdown structure 107, 109
Triangle
see Project triangle

Uncertainty
see Risk
Unexpected issues
dealing with 210–2
see also Risk
Unknown unknowns 37, 38, 40
see also Known knowns; Risk; Known unknowns
Updating your plan 39, 109, 208–9
see also Tracking

Vision board 19
Visualisation
vision board 19

visualisation technique 18–9, 305–6
Viva 305–6
Viva
cognitive behavioural therapy techniques 305
checklist 307
dealing with nerves 304–6
definition of 294, 303
devil's advocate technique 300–2
literature map 297–9
literature review 297–8
on the day 307–8
planning for 294
power poses 308
practising for 299, 303–4
preparation 294–8
rehearsal 303–4
risk assessment team 140
speaking 303–4, 299
thesis summary spreadsheet 295–6
visualisation 305–6
well-being 306
Vocal tone 254–5
Volunteering 224

Walking in fog
see Goals
Well-being
exercise 187
final stage of PhD 275–6
mindfulness 188–9
resilience 186–9
sleep 186
social connection 59–60
supervisory support 29
template: well-being planner 280
Viva 306
What if scenarios 133
What is technique 194–5, 278, 305
What's in it for me 172–3, 201–2, 284–5, 316–7
WIBNI
see Wouldn't it be nice if
WIIFM
see What's in it for me
Work breakdown structure
benefits of 108
definition of 107
estimation 108
examples 109–10
final stage of PhD 269–70
literature map 297–8
network diagram 120–1
overwhelm 198
passive tasks 108
procrastination 198

resource needs 107
risks 108, 138
time-blocking 150
verbs 109
Viva preparation 294
see also Tasks
Working hours 6, 32, 34, 49–51, 273
  see also Ground Rules; Habit; Time management
Working practices
  see Habit
Work-life balance
  final stage of PhD 276–7
  maintaining 209, 276
  managing 45, 149–53, 154
  happiness 182–5, 276
  resilience 275–6
  supervision 29
  support networks 61–5
  time-blocking 149, 153
  tracking progress 209
  see also Happiness; Support networks
Workspace 52–4
  see also Habit
Wouldn't it be nice if 211, 269
Writing
  circadian rhythms 281–2
  concentration 29, 281–2
  creating mode 286–8
  feedback 270–1, 288
  freewriting 287
  Gantt chart 272–3
  habit 54–6
  momentum 285–91
  network diagram 120–1
  procrastination 54
  productivity 281–2
  research journal 55
  revising mode 286, 288–90
  showing up to the page 50
  templates 289
  work breakdown structure 269–70
Writing-up
  see Writing

www.ingramcontent.com/pod-product-compliance
Lightning Source LLC
Chambersburg PA
CBHW082058230426
43670CB00017B/2884